Humana Festival 2006
The Complete Plays
30th Anniversary Edition

Humana, Inc. is one of the nation's largest health service companies and a $15.2 billion Fortune 150 company.

The Humana Foundation was established in 1981 to support the educational, social, medical and cultural development of communities in ways that reflect Humana's commitment to social responsibility and an improved quality of life.

Humana Festival 2006
The Complete Plays
30th Anniversary Edition

Edited by
Adrien-Alice Hansel and Julie Felise Dubiner

Playscripts, Inc.
New York, NY

Published by Playscripts, Inc.
450 Seventh Avenue, Suite 809
New York, New York, 10123
www.playscripts.com

Cover design by Matt Dobson
Cover artwork by Heads of State
Text design and layout by Erin Detrick

First Edition: April 2007
10 9 8 7 6 5 4 3 2

LCCN: 95650734
ISSN: 1935-4452

ISBN-10: 0-9709046-1-4
ISBN-13: 978-0-9709046-1-4

This book is dedicated to Alexander Speer,
in recognition of the mighty work he's done over his 40 years
at the Actors Theatre of Louisville.

Contents

Foreword by Marc Masterson 9

Editors' Note by Adrien-Alice Hansel and Julie Felise Dubiner 11

Three Guys and a Brenda by Adam Bock 13

Natural Selection by Eric Coble 23

Low by Rha Goddess 83

Act A Lady by Jordan Harrison 123

Sovereignty by Rolin Jones 175

Listeners by Jane Martin 187

Hotel Cassiopeia by Charles L. Mee 199

The Scene by Theresa Rebeck 245

Six Years by Sharr White 293

Neon Mirage
    by Liz Duffy Adams, Dan Dietz,
    Rick Hip-Flores, Julie Jensen, Lisa Kron,
    Tracey Scott Wilson, and Chay Yew 347

Acknowledgments

The editors wish to thank the following persons for their invaluable assistance in compiling this volume:

Merv Antonio
Jamie Bragg
Joanna Donehower
Maurine Evans
Marc Masterson
Jeff Rodgers
James Seacat
Kyle Shepherd
Wanda Snyder
Alexander Speer
Zan Sawyer-Dailey

Beth Blickers
John Buzzetti
Sam Cohn
Val Day
Morgan Jenness
Carl Mulert
Antje Oegel
Chris Till
Peregrine Whittlesey
Cathy Zimmerman

Foreword

The Humana Festival is theatrical multi-tasking. There are always several things happening at once—last-minute rehearsals, writers huddled with dramaturgs, directors checking in with designers, ushers moving crowds between the three performance spaces at the Actors Theatre of Louisville. For audiences and artists alike, it's an awesome and overwhelming experience. The 2006 Humana Festival of New American Plays Anthology captures that creative energy and great variety in a published volume of plays. The group of writers who contribute to this volume features new voices, evolving voices, and the voices of old friends.

The 2006 plays are varied in their investigations and interrogations of a wild assortment of topics, genres, and styles as well. From supra-naturalism to futuristic-absurdism and dreamy biography, they represent the best of contemporary American playwriting. The vibrancy and vitality of contemporary playmaking is inspiring to all of us who work on the Festival.

This year also marked the 30th anniversary of the Humana Festival of New American Plays—a hallmark of accomplishment of which we are very proud. Simply put, we could not have reached this milestone without the remarkable support of the Humana Foundation. As our long-time partner in this effort they have offered us the generous and continuous support that allows artists to realize their dreams. As one of the longest-running corporate sponsorships of any artistic endeavor in the country, we thank them for their inspiring confidence in continuing to support the mad swirl of artistic creation contained in these pages.

—Marc Masterson
Artistic Director
Actors Theatre of Louisville

Editors' Note

Every year, we at Actors Theatre of Louisville read some 750 plays, looking for the most engaging and vital work of American playwrights. In 2006, our lineup included seven full-length works and three short plays that offered a peek into the achievements and preoccupations of the sixteen playwrights we featured this year. We curate the festival with an eye towards diversity—of theme and tone, of the concerns of the characters and the ways they explore them—but over time, a conversation among the pieces begins to reverberate. What's striking this year, looking at the plays that filled out the Festival, are the ways they all offer different ways of reordering the audience's perspective—that delicate and seductive trick of theater to teach an audience to watch characters in front of them with wholly new eyes, from the total world writ small in Chuck Mee's delicate and searing theatricalization of the life, process and vision of American collage artist Robert Cornell to Theresa Rebeck's stomach-wrenching comedy that ultimately reveals itself as a morality tale of our times.

These shifts can start as externally as the Depression-era men of Wattleburg, MN, who don lady clothes for the Christmas fundraiser that was never supposed to be more than a lark. But as Jordan Harrison's *Act a Lady* continues, and all the townsfolk start inhabiting their new clothes and thinking about the ways their lives don't fit their skin, everyone in the town starts to see themselves, and their neighbors, a little differently. On the other hand, Theresa Rebeck's vicious comedy *The Scene* explores the cultural effects of a persistently crushed perspective. Charlie, a middle aged and out-of-work actor, finds his life totally changed when he tries to live his life as large as the stars whose faces are plastered across Times Square.

Sometimes the perspective quick-change is acute, as in Sharr White's *Six Years*, which offers glimpses of a marriage of a post-WWII couple every half-dozen years, some of which seem to have dragged on with restless inevitability, some of which prove to have changed this couple forever. The end of the play finds Phil and Meredith thirty-six years and a world away from where they started, returning to the same words they tried to make sense of the world with when they were younger. *Hotel Cassiopeia* by Charles L. Mee leads the audience through more radical shifts, from the outside of Joseph Cornell's carefully wrought boxes to the interior of the evocative worlds-in-miniature that traveled further in Cornell's imaginings—to Hollywood, Paris, the stars—than the man, who left Queens and Manhattan once in his adult life, did himself.

Natural Selection is Eric Coble's story of a man who learns to look with new eyes on the world when he steps out of his office for the first time on a hunt to restock the Native Pavilion at Culture Fiesta. As the play progresses Coble's slightly askew version of the Florida of the near-future feels closer and closer to home and today. *Low,* Rha Goddess's one-woman investigation of a woman battling for her mental health, turns its eye to changing the audience's perspective instead of its characters'. In a society that makes it easy to overlook the people who fall through the cracks of family and social services, her play tries to change a potentially invisible homeless woman off her medication into a human with a story and situation, tries to reawaken a communal compassion that can take in a world that seems to have gone collectively mad.

Neon Mirage explores the images of Las Vegas, insubstantial but irresistible, that form the basis of our masochistic love affair with the very American dream of infinite possibility. Over the course of their investigation of the get-rich-quick capital of America, the show's multiple writers find humor, pathos and plenty of excuses for a floor show, reflecting back the ever-changing meanings of being American today. The Festival's three ten-minute plays also variously but vigorously attack the live-action challenge of making the familiar bracing and new. Rolin Jones's play *Sovereignty* starts with a sunny subdivision and exposes the complexity and complicities of being a good neighbor, on your street and in the world. In Adam Bock's play, *Three Guys and a Brenda,* the men are played by women, infusing this comedy with tenderness and insight into the complexities of even seemingly simple romantic interactions. *Listeners,* Jane Martin's blistering comedy, gives your average angry liberal a chance to reach through the haze and doublespeak separating her from the Guy In Charge, with extreme (and eye-opening) consequences.

What begins each spring with piles of envelopes and photocopies ends, a year later, in your hands. In this book you'll find the plays from our 30th annual Festival, vibrating with the energy of these amazing writers, echoing with the work of the relentlessly dedicated staff of the Actors Theatre of Louisville, and made possible through the sustained and sustaining generosity of the Humana Foundation. In a culture where more and more entertainment is individualized, and doesn't need to reflect anything more than our own image, these plays have offered a welcome antidote. Theater is an art form of radical compassion, where writers ask an audience to care about strangers for a while, to discover that lives we thought were very different than ours have something to show us about this hard work of being human. We feel lucky and grateful to introduce these plays to the canon of the American Theatre.

—*Adrien-Alice Hansel and Julie Felise Dubiner*

THREE GUYS AND A BRENDA
by Adam Bock

BIOGRAPHY

Adam Bock's plays include *Five Flights* (Rattlestick Theater, 2004; San Francisco's Encore Theater, 2002; Glickman Award winner; published in *Breaking Ground*, American Theater Critics Award nominee, Elizabeth Osborn Award nominee, two BATCC Awards); *Swimming in the Shallows* (Shotgun Players; 2000 Bay Area Theater Critics Circle Awards for Best Original Script, Best Production; Clauder Competition Award-winner; L. Arnold Weissberger Award nominee; LA Weekly nominee; GLAAD Media Award nominee; TimeOut NYs Top Ten; Second Stage's Uptown Series in New York City, summer 2005). Mr. Bock helped Jack Cummings III develop *The Audience*, nominated for three 2005 Drama Desk Awards including Best Musical. Other plays include *The Shaker Chair*, (Actors Theater of Louisville, 2005 Humana Festival; Kesselring Prize nomination); *The Typographer's Dream* (produced in New York City, San Francisco, Edinburgh Fringe Festival, Berkeley in 2006); *Thursday* (produced in San Francisco with a 2003 NEA grant); *The Drunken City* (Kitchen Theater in Ithaca, New York, 2005); *The Thugs* (premiered at Soho Rep in NYC, 2006). Mr. Bock is an artistic associate at Shotgun Players and Encore Theater, and is a member of MCC's Writers Coalition.

ACKNOWLEDGMENTS

Three Guys and a Brenda premiered at the Humana Festival of New American Plays in April 2006. It was directed by Frank Deal with the following cast and staff:

JOE	Suzanna Hay
BOB	Keira Keeley
RANDALL	Cheryl Lynn Bowers
BRENDA	Sarah Augusta
Scenic Designer	Paul Owen
Costume Designers	John P. White
	Stacy Squires
Lighting Designer	Paul Werner
Sound Designer	Benjamin Marcum
Properties Designer	Mark Walston
Stage Manager	Debra Anne Gasper
Asst. Stage Managers	Heather Fields, Paul Mills Holmes
Dramaturg	Julie Felise Dubiner
Assistant Dramaturg	Jamie Bragg

This play was developed with the support of The 24 Hour Plays.

CAST OF CHARACTERS

BOB, a man, played by a woman
JOE, a man, played by a woman
RANDALL, a man, played by a woman
BRENDA, a woman, played by a woman

SETTING

At work.

Suzanna Hay, Cheryl Lynn Bowers, and Keira Keeley
in *Three Guys and a Brenda*

30th Annual Humana Festival of New American Plays
Actors Theatre of Louisville, 2006
Photo by Harlan Taylor

THREE GUYS AND A BRENDA

Before this, BOB, JOE *and* RANDALL *were watching TV waiting for their shift to start.*

Now: BOB *and* JOE *are onstage. They are crying.*

RANDALL *walks across stage, crying. Exits.*

BOB *and* JOE *continue to cry.*

RANDALL *walks onstage. He is still crying. He has a roll of toilet tissue. He hands out tissue. They are all crying.*

BRENDA *walks across stage. They try not to/don't cry when she is onstage. She exits.*

They cry again. Deep breaths.

They sniff. They sniff. They sniff.

BRENDA *enters.*

BRENDA. You guys are on second shift right?

JOE. Yeah Brenda.

BOB. Yeah that's right.

BRENDA. Joe, then when your shift starts, then you and Bob are going to show Randall what to do with the new machine, ok?

JOE. Ok.

BRENDA. Ok?

BOB. Yeah ok.

JOE. Ok sure.

BRENDA. Ok then.

     (*Exits.*)

JOE. (*Deep breath, doesn't cry.*) Fucking animal nature shows.

BOB. I know.

JOE. They get me every time.

RANDALL. She's so beautiful.

JOE. She is.

BOB. She is Randall.

JOE. Yes she is.

RANDALL. Isn't she Bob? She's beautiful!

BOB. She is Randall.

RANDALL. I have to tell her she's beautiful.

BOB. I don't know Randall.

JOE. I don't know.

BOB. What do you think Joe?

JOE. I don't know about that Bob.

BOB. Yeah me neither I don't know either.

JOE. Might not be appropriate. In the work environment.

BOB. Right.

JOE. Right?

BOB. In the work environment.

JOE. This being work.

BOB. Right.

RANDALL. I have to.

BOB. Well if you have to, you have to.

JOE. That's right.

BOB. If you have to, you have to.

JOE. Right.

BOB. Right.

JOE. But I don't think you're going to.

BOB. Nope.

JOE. Right?

BOB. Nope!

RANDALL. I have to.

BOB. Joe here might.

JOE. That's something I might tell her.

BOB. Right. Joe might.

JOE. I might. I might say something to her like

BOB. Like

JOE. "You're beautiful!"

BOB. Right!

JOE. But I don't know whether you'd say something like that.

RANDALL. I am too. I am too going to say something like that to her!

JOE. Well.

BOB. Well.

JOE. Well ok then.

RANDALL. Because I think she's beautiful.

BOB. Well.

JOE. Ok then.

RANDALL. And I'm going to say it.

BOB. Ok then.

JOE. Ok.

(RANDALL *exits*.)

JOE. Think he's going to tell her?

BOB. Nope.

JOE. I'm not watching any more of those nature shows. They're too sad.

BOB. Yeah I know. Me neither.

JOE. They're too fucking sad. They make me sad.

RANDALL. (*To audience*.) Thing that's hard about being a guy? You always have to tell the girl "Hey you're great" or "Hey I think you're great" or "You're great" or "You're great" and "Would you maybe want to go out?" and that's hard. Plus it's hard to have to shave all the time. That's hard too.

JOE. (*To audience*.) Plus it's hard to pick a good deodorant.

RANDALL. (*To audience*.) Yeah that's hard too.

JOE. (*To audience*.) Plus guys? Plus we have to carry everything.

RANDALL. (*To audience*.) Right.

JOE. (*To audience*.) Especially heavy things. Like sofas.

RANDALL. (*To audience*.) Yeah that's hard.

BOB. (*To audience*.) Plus

JOE. (*To audience*.) Plus you have to drive all the time.

RANDALL. (*To audience*.) Yeah. And that.

BOB. (*To audience*.) Plus

JOE. (*To audience*.) You have to drive on really long trips, to the beach, to visit your family, and then back from the beach. And if a tire blows you have to take it off, you have to put the spare on. Plus you have to pay.

RANDALL. (*To audience*.) For everything.

BOB. (*To audience*.) Plus

JOE. (*To audience*.) Plus sometimes you don't understand something and that can make you feel stupid and so you have to pretend you understand it. That can be hard. (*Pause*.)

BOB. Yeah.

RANDALL. Yeah. (*Pause*.)

JOE. (*To audience*.) That can be hard. (*Pause*.)

RANDALL. (*To audience*.) Mostly it's hard though saying "I think you're great" and "Would you maybe like to go out" and then you have to wait and find out what the answer is. That's hard.

(BRENDA *enters*.)

RANDALL. Um. Brenda?

BRENDA. Give me a second.

(BRENDA *exits.*)

RANDALL. Guys. Don't bust my chops.

JOE. I didn't say anything.

RANDALL. Don't bust my chops.

(BRENDA *enters.*)

RANDALL. Hey Brenda?

BRENDA. I said just give me a.

(*She exits.* JOE, BOB *and* RANDALL *stand.*
RANDALL *looks at* JOE *and* BOB.
BRENDA *enters.*)

BRENDA. Yeah ok?

RANDALL. Oh yeah so. Um.

BRENDA. Yeah?

RANDALL. Guys?

JOE. Oh yeah.

BOB. What?

JOE. Ok. Come on.

BOB. What?

JOE. Bob come on.

BOB. Oh yeah yeah ok!

JOE. Ok!

BOB. Ok.

(*They exit.*)

RANDALL. Yeah so Brenda?

BRENDA. Yeah ok?

RANDALL. So.

BRENDA. I have work Randall.

RANDALL. Um.

BRENDA. Yeah ok so, what?

RANDALL. Um.

BRENDA. I have work.

(*Turns to exit.*)

RANDALL. I think you're beautiful.

BRENDA. What?

RANDALL. Um.

BRENDA. That's not funny.

RANDALL. What?

BRENDA. That's not funny.

RANDALL. I'm not being funny.

BRENDA. That's mean. That pisses me off. That really truly pisses me off.

RANDALL. No I do.

BRENDA. I have a lot of work. And you're pissing me off.

RANDALL. No I do. I think you're beautiful. I think you're beautiful like a. Like something beautiful. Like the sun in the sky. Like a lake. Like the sunshine on a lake in the early evening right before the sun goes down and everything is calm. And the water's calm. That's what I think.

BRENDA. Shut up.

RANDALL. No I do.

BRENDA. Like a lake?

RANDALL. Like the sunshine. On the lake.

BRENDA. Really?

RANDALL. Yeah really.

BRENDA. Really?

RANDALL. And I think If only I could kiss her I'd be happy.

BRENDA. Really?

RANDALL. Yeah.

BRENDA. You think if you kissed me, you'd be happy?

RANDALL. Yeah.

BRENDA. You want to kiss me?

RANDALL. Yeah.

BRENDA. And that would make you happy?

RANDALL. Yeah.

BRENDA. Just a kiss?

RANDALL. Yeah.

BRENDA. Ok so.

RANDALL. Really?

BRENDA. So?

(*They kiss. Should be a good smooch.*)

RANDALL. (*Softly.*) Yeah. That made me happy.

BRENDA. I have work.

RANDALL. Ok.

BRENDA. I have work.

RANDALL. Ok. Ok.

(*She exits.*)

JOE. (*To audience.*) I told my wife I loved the sound of her voice on the phone. And I do. I still do.

BOB. (*To audience.*) I gave my girlfriend a smooth stone I found on the side of the road.

JOE. Right?

BOB. Yeah.

> (RANDALL *smiles.*)
>
> (*The three men sit.*)

End of Play

NATURAL SELECTION
by Eric Coble

BIOGRAPHY

Eric Coble was born in Edinburgh, Scotland and bred on the Navajo and Ute reservations in New Mexico and Colorado. His plays have been produced Off-Broadway and on four continents, including productions at Manhattan Class Company, the Kennedy Center, Alabama Shakespeare Festival, Cleveland Play House, Actors Theatre of Louisville, Alliance Theater, Stages Repertory, and the Contemporary American Theater Festival. His awards include the AT&T Onstage Award and National Theatre Conference Playwriting Award. Mr. Coble is a member of the Cleveland Play House Playwrights Unit, and writes, acts, and plays with his family in Cleveland, Ohio.

ACKNOWLEDGMENTS

Natural Selection premiered at the Humana Festival of New American Plays in March 2006. It was directed by Marc Masterson with the following cast and staff:

HENRY CARSON	Jay Russell
ERNIE HARDAWAY, etc	Mark Mineart
YOLANDA PASTICHE, etc	Heather Dilly
SUZIE CARSON	Melinda Wade
ZHAO MARTINEZ	Javi Mulero
TERRANCE CARSON	Joseph Benjamin Glaser
Scenic Designer	Kris Stone
Costume Designer	Lorraine Venberg
Lighting Designer	Deb Sullivan
Sound Designer	Martin R. Desjardins
Video Designer	Jason Czaja
Properties Designer	Doc Manning
Dramaturg	Julie Felise Dubiner
Assistant Dramaturg	Joanna K. Donehower

CAST OF CHARACTERS

ERNIE HARDAWAY. A Man Who is Larger than Life, 40s.

HENRY CARSON. A Man Who is Just the Same Size as Life, 40s.

YOLANDA PASTICHE. A Woman Who Keeps Culture Fiesta on the Rails.

SUZIE CARSON. A Woman Who Keeps Her Life on the Rails, 40s.

PENELOPE. A Cheerful Chopper Pilot.

ZHAO MARTINEZ. A Man Who Isn't What He Appears, 20s.

MR. NEIBERDING. A Head-Hunter from Extreme Terror Plummet Park.

MS. FJELDSTAD. A Head-Hunter from Mega Family Christian Praise Park.

TERRANCE CARSON. Son of Henry Carson.

PLACE

Orlando, Florida, and Points West.

TIME

Next Week.

SETTING

A sparsely furnished stage representing different areas in Florida and the West in the very near future.

PRODUCTION NOTE

Natural Selection can be performed by 6-9 actors. If casting for six, one woman can play Yolanda, Penelope, and Ms. Fjeldstad; one man can play Ernie and Mr. Neiberding.

EDITORS' NOTE

In the interest of preserving both the flow of the play and indicating where changes of scene occurred in the original production, stage directions that open a scene shift are not in parentheses. Stage directions internal to the action of each scene are in parentheses.

Javi Mulero, Jay Russell, Melinda Wade, and Joseph Glaser
in *Natural Selection*

30th Annual Humana Festival of New American Plays
Actors Theatre of Louisville, 2006
Photo by Harlan Taylor

Natural Selection

ACT I

AT RISE: Darkness. Silence.
Then a COYOTE HOWL.
Faint drumming. Chanting/singing.
In Navajo. Drumming, singing louder... Louder... then it CUTS OFF.
Lights up on HENRY CARSON, *40s, in a suit and telephone headset, sitting behind a desk. Beside him stands* YOLANDA PASTICHE, *a sharp woman in a sharp suit, glasses, and headset. In a chair on the other side of the desk sits a big bear of a man in full safari outfit and headset:* ERNIE HARDAWAY.

ERNIE. So it's like the whole world's coming to an end, right? The chopper's entirely in flames now, right?

HENRY. Oh my god.

ERNIE. Debris everywhere, metal stalagmites jutting out of the black smoke, I look down and my entire arm is glittering—

HENRY. Glittering?

ERNIE. A thousand shards of glass in my skin, I'm like a walking disco ball, a crystal porcupine—

HENRY. Oh my god.

ERNIE. —and I grab the two guides—one of 'em's screaming, the other's trying to scream, but he's just spitting out blood and gobs of flesh—

HENRY. Oh god—

ERNIE. I throw 'em clear of the wreckage—twenty feet, I swear, I hurl this 180 pound man twenty feet—and the pilot—the pilot's out cold—probably 'cause her lower half has been ripped clean off—

HENRY. Oh dear god—

ERNIE. —and I'm thinking, this is what I get for letting a woman drive! But I grab what's left of her and drag her out of the crash—and no sooner am I out of the ribs of the fuselage than BOOM!!

(HENRY *jumps.*)

Reserve fuel tanks, whatever, BOOM!! I'm blown back thirty feet, face scorched, half my beard on fire—

HENRY. Oh god, Ernie—

ERNIE. But I'm already face down in the charred grass and rocks, I just rub my face in the ground— (*Demonstrates.*) BHHRRRHHRR—put out the flames—and I look around and I see, my god in heaven, somehow all of

27

us—all of us—are still alive! So of course my thoughts go to the obvious question—

HENRY. "How do I get help?"

ERNIE. "Who's going to eat who first?"

HENRY. Oh god, Ernie!

ERNIE. We're miles from *anything*, Henry! We're out in the exposed air and light—we're one little helicopter—who's gonna come looking for us?

HENRY. I know, but—

ERNIE. We were in the Adirondacks, Henry! Do you know anyone who's been to the Adirondacks since The Change?

HENRY. Well, no, but the Wilderness Channel ran a special—

ERNIE. I used to think the Montana–Texas Dust Belt was the most god-forsaken no-man's land on Earth, but I swear this whole continent, it's all gone to shit—and of course my gun's all twisted to hell, useless—my grandfather gave me that gun—

HENRY. I remember—

ERNIE & HENRY. —graduation present—

ERNIE. Useless. Then I notice the heat from the chopper's inferno is actually melting the glass in my arm—I got liquid glass trickling down my wrist—

HENRY. Oh man—

ERNIE. So I drip the glass onto the open wounds in the pilot and the one guide—it solidifies almost instantly, cauterizes the gaping veins and arteries—

HENRY. Jesus, Ernie—

ERNIE. We looked like stained glass pictures in Hell, Henry, I swear, sparkling with colors and textures man was not meant to see. And the smell—Jesus!

HENRY. I can imagine.

ERNIE. No. You can't.

HENRY. Well, I can just guess—

ERNIE. You can't guess. You weren't there, you never will be there, you will not try to impose your tiny little sensory imagination on my life.

HENRY. ...I wasn't.

ERNIE. You can't imagine the smell.

HENRY. I can't.

(*Beat.* ERNIE *stares hard at* HENRY. HENRY *waits...*)

ERNIE. What we did have was a thirty story plume of black smoke and ash rising into the clear sky. I figured if we had any chance that was it. And I still had my knife—

HENRY. The one your uncle gave you—

ERNIE. Strapped to my thigh like a second dick, my friend. I whipped that sucker out and started hacking down any and every piece of foliage I could—most everything was dead anyway—

HENRY. —the drought, the plague—

ERNIE. —throwing it all on the fire, leaves, bark, birds, woodland animals, everything—

HENRY. You saw actual living wild animals?

ERNIE. And they spotted us. Troop of Cub Scouts on one of their Extreme Wilderness Weekends—only group left dumb enough to leave the cities—

HENRY. God bless the Scouts—

ERNIE. I was delirious with lack of blood, sleep, food—I could taste it—pure adrenaline in my mouth, my throat, feel it pulsing behind my eyes—you ever tasted the secretion of your own adrenal glands?

HENRY. ...no.

ERNIE. Pray you never do. Tastes like mud, like the primordial ooze we crawled out of, mixed with blood and semen.

HENRY. No. I've never tasted that.

ERNIE. I guess I didn't stop when the Scout troop showed up, kept carving, kept moving, kept swearing—apparently I took out two kids trying for a wolf badge in first aid.

HENRY. Jesus.

ERNIE. But the point is—and I don't think this was lost on the Cub pack—I survived. I looked right into the jaws of the oblivion beast, that dread maw of eternal night, and I said—not for the first time either—"Fuck You."

YOLANDA. So you didn't collect the inventory.

HENRY. Yolanda! This man just looked into the dread maw of eternal night—

YOLANDA. And the short and curly of it is, he's been gone a month and we still have no new inventory.

ERNIE. Listen, if I need a ball-bustin'—

YOLANDA. Henry's performance review is coming up and I think he was counting on new inventory, weren't you, Henry?

ERNIE. You can be one selfish sonofabitch, you know that, Henry?

HENRY. No! I'm glad you're okay! I mean, Thank God! You're a hero! You're my personal hero, Ernie, you know that—

ERNIE. I don't wanta be your hero. I just want a little common respect.

HENRY. It's just Yolanda's right, we've got the big picture to frame here—I've gotta justify the expenses incurred—

ERNIE. Goddam women pilots. I never had any luck with women pilots. Every crash I ever had: female pilot.

(YOLANDA *gives him a look.* HENRY *is desperately scanning his laptop.*)

HENRY. The question is, can we get you back into the Adirondacks and secure the inventory before the end of the month...

ERNIE. I'm not going back.

HENRY. What?

ERNIE. I had the best North-Eastern guides in the country, Henry. They ain't gonna be guidin' anyone for at least a year. I'm not goin' into the brush without them.

HENRY. Then how am I going to get the replacement Indians for the Native American Tribal Pavilion?

ERNIE. We don't know that I would've found any anyway—

HENRY. There were multiple sightings! You know how often I get indigenous sightings outside of casinos?

ERNIE. Pretty rare, I bet.

HENRY. I get more sightings of primitive Mongolians! And you know if we're looking, every other theme park and cultural pavilion is out scouring too—

ERNIE. They won't get nowhere. I had the two best guides.

YOLANDA. We can't afford any more losses, Mr. Hardaway. Attendance is down and the mortality rate of our performers is increasingly distressing—we have yet to fully repopulate the Chinese and Madagascar pavilions—

ERNIE. You guys are WonderWorld, you can do robots for a while—

YOLANDA. We're Culture Fiesta, Mr. Hardaway. We don't do "robots."

HENRY. Genuine native people in authentic native habitats. That's what we do. Ernie knows that, don't you, Ernie?

ERNIE. I can get you some guys from the cities—I know a lot are 1/16th Cherokee—

HENRY. Do they know any tribal dances, crafts, ceremonies?

ERNIE. Not unless they involve watching T.V.

HENRY. Dang it! All the courses in cultural anthropology, museum science, interactive realism, and I'm gonna end up painting our interns brown.

YOLANDA. Not on my watch. All our performers are 100% pureblood representatives of their national origins.

ERNIE. Stop your whining. Jesus. If it'll shut you up, I got one more lead. One I wouldn't need a guide for.

YOLANDA. What.

ERNIE. There's a sportsman, mostly small game, outta Newark, he says he's seen some rurals in northern New Mexico.

HENRY. By Taos?

ERNIE. Maybe.

HENRY. They were probably re-enactors from Santa Fe—

ERNIE. He says they were the real deal. Out in the desert, hogans, sheep, the whole nine yards.

YOLANDA. Did he give you a location?

ERNIE. Not precisely, but I know the canyons he hunts. It's the best I got for you, amigo.

HENRY. I was counting on the Adirondacks.

ERNIE. You rustle up some cash, and I'll bring you back a Southwestern native.

HENRY. (*Scanning his laptop.*) We just lost a Navajo—we could use another Navajo—

YOLANDA. Another Navajo would give us more rugs. Those things sell like crackcakes.

HENRY. We've never had any Hopi or Zuni though. The Hopi Sun Prayer is beautiful, Yolanda—and actually the Zuni words for "daylight" and "life" are the same words, isn't that—

YOLANDA. Henry.

HENRY. Sorry.

(*To* ERNIE.)

You think there might be a chance they might be Hopi or Zuni?

ERNIE. I know they'll be better than an intern painted brown.

YOLANDA. You think there's a serious chance?

ERNIE. I'm sayin'—

YOLANDA. Henry's going with you.

HENRY. *What*??

ERNIE. Aw, no—

YOLANDA. You take Henry with you on the hunt or you don't go.

HENRY. I don't, I'm not—

YOLANDA. He's got vacation days.

ERNIE. Look, I've known Henry since he was wetting himself in gym class—

HENRY. I—I—I—I—I—

YOLANDA. Henry, Mr. Hardaway is still not—though he is the best in his field, I have no doubt—he is still not a member of the WonderWorld Culture Fiesta family. I authorized the last trip on his terms and we've seen how that worked out.

ERNIE. Listen—

YOLANDA. If I'm going to justify another expedition, I do it on my terms, and my terms are I want a company rep repped to make sure it's done right this time.

HENRY. Absolutely, that's a totally valid position, but I've never—

YOLANDA. It's like your dream—what is it—you have that dream of being in the desert, right?

HENRY. Yeah, but I'm always a rabbit getting chased by wolves—

YOLANDA. Well, now's your chance to live the dream, Henry.

ERNIE. Look, Ms…

YOLANDA. Pastiche.

ERNIE. It's nature. Not the indoor-processed-sanitized-air-for-your-protection-Culture Fiesta-nature, but real honest-to-God outdoor rotten-disease-plagued-no-ozone-no-laws-dead-zone-humans-can't-live-here-anymore Nature.

HENRY. I won't last twenty minutes out there!

YOLANDA. And the natives may not last *that* long! Why do you think it's so hard to repopulate the indigenous pavilions? It's because no one is indigenous anymore! If the next generation is going to see honest-to-god native people on anything other than a CD-ROM, it's going to be in Culture Fiesta. We owe that to the children. We owe it to the Natives. You owe it to yourself, Henry. Isn't one of your ancestors some big Indian hunter?

HENRY. What?

YOLANDA. You're descended from…

HENRY. "Kit" Carson, yes, okay, but—

ERNIE. The guy who killed the Navajos? You never told me that.

HENRY. It's not a fact I'm particularly proud of—

YOLANDA. My point is that bagging natives is in your blood. This is your chance to look in the dread maw and say "Fuck You."

HENRY. Yolanda—

YOLANDA. Two words, Henry: Performance. Review. I'll get your leave papers by tomorrow.

(*And she walks out.* HENRY *and* ERNIE *turn to look at each other.*)

ERNIE. How are you gonna explain this to the little woman?

Lights shift. ERNIE *exits as* HENRY *turns to see* SUZIE, *his wife, 40s, in comfortable clothes and phone headset, typing on her laptop at their dining room table, taking swigs of her bottled water.* HENRY *carries a small bouquet of flowers.*

HENRY. (*Presenting the flowers.*) Da, da-da-da-da-da DAAAA!

SUZIE. Henry. Are these real?

HENRY. Yep. The garden crew made them. They just came out of the tube yesterday.

SUZIE. They're gorgeous. Let me get a shot of them.

(*She aims her little webcam at the flowers.*)

These are so much nicer than the synth ones we have at work.

HENRY. And I bought us dinner!

(*Holds up an Applebee's bag.*)

Lasagne burritos.

SUZIE. (*Kisses him.*) Ooo, Henry—

HENRY. I thought a little romantic meal before Terrance comes downstairs from school—

SUZIE. He's actually up there in soccer practice right now. It's being webcast in real time. I was checking in on it—

HENRY. (*Looks at her laptop screen.*) How's he doing?

SUZIE. Pretty well. The coach has been instant messaging notes on what he needs to work on—

HENRY. We're so lucky Mr. Klerksdorp is willing to coach from South Africa.

SUZIE. Now if we can just find him an acting coach before his school play. Let me get a shot of you and the flowers.

(*She points the webcam at* HENRY *who poses.*)

This is going straight onto my blog.

(*Typing.*)

"6:52 p.m. B-HOE brings flowers and dinner—"

HENRY. "B-HOE"?

SUZIE. "Best Husband On Earth." My acronym for you ever since you re-grouted the bathroom.

(*She kisses him again as he opens his own laptop and sits down.*)

HENRY. Man's gotta do what a man's gotta do.

SUZIE. Most of my readers all agree—the feedback is skewing highly in your favor. And this picture of you with the flowers is darling.

(*Showing him her screen as she types.*)

"Is there a more darling man?"

(*To* HENRY.)

And the burritos are from Applebee's—I'll hyper-link to them, I'm sure they'll appreciate the plug.

HENRY. (*Looking at his screen.*) Huh.

SUZIE. What.

HENRY. Oh, I was just checking the weather.

SUZIE. Why? You're not going back out are you?

HENRY. No. Just looking at the southwest United States. Looks clear and dry. Good flying weather.

SUZIE. You're not re-tracing the butterfly migration patterns again, are you? You know they're not coming back, sweetheart.

HENRY. No. Ernie's flying out to Arizona, Utah, to look for new stock for the Native Pavilion.

SUZIE. I thought he was in the Adirondacks.

HENRY. That didn't work out.

SUZIE. Send a camera with him this time. I can post his shots in the "Can You Believe It" section of my site.

HENRY. That's a fantastic idea, honey.

SUZIE. Always thinking. You want your burrito heated up?

HENRY. Maybe I can go with him and shoot the photos myself.

(SUZIE *pauses.*)

SUZIE. What?

HENRY. Since he's going anyway, I could tag along. E-mail some pictures back to you and the office—

SUZIE. You're not going to Utah.

HENRY. Maybe not Utah, but maybe Arizona and New Mexico.

SUZIE. Are you insane?

HENRY. Did you know there's still evidence of Anasazi pueblos around Chaco Canyon, Suzie? Pueblo Bonito alone was four or five stories tall, it—

SUZIE. Henry.

HENRY. Sorry.

SUZIE. Ernie came to your office today, didn't he? You told him about the desert dream, didn't you—

HENRY. I didn't—

SUZIE. (*Typing.*) "6:54 p.m. Former B-HOE goes completely off his rocker—"

HENRY. Don't make me a Former B-HOE—I'm not a *former* B-HOE—

SUZIE. (*Turns the camera on herself and types.*) "If anyone's watching this in real-time—HELP! My husband's gone suicidal—"

HENRY. We need new natives—I'll just run get a new native—

SUZIE. Can't you just paint some interns brown?

HENRY. Suzie!

SUZIE. We're talking about the desert, right, Henry?

HENRY. Exactly—plateaus, cliff dwellings, painted sand—

SUZIE. —and how many miles to the nearest TGI-Fridays?

HENRY. I'm sure there's good restaurants in Santa Fe, Phoenix—I don't know—

SUZIE. Exactly. You don't know. How often have you left Orlando?

HENRY. I go to conferences all the time—Buenos Aires, Beijing, Cairo—

SUZIE. Places where they speak English and drink Coke-a-Cola and have cell phone reception. Not the desert. Not Wile E. Coyote country.

HENRY. I know.

SUZIE. (*Typing.*) I bet there's a Traveler's Advisory on the Southwest—

HENRY. Of course there's a Travel's Advisory—there's Advisories about the entire planet—

SUZIE. (*Reading her screen.*) Sunlight at 730% Recommended Daily Allowance, Particulate Matter at 210% RDA, new viruses reported in thirteen counties, 56% chance of Separatist activity—

HENRY. I know.

SUZIE. I am *not* going to be a single mother widow to our son.

HENRY. I know—

SUZIE. On my income! Can you imagine? Wal-Mart pays well but not that well.

HENRY. Suze—

SUZIE. You don't want to pull up the rug!

HENRY. What??

SUZIE. You said you'd pull up the carpet on the stairs to the attic this weekend—you're trying to get out of pulling up the carpet, aren't you!

HENRY. Oh god.

SUZIE. You're scared. You're scared of dust mites, aren't you?

(*Typing.*)

"Hubby'd rather face plagues and killers than pull carpet tacks—"

HENRY. Will you stop typing on your blog?? This is a private conversation—

SUZIE. My readers thrive on my private conversations—I keep it real, Henry, you will *not* edit me—

HENRY. And you won't edit me, Suzie!

(*They stop. Staring at each other...*)

This isn't my idea. Yolanda's making me do it.

SUZIE. ...oh god.

HENRY. My performance review is coming up, if I don't bring back something—

SUZIE. She's willing to kill you to restock the park!

HENRY. She's willing to risk me, not kill me, we don't know that I'll die—

SUZIE. I hate her. I hate her I hate her I hate her—

HENRY. I know. I guess it's my turn to look into the dread maw and say "Fuck You."

(*Beat. He holds her.*)

I can pull up the carpet tacks when I get back on Tuesday.

(*Pause.*)

SUZIE. What are you going to tell your son?

HENRY. I guess… I have to tell him I'm going on an adventure.

Sound of a chopper. SUZIE exits as HENRY pulls on a coat and runs to meet ERNIE, in full safari gear, and PENELOPE, a pilot in sunglasses, ball-cap, headset, and active wear. They sit in three chairs, now in a helicopter—HENRY and PENELOPE in front, ERNIE sulking in the rear. HENRY looks airsick—barely hanging on. They yell over the chopper engine.

PENELOPE. (*Shouting.*) You know what I love about the desert? It's so damn quiet! The hustle and bustle of the city starts gettin' on your last nerve, grindin' you down like a whetstone, grinding you to a pointy little spike— grinding, grinding, grinding, grinding, grinding, grinding, grinding—

HENRY. Yes.

PENELOPE. But you take a quick jump out here and it's just you and the sand and sage and sky. Almost enough to make you believe in God, innit?

HENRY. Yes.

PENELOPE. Sometimes I think if there is an Almighty, this is where He's gotta be, right? Last place anyone would think to look. But if I glance out the corner of my eye real quick I might spot Him popping out from behind a cactus or running from rock to rock. And then I think, well, maybe that was just a lizard. 'Cause if it was God, He'd have to have a hell of a high sunscreen to survive out here, wouldn't He?

HENRY. Yes.

PENELOPE. You know the other thing I love? I love that it's three-dimensional!

HENRY. …what?

PENELOPE. When you're on the ground, it's just you and terra firma, you know? Accent on the "firma." I'm in my office fillin' out paper work, accident reports, insurance claims, whatnot, I get a little squirmy, the best I can do is hop on my desk or crawl under the water cooler, you know? But up here, I feel a little twitchy, and—

(*She shoves the steering column forward and they PLUMMET.*)

HENRY. AAAAAAAAA—

PENELOPE. YEEAAAAHHHH!!

(ERNIE *scowls*. PENELOPE *pulls up*.)

Gives you a whole new world view, don't it?

HENRY. Please. Let's do two dimensions. I'm very fond of two dimensions.

PENELOPE. Office jockey, am I right?

HENRY. It's not that—

PENELOPE. Free as a bird! That's what they used to say. Back when they had birds.

HENRY. We have 34 species of birds in our aviary—

PENELOPE. Sweet. Take the controls a minute, will ya?

(*She rustles in her backpack as* HENRY *grabs the steering*.)

HENRY. Jesus God!

(ERNIE *reaches over and helps steer*. PENELOPE *sits back up with an Applebee's bag. She pulls out a sandwich and takes the controls*.)

PENELOPE. Gotta keep my blood sugar up or I pass out.

HENRY. Oh god.

PENELOPE. Curry Salmon bagel. You want some?

HENRY. No. No thank you.

PENELOPE. Heavy on the creamed spinach and cheese. You sure?

HENRY. (*Not looking*.) No thank you.

PENELOPE. (*To* ERNIE.) You?

(ERNIE *snorts*.)

Your buddy back there a mute?

ERNIE. I'm not a mute.

HENRY. He's just worried.

PENELOPE. That we're not gonna catch anything?

ERNIE. That we're not gonna live to see the right canyon.

PENELOPE. Ooo, grumpy bear! Grumpy Bear!

HENRY. He's had bad luck with pilots lately.

ERNIE. Certain pilots.

PENELOPE. Well, no worries here, mate. I haven't pulled a flamer in 8 and 1/2 months. And pretty near everyone got out of that one.

ERNIE. Christ on wheat.

HENRY. Do you think we're getting close? I'm just... All the movement and noise and cramped space—I'm not sure what a heart attack feels like, but—

PENELOPE. And I don't want to be a big Gloomy Gertie, but our fuel's in the yellow— if we don't head back pretty quick, we will be testing the ol' airbags again.

ERNIE. What is this, Pre-school Safari? You go on the hunt, you stay on the hunt, you start listening to the pounding blood in your ears and the hiss of sweat in your eyes, and you tell the voice of reason to shut the hell up.

HENRY. But, Ernie—

ERNIE. Shut the hell up, Henry. Live up to your heritage, if you die today you die like a man. Now fly into that goddam slot canyon over there. I got a feeling.

PENELOPE. That's a tight squeeze.

ERNIE. Of course it's a tight squeeze! You think the natives are gonna be wanderin' around in the open? They didn't survive this long by being stupid. They're cunning. We gotta be cunninger.

(PENELOPE *steers them over...*)

HENRY. Oh god...she's right, Ernie, this is a really tight canyon—I don't—

ERNIE. (*To* PENELOPE.) You got stealth?

PENELOPE. Bad idea, Great White Hunter. It'll use up the fuel too fast.

HENRY. You've got stealth?

ERNIE. Click on the damn stealth.

PENELOPE. I'm not using stealth.

HENRY. You've got stealth?

ERNIE. You don't use stealth, we might as well put our dicks into the rotor blades right now.

PENELOPE. That's not a problem for all of us!

HENRY. You've got—

ERNIE. Use the damn—

PENELOPE. I'm not—

HENRY. You've got—

ERNIE. (*Waving his rifle.*) CLICK ON THE DAMN STEALTH!!

(*CLICK.* PENELOPE *hits a button. The rotors go to a quiet hum.*)

PENELOPE. Jesus, I hate male back seat drivers.

ERNIE. This is stealth. I got this on my Humvee. Never know when you'll need the element of surprise.

HENRY. Where?

ERNIE. I go on a lot of blind dates.

(HENRY *gives him a look...*)

HENRY. I don't think you should be waving your gun in here.

ERNIE. Probably right. I don't know this one yet. I think this is the safety.

PENELOPE. (*Looking out.*) Whoa, whoa, whoa, what's that?

HENRY. What.

PENELOPE. Those.

ERNIE. Those are cotton bushes.

HENRY. They're moving.

ERNIE. Choppers blowing them.

HENRY. They're running away.

PENELOPE. Cotton plants don't run.

ERNIE. Then they're tumbleweeds!

HENRY. Unless I miss my guess… those are sheep!

PENELOPE. Bingo.

HENRY. Oh my god, real sheep, that means we're close, Ernie! Sheep have been synonymous with primitive Navajos for centuries—blankets, commerce, mutton—do you know how many recipes there are for mutton?

ERNIE. Will you shut up, Henry?

HENRY. Sorry.

ERNIE. Those are probably wild sheep.

PENELOPE. The wild sheep were history before the birds and horses. Professor Mutton's right. Where there's sheep there's shepherds.

ERNIE. Then keep hovering here…

HENRY. There must be three dozen of them… Oh shoot!

(*He fumbles with his cell phone.*)

PENELOPE. Don't even bother, there's no reception out here.

HENRY. Photos—this is exactly what Suzie wants on her website—

(*Trying to aim his phone camera.*)

Can you keep the chopper still?

PENELOPE. I'm trying not to ram a wall…

ERNIE. There!

PENELOPE & HENRY. Where!

ERNIE. (*Pointing.*) Human figure at 10:15—got a staff—he's a shepherd!

HENRY. Ohmygodohmygodohmygod—

PENELOPE. He's running!

ERNIE. Turn the chopper so I can get a shot!

PENELOPE. I can't!

HENRY. (*Aiming his camera.*) I can get him—

ERNIE. You're gonna get a shot of my silky white ass if you don't clear the way—

(*They're scuffling—trying to move…*)

PENELOPE. Careful! Watch it!

ERNIE. Henry—

HENRY. I'm trying—

(*THOONK! The rifle goes off.*)

ERNIE. AAAAAA!!!

(*He falls back in his seat.*)

HENRY. Ernie!!

PENELOPE. Oh my god!

(*She swerves the chopper.*)

ERNIE. Shot myself in the goddam leg!!

HENRY. Ernie!

ERNIE. Fuckin' tranquilizer dart—I hate when this happens...

PENELOPE. Native's getting away!

ERNIE. Had to get your goddam picture—

HENRY. What do we do? What do we do??

ERNIE. (*Reloading.*) I got another dart, I can... I got anotheerrrr...

PENELOPE. He's running for that little shed—

HENRY. That's a hogan!

PENELOPE. If he gets in we have to go on foot—

HENRY. We're not going on foot—

ERNIE. (*Trying to aim.*) ...just bank the starboard bow— Iganjusgeeaaaa...

HENRY. Watch the gun! Watch the gun!

PENELOPE. The guy's in jeans and flannel shirt—he's not even primitive—

HENRY. He's got sheep, city natives don't have sheep, he's gotta be the real thing—

ERNIE. Imnaafininzoaaanyy...

(ERNIE *passes out, slumped over* HENRY *and* PENELOPE—*she fights to keep steady*—)

PENELOPE. Abort mission! Abort mission!

HENRY. NO!!

(HENRY *GRABS the gun and tries to aim out the window*—)

PENELOPE. He's almost in—

HENRY. Angle me around!

PENELOPE. We're—

HENRY. Jesus jesus jesus—

PENELOPE. I can't keep her up—

HENRY. I gotta shoot him in the back, I can't shoot him—

PENELOPE. Goddammit—

HENRY. I can't—

PENELOPE. Shoot!!

HENRY. Can't—

PENELOPE. SHOOOO—

> (*THOOM.* HENRY *fires. They all freeze.*)
>
> *Lights shift.* PENELOPE *and the helicopter disappear.* HENRY *and* ERNIE *step back into Henry's office, setting down an* UNCONSCIOUS MAN *in jeans, flannel shirt, and no telephone headset. He could be Native American, could be Latino. His hands and feet are tied.*
>
> ERNIE *sits with his head in his hands, rubbing his leg occasionally, as* HENRY *gently places Navajo bowls, baskets, and rugs around the prone figure. They all look worse for wear…*

ERNIE. Christ, it still feels like a hangover.

HENRY. You should have seen me, Ernie, you would've been so proud. I, I grabbed the gun, your gun, and I got him in my sights and it was so loud, like you say, the pounding and throbbing and I completely forgot my nausea for, for an eternity it felt like, and, and I shoved you back, and I aimed, I really aimed, and BLAM-O. I just squeezed the trigger. I just pulled the trigger and Blam-O.

ERNIE. That's how it usually works.

HENRY. It did! Blam-O. And he was falling forward. Right into the dust, like in slow motion, but not slow. He just fell right over. Blam. Thump. It was instant. I was there. I mean I was *there*, Ernie.

ERNIE. So was I.

HENRY. But in here I was there. And now he's here. And we're here. And I'm still there! A little.

ERNIE. What the hell are you doing?

HENRY. I'm surrounding him with familiar objects. So when he comes to he won't be so terrified.

ERNIE. (*Looks at a bowl.*) Where'd you get this Apache crap?

HENRY. Navajo. I ordered from Trail-Of-Tears.com.

ERNIE. Nice.

HENRY. I hope they smell authentic. Natives have a very keen sense of smell, you know.

ERNIE. You might wanta pull the bar-code off the rug.

HENRY. Darn it.

> (*He does.*)

I tried not washing my hands, more grease and soil build-up, you know. And no deodorant since we got back. And I removed all the air-fresheners from my office. Shouldn't his tranquilizer be wearing off?

ERNIE. When did we give him that second dose for the plane trip?

HENRY. Eight hours ago.

ERNIE. Should be anytime now. Assuming his heart don't stop.

HENRY. Don't say that. Don't even think that. God, look, my hands! They're still shaking! I can't tell you the last time my hands trembled!

ERNIE. You let the little woman know you're back yet?

HENRY. Oh god!

(*Grabs out his phone.*)

She must be worried sick, I haven't—I didn't get any pictures! Except at the Albuquerque airport when we first landed! Oh god. She'll be furious.

ERNIE. Take some of Anasazi boy.

HENRY. I can't. He's Culture Fiesta property now. Copyright issues. Let me take some of you.

ERNIE. I don't want my picture took.

HENRY. Just a couple.

ERNIE. No.

HENRY. Ernie—

ERNIE. No!

(*In steps* YOLANDA*, as sharp as ever.*)

YOLANDA. Welcome home, Henry.

HENRY. Yolanda! Oh god! I'm so—I can't—you shouldn't be here. You should wait 'til we're in the observation room with the two-way mirror.

YOLANDA. I wanted to see our newest acquisition before the docs and costume designers get their hooks into him.

(*To* ERNIE.)

Congratulations, Mr. Hardaway.

(ERNIE *tries to stand, almost falls, catches himself on the desk.*)

Are you all right?

ERNIE. Aw, it's bullshit. My leg. Hunting accident. Nothing a good shot of gin and a piss won't cure.

YOLANDA. Well, Henry, congrats to you as well.

HENRY. He's a beauty, isn't he?

YOLANDA. Doesn't look very primitive.

HENRY. He was in a canyon. Herding sheep! I mean, you can't expect them to wear loin cloths and feathers, Yolanda.

YOLANDA. (*Kneeling beside the figure.*) Who did the clean up?

HENRY. Nobody. He's all natural.

YOLANDA. You brought him to your office without decontaminating him? Henry! What is the protocol? Why do we have regulations?

HENRY. I just—

YOLANDA. (*Quickly pulling on plastic gloves.*) We could be dealing with lice, ticks, chiggers, mice—

HENRY. I just wanted him to wake up in a friendly environment, not surrounded by guys in Hepavac suits scouring him down. Look at him, Yolanda! Isn't he beautiful?

YOLANDA. You're putting everyone in administration in jeopardy.

ERNIE. That's our Henry. Rebel, rebel.

HENRY. I'm not a rebel. I mean, you know, not all the time. Sometimes. A man's gotta do what a man's gotta do.

YOLANDA. I'm sorry, Henry, but I can't abide this.

(*Into her headset.*)

Dial Tone. Securit—

(*The figure stirs.*)

HENRY. Wait! He's waking up! Shh shh shh shh—he's waking up! Don't call security, let him get his bearings—just give me two minutes—

ERNIE. (*Pulling out his big knife.*) Besides, I got us covered if he gets frisky.

YOLANDA. How'd you get that through security??

ERNIE. I got my ways.

HENRY. Get out.

ERNIE & YOLANDA. What?

HENRY. Get outside! Please. Wait outside—You'll freak him out, I don't want him freaked out by a crowd—

YOLANDA. But—

HENRY. Five minutes! Gimme five minutes to acclimate him—

MAN. …uhhhh…

HENRY. Go!

YOLANDA. Henry—

ERNIE. You need help, just scream.

(*He's out.*)

YOLANDA. You are pushing the envelope here, Henry, and not in a good—

(HENRY *closes the door on her.*)

HENRY. Thank you.

(*He turns. The figure stirs.* HENRY *clicks on a little CD player on his desk.*)

(*A traditional Navajo song starts quietly.* HENRY *scoots a little bowl in front of the* MAN, *crouches a safe distance back from him.*)

(*The* MAN *blinks his eyes—looks around… dazed…*)

(*Quietly:*) It's okay. Um. "Ya' ta' Hey." "Dineh." Safe. You're safe. See?

(*Holds up a little rug.*)

Home? Safe at home?

(*Beat. They stare at each other.*)

MAN. What the fuck is goin' on?

HENRY. What?

MAN. Why am I tied up? I want a lawyer—I didn't do nothin'—

HENRY. No. Oh no. No.

MAN. Where am I? Get those goddam pots away from me!

(*He kicks a basket across the room.*)

HENRY. Don't kick it! Native Americans don't kick their own artifacts!

MAN. ...what?

HENRY. Tell me you're Navajo, please tell me you're Navajo—

MAN. What the hell you want to know for? I got rights. I can get a lawyer. You can't keep me here—

HENRY. Oh crap. Oh crap oh crap oh crap—

MAN. Untie me, man! I ain't done nothin'!

HENRY. Okay. Listen. Just listen. Um. Are you Native American?

(*Beat. The man looks at HENRY.*)

MAN. Navajo on my mother's side, asshole.

HENRY. Just your mother?

MAN. My dad's from Guadalajara.

HENRY. You're not even a full-blood.

MAN. What's that got to do with anything?

HENRY. You were herding sheep in the open desert! What the heck were you doing herding sheep in the open desert when you're only part Indian??

MAN. I was visiting my tia and tio on the Rez. They got sheep. Is that illegal now?

HENRY. Are your aunt and uncle full-bloods? Why am I even asking? The budget's gone! I just blew the budget!

MAN. I'm not talkin', 'til I get a lawyer.

HENRY. Darn it!

(*Beat.*)

Shoot!

(HENRY *stares at the* MAN, *who stares back. Long moments pass.... HENRY taps his fingers on his desk lightly.... Then....*)

You want something to drink? I can get you a Vanilla Cherry Lime Pepsi. Or something.

(*Beat. The* MAN *stares at him.*)

My treat.

(*The* MAN *stares. More moments pass…. Then* HENRY *laughs.*)
Surprise! This is… ah…

(*Begins untying the* MAN.)

—it's a new promotion we're doing. To, ah, to get folks into the park. Get it? "It's so much fun, you'll have to be tied down!" My understanding is rope burns disappear very quickly. There shouldn't be any lasting… redness…

(*The* MAN *sits up, now free. They look at each other.*)

MAN. Where am I?

HENRY. WonderWorld, you idiot!! Sorry! Sorry. I just assumed—Hooo! Still a little tense. My first… first marketing foray. As it were. On behalf of everyone at Culture Fiesta, allow me to welcome you to the Jolliest Place On Earth.

(*At his desk.*)

And we would like to offer you a five day pass—all expenses paid—it's all on us—including airfare back to New Mexico. We already flew you here. What, ah, what name should I fill out on the paperwork? Benally? Begay? Yazzie?

MAN. Martinez.

HENRY. Of course. Mexican.

MAN. Zhao Martinez.

(HENRY *puts his head in his hands.*)

ZHAO. Named for my grandpa. He was Chinese-Brazilian. Met my grandma in Jamaica.

(HENRY *slumps further down on his desk.*)

You shoot everyone you want to come to your park?

HENRY. (*Shoves a paper across the desk.*) I'm, ah, I'm going to need you to sign a release form. To get the tickets.

ZHAO. (*Tries to stand.*) Damn, man. What the hell'd you hit me with?

HENRY. Did I say five day pass? Let me make that a ten day—

(*KNOCK KNOCK KNOCK from the door.*)

YOLANDA. (*Off-stage.*) Henry? Everything all right in there?

HENRY. Dang it! Fine! It's all fine—we're… bonding!

YOLANDA. I need to let the de-contam guys in—

HENRY. Just a minute! We're at a very delicate stage!

ZHAO. What the hell's goin' on, man?

HENRY. (*Quietly.*) Okay. To get the tickets, this is a very special trial offer, and to get the tickets, you need to not say anything to anyone out there. Not a sound. You understand? You can smile and nod. Okay? Even if they… kind of strip you down and de-louse you.

ZHAO. What?

HENRY. Standard park procedure! Can't be too careful nowadays!

ZHAO. Look, I don't know the game here—

HENRY. No game! Just sign—

ZHAO. —but I know the smell of shit on shoes.

HENRY. What?

ZHAO. You stepped in something *bad*, man. I seen that expression on my friends before, usually right before their ass ends up in the pokey.

HENRY. I don't, I, I don't know what you're—

ZHAO. Look, man, I don't know what the hell you were doin' out there on the Rez with your Black Hawk whatever. But I know this. You want me to keep my mouth shut, it's gonna take a shitload more than a ten day pass to fuckin' Culture Fiesta.

(*Beat. They watch each other.*)

HENRY. What do you want?

ZHAO. (*Points to the CD player.*) First, can the damn chanting and drumming. It's killin' me, man. Don't you got no "Bajo Bacas" or "Norteño Pimps"?

HENRY. (*Turns off the CD.*) No.

ZHAO. I gotta be honest with you—what's your name?

HENRY. Henry. Henry Carson.

ZHAO. (*A flash of a grin.*) Carson? Henrito. I was visiting my relatives 'cause I had a lot of free time and kind of needed to lay low.

HENRY. Yes.

ZHAO. I'm kind of between things right now.

HENRY. Yes…

ZHAO. I'm fuckin' unemployed, man. You want to keep my trap shut, you find me a job here with the Jolly People.

HENRY. I don't—technically we're not hiring right now—

(*BANG BANG BANG on the door.*)

YOLANDA. Henry, need I remind you of your increasingly perilous upcoming performance review?

HENRY. One second! I think I just gained his trust!

(*To* ZHAO.)

How would you feel about being WonderWorld's new Native American?

ZHAO. Like in a stunt show with tomahawks and horses and shit?

HENRY. Like you sit around and get looked at and do Corn Grinding dances and chants and serve fry bread and mutton to tourists.

ZHAO. Like working at McDonald's.

HENRY. More singing and rug-weaving, but yes.

ZHAO. What kind of salary?

HENRY. I don't know. We don't pay the other exhibits—just room and board—I'd have to take the money out of Native upkeep and maybe the Christmas party… maybe… ten dollars an hour?

ZHAO. You got yourself a deal, Henrito.

HENRY. Excellent!

ZHAO. But I don't speak hardly no Navajo.

HENRY. You can pick it up from discs and some the other genuine natives.

ZHAO. The Navajo ones.

HENRY. Exactly. Don't hang around with the Central Kalapuyan or Tilamook. Just stay silent at first. You're a newbie, they'll expect some fear.

ZHAO. And I don't know shit about rugs or bowls.

HENRY. Turquoise?

(ZHAO *shakes his head.*)

Don't you have *any* indigenous skills?

ZHAO. I rock at GameSplice and Brady Bunch trivia.

HENRY. (*Winces.*) Okay. We can get you books and DVD's. You can study them secretly in my office in off-hours.

ZHAO. Like a little espionage, huh?

HENRY. Oh god…

ZHAO. We used to play cowboys and Indians when we were pups in the irrigation ditches—

(ZHAO *moves like lightning, viciously "shooting"* HENRY, *jamming his fingers into Henry's ribs and neck—*HENRY *leaps back with a yell.*)

Doov-Doov! Dooh-Dooh-Dooh-Dooh-Dooh-Dooh—

HENRY. Aaaaaa—

(*It looks for a second like* ZHAO *is about to go for a major artery… then he pauses… grins a wicked grin and stands triumphantly over* HENRY *who is sprawled over his desk.*)

ZHAO. Somehow the Indians always ended up with AK-47s in our games.

HENRY. That's… that's great. Just… no shooting the tourists.

ZHAO. No way, man. I'm gonna be a good little Indian.

HENRY. Then… we have a deal?

ZHAO. The adventure begins today, my white brother.

(*They shake hands.*)

HENRY. Then let's go get you de-loused.

(*He opens the door and* ZHAO *walks out.*)

Lights shift. SUZIE *enters with her laptop and webcam, sitting down at her table as all the various locks on the front door click open.* HENRY *steps in with his suitcase. He looks frayed. She looks up at him.*

HENRY. Whoo! Wind's really picking up out there! Big storm coming... I just beat it...

(*She watches him... takes a swig of water... then goes back to her typing.*)

Okay. I'm sorry. You were right, cell phone reception was non-existent. And I had to go straight to the office when I got back. I came home as soon as I could... The weather's slowing everyone down...

(*She keeps typing.*)

I said I'm sorry!

(*She keeps typing. Pause. He grabs out his laptop, sits down beside her and quickly types something himself. Pushes a button, sits back and looks at her.*

DING! from her computer.

SUZIE hesitates... and clicks her mouse. Reads what's on her screen. Quickly types something, sends it.

DING! From Henry's computer. He reads his screen, winces. Types something fast and sends it.

DING! From Suzie's computer. She reads her screen... can't help herself—she smiles.)

SUZIE. I think the carpet can wait until tomorrow.

HENRY. You sure? I can get a crowbar—

SUZIE. You just better have some darn good photos to show for this.

HENRY. ...ah. Well.

SUZIE. Oh, Henry.

HENRY. I was too busy doing it to take a picture of it, Suzie! You know?

SUZIE. So how are you going to remember it?

HENRY. What.

SUZIE. "It." Whatever "it" was you were "doing." It's come, it's gone, you've got no permanent record, it might as well never have happened—

HENRY. I brought it back.

SUZIE. What?

HENRY. I brought him back. A native. I shot a native and brought him back.

(SUZIE *watches him a beat longer...*)

SUZIE. (*Typing fast.*) "OMG, 10:37: H. walks in the door and announces he's shot someone—"

HENRY. Tranq darts. He was just drugged. He's okay.

SUZIE. But you actually pulled the trigger?

HENRY. I did. From an open chopper. In a canyon. I did.

SUZIE. Oh my god.

HENRY. I know.

SUZIE. Oh my god, Henry!

HENRY. I know!

SUZIE. Jesus, I wish you'd gotten some pictures!

HENRY. You can come see him—the guy—he's in the pavilion—

SUZIE. But of you with the gun and the chopper! Are you all right? Oh my god, Henry, are you okay?

HENRY. I'm okay. I'm kind of great.

SUZIE. Your skin's not crisped.

HENRY. I covered up.

SUZIE. And you were de-loused, sterilized, everything?

HENRY. Everything.

SUZIE. (*Holding him, kissing him.*) I was terrified, Terrance was so terrified—
      (*Offering her laptop.*)
—read my journal—you've got to read my journal—

HENRY. I will. I just want to— I'm not quite here yet, you know?

SUZIE. Well, get here!
      (*Kissing him.*)
Get here now! And tell me about it! All about it!
      (*She sits beside him.*)

HENRY. Where should I—

SUZIE. (*Grabbing her laptop.*) Did you journal? Please tell me you journaled.

HENRY. I didn't write any of it down, I was—

HENRY & SUZIE. —too busy doing it.

SUZIE. Wild man. Look at you.
      (*She points the webcam toward his tired happy face and types.*)
"I think my husband…"
      (*Looks at him… smiles… types.*)
"—just aced his performance review."

HENRY. Well, you know.

SUZIE. Has anyone else upgraded their inventory?

HENRY. Phil and Maureen were setting up stuffed wolves in the Siberian pavilion, their eyes blink—

SUZIE. Henry! Name it! Claim it! You're the new Culture Fiesta Fattie!
      (HENRY *laughs.*)
Raise—Ching! Promotion—Ching! You're gonna be head of the whole Western Hemisphere side of the Reflecting Pool! God, I'm getting all tingly! We can refinish the kitchen again, we can—

HENRY. Well, we just introduced him, I don't know if he'll take—

SUZIE. What tribe is he?

HENRY. He's… you know, Navajo.

SUZIE. Ooo. Good one! Nice rugs!

HENRY. Yes. Yes, it sure is! Navajo's a very good one.

SUZIE. I think your son needs to see you.

HENRY. Is he in bed?

SUZIE. (*Pushing a button and showing him her monitor.*) Of course.

HENRY. We should re-adjust the camera—I can't see his feet.

SUZIE. Let's go wake him up.

HENRY. Can we?

SUZIE. He'll kill me if I let him sleep through this. Wait 'til you read his journal—

HENRY. (*Pauses.*) Huh.

SUZIE. What?

HENRY. Whenever… ah. Whenever the chopper would tilt or plummet or anything… I'd think "I can't die. I have to get home. I have to see Terrance and Suze." And, ah. I did it. I got home.

SUZIE. (*Holds him.*) B-HOE.

HENRY. I'm an okay-HOE.

SUZIE. You came back. Is there anything better a husband can do than come back?

(*She kisses him.*)

Let's go show your son what a father looks like.

(*She leads him off. We hear the first clap of thunder.*)

Lights shift. HENRY *immediately reenters in a fresh business jacket and briefcase, straightening his tie and hair while a slick man and sweet woman in suits and headsets, carrying briefcases, come out to surround him. These are* MR. NEIBERDING *and* MS. FJELDSTAD.

MR. NEIBERDING. Mr. Carson!

MS. FJELDSTAD. Good morning, Mr. Carson!

MR. NEIBERDING. It's my understanding you've recently procured a new exhibit for your Native Pavilion.

MS. FJELDSTAD. Congratulations, Mr. Carson!

HENRY. …thank you.

MS. FJELDSTAD. I'm Danita Fjeldstad. We met at a conference in Dublin.

MR. NEIBERDING. I'm Jerry Neiberding from the auction in Mogadishu.

MS. FJELDSTAD. (*Handing a card.*) I'm with Mega Family Christian Praise Parks.

MR. NEIBERDING. (*Handing a card.*) Personnel Manager for Extreme Terror Plummet Parks.

HENRY. Oh right. Thank you. I need to get to my office—

MR. NEIBERDING. Reason I wanted to catch you, wanted to say excellent work on the indigenous grab—

MS. FJELDSTAD. A big big salute on that one, Mr. Carson.

HENRY. Thank you. I really have to get inside. The air—

MS. FJELDSTAD. Absolutely. But I wondered if we could speak informally, avoid the secretaries and monitored phone lines and such—

MR. NEIBERDING. If I may, I wondered that first, Henry. If you'll check my ticket, I think you'll find I pulled into this garage several full minutes before Ms. Fjeldstad.

HENRY. What do you want??

MS. FJELDSTAD. Well. I think we're all aware of the skidding attendance numbers and of course the mortality rate of the performers—

(*To* MR. NEIBERDING.)

—for everyone. But I am proud to say that Mega Family Christian Praise Park is expanding our Holy History Islands of Eden—

(MR. NEIBERDING *laughs.*)

What.

MR. NEIBERDING. I believe the Islands of Eden are best known for the Singing Serpent Jamboree and the Cain and Abel Lazer-Tag—

MS. FJELDSTAD. We want to add an Old West island featuring missionaries and Mormons, and to be honest with you, we've found several authentic cowboys out of Denver, but the Native American component is proving problematic—

HENRY. Of course.

MS. FJELDSTAD. We can come up with Mexican/Native mixes, but no 100%'s like you've procured.

HENRY. Right.

MS. FJELDSTAD. Mega Family Christian Praise is prepared to pay a substantial amount for the rights to your newly acquired performer.

MR. NEIBERDING. So he can shout "woo woo woo" as he shepherds hippos onto the ark simulator? Do you have any idea who you're talking to? This is Henry Carson! This is Culture Fiesta! They do not mix time periods, they do not mix genres, they are about 100% honest accurate portrayals of honest peoples of the world, am I correct, Henry?

HENRY. That's right—

MR. NEIBERDING. Which is why Extreme Terror is preparing a new Wild West Stunt Show—totally authentic, totally period-appropriate. We don't want actors, we want *people*. Real honest-to-god western people who duke it out on horseback with rifles and arrows surrounding Fort Splash-A-Lot.

HENRY. Oh god.

MR. NEIBERDING. Can your man throw a tomahawk, Henry?

MS. FJELDSTAD. With all due respect, Henry, Mr. Nieberding is full of horse doo. The portrayal of Native Americans as strictly a warlike people has been discredited for decades. We propose to show the native in his true habitat, surrounded by teepees, animatronic buffalo, and selling drums and dreamcatchers to the guests.

MR. NEIBERDING. We offer a full educational outreach program in which we plan to act out legends, lore, and engage in a respectful discussion of animism.

MS. FJELDSTAD. We offer air-conditioned dormitories for all performers, with a reasonably equipped fitness center and basic satellite—

HENRY. He's not for sale!

(*Beat.*)

MR. NEIBERDING. I understand your hesitancy, Henry, but let me assure you that not only do we offer a terrific work environment, but our park is prepared to allow all our performers to take part in the new Va-Va-Voom Bikini Wet'N'Wild Whipped Cream Parade.

MS. FJELDSTAD. He's putting your native in an underwear show, Henry—

MR. NEIBERDING. Bikinis. And whipped cream. It would all be done with the utmost taste and respect.

MS. FJELDSTAD. Let me say that if it's fun your native wants, Mega Family Christian Praise Park is fully prepared to feature him as part of our Wubulous World of Dr. Seuss.

MR. NEIBERDING. What??

MS. FJELDSTAD. I'm just thinking off the top of my head here, but I can see "The Indian and the Sneetches in their rawhide leather breeches"—

MR. NEIBERDING. I give you my word there will be no rhyming at Extreme Terror.

MS. FJELDSTAD. "The Cat in the Hat and the Wampum Mat"—

MR. NEIBERDING. What happened to "authentic environments"?

MS. FJELDSTAD. It's the Cat's authentic environment. The Indian would come for a visit.

HENRY. Please, I can't—

MR. NEIBERDING. We'll pay shipping.

MS. FJELDSTAD. We'll give him real animal skins.

MR. NEIBERDING. We'll give him shiny beads every month!

MS. FJELDSTAD. We'll pay for his whiskey!

HENRY. No!! I can't... he's mine! I rode in the chopper. I braved the raw air. I pulled the trigger. I dragged his body back to civilization, he's mine! You take your grubby little poaching fingers out of my pavilion and go get your own damn Native American!

(*And he storms out. They stand staring... Pause.*)

MS. FJELDSTAD. Fuck WonderWorld!

(*And they're out of there.*)

(*Lights shift as more thunder rolls.* HENRY *collapses at his desk as* ZHAO *enters, now wearing a traditional purple velvet shirt with string turquoise necklace, turquoise bracelets, white pants, woven belt and headband. He carries a portable T.V. from which a fast Navajo riding song is heard.*)

ZHAO. Those guys can really dance!

HENRY. Are you even *trying* to learn the songs?

ZHAO. Why don't you watch with me? You might learn somethin'.

HENRY. I've got all the paperwork that piled up while I was gone. I still haven't read all my e-mails—

ZHAO. I can take the T.V. back to the pavilion—

HENRY. No! No books, T.V., no outside influences to contaminate the environment.

ZHAO. What about me? Am I an outside influence?

HENRY. Are you talking to the other performers?

ZHAO. Not too much. It's like they're all sittin' in the pool, just waitin' for me to wade in. They keep lookin' at me funny.

HENRY. Natives are like that. Sensitive. In touch with the earth. They operate on a different plane, between dream and reality—

ZHAO. I just want'em to teach me to make fry bread without burnin' my fingers.

HENRY. I had a dream last night. It was about the paperwork. I was back over the desert and Yolanda was sitting in the backseat telling me what to do, yapping yapping yapping, and I was trying to watch for a native—for you I think—and she just kept going on about the paperwork, and I just, I got so pissed off, I threw the papers up into the rotorblades!

ZHAO. Ow!

HENRY. Rip rip rip rip rip—shreds of paper *everywhere*. Flying through canyons, over the sand and yucca plants. It was like snow. Corporate snowflakes falling over the desert, covering everything. Covering the world.

ZHAO. Man, you oughta start hangin' out with the "performers." They'd get all over that dream in a heartbeat.

HENRY. (*Holds up papers, indicates his laptop.*) …but in reality…

(ZHAO *eagerly tries a few more awkward dance steps…*)

You gotta get better than that. And learn some the lyrics while you're at it.

ZHAO. Gimme a beer first.

HENRY. (*Pulls a can from a cooler and tosses it.*) This is your last one tonight.

ZHAO. I don't know why we're botherin'. Nobody's gonna come see us in a hurricane.

HENRY. Please. This is not a hurricane. This is light rain. You'll know a hurricane when it happens.

ZHAO. When I see bagpipes and totem poles flyin' by at 130 miles an hour.

HENRY. That's a clue. Yes.

(*He goes back to typing. ZHAO chugs the beer and tries some more steps…*)

ZHAO. You know the stories I'm humpin' most?

HENRY. What?

ZHAO. The Coyote stuff. How he tricked the chickenhawk and humming-bird ladies to sleep with him and everything. He was whacked, man.

HENRY. (*Grinning, stepping from his computer.*) Whacked. Yes. He was abso-lutely whacked! See, what's neat is Coyote's all over the map—everything from—in, in Crow tradition, Old Man Coyote actually *created* everyone else out of mud, but in the Hopi language the words for "Coyote" and "sucker" are the same word! …He actually… um. Sorry.

ZHAO. What.

HENRY. This is where people usually tell me to shut up.

ZHAO. Not me, man. I'm in for the ride.

HENRY. Well, ah, other tribes, you know, have other tricksters—uh, the Eastern woodlands tribes it's the rabbit, the Northwest coast had Raven—

ZHAO. Yeah but Coyote kicks their ass! You can't even kill him, man! He didn't even keep his life in his chest, he hid it so the otters and chickenhawks and even his own wife could like—

(*POUNDING on Henry's desk, in his face.*)

—POUND HIM TO A THOUSAND BLOODY BONY PIECES AND HE COULD COME BACK!! AROOOO!!!

HENRY. Zhao!

ZHAO. Sorry, white man.

HENRY. No one can know you're here. Please.

ZHAO. I forgot.

(ZHAO *spins away and starts fancy-dancing, heavy steps in a fast rhythm, suddenly pretty damn graceful.*)

HENRY. What are you doing?

ZHAO. Dancing.

HENRY. A minute ago you were stumbling around…

ZHAO. (*Grins.*) Some tribes dance to bring on the end of the world, am I right?

HENRY. Right—and some to get to the next one—

ZHAO. Get over here, Henrito! Come dance with me, man—

HENRY. I can't—

ZHAO. (*Still stepping.*) Try!

HENRY. (*He's up.*) …I don't—

ZHAO. Try!

(HENRY *is on the verge…*)

Tell me more stories, Carson-man! Fill me up!

(*Henry's phone rings. He checks it.*)

HENRY. Shoot. It's Suzie. What time is it—I have to get home.

ZHAO. (*Stops dancing.*) That sucks.

HENRY. We can talk more later. Come on. I have to get you back to your pavilion and lock up.

ZHAO. (*Sits down with his small T.V.*) I got a lot of discs to read, bilagaana. Words to learn.

HENRY. I know. I just—

ZHAO. You want me authentic or not?

HENRY. (*Takes a card from his desk.*) Here. Here's a temporary backstage pass card. It'll get you back into your pavilion when you're done here.

ZHAO. (*Takes the card.*) Stay and tell me one more story. I'm still empty, man.

HENRY. I have to get home!

ZHAO. I need to learn! Not from these—

(*Holds up a box of CD-ROMS.*)

From you. I need you, Henrito.

(HENRY *pauses.*)

HENRY. Well. I mean if you want to, we could keep talking at my house.

(*Beat.*)

ZHAO. You inviting me home for dinner?

HENRY. I guess I am. Yes.

ZHAO. What do you and your woman eat?

HENRY. I don't know. Whatever Suzie microwaved. Maybe some sushi or stuffed cabbage.

ZHAO. (*Stops dancing.*) Damn. All we get here are sandwiches and chips and a pickle.

HENRY. Well.

(ZHAO *looks at him.*)

That's how it works.

(ZHAO *stares at him.*)

Look, I'm sorry, but I'm offering you something better—

ZHAO. You promise no sandwich and chips and a pickle, right?

HENRY. I promise.

ZHAO. Okay. Let's try the Carson Cuisine.

(*He turns off the little T.V. Low rumble of thunder...*)

Lights shift. HENRY *unlocks and walks through the door to his house, waving to* ZHAO *to wait outside—he leaves the door ajar as* SUZIE *stands looking at her laptop.*

HENRY. Hey, Honey, I'm home—

SUZIE. (*Beckoning him over.*) Look at this site. Tell me what you think of this site—

HENRY. Actually, first you should—

SUZIE. You've got to see this before Terrance finishes orchestra... Mr. Indian Hunter.

(*She drags him to her laptop.*)

It's all native rituals, Henry. Native rituals to prepare for the big hunt—it's called LoveSnake.com.

HENRY. (*Looking at her screen.*) This is a porn site!

SUZIE. They're tantric Native rituals. It seems very authentic. Positions, face-paintings—I mean, I'm not sure we want to go there—I'm not as flexible as I used to be—But I thought maybe on the eve of your performance review...

(*She pulls open her blouse to reveal her bra just as* ZHAO *walks in behind them...*)

ZHAO. (*Waves.*) How, man.

SUZIE. Oh my god.

(*She reflexively backs up, trying to button herself back up...*)

HENRY. There's some other rituals I should probably tell you about. Like inviting someone over for dinner. This is... Leonard. Leonard Yazzie. The new Navajo.

SUZIE. Ah.

HENRY. This is my wife Suzie.

ZHAO. (*Offering his hand.*) How you doin'?

SUZIE. Um—

HENRY. (*To* ZHAO.) You can meet my son when he's back from orchestra rehearsal.

ZHAO. That's cool.

HENRY. (*To* SUZIE.) He's picked up a lot of English.

SUZIE. That's wonderful.

(*Subtly backing up to touch her laptop.*)

Henry usually just brings home pots and arrowheads.

HENRY. Had a heck of a time convincing Ahmed to let us through our gate. I'm just inviting him home for dinner—the crap they eat at the pavilion, it's just crap. Right, Leonard?

ZHAO. Pretty bad, yeah.

SUZIE. Well.

(*A little too loud.*)

Would you like a sandwich? We have chips—

HENRY. I thought I could microwave something.

SUZIE. Let me!

HENRY. No, I'll do it.

SUZIE. But—

HENRY. I'll do it!

(*Quietly.*)

It's your chance to visit the desert with me, Suzie. To kind of be there.

SUZIE. Honey…

HENRY. Think what your readers will say!

(HENRY *darts out.* SUZIE *and* ZHAO *look at each other. She smiles and unconsciously touches her laptop like a security blanket.*)

ZHAO. Where's your son play orchestra?

SUZIE. Upstairs. He's in a video-conference orchestra. He plays clarinet.

ZHAO. That's a good instrument.

(*Pause.*)

SUZIE. You must have played a lot of flute on the reservation?

ZHAO. No.

(*Pause.*)

SUZIE. That's so exotic. To be from the desert.

ZHAO. It's okay.

(*Pause.*)

SUZIE. Florida must seem like another planet to you.

ZHAO. It's wetter.

SUZIE. Of course.

ZHAO. More mosquitoes, less stink bugs.

SUZIE. Well, it was a swamp. You know. Before we paved it over.

ZHAO. It keeps raining, it'll be a swamp again.

SUZIE. Right!

(*She laughs. Quickly starts typing.*)

ZHAO. What you workin' on?

SUZIE. My blog. I just realized I needed to finish an entry.

ZHAO. Oh yeah? What's your site?

SUZIE. SuzieC4real.com.

ZHAO. That's cool. My cousin had a blog.

SUZIE. Really?

ZHAO. He eventually turned it into a porn site. More money.

SUZIE. Ah.

ZHAO. He started by recordin' his own stuff with girlfriends on his webcam. Kind of spiraled from there.

SUZIE. Really.

(*She subtly inches her webcam away. Pause. She takes a drink of bottled water.*)

ZHAO. It's called LoveSnake.com.

(*She spits her drink all over her laptop.*)

SUZIE. Oh god!

ZHAO. I haven't seen a girl spit like that in a long time—I'll dry it off—

SUZIE. It's all right, it's all right—

(*He tries to use his shirt-sleeve to dry the screen,* SUZIE *trying to block his view of the screen—He playfully moves around her, under her arms—they're increasingly tangled up…. And* HENRY *comes in with plates of food on a tray.*)

HENRY. Ah…?

ZHAO. She was showin' me her blog—

SUZIE. —he was telling me about his cousin's porn… site…

HENRY. Ah.

ZHAO. Your wife's got a good mouth, man. She's good with the spit.

SUZIE. I was taking a drink—

HENRY. Well, I brought dinner!

(*He sets down the tray.*)

Instant Sloppy Joes. Beats sandwiches anyday.

(*Pause. They sit looking at each other…*)

Although… I guess… it kind of is sandwiches. But no pickles.

ZHAO. No, I like sloppy joes. They were always my favorite lunch at school.

(*He takes a sandwich already overflowing with sloppy joe mix.*)

That and we had somethin' called "Surprise Burgers," they were like this sealed white bread roll with something inside. But you never knew what 'til you bit in.

SUZIE. Oh god.

ZHAO. It was usually just chuck and onions or whatever. But we were always pretty sure we'd get a mouthful of pus and blood and snot or something.

(SUZIE *and* HENRY *stare at their own sandwiches...* ZHAO *pauses, ready to take a big bite.*)

Sorry. Do you guys do a prayer or something?

HENRY. No.

(*Laughs.*)

No, no. We just dig right in!

(*Putting sloppy joe mix on his bun.*)

Should we get Terrance?

ZHAO. Yeah, get your boy down here—I'll show him how boys play out on the rez—

SUZIE. On the other hand, there's something to be said for his staying upstairs and giving us a chance to talk as grown-ups for a while!

ZHAO. I like grown-up talk too. Ho' zho' ni'!

(*He takes a HUGE BITE—juicy red meat and sauce pour out the other side of the bun onto the plate and table, staining his hands and face.*)

SUZIE. What's that mean?

HENRY. Beauty. Ho' zho' ni'!

(*And* HENRY *takes a massive bite—more red glop splatters around.* ZHAO *laughs with his mouth full.* SUZIE *picks up a napkin and goes for Henry's face.*)

No! Eat your sloppy joe!

SUZIE. But your face, Henry—

HENRY. Eat, woman!

(*He takes another huge bite, as does* ZHAO. SUZIE *hesitates... sees the others enjoying themselves immensely... and takes a huge bite. Meat and sauce go everywhere.*)

HENRY & ZHAO. Yaaaahh!!

(*More big bites—they look like wild animals.* SUZIE *laughs.*)

HENRY. We gotta get Terrance down here for this—

SUZIE. No! After all we taught him about "polite bites"—

HENRY. Exactly!

(*Calls out.*)

Terrance—

SUZIE. Shh! SHH!

(*She laughs, stops him, putting her hand over his mouth, leaving red stains on his cheeks.*)

(*Beat. She looks at him.*)

Oh my god. You look like a wild animal.

(*He watches her... scoops out sloppy joe mix on one finger... and puts a mark on her nose.*)

HENRY. So do you.

(*She hesitates...*)

SUZIE. For the Performance Review hunt tomorrow?

(*HENRY nods. They stare at each other.... She gets more meat... and draws a line down his throat. He does the same to her, pauses... then down across her chest.*)

(*She dabs red around his lips and kisses him slowly...*)

(*And in a frenzy they TUMBLE behind the table, making passionate noises.*)

(*ZHAO watches them. Takes a small bite of his sandwich.*)

(*A child's voice crackles over an intercom.*)

TERRANCE'S VOICE. (*Voice-over.*) Mom? Dad? Is dinner ready?

HENRY & SUZIE. (*Shouted from behind the table.*) NOT YET, HONEY!!

(*Thunder outside. They go back at it.*)

(*ZHAO scoops up some red mix on his finger... looks at it... and drags careful lines across his cheeks and forehead—war paint in red dripping hamburger...*)

ZHAO. Ho' Zho' Ni'.

(*HUGE CLAP OF THUNDER. Blackout.*)

End of Act I

ACT II

Thunder. Lights up on Henry's office, as at the top of Act I.

But now HENRY leans back in his chair like the king of the world, eyes shut, in a headset and casual shirt with no tie. There may be some slight red stains still around his mouth.

YOLANDA, in an even sharper business suit and headset, sits across from him with her palm pilot.

YOLANDA. Henry.

(*HENRY, lost in thought, continues smiling like the cat that ate every damn canary in the shop.*)

Henry. I've only allotted five minutes for this performance review.

(HENRY *opens his eyes.*)

I suggest we start.

(HENRY *spins his chair lazily.*)

HENRY. I suggest I agree.

YOLANDA. Are you all right?

HENRY. (*Shoots his forefinger at her, grinning.*) Locked, loaded, safety off.

YOLANDA. Right. Then let's get right to it. Your first three quarters were marked by a solid level of work in the face of some challenging circumstances. The death of old Nathan Takoda and having to put down Wikimak in the Canadian portion, coupled with the lukewarm reception to the Nike moccasins and Native Bobble-head Dolls.

HENRY. It's like scaling McKinley, you know? Always looking for the next chink, the next foothold—

YOLANDA. Well, your visitor numbers stayed constant with those of the South African and Ukraine pavilion, if not in the German and Italian stratosphere.

HENRY. And let's be honest. They have all that beer and pizza. Spring Break alone sets them—

YOLANDA. Never-the-less, you showed adequate progress toward the company's goals.

HENRY. Damn straight.

YOLANDA. Then the fourth quarter starts.

HENRY. As it inevitably does.

YOLANDA. It certainly didn't go unnoticed that your willingness to personally acquire a replacement for Nathan Takoda was unparalleled by any other Culture Fiesta manager—

(HENRY *jumps up, pacing.*)

HENRY. Jesus, Yolanda, you should have been there, *all* the managers should go out in the field for inventory—to actually hold the rifle—

YOLANDA. Yes. We've heard. I think you should sit down now.

HENRY. Whoo!

(*He sits.*)

YOLANDA. Since your return, however, some of the work habits of your division have… faltered.

HENRY. …What do you mean.

YOLANDA. For one, we still don't have the complete paperwork from your expedition. Your Release Forms 380, 461, Extenuating Expenses CE—

HENRY. Those are coming—

YOLANDA. The physical reports on your acquisition. His final DNA Form 816, Lineage Forms B and D, skill set forms A2, B4, and C3—

HENRY. —on their way—

YOLANDA. And productivity, Henry. Your new native isn't weaving, isn't throwing pots, isn't making sand paintings—

HENRY. He's new—

YOLANDA. He better get up to speed. You could have selected any Native American, you selected him, there has to be a reason.

HENRY. I—

YOLANDA. I don't have to know that reason, but I do have to have the paperwork to back up that reason.

HENRY. You will—

YOLANDA. And since the arrival of the new acquisition, the other natives appear to not be meeting their own productivity standards. So where are your weekly P-VAL forms to monitor and address the situation—

HENRY. I don't—

YOLANDA. This new global storm alert is already kicking us in the sweet-meats, we cannot lose one more visitor—

HENRY. I—

YOLANDA. You don't want to become Alan Donaldson, do you?

HENRY. No!

YOLANDA. The day the Native American Pavilions become the Latvian Pavilion, is the day I turn in my resignation and blow up all of Culture Fiesta.

HENRY. I think—

YOLANDA. Is that what you want, Henry? To blow up Culture Fiesta?

HENRY. No!

YOLANDA. Then where are your 380's, 461's, A2's, and P-VALS?

(HENRY *lunges over the desk at her.*)

HENRY. Will you give me a chance to answer??

(*Beat.*)

YOLANDA. I prefer to hold performance reviews with both parties seated, Mr. Carson.

(HENRY *sits.*)

And this is a discussion, not an argument.

HENRY. I'd like to discuss—

YOLANDA. They may eat this shit with mustard at Mega Families and Extreme Terror, but this is *Culture Fiesta*, Carson.

(*Beat. They stare at each other.*)

HENRY. I know that.

YOLANDA. I'm afraid I can't recommend you for your annual raise, much less promotion.

HENRY. Is it my turn to discuss now?

YOLANDA. There's a space at the bottom of your evaluation for "Employee Comments"

(*And she walks out.*)

Lights shift and HENRY *leaps over to* SUZIE *who enters with her laptop into their dining room. Her face is now clean again.*

HENRY. We did the hunt rituals! Didn't we do the hunt rituals??

SUZIE. Yes!

HENRY. Who does she think she is?? I'm the Culture Fiesta Fattie!!

SUZIE. Complete bitch.

HENRY. Alan Donaldson! She compared me to Alan Donaldson in Latvia!

SUZIE. I hate her. I hate her I hate her I hate her—

HENRY. I swear, Suzie, every time she said the words P-VAL or B4 or 461, I just wanted to leap over the desk and rip her frickin' throat out with my frickin' teeth! RAARRR!

(*She stares at him.*)

You know what I'm talkin' about, right? You work for Wal-Mart! RAAA!

SUZIE. RAAA! Absolutely! ...But you didn't actually rip her throat out, did you, Henry?

HENRY. I grabbed the fattest blackest dry erase marker I could and I scrawled "FUCK YOU" on her evaluation! That's my Employee Comment!

SUZIE. ...and did you turn that in?

HENRY. Tomorrow morning. First thing. On her desk. BAM. RAA!

SUZIE. RAA! I think you should shred that evaluation and ask for a new one.

HENRY. What?

SUZIE. Let's sit down.

HENRY. I don't want to sit down.

SUZIE. Henry, Terrance is going to come downstairs from his swimming lessons any minute—

HENRY. And it's time he saw his real father! A father who stands up to the corporate staple-heads and says "F.U.!"

SUZIE. Well. I also kind of want him to see a father who's still employed.

HENRY. There are more important things than being employed, Suzie!

(*She stares at him.*)

...aren't there?

SUZIE. Two words: Health. Insurance.

HENRY. What kind of health are we insuring?

SUZIE. Henry, it's okay you didn't get the raise, I can work more hours—they're always asking me to—I can sell ad space on my blog—we don't have to get ahead, but we have to keep where we are.

HENRY. What about "complete bitch"—what about "I hate her I hate her I hate her—"

SUZIE. I do! Just because you hate someone doesn't mean you can't work for them! Henry. You're doing what you love, right?

> (*Beat.*)

Right?

HENRY. Yes.

SUZIE. It's going to be the same everywhere, honey. They're going to ask for paperwork and forms—

HENRY. Not in the desert.

SUZIE. Then take vacations in the desert, Henry! That's what vacations are for, to escape the hell you go through to get them! But when you come back, you'll still have food and clothes and air-conditioning... I want you to be happy, Henry. I do. But I want us all to be alive.

HENRY. You know when I was alive? When you streaked my face with war paint. When you created a mask of blood and meat. Henry was gone. Henry and Suzie were subsumed.

SUZIE. (*Holding him, smiling.*) I know. But that was here. In our home. What's acceptable on our floor and what's acceptable in your office are two different things.

HENRY. But—

SUZIE. I understand the need for adventure, honey. I go crazy on my blog sometimes. I'll just write wild run-on sentences and report rumors I read on other sites without even verifying them. But it's controlled. The world's too small, sweetheart. There's no room for epic adventures.

> (*Kisses him.*)

You're an astonishingly good man, Henry. Please fill out the B4's, 461's, and P-VALS.

> *Lights shift. Thunder.* SUZIE *leaves as* HENRY *slowly walks to his desk... picks up a sheet of paper with the words "FUCK YOU" scrawled in thick black letters.... He looks at the sheet a moment... and quietly feeds it into a shredder [or crumples and tosses it]. He leans on his desk as* ZHAO *walks in behind him, still in traditional dress, but listening to an iPod. He flops down on a pillow.*

HENRY. (*Holds up various papers.*) Can't you at least fill in the skill set forms?

ZHAO. Why?

HENRY. Because I'm already filling out your lineage, health and psych forms!

ZHAO. So how crazy is this "Leonard Yazzie"?

HENRY. Zhao.

ZHAO. I'm cruisin' to this music, man. The Bluebird Song, Slow Round Dance. It speaks to me. In here.

(*He pounds the rhythm on his chest.*)

HENRY. It's gonna stop speaking anywhere if we don't get our ducks in a row.

ZHAO. (*Laughs.*) "Ducks in a row"

HENRY. Zhao!

ZHAO. I'll do it tomorrow.

HENRY. It's always tomorrow.

ZHAO. Must be a cultural thing, huh?

HENRY. Listen—

ZHAO. Chill down, Henrito. We're only gettin' a few people a day anyway.

HENRY. They'll come back. The rain will stop and they'll come back.

ZHAO. The old guys in the pavilion…? They say the rain ain't gonna stop this time.

HENRY. Oh, where'd they get that—their extrasensory Native Doppler Radar?

ZHAO. Careful.

HENRY. Well, I mean, geez.

ZHAO. Those old guys know shit.

HENRY. Then why aren't you learning from them?

ZHAO. I am. We're learnin' from each other.

HENRY. Then weave a damn rug! Make a pot or a dreamcatcher!

ZHAO. They're lookin' past that stuff now.

HENRY. What do you mean? They love doing crafts. They always smile and nod—

(ZHAO *laughs.*)

They were fine 'til you got here. Everything was fine 'til you got here.

ZHAO. I wasn't.

HENRY. Morale's going down the toilet. No one wants to work—

ZHAO. What can I say? They dig my style.

HENRY. The natives are getting surly.

ZHAO. Henry, Henry, Henry, man. Ya'ta' Hey, man. Breathe.

(*Offering earphones.*)

Listen to the music.

HENRY. I don't have time to listen to the music!

ZHAO. Then come with me. I'm on a hunt tonight.

HENRY. What?

ZHAO. I'm goin' foraging the Eastern Asian pavilions. I was cookin' with the western Europe guys last night.

HENRY. What??

ZHAO. That German beer knocks your moccasins off, man. And the Spanish coffee! I could almost forgive 'em what they did to Colorado and Mexico for that coffee—

HENRY. You can't. You can't visit other pavilions!

ZHAO. How come we got no rides, man? The Norwegians got this wooden boat trip past trolls and vikings and crap. How come the Native Americans got no ride?

HENRY. You've got a splendid movie—

ZHAO. We got no ride! You could do a little covered wagon train through history—past the Trail of Tears, the Long Walk, Wounded Knee. At the end you could sell little scalps and blankets infected with TB and whooping cough!

HENRY. See, this is why we find performers with limited English skills.

ZHAO. You wanta boost morale, put in a roller coaster or stunt show, man.

HENRY. How'd you get in the Norwegian pavilion?

ZHAO. I don't know. Someone gave me a pass.

HENRY. This doesn't happen. The tourists move from world to world. You stay put. Pure, untainted.

ZHAO. So I can be authentic?

HENRY. Exactly!

ZHAO. You don't want authentic, you want frozen. You want to pick a time and say "There. *That's* who they were. That's the real them." So I get to dress up like this. Except we didn't start dressin' this way 'til we started hangin' around with white people. The Indians before that were the "authentic" ones. Except they didn't start actin' that way 'til they got to the southwest. So the ones before them are the *real* authentic ones. Except...

(HENRY *stares at him.*)

We move, Henrito. We keep jumpin' from world to world takin' pieces of everywhere and everyone we ever been. It's all real. It's all "authentic."

(HENRY *keeps staring at him...*)

Why you gotta make my job so hard?

HENRY. ...Excuse me?

ZHAO. The egg's crackin', man, all you gotta do is get outta the way of the hammer.

HENRY. Look, the, the only thing cracking is my patience—

ZHAO. You invited me into your home, Henrito. We sloppy-joed together! Don't you dare dam that up—

HENRY. What's acceptable on my floor and what's acceptable in my office are two different things.

ZHAO. The Italian and French girls don't think so.

HENRY. No more. Give me back the pass.

ZHAO. I must've left it in my other loin cloth.

HENRY. I'm not kidding around. If anyone caught you crossing borders—

ZHAO. They don't catch me. I'm on stealth, man. My paws are silent and my breath is clear.

HENRY. Give me the pass.

ZHAO. Or.

HENRY. You're my employee. Not Culture Fiesta's. Mine. They may eat this shit with mustard on the "rez," but this is Henry Carson Land. You like the music, you like the old guys? You play by the rules. Or you'll be back on unemployment in Tucumcari.

(*Pause.* ZHAO *and* HENRY *watch one another…*)

ZHAO. Then I'll see you there. 'Cause once I go on T.V. about how a guy from WonderWorld shot me in the back while I was helping my old auntie and uncle, and he dragged me to work as a glorified robot—

HENRY. You ungrateful sonofabitch—I selected you—

ZHAO. You want me to "get my ducks in a row"? You better fasten your fuckin' seatbelt, asshole. You wanta keep on filling out skill sheets and psych forms, keep fillin'—I just wanta be there when you see what water does to file cabinets and hard drives.

(*He starts out. Pauses. Turns.*)

And I selected *you*, Henry. Not the other way round. I'll say hey to the Thai and Burmese girls for you.

(*And he leaves.*)

(HENRY *stares… blinking… as* YOLANDA *enters in a different area, on her headset.*)

YOLANDA. Henry, the rain seems to be shorting out the animatronic wolves and badgers—they just shot sparks from their eyes at some priests from Portugal.

HENRY. …I'm on it…

(SUZIE *enters in a different area, on her headset.*)

SUZIE. Henry, can you Google and zip some more sites home? Terrance wants to finish up the beadwork on his costume for the school play.

HENRY. ...on it...

(ERNIE *strides into a different area with two glasses of alcohol on a small bar table, on headset, with band-aids on his face and one severely bandaged hand.*)

ERNIE. I'm throwin' myself a goin' away party, amigo. Wanta join?

HENRY. Absolutely!

Lights shift as the women leave and HENRY *hurries to sit beside* ERNIE, *drinking. Low thunder.*

I mean, that's where it was real, wasn't it, Ernie? The chopper scraping the canyon walls—your body slumped over mine—the pilot's fighting, *fighting*, to maintain control—and I'm there with the gun—

ERNIE. I know.

HENRY. And I've got this one shot, it's now or never, the guy's almost into the hogan—sheep scattering everywhere—like cotton plants exploding in the wind—

ERNIE. Yeah.

HENRY. And Boom! I pull the trigger, BOOM!

ERNIE. That's what I hear.

HENRY. And the guy goes flying through the air—Whoosh—THUMP! Just like that, WHOOSH... THUMP!

ERNIE. This was a real peak experience for you, wasn't it, Henry?

HENRY. God, yes! Wasn't it for you?

ERNIE. Honestly, not so much.

HENRY. Every sound, every smell—

ERNIE. Now this trip I got comin' up, outside Philly—*that's* gonna be a clusterfuck on a D-Day scale.

HENRY. What are you doing?

ERNIE. I'm goin' after bats for a collector out of Montreal. Once every seventeen years these blue-headed somethings pass through this river valley—or what's left of 'em—this'll probably be their last run—just a dozen or so left—good as dead anyway, so of course this guy wants to stuff 'em—

HENRY. I guess that's best.

ERNIE. But here's the fist up the rectum: only way to get 'em—hangliders.

HENRY. No!

ERNIE. Swear on my father when he dies.

HENRY. Wow.

ERNIE. Gotta come in silent behind 'em, through 'em, and use these needle guns to leave no visible marks. Course it's stormin' there too, winds at 60 m.p.h., no visibility, and I'm gonna be danglin' off Ben Franklin's kite shooting steel at targets no larger than my nutsack.

HENRY. Jesus.

ERNIE. So see, shootin' some poor fleeing sombitch in the back? My nephew's done that eight times and he just turned twelve.

HENRY. When do you leave for the bat hunt?

ERNIE. Assuming the swelling in my hand goes down—

HENRY. What happened?

ERNIE. Guy hired me to take care his termite problem. So of course I start riggin' up a makeshift flamethrower out of a can of hairspray... didn't work out like we hoped. But my point is, if I can fly, I leave tomorrow night. Also assuming my plane can get out of this soaker. I hear we're losin' the entire gulf coast.

HENRY. I can be ready by then.

ERNIE. What?

HENRY. I want to come with you.

ERNIE. One drink and you just buy your ticket to fuzzy-wuzzy elf-land, don't ya?

HENRY. I'm not drunk! I want to go see the bats!

ERNIE. Stick to the natives, Henry. You had your adrenaline rush, more than most jerks will in a lifetime. Count your blessings and go check your E-mail.

HENRY. My E-mail's killing me, Ernie. I don't even see the words any more. I just see black lines in random shapes on a gray screen, forcing themselves into patterns, trying to mean something—anything—trying to stitch together the wounds to hold in the scream about to vomit out of the meaningless void!

ERNIE. No more Shirley Temples for you, pal.

HENRY. I need to get out, Ernie! I need to escape!

ERNIE. Henry. You got responsibilities. And you're a man. A man toughs it out.

HENRY. A man runs away! When the going gets tough, men run off and have adventures!

ERNIE. I am not gonna sit here and listen to you denigrate male motives.

HENRY. I'm not denigrating, I'm admiring! I want to be me again, Ernie. The genuine honest-to-God Henry Sumner Carson.

ERNIE. Your e-mails are the real Henry Carson, Henry. Get over it.

HENRY. And the real Ernie Hardaway is a blowhard who can't actually *live* in the real world either, he just likes to visit and steal something and run home like everybody else, except that he shoots himself and sets himself on fire—

(*CRACK! ERNIE decks* HENRY, *who crashes to the floor. Pause.*)

ERNIE. I liked your mother, Henry. She was a fine upstanding woman who baked the best pecan sandies this side of the Gulf. And she treated me with respect even when everyone else was calling me "hoodlum" and "vandal" and "goat fucker." It's in honor of her memory that I don't rip your spinal cord out and play it like a flute in the Main Street USA Electric Parade. Get back to your office.

(*He stalks out.* HENRY *pauses on the floor... feels his face... and staggers to his desk as*)

Lights Shift and SUZIE *enters into a different area, looking at her handheld monitor, on headset.*

SUZIE. Henry! Are you coming home or aren't you?

HENRY. I, ah…

SUZIE. Terrance's school play! It's starting! I thought we were going to watch together!

HENRY. We can.

(*At his computer.*)

Where is it?

SUZIE. At the school's site—click on "Arts in Education." I wanted us to sit on the couch and watch…

HENRY. Did he get his costume together?

SUZIE. He said he did.

HENRY. (*Reading his screen.*) "The Third Grade Class proudly presents—"

HENRY & SUZIE. "—The History of Florida: From Savage To Civil"

HENRY. Look at all those kids—are they all eight-years-old?

SUZIE. The next generations of Americans, sweetheart. Aren't they incredible? Kids from every background, every country—

HENRY. Are they actually in the same room?

SUZIE. They're green-screened in from all their different houses.

HENRY. But where's Terrance? I don't— there he is! I see him! Oh, there's my boy!

SUZIE. Are you recording this? I'm recording this—does his Indian costume look good?

HENRY. (*Touches the screen, quietly.*) …Ho' Zo' Ni'.

(YOLANDA *storms into Henry's office with her palm pilot.*)

YOLANDA. Henry! Why aren't you answering your phone?

HENRY. Look. Yolanda. My boy. My son's playing a native with the other kids, not *with* the kids, just in his room, but he made the leather breeches and feathers himself—we researched them together online… just the two of us…

YOLANDA. Cute.

(*Pushes a button on his keyboard.*)

But we've got a crisis.

HENRY. Hey!

YOLANDA. (*Pointing to his monitor.*) The Japanese pavilion. What do you see?

HENRY. That's not the Japanese pavilion—there's…

HENRY & YOLANDA. …cactus.

YOLANDA. Exactly. Somebody tore the banzai trees out of the rock garden and replaced them.

HENRY. Oh… crap.

YOLANDA. And you'll notice the Japanese performers are handing out beads and arrowheads instead of kites and brown rice toffee.

HENRY. Why are they doing that?

YOLANDA. (*Pushes a button.*) Maybe for the same reason that in your own pavilion—

HENRY. —the Indians are giving out jugs of saki??

YOLANDA. To the kids. In the rain. Somebody opened the ceiling and let the rain flood over the desert.

HENRY. No!

YOLANDA. My sentiments exactly. Get'em into line. Now. I have my hands full with the stupid flooding at the Netherlands pavilion—there aren't enough little Dutch boys with fingers for all the dikes.

(*She types.*)

HENRY. (*Typing.*) I do not believe this…

SUZIE. (*Watching her screen.*) There he is!

HENRY. What!

SUZIE. He's on! Terrance is coming out to confront the Spanish for the first time! Aren't you watching?

HENRY. I'm split-screening—we're having a little emergency here—

SUZIE. Oh god, look at him—he's about to lose all of Florida and he doesn't even know it.

HENRY. No! Tell him no!

(*Shouting at his monitor.*)

Run! RUN! Sink their boats and drown them in mud and use their helmets for piss pots but DON'T SHAKE HANDS!

YOLANDA. (*To* HENRY.) What the hell's wrong with your SurroundVision-360 history movie?

HENRY. What.

YOLANDA. It's running backward—apparently the settlers are fleeing back East while the Natives re-take the continent.

HENRY. Oh my god. ...He's doing it. How's he doing it?

YOLANDA. Who?

SUZIE. That's it. Ponce De Leon just took it all. Bastard.

   (*Typing.*)

I'm going to I-M him.

HENRY. Ponce De Leon?

SUZIE. Terrance! He was brilliant! Weren't you watching him?

HENRY. I couldn't— I'll call him in a second—

YOLANDA. Holy Shit!

HENRY. What?!

YOLANDA. (*Reading her screen.*) Your animatronic roadrunners are trying to mate with the penguins in the Arctic pavilion.

HENRY. Oh dear god.

SUZIE. Henry.

HENRY. What.

SUZIE. You did just watch your son's school play, didn't you?

HENRY. I did. Mostly.

SUZIE. Then you darn well better watch the recording before you get home. I'm making Lo Mein and Cheese to celebrate, and when he asks you— ...Henry? Hello? Henry, are you there?

HENRY. Suzie? Hello, Suzie?

   (*To* YOLANDA.)

Something's wrong with my phone, it—

   (*On his screen.*)

What are you doing?

YOLANDA. What?

HENRY. What are you doing to my files?

YOLANDA. I'm not doing anything!

HENRY. Someone is. They're disappearing.

YOLANDA. (*Pauses.*) What?

HENRY. All my Native Americans. Their files are vanishing.

YOLANDA. (*Pushes him aside and types on his computer.*) No one has access to those files but you—

HENRY. I know…

YOLANDA. Oh sweet Jesus…

HENRY. What!

YOLANDA. (*Watching her screen.*) —the South American natives are going… what the hell is happening?

HENRY. I don't even have those files, you can't blame me—

YOLANDA. (*Pressing keys.*) The sub-Saharans… Australians… Iranians… Jesus, every record on every nationality… is vanishing. Henry. …what the hell is going on?

(*Lights flicker. They look up.*)

HENRY. I have a really strong guess.

(*Thunder. Lights flicker.*)

YOLANDA. (*Reading her palm pilot.*) …and management's all heading for the helicopters… Goddammit! They are so not evacuating without me!

(*And she's out of there.*)

HENRY. Wait! I know who's responsible—I can find the guy responsi—

(*He turns straight into* ZHAO, *now wearing his old flannel shirt and jeans again, soaking wet.*)

—aaAAAHH!!

ZHAO. Boo, Bilagaana.

(*He stalks in, pacing, …tense—*)

HENRY. I didn't hear you—

ZHAO. My paws are silent, my breath is clear.

HENRY. What did you do to the files?

ZHAO. It ain't me. It's the storm.

HENRY. Did the storm put jugs of saki in our pavilion too?

ZHAO. No, that was me.

HENRY. Why are you doing this?? You're destroying everything I spent my life working for!

ZHAO. Isn't that why you brought me here?

(*Beat. They look at each other.*)

HENRY. Look, I want to run, I do, I want to get the heck out of here and start over, but not like this!! I do not want to be the damn rabbit!! I will not let you be the wolf and me the damn rabbit in the damn desert getting eaten by the damn wolf—

ZHAO. Then be a Cherokee rabbit. They're smart, right?

HENRY. Yeah, well, I don't feel very smart right now.

ZHAO. Then get busy. My guys are ready to go.

HENRY. What guys?

ZHAO. Everybody. Every "performer" in every pavilion. They're followin' me. We're leavin'.

HENRY. No. Not in the middle of a storm. They need to stay safe where they belong—

ZHAO. Where they belong??

HENRY. We've always kept them warm and dry and well-fed and clean—

ZHAO. Goddammit, Henry! I thought we were past this!!

HENRY. Past what? Past me caring about the natives I'm supposed to take care of?

ZHAO. Who said that was your job? Who. Ever. Said that?? You made that job up for yourself! Like you made up this whole fuckin' park, this whole fuckin' country! Everything you spent centuries makin' up is all bein' unmade, Henry. Open your eyes. You live in a vacation land and take vacations to the real world. How long did you think you could keep that up??

(HENRY *stares at him...*)

(*Holding* HENRY's *stare.*)

This isn't no ordinary storm. It's takin' apart the whole WonderWorld piece by piece, file by file. Every wall is cracking, every pavilion is flooding. If we stay in this park we are all gonna die. You *know* that.

(HENRY *pauses, staring... and nods.*)

HENRY. (*Pulling cards from his desk.*) Here. Here. Take these passes, open every pavilion, tell everyone to get to the staff exit behind the Arctic Ice Cream Shoppe. I can use my ID to hold open the gates and shutters. There should be only one guard there and if I tell him I have authorization, by the time he proves otherwise, you can be gone.

ZHAO. ...I can do that.

HENRY. You'll need vans.

ZHAO. No. We walk.

HENRY. What?

ZHAO. I know where we're supposed to go. We'll walk.

HENRY. Nobody walks anywhere in Florida on a good day! Much less in a hurricane!

ZHAO. Those theme park guys weren't idiots. They built on some of the highest land in Florida. We just have to walk to the highest of the high.

HENRY. Okay. That actually makes some sense.

ZHAO. And you're comin' with us.

HENRY. I, ah... ah—

ZHAO. Henry. You been waitin' your whole life for this chance.

HENRY. ...I know.

ZHAO. I been waitin' too. You know how long I had to sit in that goddam canyon waitin' for you to show up that day?

HENRY. ...Who are you?

ZHAO. (*Grins.*) I think you know.

(*Quietly, like a coyote.*)

Ar-ar-aroooo.

(ZHAO *smiles at* HENRY.)

HENRY. Why were you waiting for me?

ZHAO. I need you. We need you.

HENRY. I thought you just said you didn't want anyone taking care of you.

ZHAO. We don't need a parent. We need a partner. And I wanted that partner to be the descendent of "Kit" Carson.

HENRY. ...who told you that?

ZHAO. (*Grins.*) Your great great great great grandfather burned our crops and shot our children and starved our people until they could be rounded up and locked away. I want him lookin' up from Hell to see his great great great grandson walkin' out of here hand in hand with a bunch of Indians and foreigners.

HENRY. My wife and son come with me.

HENRY *turns fast to* SUZIE *who enters typing on her laptop nervously as* ZHAO *walks away. Thunder.*

Suzie!

SUZIE. (*Runs to him.*) Thank god you're home— I've been trying to call you—

HENRY. Get your bags. We're leaving.

SUZIE. What are you talking about? I just put the Lo Mein and Cheese in the oven—

HENRY. It doesn't matter. We have to go. Now. Get Terrance—

SUZIE. What do you mean it doesn't matter? This is the greatest moment in his eight-year-old life. That's his favorite food. And we have to fix some leaks, some cracks—water is getting into the rooms upstairs—

HENRY. —and there's already an inch of water in the garage—I know, we have to leave—

SUZIE. But ExtremeCloud.com said a hurricane was blowing in from the East, moving in from the North—that was an hour ago—

HENRY. What do they say now?

SUZIE. I don't know. All internet connection is gone. I've been typing into the void for 40 minutes now.

HENRY. Oh jesus...

SUZIE. But we have batteries, we have duct tape, I don't—I, I—

HENRY. I want my son to be with all the other children.

SUZIE. ...what?

HENRY. I don't want him locked in his room green-screening with his classmates, I want him *in* the room with the other children, *I* want to be in the room with them, I want all of us to be, really be in the real world in real time with each other. And I don't think we can do that here. Not anymore.

(*Holding her.*)

Suzie. Look at me. It's really unfortunate that my mid-life crisis happened to coincide with Armageddon. But it's all of us. The earth itself is shedding everything artificial—I'm just in the middle of it—

SUZIE. I've ordered us some meds from GentleSmile.com. They'll be here tomorrow morning. I think, I think if we just get through the night, I think we can get the train back on the tracks—

HENRY. The tracks are leading us over a cliff!!

SUZIE. If we were really going toward a cliff, don't you think the news would tell us?

HENRY. What do your readers read you for?

(*She stares at him.*)

Suzie. What do your readers read you for?

SUZIE. ...I keep it real.

(HENRY *nods and stars taking off his headset, and ID badge.*)

HENRY. And in a couple of hours GentleSmile and performance reviews and health insurance and blog ads, none of that's going to be real anymore. If you want to keep it real, if you want our son to keep it real, you'll take my hand and Terrance's hand and we run. We run for higher ground as far and as fast as we can. Now.

(*Pause. She looks at him... and slowly closes her laptop. Sets it down and moves to him...*)

(*Holding her.*) I think it's really likely... that his third grade play was the last hurrah of civilization.

BOOM. *Thunder. Lights shift. Sound of heavy rain...* HENRY *and* SUZIE *exit as* ZHAO *walks onstage, possibly tearing everything apart, knocking over what's left of the furniture in the lightning—and he crouches.* HENRY *stumbles back out in his rain poncho and a broken umbrella, covering his mouth, trying to cover his exposed skin—he's at his end...*

Jesus! There's alligators over there! Tell the Estonians to get away from the alligators!

ZHAO. The animals are all comin' too. They can feel it.

HENRY. There's dogs and cats—someone said the Malaysian group found Cotton Mouths—

ZHAO. We just keep out of the animals' way, they'll keep out of ours.

HENRY. So what's the plan?

ZHAO. Be handy if we had an ark, wouldn't it?

HENRY. I'm serious! You're troop leader Moses! You get us out here in a swamp with poisoned air and water, and thank god the sun's not shining, but that's only 'cause a hurricane is coming! If this isn't the end of the world I'm gonna kill you!!

SUZIE. (*Off-stage.*) Henry!

(SUZIE *enters in a rain coat, holding scraps of paper and a broken umbrella, trying to shield her 8-year-old son. This is* TERRANCE, *who blinks uneasily but calmly, staying close to his mother.* HENRY *runs to them.*)

HENRY. Terrance! Get covered, stay covered! Are you okay?

SUZIE. No, we're not okay, there's animals and people—

HENRY. I know.

SUZIE. And you can forget trying to write everything down! The scraps of paper keep melting in the rain or blowing away—whoever thought this was an effective means of communication—

ZHAO. (*Moves forward.*) So this is the son of Carson I been hearin' so much about.

(SUZIE *tries to pull* TERRANCE *back, but* HENRY *holds him.*)

HENRY. This is my son. Terrance. Terrance, this is Zhao.

SUZIE. I thought you said his name was Leonard?

ZHAO. (*Kneels beside the boy.*) Hey, little brother. Welcome to the world.

(*He offers a hand.* TERRANCE *pauses… then shakes his hand.*)

What world is this, Henry?

HENRY. What?

ZHAO. This isn't the first world, is it?

HENRY. …which tradition?

ZHAO. Navajo. What world is this?

HENRY. It's the Fifth World. The Land of the Rainbow.

SUZIE. What difference does that make?

ZHAO. The Dineh—us Navajos—didn't even begin to look like this, like humans, 'til the Fourth World. Our little dead dust bodies were nothin' 'til the Wind blew into us, brought us to life through our fingers, left its kiss in the trails of our skin.

(*He touches Terrance's shivering cheek.*)

HENRY. Fingerprints. Right.

ZHAO. And we've been movin' ever since, from world to world to world, lookin' for a home.

SUZIE. And what does that have to do with us?

ZHAO. (*To* HENRY.) You should be honored, man. We selected you.

HENRY. Why me?

ZHAO. To get us all in one place for the journey. And because you know all the stories. We gotta tell it like it really was in this world—how your people killed my people and my people killed your people. We gotta start from real in the next one.

(*To* SUZIE.)

And we need someone to write it all down.

ERNIE. (*Off-stage.*) There'll be plenty of time for writing back in the zoo, pumpkin.

(HENRY, TERRANCE *and* SUZIE *jump as* ERNIE *stalks in wearing a rain poncho and safari hat, holding a rifle, followed by* YOLANDA, *in a Culture Fiesta rain poncho.*)

HENRY. Ernie! …Yolanda? Oh my god! I thought you were evacuating!

ERNIE. (*Points his rifle at* HENRY, *who stops.*) I came to bring back stolen property. It was a fun little field trip, but it's time to get our lunchboxes and get back on the bus.

(HENRY *pushes* SUZIE *and* TERRANCE *behind him.*)

HENRY. What are you talking about?

YOLANDA. Word's out on your little excursion, Carson. You certainly know how to turn in a resignation notice, don't you? I ran into Mr. Hardaway at the airport and he's agreed for a small fee to conduct a fugitive round-up—if this doesn't get me a V-P post when this thing blows over—

HENRY. It's not blowing over—you can come with us, we're leaving the make-believe and getting real—

ERNIE. I don't care if you're in Santa's workshop with two dollar whores, you're comin' back to the park, or what's left of it.

ZHAO. Not today, Bilagaana.

ERNIE. What'd he just call me?

HENRY. "White Man."

ZHAO. Anyone who ain't part of the tribe. And you definitely ain't part of the tribe.

ERNIE. And I thank my lucky Froot Loops every damn day for that.

YOLANDA. Give the word to all the soaky natives, Henry. We're going home.

HENRY. …No.

ERNIE. What?

HENRY. They're not going back. We're not going back. We're not like you.

YOLANDA. Henry…

HENRY. Whatever happens to them happens to us.

(*Beat.* HENRY *covers Terrance's ears.*)

Fuck You.

ERNIE. (*Cocks his rifle.*) Well, somethin' bad is gonna start happenin' to them in ten seconds—

ZHAO. Go ahead. Start with me. Shoot.

HENRY. Zhao!

SUZIE. Oh god—

ZHAO. He can put more lead in me than rez drinkin' water and I'll still be standin' here. Coyote don't keep his life in his body.

HENRY. You're… Zhao, you're Zhao—that's a Coyote trick, you can't—

ERNIE. I don't care who he is. Now he's an example.

(*And he pulls the trigger. But nothing happens. Wind grows louder.*)

Oh, of all the times for Rosemary to jam up—

ZHAO. (*Howling.*) Ar-ar-aROOOOOO!

SUZIE. (*Covering* TERRANCE.) Oh god—

(ERNIE *throws down his gun and draws his hunting knife.*)

ERNIE. More than one way to skin a prick—

ZHAO. Try it!

HENRY. Ernie, No!

ERNIE. I will not be mocked by a red man with an animal fetish!!

SUZIE & HENRY. No!

(ERNIE *charges*—HENRY *tries to hold him*—ERNIE *shoves* HENRY *aside but trips—and falls on his own knife. It sinks into his gut.*)

HENRY. ERNIE!!

YOLANDA. AAH!

ERNIE. Oh, for cryin' out loud…

HENRY. Ernie, Jesus, Ernie—

ERNIE. Don't touch the blade! Leave it in! Christ. I wonder if I hit anything major…

HENRY. Zhao! Yolanda! Help me! Help me!

(SUZIE's *still covering* TERRANCE, *not letting him see…* YOLANDA *is backing away…*)

YOLANDA. Oh god oh god oh god—

ERNIE. Ow. Ow ow ow…

(ERNIE *rolls over to lie down.*)

HENRY. We gotta get a doctor—

ERNIE. All the places I ever been stabbed… I don't think I ever took one in the gut… not like Grandma…

(ERNIE *closes his eyes and lies there breathing heavily through gritted teeth as* HENRY *and* ZHAO *kneel beside him…* SUZIE *holds* TERRANCE…)

YOLANDA. He can't sue, can he? This isn't WonderWorld property, he can't sue WonderWorld—

HENRY. Yolanda, get over here and help!

YOLANDA. I'm not authorized, I can't touch the body without a PE-36, and E-Release, a—

HENRY. Yolanda! Look around you! Get over here!!

(YOLANDA *hesitates…and does… trying delicately to help.*)

SUZIE. Here. Use my papers, make a bandage, use my coat—

(HENRY *pulls off his coat too and covers* ERNIE *with it—more Thunder… but growing fainter…*)

ZHAO. (*Looking up.*) It's starting. Get your boy ready, Henrito.

HENRY. (*Going to* TERRANCE.) How can I get him ready??

(ZHAO *crouches beside* TERRANCE, *talking directly to him.*)

ZHAO. (*To* TERRANCE.) Back in the Fourth World, Little Carson, First Man and First Woman were just gettin' the tribe together, and then one day—WHOOOSH—the sky stoops down, and ROARRR—the earth rose up to meet it. And in that place where they touched, right there, Coyote was born. And he didn't howl, he didn't play. He ran right over to the Dineh. He was to always be with them. To help them. His only job. What he did in his off-hours was his business. He had a temporary pass to the whole park. But that was until First Man and First Woman got into an argument with Tie-holtsodie, a water spirit, and ended up pissin' the spirit off pretty bad. But the tribe keeps on like nothin's wrong, like they got all the time in the world—

HENRY. —and then the animals start showing up.

(*They all look at him.*)

From all over, terrified, they start gathering around the Dineh. Because the water's coming. The first day they see the flood rising from the East. The second day the North. The third day the West and the fourth day the South. They were trapped.

ZHAO. Until Coyote gets this idea—he plants a reed in the ground and it grows—grows and grows into the sky, this huge hollow reed with a hole in the bottom of the east side. And the whole tribe climbs in, they take the animals, the soil from the Sacred Mountains, and they climb. They climb for their lives. As fast as the water rises, the reed grows, climbing, climbing, until Crack! Smooth and hard. They hit the sky. And Coyote grabs Locust and

Badger and they dig, man, they dig like fire, like claws, like God himself, 'til they break through. To here.

HENRY. The Fifth World.

(*Beat.*)

ZHAO. We been here a long time and had a lot of adventures. But the water's risin' again. It's time to go.

(*They watch each other. Sound of rain.*)

HENRY. Time to go to the Sixth World.

SUZIE. (*Looking out.*) Everyone's coming in… the animals—

ZHAO. The heart of the storm is about to hit.

HENRY. Suzie—Terrance—grab hold of something—

ZHAO. (*Looking up.*) When the eye passes over, we're out of here.

(*Wind howls louder…*)

HENRY. We're gonna be torn limb from limb…

ZHAO. Can you taste it?

HENRY. What.

ZHAO. In your mouth.

HENRY. I do. I do taste something.

ZHAO. That's adrenaline.

(*The wind howls louder… They look around…*)

HENRY. (*Yelling over the wind.*) I'm scared.

ZHAO. (*Yelling back.*) Me too. …can you dance?

HENRY. What?

ZHAO. The Blessing Way—

(ZHAO *starts to step, rhythmically*— *We hear faint Navajo chanting in the distance…*)

(*Spoken.*) …"With beauty before me, I walk.

With beauty behind me, I walk.

With beauty below me, I walk.

With beauty all around me—"

HENRY & ZHAO. "—I walk…

It is finished in beauty.

It is finished in beauty.

It is finished… in beauty."

(*Beat. They look at each other.*)

ZHAO. In the Sixth World, we dance, Henry.

(*Wind howls louder—lights grow brighter…* ZHAO *dances—Chanting grows louder, building with the wind—Louder…. And* HENRY *takes a step. Another.*

*Following Zhao's lead—Music grows—*SUZIE *and* TERRANCE *watching them...* YOLANDA *holding* ERNIE.... *Wind* HOWLING—*Lights Brighter.... The two men are dancing—Dancing... Dancing... Silence. Blackout.*)

End of Play

LOW

by Rha Goddess

BIOGRAPHY

Rha Goddess is a performing artist and social/political activist. Her work has been internationally featured in several compilations, anthologies, forums and festivals. Rha's debut project, *Soulah Vibe*, received rave industry reviews from Ms. Magazine, The Source, XXL, Interview, etc.. *Time Magazine* called it *"...one of the year's coolest records."* As Founder and CEO of Divine Dime Entertainment, Ltd., she was one of the first women in Hip Hop to create, independently market and commercially distribute her own music world wide. In May 2000, *Essence Magazine* recognized Rha as one of 30 Women to Watch in the new millennium. In 2002, BAM's prestigious Next Wave festival's NextNext series, chose her as one of six artists deemed to be influential in the next decade. Her activist work includes Co-founding the Sista II Sista Freedom School for Young Women of Color, and being the former International Spokeswoman for the Universal Zulu Nation. Rha has also been an encore featured keynote in the *Women & Power Summit at Omega Institute* along with Iyanla Vanzant, Eve Ensler, Anita Hill, and Eileen Fisher, Jane Fonda, Alice Walker, Eve Ensler, and Marion Woodman. Rha's current projects include being the Founder and Project Director of The Next Wave of Women & Power/"We Got Issues!" and working on a modern trilogy entitled, *Meditations With The Goddess. Low*, Part I of the Meditations Trilogy, premiered at the 2006 Humana Festival for New American Plays.

ACKNOWLEDGMENTS

Low (Meditations Trilogy Pt. I) premiered at the Humana Festival of New American Plays in March 2006. It was directed and developed by Chay Yew with the following cast and staff:

LOWQUESHA, ET.AL ....Rha Goddess

Sound Designer ....Darrin Ross
Lighting Designer.. Sabrina Hamilton
Set Designer .... Mikiko Suzuki McAdams
Composers...Darrin Ross
                                                          Rha Goddess
                                                          Baba Israel
Stage Manager, Technical Director ....Sarah Goshman
Dramaturg ....Mervin P. Antonio
Assistant Dramaturg...Jamie Bragg
Project Management, Tour Rep..... Cathy Zimmerman, MAPP

Presented by special arrangement with Multi Arts Projects & productions. *Low* is a co- production of Divine Dime Entertainment, Ltd. and Sasha Dees for Made in da Shade. *Low* is made possible in part with grants from the Doris Duke Charitable Foundation, Jerome Foundation, Meet the Composer, the NPN Creation Fund, Fonds voor Amateurkunst en Podiumkunsten (FAPK), and Theater Instituut Nederland (TIN). Association of Performing Arts Presenters *Next Steps Program*, New York State Council on the Arts, and the Kentucky Foundation for Women. *Low* has received commissioning support from 651 ARTS, Brooklyn, NY; and New World Theater, Amherst, MA. Crucial developmental residencies have been provided by the Actor's Theatre of Louisville (Louisville, KY), New York Theatre Workshop, Center for Creative Education (Stone Ridge, NY), The Hourglass Group and North American Cultural Laboratory (Highland Lakes, NY). *Low* will tour internationally during the 2006-2007 and 2007-2008 seasons.

CAST OF CHARACTERS

LOWQUESHA GODDESS, a 25 year old Blacktina, round the way— Hip Hop B-Girl/MC from the Brooklyn. Born and raised on true school and new school Hip Hop. High energy, intelligent, street smart quick tongued & tempered, courageous, vulnerable, strong spirited, confrontational…a survivor.

SETTING

The present, Brooklyn, NY.

Rha Goddess
in *Low*

30th Annual Humana Festival of New American Plays
Actors Theatre of Louisville, 2006
Photo by Harlan Taylor

LOW

1. SAYING GRACE

LOW. It is Sunday, I am 8
And I am sitting at the table
I have been left here with my sister Anna
Because I did not clean my plate
I smell half eaten turkey bones
With dry cranberry sauce
Mashed potatoes and cold gravy

But mostly, I smell cinnamon
And the cold soggy, wrinkly
Skin that holds mushy orange flesh

I will not eat it, no matter
How long I have to sit here
I like school, but I will be absent
Tomorrow—I will be right here
Still refusing to eat it.

"Hurry up and get it over with"
Says Anna, raising the left side of her
Lip—I can see her fangs,
She's such a bitch sometimes

"I ain't eatin it!"
"Yes you are" She says
"Eat it now before I come over there and make you"
"No!" (*Gestures.*) I say "you ain't the boss of me….."

And she scoops the pumpkin colored mush
Into her hands and splats it onto my face.
I gag for air as the disgusting slop goes
Up my nose.

Anna is laughing hysterically

"I hate you!" I scream
scooping my own glop to sling
I grab another and another
As Anna runs around the
new dining room table
cackling like a witch

This time I grab yam guts in
Both hands and sling them
At the same time, at last
I hit my target.
The orange sludge slides down the side of Anna's
head and lands right top of her Sunday blouse

"Look what you did stupid!"
All of a sudden we look
Around the room, there is
Sweet potato everywhere

Oh shit! Anna says
We better hurry up and clean this
Up before Mommie gets back.

That night,
I am the room I share with Anna coloring

The first time I hear it
I think it's coming from the

TV Ay! Ay! Ay!

ANNA! Come here right now
Even before Anna can reach the
Front room I hear my name
"Low did it mommy-you know how
you told her to clean her plate…"

I am off my bed and out the
the door, I come in at the top
of my lungs, "No Mommie!
Anna started it, she threw
Yams in my face."

Neither one of us can
Finish because Mommie
Has left the room—

We stare at the walls and the carpet
With the light on
they look disgusting
we stare at one another knowing
what will come next,
Run!

Mommie's footsteps are
already back on the
hall, She grabs Anna first

thank god, I see the extension
cord whip through the air and come
down on her legs and back

When you are being hit with an extension
Cord, it feels like you are
Being lit on fire
The cord leaves large red whelps
And mommie
Hits hard enough even to mark
my chocolate flesh

the storm is over and Anna and
I are on our knees with a
Buket of Mr. Clean and water
Trying to get the dried
Yam out of the rug

I will not touch another sweet potato
As long as I live.

2. 5ᵗʰ GRADE ASSIGNMENT

TEACHER. Children, today I have the most exciting assignment for you
in honor of independence day each of you will create a family tree
All of us have immigrated to this country from somewhere else
so go back across the ocean and tell us where you are originally from...
and remember to have fun with it!

LOW. Dwight who sits in front of me, we call him Blackwatch because he's
always wearing Dakshkis and raising his fist like this, (*Gestures.*) is about to go
off—he says when his dad finds out about this he's gonna come to school
and shut the teacher down for giving such a racist assignment—"Black
people were sold in bondage that's how we got here! To subject me to such
humiliation as to make me admit to the entire class that I don't know where I
come from is cruel and unusual punishment"

LOW. Whatever! I'm still trying to figure out how to get some more
branches....momma swears she was an orphan. So that means it's just me,
Mommie, Anna, and maybe Rosa her best friend.

Wait I know! I'll do a whole section on my uncles, you know, Mommie's
men friends? Let's see first there was Juan, the mortician who smelled funny
and always picked his nose, then Arthur with the really thick glasses who
studied the Bible while on the toilet, then Hector who cried, every time
mommy asked for money, and Willie and his 10 dirty ass kids who always
had they hand out, and um Luis who bought mommy a red spandex dress
and usta sing "the blacker the berry," then Danny, then Harold, then Melvin,

no wait I think it was Harold, Melvin, Bobby, then Danny, then Charles, then Rudy, then Paul, hmmm, no then Jimmy, then Paul, and then Victor who wore panties and changed his name to Jasmine when they broke up, and my most favoritest of them all; Jonnie B. Jonnie B was the shit! I could tell mommie really loved him too. He usta make the best barbeque chicken and fried plantanos, we ate real good when he was around. Always bringing me candy, and teaching me funny songs, he even knew how to argue, which was most important because mommie is a professional, he'd just go, "looka here, anytime you do want my lovin' just let me know, I'm sure I can find somebody'll help me eat these pork chops." Next thing I knew she'd be laughing and he'd be in the kitchen cooking up a storm...Mommy could never stay mad at him. But then one day he just stopped, no big scene, no last supper, he just disappeared. After he left, Mommy got real quiet, and there were no more uncles for a long time. I think she's hoping he'll come back, but I don't think he will.

Wow, look at my tree now!

3. HIGHER LEARNING

LOW. I am 16 and I am in Ms. Murphy's class
Ms. Murphy teaches English. English is my favorite
subject accept I don't like her. She's always
talking about how Black and Latino authors were
influenced by White ones, like White people
where the first and only people on the planet to ever
do anything right.

So most days I just ignore her lectures, but
I always read the books.

Jonnie B told me that lots of blacks and latinos
have done great things for America, but he says
they'll never tell you that in school. So when
Ms. Murphy announced that we were going
to do the Harlem Renaissance, I asked if I could
Read a poem by Langston Hughes and she said
Of course I could.

Johnie B, told me all about him, he was this really
Great poet who wrote about the struggles
Of being Black in America during the 30s and 40s and 50s
He gave me a book of his poetry that I still keep under my pillow.
We haven't heard from Jonnie B in a very long time
I've been re-reading the book because I miss him.

When Ms. Murphy starts to talk about Langston

I raise my hand but she ignores me,
And keeps going on and on about
How Langston got his inspiration from Walt Whitman

I got so pissed off,
I took my hand down
Took out his book
And started reading to
Myself. (*Starts reading "A Dream Deferred" aloud.*)

MURPHY. "Lowquesha, did you want
To say something?"

LOW. Forget it!

MURPHY. "why don't you tell us
How you learned about Langston Hughes?"

LOW. I keep reading my poem aloud, like I don't hear
her

MURPHY. "What's that you're reading?"

MURPHY. "Give it to me. You can pick it
up at the end of class, but right now
you're supposed to be paying attention."

LOW. I go to put the book away cause
There is no way in hell, I'm letting
Her have this book
She tries to snatch the book out of my hand
And it rips.

I jumped up and smacked her in her face.

"you fuckin bitch! Look what you did!"

Now she's telling one of the white students
To run down to the office and get the
Principal.

"don't you tell me what to do, it's you're fuckin
fault you got smacked in the first place."
You not supposed to put your hands on me!
You not supposed to put your hands on my stuff either
You racist bitch!"

The principal who has just walked in
motions for Ms. Murphy to come into the hallway
She looks like she's about to cry

After a few minutes

He swings open the door

I grab my stuff and storm out....
They gonna call Mommie,
But I don't care
She'll take my side,
I know she will

4. No Type A Remedy

DR. LONG. Hi Lowquesha, my name is Dr. Long

LOW. He is big and hairy with curly hair and a beard and mustache,
His smile is warm and friendly
I almost forget whose side he's on.

DOCTOR. so I hear that you haven't been sleeping

LOW. (*Gently shakes head.*)

DOCTOR. what about your appetite-are you eating?

LOW. (*Gently shrugs—turns up hands.*)

DOCTOR. how are you feeling right now?

LOW. (*Big shrug.*)

DOCTOR. happy, sad, angry, nervous, anxious, irritable?

LOW. (*Pause—thinks—begins to look around the room and touch things.*)

DOCTOR. Lowquesha, do you have difficulty remembering or keeping track of your thoughts? —Oh, please be careful with that.

LOW. (*Looks caught—gently puts object down.*)

DOCTOR. how are things at home?

LOW. (*Starts to walk around—arm moving.*) okay...

DOCTOR. okay like how?

LOW. I don't know, some days it's okay, like okay and some days it's like really bad my mother can be a real bitch sometimes so can my sister Anna.

DOCTOR. Lowquesha, do you ever feel depressed or lethargic? Lethargic means you have very little energy....

LOW. (*Turning to face him, crossing arms like "I know."*)

DOCTOR. I understand you are having problems in English right now

LOW. No, it's just I don't like my teacher—ooo, is that your wife?

DOCTOR. yes, that's my wife—so why don't you like your teacher?

LOW. cause she don't respect me, she always be trying to put me down in front of the class, fuckin bitch.

DOCTOR. so yelling at your teacher makes you feel good?

LOW. (*Quiet.*) can I tell you the truth? It felt really good to smack her!

DOCTOR. what else makes you feel good?

LOW. Rapping, you know, spitting lyrics over a beat.

DOCTOR. hmm, can you give me an example?

LOW. Public Enemy? (*Sucks teeth.*) Will Smith?

DOCTOR. Oh, rapping I got it...what else makes you feel good?

LOW. huh? Um, being with my boyfriend

DOCTOR. do you see him often?

LOW. sometimes I cut class to be with him, we…you know….

DOCTOR. really?

LOW. (*Nods.*)

DOCTOR. Lowquesha, I want to do some tests just to make sure, but I think I have a sense of what is going on with you and I believe that we can help you feel better.

LOW. so I'm not in trouble?

5. MEETING DARNELL

LOW. I was at my girl Shawna's
She was having a little celebration
For Junior who just got outa jail
Everybody always liked Jun from when he was little
Shawna been in love with him since the 2nd grade.

Me and Jun had a little thing
kept it on the down low cause
Niggas talk too much
I wasn't in love with him
I was just in a bind and he
helped me out—so I had to show my gratitude.

The house was packed, cause all Jun's boys came through
Some from around the way, some from being on lock and some other
dudes he met when he was doing that music
thing.

The Ole E is flowing, and Jun is holding court, reminiscing.
Eventually, memory lane leads back to me.

Jun ain't crazy, Shawna would kill us both

So he ain't saying shit out loud….but I can
tell he's talking because as soon as he's done gesturing
Niggas is looking at me like "what's up shorty?"
"and that's my word" was all you heard him say.

Now, one of the music ballers is giving me the extra eye
He's rocking a cobalt blue leather baseball jacket with a
Mini afro and those sculpted sideburns that I love
thick juicy lips, that blush red in the middle with a natural
brown outline—he licks for my benefit.
Eyes are dark, lashes long, jawbone strong—just the way I like um
Yea, he's definitely clocking, and Yea, he's definitely cute

I find a reason to walk past, I can tell exactly when he's gonna put his
Hand on my arm too,
It will be just before I get totally out of reach
Done so as not to be obvious to the other brothers
Who by that time are through looking at my ass.

He doesn't say anything, just holds on like he know me
Then quietly releases before I blow up his spot….I move deeper into the kitchen
Then turn and give him a fly girl smile

Then all dem niggas start laughing, and I hear his
Name, "Yo, Darnell, pass that libation," he obliges
Pretending not to feel me looking- but the deal has already been
inked as my man Dinero would say……….

Three hours later we in the back of his whip
and he is totally handling his business
no small talk, no profiling, and no pretending
just a straight up—"let's do this"
I'm feeling good, cause it's nice to be
Wit a guy who knows what he's doing
Things are getting freakier by the minute
But that's all right with me…cause I know
Just how to play it….

I let him start to feel it
Let it start to get good
And then I pull away and
say—"hold up"—he looks
like he's about to explode
"you feelin me special—or is this
just some everyday shit?"
I wanna know before I let
This go any farther

He's caught and we both
Know it—cause ain't now way
He turning this down
I slowly start to pull my pants up
"Whhhoaaa Shorty, slow down"
Allright, let's talk…I smile in the dark

6. TAKING MY MEDICINE

LOW. You see these labels? I know them in my sleep!
And there is no fuckin way I can take all of this
shit and be normal…….

Warning! Do not take on an empty stomach. Warning! Do not take while operating heavy machinery Or driving an automobile. Warning! Do not mix with Alcohol. Warning! Do not exceed the recommended dosage. Warning! Do not refill this prescription unless you call this number first.

The blue ones make me feel dizzy, and give me tunnel vision like I've been running around with my neck up my ass if I combine them with the round ones I get the head bobbles and really bad gas which the square ones turn to full blown diarrhea.

If I take the round ones with the pink ones, and the squares, I get the hiccups, every thing becomes gray and fuzzy, my face twitches and I can't get out of bed

The green ones, make my tongue thick, make my speech slur, and my mouth overflow with saliva combined with the blue ones make me blind and jittery and I don't want any food or sex.

I take the blue ones every other day because they are really expensive and a half of pink one gives me the same affect.
I take 1 green a day which I cut it in half to give me two treatments.

I won't take the green ones when I see Darnell
I will take an extra blue when I deal with my mother
And I will only take a half of the round one when I go to work
I wish there was a pill that made me pretty.

7. YOU THINK YOU LOOK GOOD?

LOW. Today, is a good day
I am staring at my reflection
In the mirror
I can see the mystery in my eyes
And a subtle glow in my skin
My breasts, my hair and my smile

Are all pleasing to me
Today, I fully accept who I am

LOW MEAN. Bitch please, wasn't you just on your knees
Wit a knife at ya life, cause the nigga
didn't leave you a message, Low, you don't get
it! He don't give a shit about you—why you stressing?

LOW. Hey! Don't start okay! Nobody's talking to you
so shut up!

LOW MEAN. Low, I'm doing you a favor
Even though he talk a good game
He a playa-freak what he said, I don't care
You betta watch what he do—is he good to you?
Down for you? Real wit you? True?

LOW. I'm not listening to you
I'm not listening to you
I'm not listening to you

LOW MEAN. Yea, okay whatever,
But you ain't clever you don't even
make him pay when he treat you like
scum—how you let him dis you,
lie—then dismiss you. Yo Low,
come on! Why you actin' so dumb?

LOW. Shut up! You don't know what you're talking
About, Darnell really does care about me
He's just busy

LOW MEAN. Pretend all ya want
But I deal in the real
And the real deal—is you ain't never been
the one, beg and plead
All you wanna, call and chase
If you gonna—but the truth is the truth
So, girl you can't front—

LOW. John—You see Darnell?
You told him to call me right?
Yo, Monifa dis Lowquesha
Darnell come to class last night?
Yo Jamal, where ya man at?
Hey Sal, he come to work today?
Yo, Biz, what the deal, D ain't come around your way?

LOW MEAN. Low, why you wasting the pretty?
You don't need that nigga's

Pity, you too fly to be sittin'
by the phone. Fuck him! Keep um guessin
that's when He'll start sweatin, when
he realize that you gotta life
Of your own!

LOW. Hey Misha, seen your brother?
Yo, bitch this is WIFEY!, betta not be runnin' wit my man!
Darnell? Why you ain't call me? Busy?
Doin what? And you couldn't take two seconds and call me back?
You fuckin' up!

LOW MEAN. (*Starts laughing.*) Um Hmmmmmm

8. HIGH AND DRY

(*Sung 2x.*)
LOW. Oooo Watch that glare! Watch that glare! Watch that glare!
Whaat peep that shine! peep that shine! Peep that shine!

Standin in the Waldorf Astoria
In my red leather looking mighty Blaouh!
Limo pick me up at a quarter to three
Take me to the studios of MTV

Gotta interview wit Carson on TLC
Gonna talk about hit what?—number 3

Beyonce' betta watch her back
Climbing up the charts movin mighty fast
Waving to the haters—how you like me now?
Rollin wit the majors' in a drop DL
Busta Rhymes, Method Man, Nasty Nas
LL, Jay Z, Lincoln Park
All want me to come lace 'day tracks
Cause they hooked on this lyrical acrobat

Oooo Watch that glare! Watch that glare! Watch that glare!
Whaaat?! peep that shine! peep that shine! Peep that shine!

Breakin all kinda records
Imma rising star
With my hot butta flow
I'm raising the bar
Gotta fly hook to put me on top
Crossing over to R&B and POP
Buzz so loud you can barely hear
Taking over the grammy's this year

RECEPTIONIST. Lowquesha, there you are, Dr. Green will see you now.

9. Can I Help You?

LOW. Hi, can I take your order?

Yo, let me get a grande' double shot expresso latte wit a shot a vanilla

Mira, I need a caramello, frappachino extra thick wit chocolate sprinkles
No scratch that, make it an iced grande mocha nut frap, extra thick wit caramel sauce

Yea, can I get a grande soy chai latte, extra hot no foam
And a Venti vanilla hazel nut roast, wit a shot a cinnamon dolce

Yea, I need a Tazo calm and a expresso con panna and, make um stand tall please

When people ask me what I do, I tell um I talk to addicts all day

Suits and ties
Wigged out college heads
Hip Hop wannabees
Constructionites
Ghetto Bougie Paris Hilton's in waiting
Thug Mugs hooked on the summer drinks
The whole rainbow.

And all of them are anxious
Stressed out—Hyper excitable—high octaine withdrawal—
Having—Fuckin' Fiends!

I know they never talk about this shit,
But coffee is DEEP

Yea, let me get a marble mocha mocchiato, grande, wit a shot of expresso, and whip it high!

I love doing the register
and calling out the orders
I use um to practice my fast diction
Any MC worth her salt has got to be
Able to spit fast and clear, feel me?

When I am on the register and it's really busy
I gotta represent!

Especially for them stick up the ass Wall Street types

This is how I do them,

Hi, can I take your order?

Yes, I'll have a Venezula Sunrise, with a hint of soy, easy on the foam

What size sir?

Make it a grande

Yo, Felippe, I need a Venis Sun, smack it with a fake cow and wipe it's mouth! Oh yea, and make it a step child.

He's rollin his eyes now cause he's sure I fucked up his order!

He's like no, I asked for a blabbydy blah blay-blah blah blah......

I say sir, I got you...

He's back five minutes later,

"This is not what I ordered!"

Are you sure you didn't take someone else's drink sir?

"get me the manager!"

My shift manager Don, is some young up and coming
from Connecticut
Who's studying poly sci at NYU

He takes one look at the guy and knows what happened.

Of course my man walks out with free coffee

Hi, can I take your order?

Felippe' I need a Venti white chocolate moca shhh-huh? Latte- latte, scratch it's a grande cinnamon dolce e and a Venti—latte-soy-gingerbread latte extra foam, foam—scratch no foam

Don is on my ass now, cause I'm fuckin up....I promised to work a double shift today...and we're in the middle of a noon day rush...

I can hear him correcting me in the background with each order

Yo, can I get a Cinnamon Gingerbread shit! Scratch a grande, Vanilla latte no tall vanilla latte and a grande peppermint mocha with a shot of Java chip sorry with a shot of java chip light and chocolate sprinkles.

It's mad busy, the line is damn near out the door, and I can see people looking at their watches, anxious, high octane withdrawal, don't wanna hear my sob story about why I can't get it right Fiends—who need their fix so they can get through the rest of the day.

Hi, can I help you?

I'm sorry, so you want a tall black coffee, a grande tazo refresh, and a venti soy latte w/ extra foam?

At the end of my first shift, Don pulls me aside, I try to focus on the words after a while I don't have to, something about because I can't make the coffee, him needing people who are versatile ......

It ain't til I'm on the train that I realize what I did, I look in my case and the other half of my round pill is missing.

10. HAVE MERCY

LOW. His dick is in my mouth but I don't feel it
Feel him cause he don't give a shit about me
My head bangs against the door with every thrust
Which is every fuck you spelled backwards
This is why I blew up his phone
Got my hair done, put on lipstick
This is why I made Shawna lend
Me her gold blouse this is why
I made small talk with
His mother, this is just how bad
I want to go out, but we never
Made it to the restaurant, so I'm settling for drive
thru instead. He got the big mac,
and I am left with a happy meal
This is why I hound
His boys call his job befriend his sister
This is how bad I want to be
Down, in love with him lust with him
Feel more than used by him
And here he comes, spewing
Guilt, pity and relief all over
My face, rubbing in just how dirty
And desperate I am, just how crazy and fucked
Up I've been because he and I both
Know I'll be at it again tomorrow
This is why I threatened that Bitch
And told her to call me Wifey
Cause I get quality time
Yea, I got a front row seat
And he be doing me, just
Like this.

11. SLAY ME

LOW. I am a piece of shit!
A good for nothing
Dirty cunt-butt fuck ugly
Stupid, screwed up
Crazy desperate bitch

I can't keep a job
I can keep a man
I can't do anything

I ain't ever gonna be no real MC
I sound like shit—I can't even
keep a menial ass job slinging coffee at
Starbucks how the hell do I think
I'm gonna be a rap star?

Fuck it! (*Pulls knife.*)

He promised me I could have dessert
I really wanted the crème brule
Why would he say he was gonna take me?
All we did was fuck in the back of his car....
Why would he lie like that?

12. I Don't Feel Well Today

LOWQUESHA. I don't feel well today.
And I'm just letting you know. okay?
Some people get offended when I say that,
Like it's about them.......
Why some people always think it's about them?

It's just that some days, I don't feel so good.
And I'm trying to be considerate and let you
know.... so that you could stay away
So that you had some warning so that you'd know, that
now might not be a good time to start no shit!

I would appreciate it if you said it to me,
Cause I know what it's like not to
feel so good.........no, I do, really.

But this bitch here? Been told, but
She don't listen I be telling her:

MA, I'm not feeling very well today,

I'm not feeling well, and I'm not feeling you
So can we talk about this another time?
She still talking—running her mouth—like I didn't say anything,
Following me around the house, like she don't know I'm liable
to.....MAAAA! I don't give a fuck about ya bag a cheese doodles
I don't remember if I ate them or not, I might have, I'm sorry, I'll buy you a new
Bag tomorrow, but right now, what I really need is for me to lay down and

For you to shut the fuck up!!!!!!

She still talking, only now she's
Diggin in the crates of past bullshit
Like more ammunition is gonna help her cause
I'm so inconsiderate, blah blah I always do this...blah blah, blah blah
Yo, I swear I hate that shit, even when I'm
Feelin' well. If you mad at me about something...
Stick to what you mad about don't be tryin' to
Build no federal case......over a fuckin' bag
A cheese doodles? Naw, for real, over a fuckin'
bag a cheese doodles!! UM! AK! RAT! SHT! FUTG!
YOU FUCKIN BITCH! YOU FUCKIN BITCH! YOU FUCKIN BITCH!
Now her eye is swole and her lips is bleeding
and I can hear them banging on the door....

And here I go, back in the hospital, all
Because, a stupid bag of cheese doodles was
missing.......

13. SLOW MOTION

LOW. Ummmmmmmmmmmmmmmmmmmmmmmmmmmmmm'
What
Was
I
Saying?
This is drugs
This is my brain on drugs
Do you
ever wonder
who
Was the first
person to pick
Their nose?
Everybody does it now
But who
Was
The
First?

I bet
It was
A man

Cause they

Are always
Digging
And
fiddling
With
themselves
at the
most
inappropriate
times

He must
Have
Done
It
In
Public

So
That
Other
People
Could
See
And
would
know
exactly
how
it
was
done

or
maybe
it
was one
of those
things

where
a bunch
of
people
got
the idea

at the
same time

You
know
like
Spontaneous
Inspiration?

Either
Way
I am
Just
Happy
That
In times
Like
These
I
Can
Have
Something
To
Do.

14. HAIL MARY

LOW. Hello Mommie…
I'm coming home
They just released me
I don't have my keys so I just want
To make sure you'll be there
I'm really hungry …can you make
Me some chicken with rice and beans?

MOMMIE. I just get off the phone with Dr. Green
He say you getting worse,

You always been strong willed Low
You do what you please
It's just too much

LOW. What are you saying to me Ma?

MOMMIE. I don't know all about this what he's saying
All of the time we fighting

I don't know where I go wrong with you

Look at your sister, she doing good

Even though she don't call me
Or sometime say mean things that
Hurt my feelings, she got her own life.

LOW. Mommie, what are you saying to me?

MOMMIE. Do you know how long it take my eye to heal?
2 weeks I was shamed to go to work,
3 days I stay home
But I need the money so I go in
You hurt me very bad Low on the inside

I don't feel to trust you
I'm not sure I can take care of you

LOW. Stop talking crazy….you're scaring me!

MOMMIE. (*Silence.*)

LOW. Mommie, I'm hanging up the phone
Right now, and I'm coming home!

MOMMIE. I pack up your things and
Give them to your friend Shawna down the hall

I won't be here so don't ring the bell
And don't ask Hector because I tell
Him not to let you in.

I can't take care of you anymore

LOW. Mommie, where am I supposed to go?! Listen, I'm sorry I hit you
but you wouldn't leave me alone. And I'm sorry I just yelled at you.

Mommie, please don't do this…I promise I won't argue with you anymore

MOMMIE. I hang up now

15. LOW FREESTYLE—BATTLE SONG

LOW. Battle song
I'm getting my battle on
Yo, when things go wrong
I get my battle on…..

High steppers
Come on get ya weapons
We bout to do this shit
For go-getters
We bout to catch wreck
From trend setters

I'm getting
The fuck outta dodge
before I wet her
You got hell real quick
For killing ya moms
Word to the Bible
I'm about survival

How you gone dis me
Over cheese doodles
How you gone dismiss me
After all we been—through?
Just goes to show
That blood ain't thicker
Nothing
Curb ya own daughter
Now she's got to rough it

These streets is mean
So I got's to be tougher
I usta love her now
Fuck my mother!!

Kicked me out
To fend for—my-self
Kicked me out
Even though I need—help

She broke my heart
But I can't fall apart
Word to the Bible
It's all about survival

Battle song
I'm getting my Battle on
Yo when things go wrong
I get my Battle on

16. ON THE DOWN LOW

LOW. I am dreaming of
A beautiful bathroom
It has a Jacuzzi
And lots of Hollywood
Star lights around the mirrors
The porcelain belly of each sink gleams
And my image is reflected in the chrome fixtures

I am sitting on the toilet
I have had a full night
Of wine and drink and people
My belly is full and all it
Wants to do is release.....sssssssssssssssssss

My first night on the street
I had this dream
And peed all over myself
I didn't even realize it
Until the morning
Buried beneath the cardboard
Wooden crates and tarmac
The dumpster's charity made me invisible
And I took my very last pink pill
So I could sleep.....

The pavement's chill
Seeped into my bones
And I woke up
Wet and frozen

I need to change
I ain't got much shit with me,
Only another pair of pants
And a shirt and two panties
I figured that wherever I wound
Up, I'd be able to rinse my bra and socks.

McDonalds doesn't open til 7am
And their public bathroom is disgusting
I stay crouched beneath the dumpster
Cause I don't want no trouble
Try not to think about
How foul this is
How nasty my skin feels
How badly I smell

Try to imagine myself
Back in that bathroom
I peal off my clothes
And step into the Jacuzzi
The water is warm and smells
Of rose and lavender
I am washing my hair
And it feels soo good

"Hey, get the fuck outta there!"

Some white guy's yellin at me
In a dingy burgundy shirt

"Oh shit, goddamit—you fuckin' smell like piss"
"get your skanky ass out of here…"
I am trying to figure out how to ask him
"Um can I please use the bathroom…."
"Bitch, if you don't get the hell away from me,
I'm gonna fuck you up!"
"Please sir….I really need to "
"If I let you use the bathroom I'm gonna have to clean up after you"
I shake my head, no, I'll clean, both of the bathrooms if you let me
Wash and get some breakfast"

He is looking around-contemplating
If he's getting a good deal
"Tell you what, I'll let you wash and eat
if you clean both of the bathrooms and suck me off"

I step out of the Jacuzzi
And wipe the steam from the mirror
I look into my eyes
I look so peaceful….

18. GUTTER

LOW. On my fifth day in the street
I got desperate
I was so anxious
My face began to twitch
Like crazy and I knew
That the medicine was
Almost out of my system

I had to move from the
Alley behind McDonalds
Because the manager
Told all the guys
What happened
And they would be out back
Lined up offering me
Cheese burgers and French fries to
Do it to them.

I got tired of eating
McDonalds though
I kept seeing posters

For that movie
Super Size Me
And one day
I snuck into
The theater
And watched it

Now, I'm near a vegetarian
Restaurant, but they don't
Throw as much away
Cause of all that recycling
Bullshit.

Trying to keep my mind
Off the drama I be writing
Rhymes on paper bags, pretty
Soon I'll have enough for an album
The days out here pass so slow
I had to move from out my
Neighborhood so that
People wouldn't recognize me
Funny, but when I can get into
A bathroom and stare at myself
In the mirror
I don't barely recognize me either

Mommie still hangs up
When I call her
I don't even bother with Anna
I know Shawna would take me
In if Junior wasn't there.

I can't let Darnell
See me like this
I keep trying him
But he don't never pick up
Or call me back
Pretty soon they gonna cut my cell phone off
And then he won't have no
way to get at me.

I been finding so many
Pennies on the ground
And the old timers, like John
Sometimes let me help
Them with the bottles

I buy soap mostly

Cause I just can't stand to stink

I try not to look to
Too dirty which is
A sure fire way to get
The cops on your ass

One of them is already trackin'
I think he knows about my
Mickey D's hustle
But I ain't fuckin with 50 like that

I been thinking about checking
Myself in-but I gotta wait till
Shit gets really bad, cause
Otherwise they put you
In the dungeon at county and make you wait
For a bed.

I had a friend who got put there
And woke up with some dude
On top of her-she spent the next
3 days runnin from his ass

I don't know if I can fuck wit
County.

I'll just have to wait
Til I feel the shit coming on and fall through
the door
This way they gotta take
Me……..

19. RED DRAGON

LOW. I am sitting on the train on my way to see Anna
I am sitting across from this well dressed man
who is eyeing me

he is probably a very nice man
who is really concerned

but I don't like the look on his face

You think you know me

You make assumptions about my life
And go Wow, isn't that
Interesting?

You think your pity

Is something I need
To be normal, okay, acceptable

While you watch me
While I sit here
With my guts hanging out

While you watch me
While I sit here
Pointing to all the sore spots

Don't feel bad for me
Don't feel shame for me
Do not even remotely
Think you understand

Because while you nurse
Your bleeding heart, motherfucker

I'm going flying!
On the back of a red dragon
Whipping through the flames
Of this cruel world
Laughing my ass off

I am above all of this
Lifted out of
My misery instantly
And on a daily

All I gotta do is
Say the word
And I got a ticket to
Ride.

I am moving
Way to fast for
Any of this shit to matter

Feel the tough scales between my legs
Hear the snarl and grunt of this beast
Edging on the galaxy with a Ya!

I go faster, faster faster
Until I am a blur to you
Something you can't even
Make out in the distance

Whizzing past purple planets
And indigo people burning
Medicinal herbs to help

Me remember
Who I am,
Who I was
Before all of this

My soul fills the air
My conviction rises to
The roof of my mouth
Fantasies surround me in
Technicolor screaming
Pick Me! Pick Me!
I will make you Happy!

I am soaring so high
Looping, diving, swerving
Spinning so fast
My path is invincible
My mouth is open
Wide and I am catching
Stars between my teeth

Then spitting them back
Into the sky like Pu-Pow! Pu-Pow!
And I am making
My original sound
Orchestrated by
The Tango of heart and lungs
Brewed in the fire of my belly

My spirit marinates
In the swirl of it all

Oh I wish you could see what
I see when I get way up high

You wouldn't be so quick
To judge me with your sorrow.

Cause I can leave this place
Like that (*Snaps fingers.*)
Anytime I please.

20. SMALL TALK

LOW. I don't do Manhattan
Unless I'm clocking paper
And since my money and circumstances
Is really strange right now

I am definitely not trying to be here
I walk past the tinted windows
Eyeing knuckleheads behind velvet
Ropes that draw the color lines
On their own people
You've come a long way Sis
From extension cords and
Sweet potatoes
You rockin full length leather
Got your hair straighted
Pulled back and wound up tight
I can tell you been fucking a white boy
You don't even need to say it
Did he teach you how to hold your nose like that—in the air?
I am clearly riding your coattails tonight.

Mommie would lay down and die
If she knew
But she ain't seen you either
Maybe that's why she's trippin

"Order anything you want....it's on me"
I wanna say "fuck you" as
I sit there trying not to look homeless
I want to show some form of dignity
While you wave your perfectly manicured
hand in the air golden bangles dance
and I think of our childhood playgrounds
and hoola hoops.

What the fuck happened to me?
Yo, what the fuck happened to you?
I will sit here for the next hour and try not
To wolf this meal down, the most I have had in
over 3 days, I will excuse myself now and go to
the bathroom so that I can wash my ass surrounded by
ceramic tile and scented candles...I will pretend that
all this shit is mine until I return to the table
and see your pity being served then you will
open your mouth to get your conscience out of
the way.

"Listen, it's just not a good time for me,
things are hectic at work, I'm up for a promotion,
and I'm really tryin' to focus right now, you know?
I'm sorry Mommie kicked you out, I know she can be
A real Bitch sometimes, can't you stay with Shawna

till she calms down?"

"Listen, (*she is whispering*) don't look at me
like that! Nobody told you to hit her,
you promised all of us you'd take your
medicine."

I watch her lip curl
Peep those fangs
And realize ain't a damn
thing changed.

I will not cry in this
Stuckup-fucked up restaurant
Where everybody smiles and
Rattles off reasons why the world
Should suck their dick

And they have no idea
How dumb they really
Look to people like me.

I will not be a homeless
Crazy bitch who's been
dissed by her sister
At least not until I get back to Brooklyn
Where I can be assed out on my own
terms.

This chicken is cooked just how
I like it—crispy on the outside
But real tender on the in
And the potatoes are whipped
with garlic and butter
it all tastes so good
and right now all I wanna do
is forget about how bad
I feel and just pretend
That we are sistas
Catching up

"Low, your face is twitching"
Yea, I say it's from the stress (*Touches cheek.*)
What are you gonna do?
I don't know, (*Shrug.*) I been thinking about checking myself in.
"Will they take care of you?"
Depends, if I can get transferred out of County to a better place
It will bide me some time, at least until I can figure out my next move

"here" she reaches into her purse, leans over and shoves a $100 bill into my palm
I sit there, and for the first time in seven days I feel
Safe enough to cry.

21. SOMEBODY FUCK WIT YOU

LOW. *SOMEBODY FUCK WIT YOU…(Give Petey a lisp.)*

Somebody fuck wit you act like you Crazy!
Somebody fuck with you act like you Crazy!
Crazy! Crazy! Crazy!

That's Petey he's originally from Chicago,
He was let out of some hospital upstate when
the budget cuts happened.

He's yellin at the passing cars
Because he thinks they are ghosts
Trying to swoop in and take his
Soul.

Out here, there are generally
Three kinds of people

1. The Druggies
2. The Crazies
3. And The Really Unfortunate

The Druggies are strung out, mad desperate, and can't be trusted.
I don't mess with them, unless I need weed.

The Crazies are crazy, like Petey but they can't help it, most of um need medicine, but can't get it. They ain't dangerous really.

The really unfortunate are good people in fucked up situations, divorce, fire, lay offs, evictees, that would be me.

Most of the old timers are in this last category. They may have started out in the others, but it takes a lotta smarts to survive all those years on the streets. You can't be living foul and expect to make it.

Everybody knows how bad the shelters can be, so we all take their chances out here.

Somebody Fuck With me! Now Petey's taking off his clothes and throwing them at the cars

And I went CRAZZZZZZZZZYYY!!! And there he goes running up the street
Buck naked!

22. PRIDE

LOW. On my 21st day in the street
I stopped sleeping
The left side of my face became numb
And I had this constant sinking feeling
in the pit of my stomach
My back and legs felt like
they were on pins and needles
and somebody wouldn't stop whispering in my ear
I knew I was fucked up, but I was trying
to hold on.

Petey got the shit beat out of him
a couple of nights ago—there's
a crew a kids going around
attacking homeless people
Somebody told me they
even been throwing gasoline
and setting them on fire.

John and the rest of the old timers have
gone underground until things cool down.

I didn't go with John because I knew that
once I crossed that line and entered
that world, I would be saying to myself
this is who I am now.

So it's just me and a couple a prostitute
Drug fiends still up here in the alley.

I don't think I can do this anymore.....
I try to stand up but there is this racing pain
That keeps shooting up and down my legs...
I grab onto the dumpster and pull myself onto my feet.

Fuck it! I'm going in!

When you get locked up
Or brought in by the police
They automatically take you to county
And they assign you a counselor
Problem is most of um
If they really trying to do their job
Don't stay long
The conditions at county is so fucked up
You got to be in really bad shape

to the point where you don't even care

So I go to the free clinic instead

The line for psyche is damn near out the door
And half of the people I can tell are out
here just like me they been drying out hoping to get rushed
into a bed, hoping and praying that the demons will swoop in
just in time so they can cut the line...

If I am belligerent they will make me wait longer
Even if they think I'm symptomatic
People's personal shit is always in the mix

I am falling, slipping, sinking
something blaring between my ears
10 fingers not enough to grip safety
but willing fingers to hold on
I'm going DOWN
heart beat inside the soles of feet
black gapolyghouls slither past my
periphery they are the ghosts of foul
shit—revisiting bad circumstances
bearing my name
quick shutter images, fast frame
my bullshit flies before me
sinking dips lower, turns
somebody's
breathe hot sa-liva mixes
molten tones and phrases in my
ear and I can't tell if they're really here
or in my head....don't cut the line,
don't cut the line, don't cut the line

Oooooooooooaoooaoaoaoaoaoaa
Aoooooooooooooooooaoooooooaaaaa
        (Motions as if brushing off the demons.)

All of a sudden SILENCE
I can't hear anything
Then my skin on fire being pricked
With a thousand needles
AAARAAAAAAGRH....

23. GET THE FUCK OUT MY FACE
        Musical overdub. Full scale brawl with self.

LOW. *Hard rock enough to put a knot on your dome single-handed*

When I got toe to toe- even the most masculine can't stand it
Papie Chulo think he a gangsta, now you know he got slanted
And all that macho shit he was talking before yo, it's stranded......

ILL—whenever I flip the lyric
ILL—when it comes to this
"Hands on" business
ILL—motherfucker don't you
Even try it

I'll leave you devastated, emaciated, annihilated,
Toxic wasted, hella frustrated,
Eat down fro m the beat down
And deeply violated.

Blaw! Rock your spot
Welcome to the school of
Hard knocks and thick plots
Help that ass to the concrete
With a red dot-X marks the spot

Guess how many dogs
I drop in a week
They'd tell you but they too weak
To speak anymore
Blasphemy
Popped shit got smacked up nastily

If you know what's good for you
Betta stop askin me...

22a. PRIDE

LOW. My teeth start to chatter
Arms and legs sensing beef involuntarily thrust back

Thrashing, thrashing, back the fuck up off me, I don't care
ghosts, demons, and orderlies........

Convulsing convulsing, convulsing, convulsing I am being
held against my will, they are invading my house

GET THE FUCK OFF MY PROPERTY!!!

Holding, holding, get the fuck!
(spitting-spitting) buzzing buzzing

(STRETCHED-STRETCHED-STRETCHED) *(Done in sound.)*

I fly up into the air, soaring towards the sun
Turned blazing shimmering magnet

Lifted-way up-high-back into the SILENCE
Suspended in ……..
DROPPED falling, spinning, swirling
Down, full momentum whoosh
Turning-SLAMMED back into my body

Incredible pain
Heads blurred, faces contorted with concern
Moving in around me

I am sitting in a wheelchair in the hallway
My hands and legs are tied up...

What was I saying?

24. ON LOCK

LOW. I feel myself being wheeled out, put into a van and transported,
I hear them say that the other hospital is full so they're taking me to county

I hate county

I wake up the next morning
In a room with white bare walls
On a hard-ass twin bed
My wrists are killing me
And my tongue is swollen
I feel like I have been hit by a truck

I slowly get up, moving slowly
Moving towards the small closet
where they have
Stored the rest of my bullshit
Even my cell phone which is off now
is still in my bag.

There is a small desk with a couple
Of towels neatly folded
And a tiny bar of soap

I go down the hall, moving slowly

to find the bathroom
and showers
I can't wait to feel the warm

Hey! Get Back in your Room!

Eyes flicker, try to focus on
this massive wall moving

hands take liberties

Strong arming me
Back to my room

Something very small inside
Screams "get the fuck....."

But I can't find it.

"Hey, ya not supposed to be going to the bathroom
by yourself—if you crack ya head—I could lose my job
And I ain't losing my job on account of you—
Stay right here and I'll get the nurse."

Suddenly, staying in bed seems like a much
Better idea

Hands, pulling away the sheets
Soft Jamaican accents float
Through the air.....

Lowquesha, why ya pee all over yaself?!
Why didn' ya call me?

Come, I gotta change the bed

Lifted, coaxed gently onto the floor
I smell ammonia

Shuffling, shuffling

Hold onto the rail chile—
Stay along the wall

The rush of the water,
feels so good on my skin

I am handed another pill

25. PARANOIA

> *LOW in a very drugged-up state.*

LOW. You can't touch me can't hold me
Don't own me, control me—never!
Keeps my eye on the sparrow, stone cold thug
In da marrow, beyond chemically impaired
And I'm still spittin' arrows—Climbing Jacobs ladder wit rhymes badder than
an angel, who be doped up on some ole straight and narrow
save the forty libation for your own situation
cause even in the hardest times I still
draw power. Dis is about elevation to the next

level, combatin the demons and devils who anticipate my arrival
I keeps it moving through the darkness, jagged edges and marshes
Cause at the heart of the matter is always survival.

My soul transcends the fragmented flesh of me
And I'm ill to the inth degree but where my
Spirit lies these earthly curses are shamanic gifts to me
Crafty with the verbals, lyrical herbals I got the remedy
Buts it's rooted in rhymes… and I gotta wait a few more life times till humanities
understanding can catch up to me.

In the meantime, I pace padded cells dousing hells towering infernos
with poetry….my shits episodic stronger than any narcotic
and you best believe you ain't heard the last a me.

End of Play

ACT A LADY
by Jordan Harrison

BIOGRAPHY

Jordan Harrison's plays include *Kid-Simple*, *The Museum Play*, *Finn in the Underworld*, *Act a Lady*, and *Amazons and their Men*. His work has been produced and developed at Actors Theatre of Louisville, American Theater Company, Berkeley Repertory Theatre, the Edinburgh Fringe Festival, Geva Theatre Center, New York Theatre Workshop, PlayLabs, Playwrights Horizons, Portland Center Stage, Seattle Repertory Theatre, Signature Theatre Company, Soho Rep, the SPF Festival, the Tokyo International Arts Festival, and the Williamstown Theatre Festival. He is the recipient of the Heideman Award, the Weston Prize, two Jerome Fellowships and a McKnight Grant from The Playwrights' Center, a New Works Grant from the Rhode Island Foundation, and a 2005 NEA/TCG Playwright-in-Residence Grant with the Empty Space Theatre. *Act a Lady* was a finalist for the Weissberger Award and the winner of an Arch and Bruce Brown Playwriting Award. Jordan has received commissions from South Coast Repertory and Guthrie Theater/Children's Theatre Company and has been a resident playwright at Theatre de la Jeune Lune and the Sundance Playwrights Retreat. With Sally Oswald, he edits the annual *Play: A Journal of Plays*. A graduate of Brown University's MFA Playwriting program, he is a resident playwright at New Dramatists.

ACKNOWLEDGMENTS

Act a Lady premiered at the Humana Festival of New American Plays in March 2006. It was directed by Anne Kauffman with the following cast and staff:

Act One

MILES / LADY ROMOLA	Paul O'Brien
TRUE / COUNTESS ROQUEFORT	Matt Seidman
CASPER / GRETA THE MAID	Steven Boyer
DOROTHY	Suzanna Hay
LORNA	Cheryl Lynn Bowers
ZINA	Sandra Shipley

Act Two

LADY ROMOLA	Paul O'Brien
COUNTESS ROQUEFORT	Matt Seidman
GRETA THE MAID	Steven Boyer
DOROTHY / MILES	Suzanna Hay
LORNA / TRUE	Cheryl Lynn Bowers
ZINA / CASPER	Sandra Shipley

Scenic Designer .... Kris Stone
Costume Designer .... Lorraine Venberg
Lighting Designer .... Deb Sullivan
Sound Designer .... Benjamin Marcum
Original Music .... Michael Friedman
Properties Designer .... Doc Manning
Dialect Coach .... Rinda Frye
Movement Coach .... Wendy McClellan
Fight Director .... Cliff Williams III
Stage Manager .... Debra Anne Gasper
Assistant Stage Manager .... Heather Fields
Dramaturg .... Adrien-Alice Hansel
Assistant Dramaturg .... Jamie Bragg
Casting .... Paul Fouquet, Elissa Meyers Casting
Directing Assistant .... Pirronne Yousefzadeh

Act a Lady was originally commissioned by The Commonweal Theatre Company and was written with the support of Jerome and McKnight Fellowships at The Playwrights' Center. With gratitude to the many wonderful actors, designers, dramaturgs, and directors who helped to develop the play in workshops at Commonweal, the Brown University/Trinity Rep Consortium, the Illusion Theater, Portland Center Stage, the PlayPenn Conference, Playwrights Horizons and in readings across the country.

This play is for Annie Kauffman, Michael Goldfried,
Adam Greenfield, and Peter Rothstein.

CAST OF CHARACTERS

MILES, a small business owner, 40s,
also plays LADY ROMOLA VON PLOFSDORF

TRUE, a tanner, early 30s,
also plays the COUNTESS ROQUEFORT

CASPER, a photographer, 20s,
also plays GRETA THE MAID

DOROTHY, a sometime accordion teacher, 40s

LORNA, a make-up artist, late 20s

ZINA, a director, ageless

Note on Act Two: For most of the second Act, the three male actors remain in their play-within-the-play personae: Countess Roquefort, Greta The Maid, and Romola Von Plofsdorf. (Additionally, the actor who played Miles cameos as the Vicomte Valentino Ufa.) In addition to playing the female characters, the actresses now play the male characters from Act I: The actress playing Lorna now plays True, Dorothy plays Miles, and Zina is Casper.

SETTING

1927. A very small town in the Midwest.
A kitchen. A dressing room. A stage.

PRODUCTION NOTES

Very Important: A red velvet curtain rises and falls on the play-within-the-play. This curtain is lush, red, old school. Scalloped?

On the Music: Dorothy sings two songs. I highly recommend Michael Friedman's compositions for the Louisville production. Please inquire to Playscripts, Inc. if you're interested in using these for your production. In case you decide to use your own composer, a few words on the feeling of these songs: They are passionate anthems written by a woman who is completely uncomfortable expressing passion. The songs are simple and catchy and a little beautiful and a little rough around the edges. They shouldn't be too churchy—rather, think of protest songs, think of the Carter Family, think of a polka band. The actress playing Dorothy need not, of course, be a virtuosic accordion player (although some musical ability helps), so long as she plays with conviction.

On the Cross-Dressing: In the play-within-the-play scenes, the drag should be devoted, meticulous, "well-acted" (from a certain late-19th century school of melodrama), ridiculous when necessary, but always dignified. It is the ideal performance the Midwesterners would give, not the actual one.

Matt Seidman, Paul O'Brien, and Sandra Shipley
in *Act a Lady*

30th Annual Humana Festival of New American Plays
Actors Theatre of Louisville, 2006
Photo by Harlan Taylor

ACT A LADY

ACT I
Scene 1

MILES, CASPER, *and* TRUE *in a country kitchen with* DOROTHY.
Perhaps she's busy cooking supper. A big red accordion sits on the kitchen table.
The following quite rapidly:

MILES. A play

DOROTHY. A play?

CASPER. A play

TRUE. A kind of

MILES. Pageant, like.

TRUE. Thirty of us gents

CASPER. Cast o' thousands

MILES. Cast o' thirties

CASPER. In fancy dress

DOROTHY. "Fancy?"

CASPER. Real fancy dressed up.

DOROTHY. Like for church dressed up?

(A pause. The men look at each other.)

DOROTHY. Shirttails, suspenders…

CASPER. Well no, not

MILES. Casper

CASPER. What

DOROTHY. *(To* MILES.*)* No?

TRUE. No

MILES. No. In fancy-type women-type clothes. *(Pause.)*

DOROTHY. You're wearing women clothes in public.

CASPER. For a good *good* cause

TRUE. Righteous good cause

MILES. For the kids for Christmas.

TRUE. Never ever 'cept for the kids.

CASPER. *(With a hint of excitement.)* Santa's coming.

MILES. Whole town of kids on the Nice list only a coupla' Naughties but even them Nices at heart. So the Elks decided: a fundraiser.

TRUE. Gotta have lots of toys with such a long long list o' Nice.

DOROTHY. Gonna stand up in front of the whole town and wear women clothes.

MILES. I'm not saying it's natural but

TRUE. Can't close your heart to the kids, Dot.

CASPER. Just think of the kids, Dot.

MILES. Dorothy.

DOROTHY. You expect to wear *my* lacies?

MILES. Dress, hat, maybe stockings. Just enough to make the illusion.

CASPER. Garters, lacies, pointy-like brassiere.

TRUE. It's about the French revolution.

CASPER. Stuffies most likely. Can't make a lady without stuffies.

MILES. (*"Be quiet."*) Thank you Casper.

CASPER. (*Backpedaling.*) For the kids.

DOROTHY. Anyone else says "kids" and I'll clock 'em with my stirring spoon. What's for the kids about their dads prancing around like some kinda mix-up moonshine walkarounder sugar-plum manhattan fancyman, now what

about kids

is that,

huh Miles Cuthbert?

MILES. Um.

DOROTHY. Can't hear you.

MILES. Other wives helping out.

DOROTHY. Other who.

MILES. Linda Lottie Lucy Blanche.

CASPER. It'll be fun

TRUE. Be lotta fun

MILES. It's for *fun*

TRUE. Don't miss out.

DOROTHY. I thought you said kids.

CASPER. Fun and kids

MILES. Yeah

TRUE. Both

CASPER. And lacies! Marie Antoinette-style.

MILES. (*Stepping in front of* CASPER.) And one last thing we were wonderin'

DOROTHY. Oh you were *wond*erin'

MILES. Just ponderin' really

DOROTHY. What is it Miles.

TRUE. (*Charming.*) Whether you might grace us with you and that sweet singing accordion.

DOROTHY. You mean to involve my accordion in your infernal descent.

CASPER. Tough to dance without music.

DOROTHY. Dancing?

CASPER. Just a little two-step, little tango.

MILES. We'll just need a little outta the bank.

(*She turns away, trying not to lose her cool.*)

MILES. Just a few dollars, to get the whole thing on its feet.

DOROTHY. Funds for a fund-raiser.

MILES. We'll skim it off the down payment on the store. Make it right back and then some.

DOROTHY. You're telling me lady-clothes, dancing, and *gambling* all baked in one big clove-foot casserole.

MILES. I swear sweet Dorothy my wife of twenty years Dorothy I swear I'll never ask you anything again.

CASPER. Dorothy

TRUE. Dorothy

(*Pause.*)

DOROTHY. When's this devil thing start practice?

MILES & TRUE. (*Quickly.*) Tuesday.

CASPER. 7 p.m. sharp!

DOROTHY. What you just said, Miles…

MILES. Tuesday?

DOROTHY. You said you / won't never

MILES. (*Overlapping.*) Won't never gonna ask you nothing again.

DOROTHY. Gonna want that in writing.

Scene 2

Lights down to a spot on DOROTHY. *An internal scene, a step outside of time. She turns away from the stove and runs a hand tenderly along her bright shiny accordion.*

DOROTHY. Gotta have fleet fleet fingers for playing the accordion with. I tell my students maybe you can *play* with little shorty fingers but you can't never be truly great. Better to kick a football with fingers like that, little Jimmy, little Suzie. Maybe one in every thirty of them gonna make something o' themselves on the accordion. Sometimes they take it hard, but I know I'm saving them more hard down the road.

(She wiggles her fingers: looking at them, their power.)

Pa started me early. Right outta the crib, so the weight feels just *right*. And with my fingers on the keys, it's like I've got eighty fingers rather than eight, blacks and whites, shiny.

(She plays a nimble little riff, up and down the scale.)

I know eighteen songs by heart and I can fake at least forty if you hum along to help me off. Here's one I wrote. Naturally, this is one I know by heart. *(She plays us a song, Singing.)*

> it's a high high time when i got time to lose
> it's a high time when i wear my high shiny shoes
> wear my high shiny shoes for stepping on
> the bad bad devilman's toes.

That's the start to one I wrote. I like how it's a surprise at the end of the line. Thinking this is just a night for dancing in fancy shoes but really it's for stomping out sin. To me that's art. When you think you know how to see something but when you're done you see it someway else. Now tell me what's art about a gent in a dress, that's all I'm asking.

I mean to play in their fancy freakshow and I mean to play my best. I'll play until Miles comes crawling back to me, touches me on both knees and wrinkles my stockings, looks up at me, puppy-dog face, and says "Dottie I was wrong. I been making myself the fool, Dot, you were right all along." And I'll say no, Miles honey, you got bit by the vaudeville bug and you *shined* in fronta those footlights, Miles you shined like a star you could never play the fool. But I'll be smiling inside, ear to ear, and isn't that the best kinda winning?

MILES. *(From off.)* Dottie? Come up to bed. We'll put it in writing tomorrow.

DOROTHY. *(Crafty.)* Coming right up, Miles, my sweet sweet prince.

Scene 3

The red curtain rises for the first time to reveal: The play within the play.

LADY ROMOLA *in the well-appointed drawing room of the Countess Roquefort, with the maid,* GRETA. *In the Paris of Louis XVI.*

Although their make-up may be incomplete [given the time restrictions], the male actors speak with impeccable diction and move fluidly. Perfect ladies.

GRETA THE MAID. Madame will be so angry, oh she'll be furious.

LADY ROMOLA. Then we mustn't *tell* her, Greta. Not just yet.

GRETA THE MAID. When Madame is angry, her face gets as red as the inside of a spring fig.

LADY ROMOLA. ?

GRETA THE MAID. Very very red.

LADY ROMOLA. Then you must help me, Greta. Help me protect her from infirmity, from her own melancholic humours, can you do that for me?

GRETA. Sister Temperance told me every lie we tell is a skinny-dip in the lake of fire.

ROMOLA. Silly, stupid girl. We are not *lying*, we are simply holding truth at bay…until the right moment.

GRETA. How will we know the right moment?

ROMOLA. When she seems most at ease, be-suppled with the elixir of my company. Now take this (*It is an embroidered handkerchief.*) and stand in the corner at the tea tray, and stuff the kerchief in your craw if you feel any truths bubbling up. I'll take care of the rest.

GRETA. Won't she be able to read the terrible secret on my visage?

ROMOLA. My dear simple Greta. No one can read anything on that protuberant brow but your unmistakable descent from the baboons.

GRETA. Madame is clever. She'll see it on my face just the same.

ROMOLA. She'll see *nothing*. Your mistress is far too preoccupied with her own fading grandeur, her mothballed dynasty. *Les Roqueforts.* Stripped of their glory, Les Roqueforts now lie heir-less, their cologne run dry, stinking like some kind of pungent cheese.

GRETA. What makes you think you can insult my mistress as you stand in her very drawing room? What makes you think you'll get away with this in the *chambre* of the Countess Mathilde St. Roquefort?

COUNTESS. Get away with what, pray tell?

(*Enter the* COUNTESS ROQUEFORT. *She is rather stunning: Fan, beauty mark, blood red dress.*)

GRETA. Madame!

ROMOLA. Mathilde, my dearest ladyship.

COUNTESS. Romola, my sincerest confidante.

ROMOLA. Mathilde

COUNTESS. Romola

ROMOLA. Mathilde

COUNTESS. Romola, do you come bearing any particular pleasantries or shall we stand here like a couple of Roman senators hurling each other's names back and forth with vainglory, little aware of the fraternal daggers approaching from behind?

ROMOLA. The mind races to keep up with your similes, my ladyship.

COUNTESS. (*Savoring the "p" at the end.*) I think you keep well enough *up.*

ROMOLA. I'm afraid I studied needlepoint instead of the ancient languages. (*Rather pointedly.*) Father wanted me to make a *suitable* match.

(GRETA *is saying something into the handkerchief—stifling the secret, as in-*

structed.)

COUNTESS. Greta, what is that? I can't understand a thing you're saying with that thing in your mouth.

GRETA. Nothing, Madame.

COUNTESS. Romola, is that a new emerald around your neck?

(ROMOLA *has been conspicuously fingering the huge emerald.* GRETA *talks into her hankie.*)

ROMOLA. (*Very pointedly.*) The Vicomte Ufa has impeccable taste.

COUNTESS. Valentino Ufa, the foreign dignitary?

(GRETA *talks, loudly, into her hankie.*)

ROMOLA. The very.

COUNTESS. But the Vicomte has already promised his very sizable emerald and his heart…to me.

GRETA. (*Breaking point.*) Deceit, Madame! Wicked deceit!

ROMOLA. (*Calmly.*) You may as well know: The Vicomte has come to an understanding after a private conference with my father the President of the Banque Limoge and we are to be married on the first of next month.

COUNTESS. You and your father?

ROMOLA. Valentino and I, I and Valentino.

COUNTESS. (*To* GRETA.) Give that here, girl.

ROMOLA. Don't fret, dear. You're to be invited, of course.

(THE COUNTESS ROQUEFORT *puts the handkerchief in her mouth and we hear her muffled screams.*)

ROMOLA. Perhaps I'll even make you one of my bridesmaids.

(*A more unbridled wail from the* COUNTESS *as the red velvet curtain falls.*)

Scene 4

The very beginning of rehearsal.

Spot up on ZINA, *the director. A rather severe-looking woman with a certain Louise Brooks-meets-Weimar flapper fashion flair. An exotic bird in this town. She speaks as if to the assembled cast.*

ZINA. (*Mit sturm und drang.*) The tale of a headstrong woman torn between love and society, keenly aware of the commerce of her own body, with the French Revolution as its backdrop!

The sad-eyed Mathilde St. Roquefort. The elegant Mathilde who must kill for love. Has any of *you* ever killed for love? (*Pause.*) Has anyone ever been in love? Raise your hand if you've ever been in love. (*Pause.*) Okay raise your hand if you ever *liked* someone a whole awful lot. Good, good.

The story of the Countess Roquefort is an old and tragic one, and—in a sparkling new adaptation by me—we intend to do it justice. Maeterlinck failed, Meyerhold failed, the great and noble Mistletwerpe failed miserably but we

will

not

fail.

(*She reigns herself in.*) It won't be easy. Three *weeks* of rehearsal: Not how we prefer to work on the continent. But in this mere fortnight and a half, you will submit to an exacting regimen of Dell Sarte technique, gymnastics… (*Perhaps she performs a rather lumbering cartwheel.*) …trampolining, music appreciation, and of course, the modern dance. (*She strikes an oblique Isadora Duncan-like pose.*) …until every one of you are flawless specimens of stage beauty.

Why have so many attempted this classic tale of becoming? One-hundred years before Nora gave up her macaroons, the Countess left the comforts of her own *modus vivendi*. Many have found that the story wakes them from their own drawing rooms, out into the sunlight of self-awareness. (*Fierce.*) Are you brave enough to let it wake you?

I could use some coffee. Someone was getting my coffee. Where's the girl with my coffee?

MILES. Ma'am?

ZINA. Miles, is it?

MILES. Coffee's five miles down the road at the Big Steer.

ZINA. Then, Miles, we must *endure.*

Scene 5

Lights down to a spot on MILES. *He speaks out.*

MILES. We done a lotta spectacles here in Wattleburg. We done *The Merry Widow* we done *The Purloined Letter* we done *The Stymied Sinner* we done *The Contented Cockerel* we done *The Purblind Porpoise* and we done it all in rep.

We done the *Henrys* Part IV, Part IV Part Two, and Part VI Part One with swords made by Olaf down the street at the smith shop, made a bona fide clang clang clang. You better hope you didn't get sat in the front row or else clang clang clang.

Seen a whole lotta directors come through town and go but I've never seen nobody like her. She got strange ways, she got a not-so-ladylike step. She wears *britches*, like she means to fly with the Red Baron. Where most people got blood she got coffee and gin.

Me and the Elks think it's important to have art here in town so we spare no expense. We ship in the best of the best of the cream of the crop. Art is supposed to *cost* something, I think. Not just money—I mean what you spend of yourself. But that Zina is making it cost in ways we never imagined: real silk for the dresses, dialect coach. She even hired a lady for face paint, real expert—I'm surprised we could get her. Local girl who made good, working in the moving pictures.

(*Light on* LORNA *the make-up lady, a fresh-faced, chipper, thirtyish woman.*)

LORNA. Miles, pop quiz: what kinda skin you got?

MILES. (*Surprised by the question.*) Um, white?

LORNA. I mean you got oily skin, dry skin, combination skin?

(*He checks his face with his hands.*)

MILES. Dirty.

LORNA. I can tell this is gonna be a special challenge.

MILES. Don't you think we're going a little far with the face paint?

LORNA. Thought you wanted to be ladies.

MILES. (*A reflex reaction.*) We don't want to be ladies! Just gents in skirts—so everyone knows it's just for fun.

LORNA. So, you're scared there's a lady in you waiting to get out.

MILES. If there's lady in me, Lorna, there's lady in everyone.

Scene 6

LORNA. Fellas.

A spot on LORNA. *She might demonstrate make-up application on her own face as she speaks. Quick talker.*

LORNA. The first start to being pretty is powder for that nice even tone. Don't know nobody who gotta nice even tone without the helpa powder 'cept maybe the Chinawoman who works down in the laundry. Asked her once how she gets such fine even tone and she touched my cheek—her hand just shot out from behind the counter and stretched my cheek-skin between her thumb and pointerfinger like that, and she said: "Peaches and cream." Peaches and cream is all she said but I knew somehow that meant "You're all right, Lorna—you be happy with what you got." That was nice. But that's a whole other story.

First start to being pretty is powder and you use the powder puff here, puff puff puff anywhere and everywhere but 'specially wherever it's—darn it, darn it. Darn it I shoulda started you all off with *shaving*. Shaving for the boys, gotta shave real close first or else you'll end up looking like you're some kinda sideshow act let out on the loose—which is okay if that's what you want but that's not what we want. Illusion we want. Elegant we want. *Ladies* we want.

I know, I'm a dreamer, I know, that's what they call me. But I think when we get all your wives and sisters and momfolk lined up opening night they're gonna see I've been dreaming real. Now, third step after shave 'n powder is gonna be your eyes. Big big eyes to put Pickford to shame. You do wanna look pretty, right fellas? (*Pause.*)

> (TRUE *is visible now.*)

TRUE. (*Humoring the pretty girl.*) Sure do, ma'am.

LORNA. Thank you, True.

TRUE. 'Pleasure.

LORNA. Now get to yer dressing rooms and try out that puff puff puff!

> (*But* TRUE *doesn't leave.*)

TRUE. So… (*They look at each other.*) What's it like out there in the movies.

LORNA. I don't have to do much. Their faces aren't like ours, they're better. Clara Bow, the Sisters Gish, Mary Pickford—they got this fine layer o' peach fuzz on their faces. You just turn on the spotlight and those little blonde hairs bounce back the light like a heavenly halo. I didn't have to do much. Sometimes you gotta put more light on the star so everybody knows that's the star, but those Gishes got a light all their own.

TRUE. Huh.

LORNA. Yeah.

TRUE. You're kinda like that in this town—walking around with a halo.

LORNA. I heard you know how to *talk*. I heard yer trouble.

TRUE. You heard / from who.

LORNA. (*Overlapping at /.*) I heard you were trouble for some girl ten years back. (*Awkward pause.*)

TRUE. I was young. Today I wouldn't never have run.

LORNA. Like the villain. You're not like that, you were born the Good Guy, the…Rudolph Valentino.

TRUE. How do you tell him? Gotta halo?

LORNA. You can always tell the Good Guy by his moustache: Either it ain't as twisty or… (*Re:* TRUE.) he got none at all.

> (*They look at each other, hard. Seems like he's just about to kiss her.*)

LORNA. (*An escape.*) I heard it was liquor that made you rabbit.

TRUE. Guess that won't happen no more with the Ladies' Christian Temperance Union on the night prowl.

LORNA. I heard you got your ways.

> (*He touches her on the cheek.*)

LORNA. I heard you find many an occasion to visit the Canada border.

TRUE. Duck hunting.

LORNA. I heard, is all.

TRUE. Somebody's doing a whole lotta talking.

Scene 7

The play-within-the-play. The red curtain rises to reveal GRETA *alone in the drawing room. She removes a letter furtively from her décolletage and starts to read.*

GRETA. "Greta my dearest darling, meet me this evening at midnight—

(*We hear a horse's whinny.* GRETA *conceals the letter and eavesdrops on voices off.*)

COUNTESS. (*Off.*) What a shame you must take your leave so soon, Romola.

ROMOLA. (*Off.*) I'm afraid I fatigue so fast these days: An emerald *this* splendid is a heavy burden indeed.

COUNTESS. How fortunate, at least, that your neck is thick enough to bear your hundred-carat hypocrisies.

ROMOLA. (*With faux-sympathy.*) Your metaphors are as desperate as your fortunes, Mathilde.

(*Quiet, and* GRETA *dares to start the letter again.*)

GRETA. "Greta my dearest darling, meet me—

ROMOLA. (*Off.*) Don't fret, my dear— Money isn't the only way to attract men. I'm sure with your *pass*able looks, you'll soon turn the head of some cobbler, or perhaps a chimney sweep?

COUNTESS. (*Off.*) Yes, yes. I'm certain things will look up for me *quite* soon.

(*At last,* GRETA *seems to have time for the letter.*)

GRETA. "Greta my dearest darling, Meet me this evening at midnight on the Île St. Louis. I shall be wearing a crimson ascot, and you, your raw silk snood. I can see it even now as I describe it, like the inexorable conjunction of two impeccably dressed planets. I know it must be torture for you to work right under the nose of my two unctuously enterprising would-be-brides. How you—"

COUNTESS. (*Off.*) Bon voyage, pet!

(*The sound of bells, Romola's carriage departing.* GRETA *secrets the letter into her décolletage. The* COUNTESS *re-enters and crumples against the door.* GRETA *busies herself with a feather duster.*)

COUNTESS. I thought she'd never take her leave. I swallowed my pride and wished her every happiness. Well what is it, Greta? You're white as a cadaver.

GRETA. Nothing, Madame.

(GRETA *is aggressively dusting the windowsill. Feathers flying.*)

COUNTESS. That's right, girl, make yourself practical.

(GRETA *has seen something—looking off into the audience, describing the events playing out in imaginary space. [We might notice the* COUNTESS *disguising her pleasure at all this.]*)

GRETA. Oh Madame, an accident in the street, oh horror! Lady Romola has been thrown from her carriage! It is the wheel, the wheel fallen off its axel, oh! The mare is caught in the carriage-straps and—it's *trodding* on her. I can still see her poor little arms flailing against the blows but— for naught, for naught.

COUNTESS. (*Feigning surprise.*) Oh, what a world!

GRETA. What's that thing behind your back, Madame?

COUNTESS. What thing where?

GRETA. That greasy rod betwixt your fingers.

COUNTESS. Merely a walking stick, Greta. (*She demonstrates, although the spoke is much too short to be a walking stick.*) I think I will take my afternoon constitutional soon.

GRETA. It looks like the spoke from a carriage wheel.

COUNTESS. I'm sure you must be mistaken, Greta.

GRETA. With all due respect, mistress, I don't know why you prevaricate. I'm thirsty as you for the blood of that vicious she-beast, that buxom barracuda, that—

COUNTESS. That's enough vengeful outrage for one scene, you fickle little halfling. We women are not blood-thirsty, we're just…resourceful.

GRETA. (*Memorizing this euphemism for future use.*) Resourceful.

COUNTESS. But, oh dear, when the authorities discover Romola's grisly, trodden corpse in the street they're sure to suspect my intervention, unless…

(*She offers the spoke to* GRETA, *while looking the other direction.*)

COUNTESS. …Unless some brave soul were willing to suffer the gallows on my behalf. (*Enticingly.*) Gallows…

GRETA. I know no such soul, Madame.

COUNTESS. (*Elegantly abstract again.*) Oh what to do, where to go?

GRETA. Perhaps if you disguise yourself as a boy?

COUNTESS. I know what to do, I will disguise myself as a boy! Yes, I will dress myself in the raiment of a humble apprentice and…

GRETA. And cross the border before anyone's the wiser.

COUNTESS. And stealthily cross the border to friendly Lichtenstein!

GRETA. (*Aside.*) Madame is most suggestible in her aggrieved state.

COUNTESS. I am most suggestible, yes!

GRETA. And wait to send word to the Vicomte, only after you're at a safe distance. A great…*far-off*…safe distance.

COUNTESS. Absence makes the heart grow fonder, they say!

GRETA. Alas, Madame, you're sure to be recognized with your wondrous tresses.

COUNTESS. And yet Greta, I must chop off my wondrous tresses.

GRETA. The poor are always with us, Madame.

COUNTESS. Why, we'll give them to poor bald little orphan children, Greta. Just think! Poor little children running about with my lustrous curls, oh happiness!

GRETA. Truly the heart melts, Madame.

(The red velvet curtain falls.)

Scene 8

Lights down to a spot on TRUE *in the dressing room. [He might simply remove his* COUNTESS *wig and step outside of the scene, the red curtain falling behind him.]*

TRUE. Back in the merchant marines, I remember a fella who put two coconuts on his chest and called that a lady. Entered himself in the cadet talent show, strummed on a banjo missing a string and sang *"Under the mango tree..."* He didn't look pretty, no, far from, with a big mouth drawn on like the south sea natives, it weren't half pretty. But I remember everybody leaned forward in their chairs, like they watched it sorta *different* because of how he looked. Guess it had the interest of something uncommon. Like a magnet—it's hard to explain. He put on those two coconuts and suddenly everyone with their eyes bigger than if he were a hunderd-percent lady swishing in that grass skirt.

I got no problem wearing a dress, 'less it pinches. I just don't know if I call it *art*. I know: what right I got to judge? I tan I'm a tanner I tan things I tan. But one time my partner Knox and I stuffed two otters right outta the Stick River and mounted them like you couldn't hardly tell they weren't alive. Like we put the life back in them 'cause of how we posed them. Nobody could say that wasn't something to see.

I guess I never thoughta myself as something to see. But if that Zina wants a tanner for a Countess, I'll do my best to make 'em lean forward. And it's better than watching paint dry, and that blue-eyed Lorna sure knows a thing or two or three about pretty.

(Light returns. CASPER *is there.)*

CASPER. That was real good, True.

TRUE. Thanks Casper.

CASPER. You make a real good woman.

TRUE. You know, I was sorta hoping it'd be *hard*. I sorta hoped I wouldn't be any good.

CASPER. Why?

TRUE. Like that'd mean I was a real man.

CASPER. You're the realest man I know.

(*This hangs in the air.*)

TRUE. Casper I'll see you later. (*Re: his makeup.*) Think I got my eyes on crooked again. Gotta find Lorna before the take-five is up.

Scene 9

Spot on CASPER. *He has his camera with him. Brisk, wide-eyed—not reflective:*

CASPER. That True is a mystery-type figure. He wears six brass pins on his hat, on his railroad hat, one-two-three-four-five-six, all different kinds of shapes and colors. Someday I'll ask if they stand for something or what. That True knows things. He's more clever than he lets on. He showed me a place under the floorboards where he keeps a bottle of pumpkin gin for the extra-long rehearsals. Sometimes it stinks on him strong, but I don't mind.

I'd like to take a portrait of that True. That's a hard face to know, good challenge for a photographer—think I'd use a soft light from the side so he doesn't crinkle his eyes like he likes to. Put the light low, open the aperture and see into those eyes.

That True looks like everything has happened to him and he don't care if nothing ever do again. He must look at me and think: That Casper look like nothing and no one ever happened to him. True and Casper, Casper and True.

When I think on something I'd like to do or somewhere I'd like to go, it rises on my face like 6 a.m., red and hot and—no disguise. Playing poker, you could look on my face and say "That face looks like a Pair of Fours kinda face." (CASPER *is looking in the dressing-room mirror—posing with his feather duster, perhaps.*) Greta's different. Greta's gotta be good at keeping secrets.

(DOROTHY *is there with her accordion. Light returns.*)

DOROTHY. See something you like, Casper?

CASPER. Ma'am?

DOROTHY. Looks like you're searching yourself for clues.

CASPER. (*Good save.*) Just...plannin' my next shot. Photographer's gotta know just how light hits the face.

DOROTHY. Don't go pointing that thing at me.

CASPER. (*Still pointing it at her, framing shots.*) I was thinking I'd get us some newspaper shots. Plus, preserve the artistic process for future generations!

DOROTHY. What interest does some future generation got in your silki-fied heinie?

CASPER. I really don't know Mrs. Cuthbert.

DOROTHY. You seen my husband, Casper?

CASPER. Thataway, ma'am. Rehearsing the Big Death Scene. Next up, the Big Love Scene!

(*This stops her in her tracks.*)

DOROTHY. What're you hollering about?

CASPER. You know—Act Two. Greta and Valentino?

DOROTHY. You and my husband.

CASPER. Nobody else fit to play Valentino. He's the only one who can do the voice: "My dearest Greta." Kinda nervous—I never kissed nobody in real life. (*Pause.*)

DOROTHY. You always say everything that comes into your head Casper? (*She stalks off toward the rehearsal.*)

CASPER. (*Small.*) Yes. Yes indeed I do.

Scene 10

Rehearsal. [Please note that this scene is not behind the red curtain: no foot-lights, no magic.]

ZINA *directing* TRUE *and* MILES *in practice shifts and heels. They are stilted, in voice and movement—just the occasional glimmer of the fluency to come.* LORNA *looks on from the wings.*

ZINA. Again!

TRUE. "Why, for love—why else do we do anything?"

MILES. "Then you've come only to gloat, to putrify my last hours with your insufferable smuggery?"

TRUE. "I came only for what is mine."

MILES. "Oh! If only I had the strength left to resist you!"

(*They end up in a very masculine-looking skirmish. Fisticuffs, almost.*)

ZINA. All right, hold.

(LORNA *breaks into applause.*)

ZINA. How'd that feel?

MILES. Pretty good.

ZINA. Interesting.

MILES. Yeah?

ZINA. We'll try it again. And this time, try doing something *elevated* with your body.

MILES. This body won't do nothing elevated.

ZINA. Something oblique, something like, I don't know…

(*She does something elevated [and pre-meditated looking] with her body.* MILES *tries to imitate.* LORNA *signals to* TRUE *from the wings.*)

LORNA. True, you got your eyes on crooked.

TRUE. I know, I know.

ZINA. (*To* MILES.) Don't forget your hands!

(LORNA *licks her thumb and smudges* TRUE's *makeup.*)

TRUE. Ouch.

LORNA. There you are. My masterpiece.

ZINA. (*To* MILES.) Don't forget your arms. They're not tree branches!

(DOROTHY *enters in a huff. She still has her accordion.*)

DOROTHY. Miles, we gotta talk.

MILES. (*Still posing.*) Kinda busy, hon.'

ZINA. Let the energy shoot straight out your fingers like you're casting a spell, like you're casting a wicked spell!

MILES. Like…

ZINA. Yes, *wicked.*

MILES. Ouch

ZINA. Yes, "ouch," use it.

LORNA. (*Whisper to* TRUE.) She's very good.

ZINA. And now, the final ingredient.

(ZINA *pulls the emerald out of her pocket. Everyone takes notice—it is the very first time they've seen it.* TRUE *wolf whistles.*)

MILES. Gotta be five hundred carats on that gal.

TRUE. Gotta be five thousand.

ZINA. It's only glass. But you can make us forget that. (ZINA *puts it over* MILES' *neck.*) You must look at your emerald as though it is the answer to the question of your life.

LORNA. (*She hasn't taken her eyes off the emerald.*) Wow.

ZINA. Like that, yes. Now, show me what you've learned.

MILES. (*Turning to* TRUE.) "Then you've come only to gloat?"

ZINA. Dorothy, give them music!

(DOROTHY *starts, grudgingly, to play a little air on the accordion—it actually does seem to lift the scene to a new level.*)

MILES. "To putrify my last hours with your insufferable smuggery?"

TRUE. "I came only for what is mine."

ZINA. Yes, yes!

MILES. "If only I had the strength left to resist you."

TRUE. "Oh, how it glisters!"

MILES. "Promise me something, Mathilde."

TRUE. "Anything, Romola, or else nothing."

ZINA. True, watch your knees.

TRUE. Ma'am?

(DOROTHY *stops playing abruptly.*)

ZINA. There's no trick to acting a lady. Just less, always *less* when you move—as if your very existence *fatigues* you.

TRUE. Women are fatigued?

DOROTHY. Yes.

ZINA. How to explain, how to explain.

(CASPER *enters.*)

CASPER. Anybody seen my snood?

ZINA. (*"Eureka."*) Be more like Casper!

TRUE & MILES. (*Turning to look at him.*) Oh...

CASPER. What.

ZINA. Study his swish.

CASPER. I don't swish!

ZINA. Regard his glide.

CASPER. I don't glide!

ZINA. Go ahead, show them your swish.

CASPER. Don't have to hear about my swish from some cut-rate director couldn't cut it on the "continent!"

(*Everyone is quiet.*)

ZINA. Give us a moment please.

MILES. Everyone back in five.

(*Everyone starts to exit. ZINA doesn't take her eyes off CASPER as the others chatter away.*)

TRUE. Lorna, would you explain that puff to me one more time?

LORNA. Again?

DOROTHY. Better bring your brass knuckles, Lorna.

CASPER. Don't leave me with her!

DOROTHY. Miles, we got business.

(*ZINA and CASPER are alone. A pause that ZINA savors, then.*)

ZINA. You've got an *advantage.* That's all I'm saying.

CASPER. Huh.

ZINA. Your edges are different than the others. Soft.

CASPER. It shows?

ZINA. It shows. Don't think I don't know about different. You'd think the Cro-Magnons at the saloon never saw a lady wear pants before.

CASPER. Probably they never did.

ZINA. There's a whole *world* out there. My world was small once, like yours.

CASPER. You were never like me.

ZINA. As you can see, I have evolved. But you make me remember. I grew up small-minded like you but I went somewhere.

CASPER. I been places with my camera.

ZINA. Places.

CASPER. Des Moines, Eau Claire, far as Lansing even.

ZINA. Take that camera and go to *Tibet,* Colombia, Persia. The only way to learn, Casper, is to put yourself in situations of great danger.

CASPER. But, the show.

ZINA. I mean after. I mean: this town's already too small for a person like you. Your home is out there somewhere, in the *wilderness.* Maybe you can fool them with a blade of grass between your teeth but I know one of you when I see you. Blade of grass in your teeth and watching yourself, how you walk down the street, but still not fooling Zina.

Miles and True, when I talk to them about how to move, on stage, it's like I'm asking them to use some sort of third arm they don't have. But you…I think around here you're used to watching yourself. (*Pause.*)

CASPER. You're a smart lady.

Scene 11

The red curtain rises to reveal the COUNTESS ROQUEFORT, *now dressed as a not-very-convincing boy page. [Perhaps she wears riding boots, a cloak, and a wide-brimmed, three-cornered hat?] She kneels at the deathbed of* LADY ROMOLA, *a great big red hoof-print marring her otherwise lovely forehead.*

COUNTESS. Poor, feeble Lady Romola.

LADY ROMOLA. Doth someone speak? Some restless ghost?

COUNTESS. This way, Lady.

LADY ROMOLA. Gentle youth, have we met in this life? Or are you rather some angelic harbinger of the welcome world to come?

COUNTESS. I am no figment, Lady, I am flesh and blood. But I bear you to that other life all the same. Know me, (*Leaning close, and removing her hat.*) Know me as an old companion.

LADY ROMOLA. Mathilde!

COUNTESS. Romola

LADY ROMOLA. Mathilde

COUNTESS. Romola

LADY ROMOLA. Mathilde, but your aspect is so changéd. Your skin, un-painted. Your hair, like something fashioned by a woodland critter for its home.

COUNTESS. The streets are filled with revolutionaries. I dared not travel in all my finery.

LADY ROMOLA. Mathilde. I fear my injustice toward you has brought fate crashing down about my head.

COUNTESS. You wrongly accuse the Fates—it was I myself who devised your most equine end!

> (*The* COUNTESS *produces the carriage-spoke from behind her back.* [*During the following, we see gestures from the rehearsal scene transformed into something elegant. We begin to hear* DOROTHY'*s accordion tune from that scene as well. Sounding more refined but still unmistakable.*])

LADY ROMOLA. But...why?

COUNTESS. Why, for love, of course. Why else do we do anything?

LADY ROMOLA. Then you've come only to gloat, to putrify my last hours with your insufferable smuggery?

COUNTESS. I came only for what is mine.

> (*The* COUNTESS *tears the huge emerald from around* ROMOLA'*s neck.*)

LADY ROMOLA. Ah! If only I had the strength left to resist you.

COUNTESS. Oh how it glisters!

LADY ROMOLA. Promise me something, Mathilde.

COUNTESS. Anything, Romola, (*A dark aside*) or else nothing.

LADY ROMOLA. Not for me, but for Valentino. Promise me you'll treat him well.

COUNTESS. The wellest.

LADY ROMOLA. Promise me you'll treat him like a prince.

COUNTESS. The princeliest.

LADY ROMOLA. And all the while, never let him know...

COUNTESS. (*Brightly.*) Of your treachery, yes, never.

LADY ROMOLA. Of *your* treachery, witch.

COUNTESS. Triple-faced harlot! Brutus in a skirt! I'll kill you again!

LADY ROMOLA. Too late, harpy, stay fast, my death is already upon me—

COUNTESS. Then you must keep hell warm for me, Lady Romola.

LADY ROMOLA. (*Her Oscar-winning scene.*)

You will meet Lucifer alone,

For I'm bound to the highest heavens!

My brow burns just thinking on't,

circled in a kind of saintly fire!

COUNTESS. That is just the horseprint on your face, dear Lady.

(DOROTHY's *accordion tune swells.*)

LADY ROMOLA. But lo, I think I hear the song of my harp now,

   Carrying me there on an isthmus of music,

   bright tones, brighter skies—

   (*She expires, with an inelegant death-wheeze, as the tune fades.*)

COUNTESS. (*Solemnly.*) No harp, no heaven—only the unmelodic bleating of some threadbare street trollop, some gypsy, pursuant of a lusterless franc, a friend to no ears.

   (*A kind of orgy of stage business, accompanied by accordion:* THE COUNTESS *clutches the emerald to her breast and kisses it. She thinks for a moment, then places a pen in* ROMOLA's *lifeless hand and writes a longhand note. As she writes, we hear her say the words "Bequeath… Emerald… Countess!". She places the note in* ROMOLA's *hands, then folds her arms across her chest in eternal repose [perhaps they are already a bit stiff with rigor mortis]. She rings a little service bell for the nurse and crosses herself before heading off into the night. The red curtain falls.*)

Scene 12

A three-ring, fast-cutting, traveling scene.

MILES *and* DOROTHY *outside of rehearsal [having left* ZINA *and* CASPER *alone].*

DOROTHY. Been hunting you all over.

MILES. Been working.

DOROTHY. Don't look much like work. Looks more like play.

MILES. Dorothy

DOROTHY. Mr. McKittrick walked mud into my kitchen this morning and asked Where's my husband at with the down payment on the store.

MILES. What did you tell him?

DOROTHY. Told him by the end of the week.

MILES. Dot, I been thinking, Dot. What about instead of the store…what if we ran the theater all year round?

DOROTHY. What if

   (DOROTHY *turns up stage quickly, as if counting to ten to keep from exploding.*)

MILES. Whole season of shows! And we'd make our way doing this.

   (DOROTHY *turns back and takes a note out of her pocket. The note from Scene One.*)

DOROTHY. Tell me what this says, Miles.

MILES. Dorothy.

DOROTHY. Read it to me. My eyes aren't so good.

MILES. (*Reading.*) "I, Miles Cuthbert, sound of body and sounder of mind do so solemnly swear that I won't ask Dorothy Cuthbert nothing more of the outlandish, cockamamie, or damn-fool sort as / long as we both shall live."

DOROTHY. (*Overlapping, from memory.*) "Long as we both shall live."

MILES. Dorothy.

DOROTHY. Knew that'd come in handy some day.

> (*Cut to:* TRUE *in the dressing room, practicing his makeup. He has the emerald around his neck from the last Countess scene.*)

TRUE. I been wondering why all the fuss about emeralds. Never seen anything so pretty you'd kill for it. So I went to the library and asked Miss Jenks what's to know about emeralds. Miss Jenks looks down her ugly long nose at me and says *What do you want with emeralds?* So I look right back down my nose at her—that's how things get done around the library. And Miss Jenks blows the dust off this big ol' book, and I open it real careful: (TRUE *closes his eyes and recites the following from memory, almost magically.*) "Emerald's precious green color is caused by small amounts of chromium and enhanced by traces of iron. These flaws are considered part of the character of the stone and are used to confirm its quality." (*He opens his eyes.*) And I thought: I like that. Something that got flaws and ain't shamed for it. Flaws to help you know you're looking at something bona and fide.

> (CASPER *is there all of a sudden.* TRUE *takes his bottle of pumpkin gin out of its hiding place under the floorboards. Maybe* CASPER *starts to affix his snood.*)

TRUE. Don't see any black and blue on you, Casper. Zina musta let you off easy.

CASPER. Not exactly.

TRUE. (*Offering him the bottle.*) Well, this'll take the edge off.

CASPER. That stuff tastes like poison.

TRUE. That's cuz it is.

> (TRUE *swigs.*)

CASPER. True, mind if I ask you something?

TRUE. Yeah Casper?

CASPER. (*Point to the pins on* TRUE's *hat.*) Do they stand for something or what.

> (TRUE *takes it off to show* CASPER.)

TRUE. This one is the shape of Norway on account of that's where my father's from and his father and his father before. This one they give you when you ride third class on the Queen Anne, that was my honeymoon. This one I found on the street and just thought "I gotta rescue that piece o' shiny or no one will." This one is volunteer fire brigade.

CASPER. Red.

TRUE. Which is yer favorite.

CASPER. (*Pointing.*) Anchor.

TRUE. (*Taking the pin off.*) Here it's yours then.

CASPER. Really?

> (CASPER *lays his head, tentatively, on* TRUE's *shoulder.*)
> (*Pause.*)

TRUE. Casper

Watcha doing?

CASPER. Just, laying my head here.

TRUE. Huh.

CASPER. (*With a yawn.*) Real tired.

TRUE. Casper.

CASPER. All I want is to stay here just a second.

TRUE. Okay.

CASPER. Okay?

TRUE. Well stay already before I change my mind.

CASPER. (*Laying his head back down.*) Oh, I'm stayin'! (*Short pause.*) How come they call you True, True?

TRUE. Guess it's on account of I could never pull off a lie. (*Pause.*)

CASPER. (*To himself.*) Me neither.

> (*Cut back to:* MILES *and* DOROTHY.)

DOROTHY. I *see* you, Miles, better than you see yourself. Mouthing your lines while you sleep. Making lady faces in the mirror. You got one foot in this world and one foot on that stage. Somebody 'round here gotta keep both feet planted *firm*.

MILES. This ain't just about money, is it.

DOROTHY. No Miles it is not. This is not just about the money we don't have.

MILES. Gimme a hint, Dot?

DOROTHY. I'm a hard-working woman. I watch my soul. I scrub it clean like the linens. I tend it like the vegetable garden. I mean to get to heaven and I want you standing there next to me, Miles. (*With great difficulty.*) I want you standing there with me, but lately I'm not so sure.

MILES. (*Embracing her tenderly.*) What's got into you, girl?

DOROTHY. (*Breaking away.*) Love scene with a man!? Are you out of your not-so-god-fearing skull!?

MILES. It's in the script. Don't mean I mean to enjoy it.

DOROTHY. Don't see you calling for rewrites.

MILES. I *kill* somebody in this play too—think I'm going to hell for that?

DOROTHY. You can go to hell for choosing this play and putting it before the whole town and calling it art.

MILES. I don't tell you what to put in your songs, Dot.

DOROTHY. I don't write songs that hurt *God*, Miles Cuthbert.

(*She stalks off.*)

MILES. No. Only songs that hurt the ears.

(*Cut back to:* TRUE *and* CASPER *in the dressing room.* CASPER's *head still on his shoulder.*)

CASPER. (*Re: the anchor pin.*) You were married?

TRUE. Don't much want to talk about it.

CASPER. What's it like being married.

TRUE. I don't remember. (*Pause.*)

CASPER. True, you mind if I took your portrait sometime? You'd make a real good portrait.

TRUE. Casper.

CASPER. I could make you look the way *I* see you.

(TRUE *stands up, retreating.*)

TRUE. I got something for you, Casper.

CASPER. Another present? (*It is a small photograph of Mary Pickford. A kind of primitive pin-up.*)

TRUE. Thought you might need something to look at.

CASPER. What for.

TRUE. Found her in one of Lorna's movie magazines. You just prop her up like this and go (*Appreciatively.*) "Look at those stems." You try.

CASPER. (*Not very convincingly.*) "Look at those stems."

TRUE. And if you squint a little, it's like you got Mary Pickford right there in your very own room.

(CASPER *squints.*)

TRUE. Must be hard, growing up here with no one to look at. You just take her outta your pocket once a day and...

CASPER. And?

TRUE. And you'll be fine.

(*And he leaves* CASPER *alone.*)

(*Cut to:* LORNA, *sewing a costume.* [*It looks like Valentino's costume, soon to be seen in Act Two.*])

LORNA. I got the best job, bringing out what's beautiful in folks. Sometimes it takes a lot of foundation. Isn't it the same thing when you got it bad for somebody? Hunting for something in them no one's ever seen. With that True, there's all kinds of uncharted territory. Places I'm not sure I want to explore. Hollywood faces: they're so smooth, you gotta make up stories to go on top of them. But around here, people got lines.

(TRUE *appears in the threshold. He whistles at her.*)

TRUE. You sure are pretty, lady.

LORNA. You sure are pretty, Mister.

(*This cools him down.*)

TRUE. I'm tired of pretty.

LORNA. What's the matter? You make a real good woman.

TRUE. (*Retreating even more.*) Pretty's got us all bent out of shape. Like we aren't ourselves any more.

LORNA. Isn't that what acting's for? Being someone else?

TRUE. But the someone else is supposed to stay *on stage*. Casper's someone else is running all over town.

LORNA. Yeah, he's a natural!

(*He moves towards her.*)

TRUE. Oof. Heels are hell on my heels.

LORNA. That means they're elegant.

TRUE. Emerald weighs a ton.

LORNA. But it makes your eyes glister.

TRUE. Someday I'll get you a real one.

LORNA. (*Playful.*) What're you saying, True? I'm not your girl.

(*They kiss.*)

TRUE. What if I ask real nice.

LORNA. You taste like moonshine.

TRUE. What of it?

LORNA. The Good Guy tastes like peppermint.

TRUE. I hate that guy.

(*Another kiss. TRUE fidgets with the hem of his dress.*)

TRUE. Funny, this.

LORNA. (*As in, "no, it's sexy."*) Yeah, "funny." Almost like there's two of me.

TRUE. And there's none of me, no True

LORNA. No True.

TRUE. Only two of Lorna…but I'm still around to watch.

LORNA. Well, "Lorna," (*They both giggle.*) I think now my hands, all four of my hands gonna start snaking up here, snaking up up.

TRUE. (*Amorously.*) Lorna. (*Not amorously.*) Lorna.

LORNA. Yes, Lorna?

TRUE. (*Pulling back for a moment.*) Think this'll make us go twisted?

LORNA. Maybe.

(*She pulls him back into the kiss.*)

(*Cut back to:* CASPER, *alone, where we left him.*)

CASPER. (*On a sigh.*) True and Casper, Casper and True…
Greta.

(CASPER *starts to apply his stage make-up, practicing his lines as* GRETA—*it seems a comfort to him. Over the course of the monologue his manner and his make-up evolve until, at the end of the monologue, he is* GRETA *through and through.*)

GRETA. "Greta my dearest darling, Meet me tonight on the Île St. Louis. I shall be wearing a crimson ascot, and you, your raw silk snood. I can see it even now as I describe it, like the inexorable conjunction of two impeccably dressed planets.

I know it must be torture for you to work right under the nose of my two unctuously enterprising would-be-brides. How you must die a little death every time you conceal your desire. Forever unable to say your love, a love forbidden by society.

Greta, my charm, my sprite, I'm afraid I must needs marry into money, but that means not we need not see each other…not. Know always that you are the true owner of my emerald, and my nights are spent mapping the illimitable constellations of the stars in your eyes.

Yours in utmost secrecy and discretion, The Vicomte Valentino Ufa."

(*A knock at the door.* GRETA *hides the letter in her décolletage.*)

GRETA. Who's there?

(*Someone who looks just like* CASPER *enters the room, dressed in male clothing. [It is the actress who played* ZINA, *now playing* CASPER. *The first time we've seen the character in all-male clothes since Scene Four.]*)

CASPER. Ma'am?

GRETA. You're bold to enter my room unannounced.

CASPER. Pardon me, ma'am, it's just—this is my dressing room.

GRETA. You needn't call me Madame, I'm nothing but a chambermaid.

CASPER. Look real elegant for nothing but a maid.

GRETA. And you look…fiendish familiar, for a bumpkin.

CASPER. Seen you too somewhere. (CASPER *extends his hand.*) Casper Logan.

(GRETA *takes his hand delicately, not shaking.*)

GRETA. You may call me Greta.

(CASPER *withdraws his hand.*)

CASPER. (*Stammering, taken aback.*) But if you're Greta—and I'm here—and you're there...then who am I?

GRETA. That is the eternal question, Monsieur Casper.

CASPER. (*To himself.*) Who *am* I.

GRETA. But this frock is rather too binding for philosophic exploits. The hour is late, and a gentleman is expecting me. Would you help me lace the back of my dress?

(*Blackout.*)

End of Act I

ACT II

DOROTHY *sings a song, accompanying herself on the accordion:*

DOROTHY.
it's a high high time when i got time to lose
it's a high time when i wear my high shiny shoes
wear my high shiny shoes for stepping
on the bad bad devilman's toes.

gnarled 'n knotty,
split-nailed 'n spotty,
you can know the devilman
by his bad bum toes.

you can know the devilman
by his bad bum toes
but you can't know a lady
by her shiny high shoes.

nail through the toe,
nail through the heel,
spit-shined bright
as an electric eel.
satin is the look
but it sure ain't the feel.
you can't tell a lady
by her shiny high shoes.

you cannot tell a lady
by her shiny high shoes
but you'll know a fine lady
by her walk, by her walk.
you'll know a fine lady
by the way she stomps
on the bad bad devilman's toes.

if you cannot tell a lady
by her walk
by her walk
if you cannot tell...

> (*The music stops abruptly.*)

you better not ask.

Scene 1

We see GRETA *at the moonlit rendezvous with her secret lover,* VALEN-
TINO UFA. *[He is played by the actor who played* MILES *in Act One.]*
VALENTINO *has a romantic mask and a romantic accent. He wears his
crimson ascot, as stipulated, and she, her raw silk snood.*

*For the first time we are outside. The red curtain has tracked off altogether, re-
vealing a more open, less familiar world. Like the forest of a Shakespearean
comedy.*

VALENTINO UFA. My dearest Greta.

GRETA. Valentino, dearest mine.

VALENTINO UFA. At last!

GRETA. At longest last!

VALENTINO UFA. I knew you at once by your raw silk snood.

GRETA. And you, by your crimson ascot.

> (*They kiss deeply.*)

VALENTINO UFA. How did you conspire to slip away?

GRETA. Madame has fled to Lichtenstein, on some inscrutable caper.
(*Faux-innocent.*) Who can say what voices buzz in her brain?

VALENTINO. Your eyes, like two black pearls harvested from the heftiest
clams by the quickest-fingered divers of the Orient. Just as I remembered.

GRETA. (*Distracted.*) Valentino...

VALENTINO. Your ears, like chestnuts, like supplest cauliflower, like two
Brussels sprouts sautéing in the creamiest goat butter. Just as I remembered.

GRETA. Valentino...

VALENTINO. Your cheek, like a new-sprouted hyacinth unwatered with
water so that it assumes the most appealing pallor. Just as I remembered.

GRETA. My love, 'tis no ordinary pallor.

VALENTINO. No, the rarest!

GRETA. (*Expectoratingly.*) I mean: My pallor is perpetuated neither by powder nor pestilence. No, I'm pale because...I've seen a ghost.

VALENTINO. My angel, what a scare you've had—a ghost!

GRETA. I've tussled with ghosts before but never like this. He was quite…solid.

VALENTINO. He?

GRETA. His name was virile with consonants. "Casper Logan."

VALENTINO. Then the specter did not have the aspect of my once nearly, now dearly-departed Romola?

GRETA. (*Preoccupied.*) Almost as if he weren't a ghost at all…

VALENTINO. You're certain, "he"? Not my ill-starred betrothed, come in search of horrible recompense?

GRETA. No, no, no. Just so long as the Lady Romola was buried with her emerald— Just so long as that measure was taken to appease her restless spirit, to ensure against any post-mortal wanderings…

(*We see a ghostly arm emerge from the darkness. The arm is wearing one of* ROMOLA's *long green gloves.*)

GRETA. Just so long as she left this world with the emerald still in her green-glovéd grasp, we should have nothing at all to fear from her specter.

(*The ghostly arm has begun to caress* VALENTINO's *cheek.*)

VALENTINO. My dear, your dear little hand is so cold on my cheek. Not as I remembered.

GRETA. My dear little hand isn't on your cheek.

VALENTINO. My dear, your breath: like a gust from the grave!

GRETA. I perfumed my breath not an hour ago.

(*The ghostly arm pulls* VALENTINO *off stage by his crimson ascot.* GRETA *doesn't notice.*)

VALENTINO. (*Ever softer, as if being strangled.*) My dear

My dear

My dear

my dear—

GRETA. Valentino? Whither have you wandered while the moon cowers behind the clouds? Valentino?

(*We hear* ROMOLA's *sepulchral voice now [since the* MILES *actor is now off stage, free to play it].*)

ROMOLA'S GHOST. (*Off.*) Snoooood.

GRETA. Show yourself to me, spirit! Do you so much fear the light?

ROMOLA'S GHOST. (*Off.*) Snooooood!

GRETA. Chthonic demon, why do you repeat that word?

ROMOLA'S GHOST. (*Predatory.*) Raw…silk…snoood.

(GRETA *touches her hand to her snood. She makes a run for it.*)

Scene 2

The red curtain returns. We are inside the theater again.

ZINA *holds the accordion.* DOROTHY *has been teaching her. An atonal gasp comes out of it.*

ZINA. Strange, slinky beast. (*Another terrible bleating.*) It breathes noise instead of fire!

DOROTHY. Don't sound so strange when you make it sing right.

ZINA. How did you tame this runtish offspring of bagpipe and piano?

DOROTHY. Takes long fingers.

ZINA. I don't have long fingers?

DOROTHY. You got long speeches.

ZINA. Tell me, Dorothy. What do people *do* around here all the time?

DOROTHY. Usually, people raise a family.

ZINA. And what do they do…when they don't raise a family?

DOROTHY. They teach accordion. (*Pause.*)

ZINA. I'm sorry.

DOROTHY. No room for sorry. I was over "Sorry" a long time ago. You take your sorry and put it to music and then it's not fit to haunt you no more. It's just a tune to get stuck in your head.

ZINA. (*Solemn.*) Yes, so it is in the Theater.

DOROTHY. Don't much like your play, Zina. I don't like what you brought to our boys. But somehow I like you, Zina, you and your britches.

ZINA. The first time I attempted a prestigious drag spectacle, I put ladies on stage beside the boys. Ladies in trousers, boys in skirts. I thought: Why should the boys be the only ones to escape what's expected of them every day?

Right away I learned: People are not so quick to laugh as they are when a man puts on a dress. Trousers speak louder *off stage*: the woman who wants to fight beside her husband in battle; the woman who wants a life in the Theater.

The stage is for skirts. Pants are a power in real life.

(ZINA *looks at* DOROTHY. DOROTHY *looks at* ZINA's *pants.*)

DOROTHY. Yes. Yes they are.

LORNA. (*Off stage.*) Girls!

(LORNA *comes running on, in a state, breaking the moment.*)

DOROTHY. What is it, Lorna?

LORNA. They're shutting us down.

ZINA. What?

LORNA. The show!

DOROTHY. The show?

LORNA. They called out the sheriff on us.

DOROTHY. They who.

LORNA. Ladies Christian Temperance Union.

ZINA. (*Ruefully.*) The *Christians*.

DOROTHY. Don't seem like their jurisdiction.

LORNA. They found True's hooch under the stage. And he promised me he'd go off the bottle.

DOROTHY. I told you: he's not the changing kind.

LORNA. Ten years, Dorothy. Aren't you never going to see him someway else?

DOROTHY. Not 'till he starts keeping his promises.

ZINA. How did the Christians know where to look?

LORNA. Somebody musta tipped them off. (*A discovery.*) Somebody musta given them a *map*…

DOROTHY. What're you eyeing me for, Lorna?

LORNA. Lying's still a sin, Dot—even when you think you're in the right.

(*Short pause.*)

DOROTHY. (*A bold confession.*) Even when you mean to save souls?

(*A feeling of melodrama here, as if the play-within-the-play has spilled into Wattleburg. Perhaps we see the footlights on the women as the lights fade. The red curtain tracks off.*)

Scene 3

The COUNTESS, *still not-very-well disguised as a boy, travels down stage. She breaks the plane of the red curtain, moving into the space formerly reserved for the real world.*

COUNTESS. I walk and I scamper and I plod and I trod 'til the ramparts of Paris give way to an entirely unfamiliar country. Lakes and lakes and humdrum lakes beyond all ocular capacity or want! (*She surveys the width of the audience, regally.*) And every person who crosses my path, a peasant: hair unpowdered, faces dirty but lifted, proud, even in the rain. And a snow-bellied skylark who alights on my wrist and sings me a tune to pass the time.

(*She whistles back at the bird and then lets it go. Perhaps she begins to flap her arms along with it.*)

COUNTESS. I watch those white wings shirring the air and I think: if only *I* could wing myself away from here! But alas, (*Seeing her drab boy's clothing*) my wings are clipped. Like the plumage of a bird, one's dress is one's principle means of attraction—like the rare scent of the snifter beetle or the intoxicating dance of the black mamba. What, then, is to become of one who meets the world in imperfect dress? Walking these shabby streets, the men look through me rather than at me. An enchantress who has lost her powers and her sense of direction.

(TRUE *approaches, played by the actress who plays* LORNA.)

TRUE. You lost, boy?

COUNTESS. (*Still out.*) But one man saw me anyway. Even in the aspect of a boy, he *saw* me.

TRUE. Nothing but farm this way. Town center's over there.

COUNTESS. (*Still out.*) My knees begin to buckle, a true gentleman! —but I feel the cool gem in my pocket and, though it be a bauble besmirched, it gives me strength.

TRUE. Ain't you got a map?

COUNTESS. (*Directly to him now.*) I have been following my nose, as they say.

Scene 4

Lights down to a spot on TRUE.

TRUE. That boy's got a swish for studying. Shoulders like an ox, but walking like a Florida flamingo. He ain't bad looking though. Is that how I look in fronta those footlights?

You ever wake up one morning and feel like a stranger in yer own skin? Like your face don't even make sense in the mirror?

My partner Knox can tell something's up. I walk in the shop today and he says, *Why you doin' all this, True? Got Blisters on yer feet. Got cuts on yer legs from shaving like some kinda sidewalk susie. Why you doin' all this for some lady show?*

And I say, *I don't rightly know, except That Lorna told me how to get pretty, so it's like I'm doing it for her. Do you get to make yourself pretty for someone?* I say. And Knox just looks at me like I'm a stranger.

(*Back to the scene, as though no time has passed.*)

COUNTESS. You seem lost in your thoughts, hero.

TRUE. I guess we're both of us lost.

COUNTESS. I'm afraid I never was skilled with the sextant. Can *you* apprehend the stars?

TRUE. You follow me, stranger. I'll steer us straight.

COUNTESS. This arid yet lake-laden land… Is this friendly Lichtenstein then?

Scene 5

ROMOLA'S GHOST. Snoooooood!

(GRETA *scurries from one side of the stage to the other and out of sight, tee-*

tering on her heels.)

(ROMOLA'S GHOST *enters, hot on her trail, but seemingly in no hurry. Her movements are dreamy but demented. She seems almost to float. She is very very pale.*)

ROMOLA'S GHOST. Buried me face down in the earth, buried me emeraldless and husbandless looking down toward China but still I clawed my way out. Scratch scratch scratch, nails to coffinsatin—griming and dirting and earthing underneath my filed fine fingernails 'till I wormed my way out. Followed a worm up and broke through to the sun. Only it wasn't sunning out, it was mooning, full-mooning in the Père Lachaise.

(*She runs* VALENTINO's *crimson ascot through her hands.*)

ROMOLA'S GHOST. Got a pretty pretty blood red pretty for my collection, now I'm searching a snood if you find a snood you find the girl to go with it. The girl. The girl. The girl won't have no using for a snood no more when I'm through with eating the space between her chin and her collarbone, her snoodplace, boring through that soft soft girl 'till you hit spine.

Dead don't talk quite the same sort as the living no more but the words are still enough, you understand? Imperfect speeching not so ladylike with the commas sounding in the wrong place but it's what feels good in my mouth these days and I wonder if it'll speak denser the longer I'm decay. (*Looking at the ascot, again.*) Believed you, Valentino. Trusted you madly but instead he played goosey-loosey with my jewel and my heart and now *I want my rightful emerald back*. I want. I want. And if six feet of dirt couldn't stop me then no chamber whore nor any of yous won't don't stop me no *marrrk*

(*We hear* MILES *calling from off stage.*)

MILES. (*Off.*) Dorothy?

ROMOLA'S GHOST. *myyyy*

MILES. (*Off.*) You seen my ascot?

ROMOLA'S GHOST. *worrrrd.*

MILES. (*Off.*) Know you're real sore at me, Dot. But can it wait till after the show?

(MILES *enters [played by the actress who plays* DOROTHY*].*)

MILES. Um. Yer real white.

ROMOLA. Where is the girl or I will eat you.

MILES. Ain't seen no girl.

ROMOLA. But you've seen my green, my emerald. I can see it flashing, still, in your dull dullard eyes.

MILES. What do you mean by paying me a visit?

ROMOLA. Slatternly serf, do I not scarify?

MILES. No, ma'am. How could I be scared of a piece of myself?

ROMOLA. *Snoooooooooooooooooooooood.*

MILES. (*Interrupting, as if he knows what* ROMOLA's *going to say—it is a kind of snooding contest.*) *Snoooooooooooooooooooood.* Dot says I know your words better than the Sunday psalms. Dot says you're too deep in my blood and bones. Dot wants my two feet planted in *this* world, so that's where they'll stay 'till I step on that stage tonight, thank you very much, ma'am.

ROMOLA. (*Very close to him.*) Where is the emerald, and I shannot visit you no more.

MILES. It went thataway.

(ROMOLA *starts to exit in the direction that* MILES *pointed.*)

ROMOLA. (*Sepulchral.*) Thataway...

Scene 6

MILES *watches* ROMOLA *drift off.*

MILES. I know how she feels. I got all kinds 'a strange noise in my head these days. 'Stead of ties I got ascots. 'Stead of dynasties I got (*Pronouncing it the fancy way.*) dynasties. Most of all I got snoods. Those ladies don't like to say anything the easy way.

How'm I supposed to keep my feet on the ground when my words are knocking around on high heels? Like right now: I never used to have question marks in my talk. Now I'm talking in question marks, you know?

My Dot hears things too. I know she does. When you got faith, it puts words in your head and your heart. Like Joan of Arc. (*Pronounced "Jonah Arc."*) Isn't it the same thing when you play a part? When you play a part, you aren't never alone. It's like you got someone else walking through your life, whispering things in your ear. Sure wish my Dot could hear the same thing.

Scene 7

The red curtain returns. LORNA *and* ZINA *at the theater, right where we left them. We hear* DOROTHY *from off in the wings, playing the accordion with fierce abandon. It sounds like something Rachmaninoff might compose for accordion. Stormy.*

LORNA. Think she's working something out.

ZINA. Yes.

LORNA. (*Confidential, like a slumber-party secret.*) When I need to work something out, sometimes I sit under the trestle and eat a whole tin o' sardines!

(ZINA *just looks at her.*)

ZINA. (*A sort of warning.*) When I need to work something out, I like to find a young person and rob them of their virtue.

(*We hear another surge of accordion.*)

LORNA. I don't think she really *meant* to shut us down.

ZINA. Oh she meant it.

LORNA. But the boys have worked so hard.

ZINA. We've all worked hard, and now… (*Quite noble.*) Now we join Rousseau and de Sade as martyrs of censorship.

(DOROTHY *is there in the doorway.*)

DOROTHY. To be a martyr, don't you have to have faith in something?

LORNA. (*Spinning to see her.*) Dorothy.

ZINA. Dorothy, I have a story to tell you.

DOROTHY. A story?

ZINA. (*To herself.*) Even the abstract Mistletwerpe was not above narrative in moments of crisis.

I was walking out of the post office today and I ran into a woman who said *Shame.* This woman pointed her finger at me and said *Shame,* a fake daisy on her hat bobbing up and down: *It's no good to have our young fellas prancing around against nature. It's the beginning of the end, it's fire and brimstone.* And I don't remember everything she said but it got very biblical.

DOROTHY. This supposed to convince me?

ZINA. I tried to explain about Shakespeare, about Ancient Greece, about *precedent,* but she kept wagging her finger at me. So, I suggested she try something more elevated with her body.

LORNA. You didn't.

ZINA. Wagging her finger, wagging her way into other people's lives. Putting words in God's mouth, as if she knows what he's thinking. And now you come in here wagging your finger at us and I think: aha, *there* is that lady.

DOROTHY. I am NOT that lady.

ZINA. Then why do you wag your way into other people's lives?

DOROTHY. You're the one doing the serious wagging 'round here, Zina. What do you know about our lives? What do you know about sun and sweat and down payments on the store. You spend your life *elevated.*

ZINA. Oh, do I.

DOROTHY. Around here, art's not what you do when you got time to waste. We don't *have* time to waste. So if you're making art in this town, you better make sure it takes you nearer to God.

LORNA. (*Rallying behind* ZINA.) It does. It do!

DOROTHY. Well he ain't any god I know.

ZINA. Do not let that lady crawl down your throat and speak in your voice! You do not wear a daisy. You told me yourself, you find art in things that would make other people hang their heads and weep. I think you can find it in our little show.

LORNA. Yeah.

ZINA. I think you can find it in the way your husband moves like someone two centuries ago.

LORNA. Yeah!

ZINA. The way he takes those big words and *tames* them!

LORNA. Dorothy!

ZINA. Dorothy!

LORNA. Please Dorothy!

ZINA. Please.

      (*Pause.*)

DOROTHY. (*"This better be good."*) I'll be looking for *art* tonight.

LORNA. I think that's her way of saying we're back on.

ZINA. We're back on!

DOROTHY. Aren't you forgetting something?

LORNA. What.

DOROTHY. Ladies Christian Temperance Union.

ZINA. Oh *piss.*

      (*Short pause.*)

LORNA. *I* know. Sheriff Pete was sweet on me in high school…

ZINA. Yes?

LORNA. Mighta gone for it too if it weren't for that harelip.

ZINA. Harelip, yes!

DOROTHY. Yes?

LORNA. I could pay him a visit.

ZINA. You could wear that dress of yours.

LORNA. Stage a little reunion…

DOROTHY. Which dress?

ZINA. With the blue flowers and the neckline to here.

DOROTHY. Oh *that* dress.

ZINA. The dress with the *powers.*

LORNA. And what am I supposed to tell him while I'm making like Pickford?

ZINA. (*Like a damsel, batting her eyelashes.*) "Sure didn't mean nothing by the liquors, Mr. Sheriff."

LORNA. (*Batting her eyelashes.*) "Bet you enjoy a drop once in a while…"

ZINA. Don't forget your arms.

LORNA. (*Using her arms.*) "…when you're looking to unwind."

ZINA. "*Please* Mr. Sheriff, we just want to put a smile on our fellow man."

DOROTHY. You two look like a couple of fat magpies waiting to get shot off a wire.

LORNA. "Please Mister Sheriff, won't you save the day?"

ZINA. Again, with the arms!

LORNA. "Please Mister Sheriff, won't you save the day?"

ZINA. You are ready. Now go act a lady!

(*ZINA whacks LORNA on the rump. She runs off, excited.*)

DOROTHY. Can a lady act a lady?

ZINA. It's something you learn, like anything else.

DOROTHY. Yeah?

ZINA. Did you come out of the crib batting your eyelashes?

DOROTHY. I *never* bat my eyelashes.

(*Again, a feeling of melodrama. The red curtain tracks off.*)

Scene 8

Outside. A fast-cutting, traveling scene.

GRETA *runs on, gasping. It takes her a while to catch her breath—she has been running for half the act.*

GRETA. They say "too young to die" and I wonder how young is too young? Certainly ten, most likely twelve, but who would pity poor Greta at bittersweet sixteen?

"She'd known her first kiss," the women will say in the Plâce Vendome. "She'd known occupational tedium and sartorial splendescence. Of what worldly experience was she deprived when the unhappy ghost chewed her in twain?"

Worst of all, I fear some part of me *embraces* my fate— What is there for me, now that Valentino is undone by the very ascot that drew me to his handsome neck? Would I return to feminine toils? Ne'er! I shall ne'er go back to those dusty rooms choked with chintz! I shall ne'er polish brass, now that I've spied golder horizons!

But what sunset can I ride into, if not on a stallion's strong back? Will ever man cross my girlish path again?

(*CASPER crosses her girlish path. He is staring down at the photograph of Mary Pickford as he walks. GRETA finds a hiding place.*)

CASPER. Miss Pickford, pretty Miss Pickford, wealthy Miss Pickford with the stars in your eyes. Gonna put you under my pillow tonight so you can sneak into my sleep and tell me how to want you. How to be with you.

True says if I stare at you long enough my imagination will figure it out. But all I can think about is how to *light* you. A flat hard light straight on, to be kind to your nose—or else a soft light from behind for casting you a halo.

I saw you in *Winds of Intrigue* and *The Cavalier Cavalier*, and *Let the Bodice Beware* was my favorite, but the movies always cut out before they tell you anything useful. The hero takes you in his arms and everything goes dark. How'm I supposed to know what to do?

GRETA. (*Heroic yet wanton.*) I'll show you!

CASPER. You!

GRETA. Shhh. I'm *eluding*. Perhaps you know the way to Lichtenstein?

CASPER. Never been farther than Lansing.

GRETA. There's a whole wide world out there, Monsieur Casper!

CASPER. That's what I hear.

GRETA. *Lichtenstein.* It's said to be a land of rich food and flexuous tax laws. But the journey is not without its perils. I could use a robust traveling companion.

CASPER. Who, me?

GRETA. Lend me your arm, Sir.

CASPER. What d'you want my arm for?

GRETA. (*Rhetorical, a little minxy.*) Why does a lady want to be with a man?

CASPER. I don't know. Why?

GRETA. What a curious, in-between creature you are!

CASPER. I am not.

GRETA. How alike we are, really. The two of us brand-new to the world.

(*Cut to:* TRUE *with the* COUNTESS, *still disguised as a boy.*)

TRUE. This here's Wattleburg, stranger. We got a general store. Got a haberdasher. We even got a spectacle tonight.

COUNTESS. A land of plenty! I would still trod the unwelcome wilds if not for your intervention, hero.

TRUE. Never been called "hero."

COUNTESS. That is difficult to believe.

TRUE. Lorna calls me the Good Guy, but I'm not so sure.

COUNTESS. Why do you keep your chin so rough, like…an animal.

TRUE. (*"You're not a lady, so hands off."*) Ladies seem to like it.

COUNTESS. Surely it's a hazard to anyone who would entertain an intimacy with your cheek?

TRUE. Maybe that's why they proceed with caution. You'll grow yer own soon, and then they'll be careful of you too.

COUNTESS. I will not grow hairs.

TRUE. (*Bemused.*) Oh no?

COUNTESS. For no delicate boy am I. You look upon a Countess!

(*The* COUNTESS *tears off her cap.*)

TRUE. Madam, I knew you looked familiar.

(*Back to.*)

GRETA. The open road, imagine it! (*Taking* CASPER's *hand.*) You can protect me from highwaymen and gypsies, while I recite cloying homilies to pass the time. And together we'll make the most resourceful team.

CASPER. (*Reclaiming his hand.*) But, the show.

GRETA. Monsieur Casper, I lived my life in small rooms like you, the dusters and teapots keeping me cold cold company. Now my pulse is always racing, my blood rushing toward survival. My dreams were filled with one man, and now *armies* of eligibles cross my path! (*Sizing up the audience.*) You'll do, and you—not so much you. Perchance you? No longer can I mask my desire behind fan or mask. (*Embracing* CASPER.) I give myself over to netherreaching roilings! (*She looks at* CASPER's *nether reaches.*) Where are your roilings, Monsieur?

CASPER. (*Staring hard at the Pickford picture.*) I don't know!

(GRETA *grabs the picture and tears it in two.*)

GRETA. Who needs that pale imitation of my gamine gams? (*She takes his hand.*) Come, monsieur!: The open road will put the blush back in your cheek and the roil in your reaches.

CASPER. I can't leave. I like it here. There's…people here.

GRETA. I see: You love another.

CASPER. It shows?

GRETA. (*Tragically.*) It shows. (*Bright again.*) Oh well. I myself no longer have the luxury of such moonlit moonery. (*Very quick.*) I must away to Lichtenstein to find the Countess to find the necklace to bury the jewel to appease poor rotting Romola before she devours me. It's surpassing simple.

(*Back to.*)

COUNTESS. Bestubbled hero. Close your eyes.

TRUE. (*He does.*) How come.

COUNTESS. A humble gift: Some can see their futures faceted in its greeny deep. Now it reflects nothing back to me but blood and betrayal.

(*The* COUNTESS *reaches into her pocket and pulls out the emerald, which seems to shine with a light of its own.* TRUE *opens his eyes and whistles at the emerald.*)

COUNTESS. Take it, stranger, and give it new reflections. Take it, stranger, and may it glister again.

(*The* COUNTESS *slips it over* TRUE's *head.* TRUE *sees the* COUNTESS' *large, male hand and grabs it.*)

TRUE. Who are you, really?

COUNTESS. (*A hand to her sternum, faux-indignant.*) I am only what I appear to be, nothing more.

TRUE. No, there is something more...

(*He runs a finger down the* COUNTESS' *cheek, leaving an unpainted line on her pale face.*)

COUNTESS. Take care, bold youth—a lady cannot face the world without decoration.

TRUE. I thought you said you got nothing to hide.

(TRUE *has started to remove the* COUNTESS' *wig, to unbutton her gown.*)

TRUE. A disguise under a disguise under a disguise!

COUNTESS. What are *your* disguises, hero?

TRUE. Didn't think I had any. That's how come they call me True.

COUNTESS. I am not speaking of truth and lies.

(*The* COUNTESS *has started to remove* TRUE's *costume as well.*)

COUNTESS. It is possible, is it not, to meet someone who discovers things in yourself you never even knew...

(*They are beginning to look more and more alike—somewhere in between male and female.*)

COUNTESS. ...I suppose we all dream that will happen.

(*A figure walks to the edge of the stage. At first it might look like* MILES, *but closer up we see that it's* DOROTHY. *For the first time, she is wearing britches instead of a dress.*)

DOROTHY. Evenin', Lord.

(*You can tell* DOROTHY *feels right in britches.*)

Scene 9

The red curtain returns. Lights out on all but DOROTHY, *who is at the theater saying a prayer. Head bent but not kneeling.*

DOROTHY. Lord, I hope it's you workin' through us tonight, and not you-know-who. Lord, help those boys get here fast and safe. Lord, help my husband be the star tonight and not the fool. He thinks those ladies *talk* to him, the way you talk to me. Help him move with purpose and feminine fatigue. Help my fingers find the right keys, good and fleet. Help this whole thing bring our town together somehow and not apart. Help it be *art* somehow, not just fellas stretchin' out my delicates. I know you got a lot on your mind Lord but Lord won't you watch us tonight.

(*She peeks upstage under the curtain, her back to us—as if looking at the assembled crowd. Glimpses of the footlights through the curtain.* ZINA *enters with many grocery bags.*)

ZINA. How does it look out there?

DOROTHY. (*Gravely.*) Full house, and I still haven't seen the boys.

ZINA. Eight minutes to curtain, and no sign of my ladies!

DOROTHY. You mean boys.

ZINA. I mean ladies.

DOROTHY. (*Re: the grocery bags.*) What's all that?

ZINA. All the tomatoes in town. (*She produces one from a sack and starts to juggle it.*) So they won't have anything to throw at us—I bought all the ammunition.

DOROTHY. This is cow country. What if they find something else to throw?

ZINA. Then we'll duck.

(*She throws the tomato at* DOROTHY. *She catches it, takes a bite.*)

DOROTHY. S'good.

(LORNA *enters.*)

LORNA. You seen my boyfriend?

DOROTHY. You seen my husband?

ZINA. You seen my cast?

ALL. No.

DOROTHY. They'll be here.

LORNA. Brought you coffee, fresh from the Big Steer.

ZINA. Extra black?

LORNA. Black as a bog.

(ZINA *takes out a flask.*)

ZINA. With a splash of gin, the way I like.

DOROTHY. Ugh.

LORNA. You put that away, Miss Zina—they could shut us down again like (*Snapping her fingers*) that.

ZINA. (*A toast.*) Here's to your triumph, my dear.

DOROTHY. Pretty darn impressive.

LORNA. When I got nervous, I just made like I was Clara Bow and Sheriff Pete was a big movie camera starin' me in the eye. It wasn't nothing. Soon as I saw that harelip start to quiver, I knew we were back on.

DOROTHY. Sheriff Pete didn't know what hit him.

ZINA. Duse herself could not have done it.

DOROTHY. She didn't have that dress.

LORNA. He even said he'd come tonight. Isn't that sweet?

(ZINA *checks her watch.*)

ZINA. *Six* minutes. And no one to play my ladies. No one, *unless…*

(*She looks the women up and down.*)

DOROTHY. Don't look at *me* like a piece o' meat. Couldn't shoehorn me into that Countess dress.

LORNA. I could squeeze.

ZINA. (*To* DOROTHY.) You're more of a Romola.

LORNA. I'm good with a fan.

DOROTHY. (*To* ZINA.) Telling me I'm not Countess material?

LORNA. Dorothy you're lovely.

DOROTHY. Countess don't mean lovely.

ZINA. I'll *hunt* those boys down if I have to.

DOROTHY. Countess means *grand*.

(ZINA *runs off.*)

DOROTHY. Countess means "I'm not going to bow for nobody."

(*The* COUNTESS *glides on from stage right, in her full regalia again.*)

COUNTESS. My ears fairly burn—does someone summon me?

LORNA. Thank goodness, True! You're on.

COUNTESS. I'm…"on?"

LORNA. Are you drunk?

COUNTESS. Drunk with love.

LORNA. Thanks hon' but—

COUNTESS. Drunk with *stubble*.

LORNA. Didn't you shave first like I said?

COUNTESS. Drunk with the stubble of a gentle plebeian.

LORNA. Yeah, *weird*, True, but you gotta get yourself on stage right away. Starting to think those Temperance gals have a point.

COUNTESS. Ragamuffin, you take me for some kind of *actress?*

LORNA. True, are you *in* there?

DOROTHY. Lorna, he's toasted.

COUNTESS. Better if you'd taken me for a common strumpet!

DOROTHY. At least he's not breaking character.

LORNA. Where's your fan, hon'? You need it for your entrance.

(LORNA *advances and the* COUNTESS *sees the emerald [still around* LORNA's *neck from her last scene as* TRUE*].*)

COUNTESS. So, peasant, you've pilfered my hero's jewel!

LORNA. Don't you remember? You said I could wear it.

COUNTESS. Or did you tease it out from under him?

LORNA. You said 'till you got me a real one. Are you getting cold feet / Mr. True?

COUNTESS. (*Overlapping.*) Surrender the gem at once, you filthy little /

magpie!

LORNA. (*Overlapping.*) True, you don't know what you're saying.

ZINA. (*Off.*) Casper, places!

LORNA. You go dry yourself up, and fast!

(*She shoves the* COUNTESS *off stage.*)

DOROTHY. That's right, you show him who wears the dress!

LORNA. (*Rattled.*) He was lookin' at me like a stranger.

DOROTHY. (*Shaking her head.*) Soon as he starts to feel something, he bolts.

LORNA. He ain't like that any more.

DOROTHY. I told you a hundred times, Lorna. You can't change a fella with a powder puff.

(ROMOLA'S GHOST *glides across the stage, unseen.*)

LORNA. And you can't change him with prayers either, Dorothy. At least, I don't see it working for you.

DOROTHY. Well, well. Maybe you *are* a Countess.

LORNA. I'm just saying—we're both of us tryin' to change our fellas.

ZINA. (*Off.*) Casper, I said places!

(GRETA *scurries on.*)

GRETA. What is this "places?"

DOROTHY. Five minutes, Casper!

GRETA. Have you seen a pale, terrible woman?

DOROTHY. Casper, you been into True's hooch?

LORNA. Whatever they got, it's catching.

(MILES *enters, dressed as* ROMOLA'S GHOST. *[Note: In this scene, MILES, TRUE, and CASPER are again played by the male actors.]*)

GRETA. Merciful heaven!

DOROTHY. Where you been, Miles Cuthbert?

LORNA. (*Seeing that he's wearing the unkempt ghost wig.*) Wrong wig!

(LORNA *runs offstage.*)

MILES. Are those my pants, Dot?

ZINA. (*Off.*) Lorna, get the bench!

GRETA. At last, Greta, your fate has found you!

MILES. What's got into you, Casper?

DOROTHY. Serious case o' stage fright.

MILES. (*Advancing.*) Take it easy, Casper— You'll do great out there.

GRETA. I surrender, spirit! (GRETA *assumes a pose of supplication.*) Feast, but fast, on my pretty neck.

MILES. He *do* have a nice neck.

(ZINA *enters from stage left, and stalks across the stage, never breaking her stride.*)

ZINA. I thought we had our Countess!

(LORNA *returns with the bench.*)

MILES. Anybody seen my cape?

(*And* ZINA *is gone, off stage right.*)

LORNA. Shoot shoot shoot, I was mending the hem down in the shop.

(MILES *rushes off stage right.*)

LORNA. Quick!

ZINA. (*Off.*) True!

LORNA. True!

GRETA. Then, I am spared again?

DOROTHY. Casper, get off the floor.

GRETA. Greta, you have more lives than a cat!

(TRUE *enters from stage left, looking exactly as the Countess did. With his fan now. He taps* LORNA *on the shoulder with it.*)

TRUE. Hey girl, how do I look? I do my eyes okay?

LORNA. That's more like it, Hon'. (*Formal.*) Now, I am ready to accept yer apology.

TRUE. Apology?

GRETA. Madame, can it be you?

TRUE. You ready for the limelight, Casper?

GRETA. (*Aside.*) Truly she has embraced the manner of a boy, if not the cloth.

TRUE. Where's your duster at?

GRETA. (*To* TRUE.) Cruel mistress, would you have me tidy the road of exile?

TRUE. No time / for fun, Casper. Get your duster.

ZINA. (*Off.*) Miles, places!

GRETA. I refuse. No longer will I live for your whims.

ZINA. (*Off.*) You heard me: Places!

(ROMOLA'S GHOST *enters, unseen. [Looking just like* MILES *did.]*)

DOROTHY. (*To* GRETA *and* TRUE.) You heard the lady.

TRUE. (*To* GRETA, *re: duster.*) You better pray it's on the prop table.

LORNA. (*Seeing* ROMOLA'S GHOST.) Miles, thank heaven!

ROMOLA'S GHOST. (*Advancing on* GRETA.) Snoood!

GRETA. Unmerciful heaven!

(GRETA *flees from* ROMOLA, *exiting stage right.*)

TRUE. (*Shouting off.*) Wrong way, Casper!

(TRUE *follows* GRETA *off.* LORNA *and* DOROTHY *grab* RO-MOLA'S GHOST. *They put the tidy wig from the top of the show on her.*)

LORNA. Sit down, Miles. You got on the wrong wig.

ZINA. (*Off.*) Casper, I already told you! Places!

DOROTHY. I'm getting dizzy.

(CASPER *enters [looking exactly like* GRETA, *of course], from the opposite direction that* GRETA *ran off.*)

CASPER. Sorry I'm late.

DOROTHY. *Real* dizzy.

ROMOLA'S GHOST. Snood?

CASPER. I was getting into character.

LORNA. (*Re:* ROMOLA'S GHOST.) Him too.

ROMOLA'S GHOST. (*Advancing on* CASPER *now.*) Snoood!

(CASPER *is, of course, unfazed by* ROMOLA'S GHOST.)

DOROTHY. Settle down, Miles.

LORNA. (*Suddenly remembering.*) Chairs!

LORNA & DOROTHY. Got it!

LORNA & DOROTHY. You go that way!

(*They run off to get the furniture for the countess's drawing room.* RO-MOLA'S GHOST *and* CASPER *are alone for a second.*)

ROMOLA'S GHOST. Where is the emerald or I will eat you.

CASPER. Did you check the prop table?

ROMOLA'S GHOST. Prop table…

(ZINA *enters from stage right, dragging the* COUNTESS.)

ZINA. That's everyone!

COUNTESS. Release me at once.

CASPER. My duster!

(CASPER *exits.*)

ZINA. No, places!

ROMOLA'S GHOST. "Places?"

LORNA. Places!

ROMOLA'S GHOST. (*Seeing it around* LORNA's *neck.*) Glory, my emerald!

COUNTESS. *My* emerald!

LORNA. *My* emerald!

(GRETA *enters.*)

GRETA. *My* emerald!

(ROMOLA'S GHOST *tears it from* LORNA's *neck.*)

ZINA. Places!

LORNA. Places!

ROMOLA'S GHOST. (*Ghoulish.*) Places?

GRETA. (*Panicked.*) Places!

COUNTESS. (*Grand.*) Places!

> (*Somehow they end up in their places, at the top of the play-within-the-play. A frozen tableau, seen from behind.* ROMOLA *holds the emerald aloft.*)
>
> (ZINA, DOROTHY, *and* LORNA *run to the wings, so as not to be seen.* DOROTHY *is poised for her first chord on the accordion.*)
>
> (*Chaos gives way, all of a sudden, to order. Just as the red curtain starts to rise.*)
>
> (*Blackout.*)

End of Act II

CODA

During the changeover, DOROTHY *sings her simplest, most tuneful song, accompanying herself on the accordion:*

DOROTHY. if i had myself a pretty little jewel
i sure wouldn't show it to you.
if i had myself a pretty big jewel
i surely wouldn't show it to you.

i'd keep it from the sun
i'd hide it from the fuzz
i'd put it in my sock drawer
where the bees don't buzz.

i'd bury it good
i'd lock it in a case
i'd draw a treasure map with a hundred million Xs so you'd have to dig holes up
all over the place.

if I had myself a sea-green jewel
i sure wouldn't show it to you.
if I had myself a mighty-fine jewel
i surely wouldn't show it to you.

i'd polish it good
i'd hide it in my pocket
i'd keep it in a safe
where you can't unlock it.

i'd take it far away
i'd take it on the lam
i'd hold its flaws right up to the light when i need to remember

just who i am.

if i had myself a light-catching jewel
i sure wouldn't show it to you.
if i had myself a glistering jewel,
i surely wouldn't show it to you.

but then what would be the point
of having that sea-green mighty-fine light-catching glistering jewel?
what would be the point if i couldn't see it shinin',
shinin' back at me in your not-so-very-sea-green eyes?

> (*Back in the kitchen.* MILES, TRUE, CASPER, *and* LORNA *around the kitchen table. Quite like the first scene of the play. The men in male dress again.* DOROTHY *walks back into the scene, already underway.*)
>
> (*A feeling of returning to earth. But everyone looks a little bit changed now: Maybe* TRUE *still has some eye makeup on;* DOROTHY *wears the britches;* MILES *helps her at the stove now; Maybe* LORNA *puts her feet up like a man.*)

MILES. Went pretty well

CASPER. Went real well

TRUE. Went pretty real well

LORNA. They stood!

TRUE. They stood?

LORNA. In the back

CASPER. Standing O!

MILES. If you say so

TRUE. "If you say so?"

MILES. Standing O is everyone standing not a few in the back.

LORNA. (*"Take it easy. "*) They *liked* it.

CASPER. They liked it.

MILES. (*Capitulating.*) They liked it.

TRUE. Nobody threw *nothing.*

CASPER. A sequel, a sequel!

TRUE. They were laughing

MILES. With us or at us?

CASPER. With us, I think

LORNA. Heard Zina's laugh.

TRUE. ZINA laughed?

LORNA. That kinda thin kinda (*Makes a sophisticated wheezing sound.*)

CASPER. Never seen Miss Jenks whoop so hard in my life.

TRUE. Sheriff Pete blew me a kiss.

MILES. What'd *you* make of it, Dot?

    (*Everybody is quiet.*)

DOROTHY. (*Turning to* MILES.) Looked almost like art, the way things turned out.

CASPER. Art!

DOROTHY. I said *almost* art, Casper.

CASPER. Almost-art!

MILES. What made it art, you think.

CASPER. Cuz of the costumes

TRUE. (*Looking at* LORNA.) Cuz of the face paint

LORNA. (*Looking at* TRUE.) Cuz of the leading lady.

DOROTHY. No.

MILES. No?

LORNA. No?

DOROTHY. No, it was art because I went somewhere and I'm still not sure I totally came back.

MILES. (*Embracing her.*) Glad you went for it, hon'. Just don't ask me what it all means.

DOROTHY. I took it to mean: you got a duty to live. Got a duty to get dirt under your fingernails.

LORNA. (*To* TRUE.) Got a duty to talk to strangers.

TRUE. (*To* LORNA.) Got a duty to hear 'em.

MILES. Gonna miss having those gals in my head.

DOROTHY. You'll have more gals to talk to soon.

MILES. You mean—

DOROTHY. With a whole season o' shows, you'll have plenty of company in there.

MILES. Dorothy?

DOROTHY. Just don't ask me how to handle them all.

    (*He embraces her.*)

TRUE. What I don't get is: how'd it end up funny? Murder isn't funny, love isn't funny, Zina isn't funny.

CASPER. *I* think love is funny. What it does to you, I mean… (*Looking at* TRUE.) and the way you can't choose it.

TRUE. Casper, don't you start that up again.

CASPER. Start what up.

TRUE. Your eyes are getting all…sparkly.

CASPER. I did like you said. I put Pickford under my pillow every night but she won't give me the right dreams. Been dreaming someone else.

LORNA. Dreams don't always lead the right way, Casper. I had a dream those movie ladies needed me out there, but you fellas need *way* more help.

CASPER. It's not that kind of dream.

LORNA. What kinda dream is it, Casper?

CASPER. The kind you can't always put into words after you wake up. But you know it was good and right.

TRUE. Close yer eyes Casper.

CASPER. (*Closing his eyes.*) How come.

TRUE. Got a gift for you. (*He looks to* LORNA, *who nods. In his own voice, not the Countess's.*) "Take it, stranger, and may it glister again."

> (TRUE *takes off the emerald and puts it around* CASPER's *neck. [Not too much ceremony here.]*)

CASPER. Why me?

TRUE. I think maybe you know what it's like to be a stranger.

CASPER. You sound like Zina.

LORNA. Where's she at, anyway? Tore outta that theater with barely a "Bravo."

DOROTHY. Next train to Chicago, she said.

CASPER. Chicago.

MILES. She got more lady shows.

DOROTHY. Gonna miss her speeches.

CASPER. (*To* MILES.) What's that train cost?

TRUE. It ain't pocket change.

MILES. Ten dollars round-trip.

CASPER. How much for one way?

TRUE. You plannin' a trip, Casper?

CASPER. I hear there's a whole lotta world out there.

> (CASPER *holds up the emerald and it glisters in the light.*)
> (*Simultaneously, they all whistle at it.*)
> (*Blackout.*)

End of Play

SOVEREIGNTY
by Rolin Jones

BIOGRAPHY

Rolin Jones' play *The Intelligent Design of Jenny Chow* was a finalist for the 2006 Pulitzer Prize in Drama. It received the 2006 Obie Award for Excellence in Playwriting, the Elizabeth Osborne Award for an Emerging Artist (American Theatre Critic's Association) and *OC Weekly*'s 2004 "Best New Play" Award. His full-length play, *The Jammer*, received a Fringe First Award for Best New Writing at 2004's Edinburgh Fringe Festival and was also produced at the 2004 New York International Fringe Festival. His ten-minute play, *Sovereignty*, was produced at the Actor's Theater of Louisville's 2006 Humana Festival. He has been commissioned by South Coast Repertory, was one of four American playwrights chosen to participate in the 2004 Old Vic/New Voices Festival in London, and was an NEA/TCG playwright-in-residence at Yale Repertory Theatre. Currently writing on his third season for Showtime's award-winning series, *Weeds*, Mr. Jones graduated from the Yale School of Drama in 2004.

ACKNOWLEDGMENTS

Sovereignty premiered at the Humana Festival of New American Plays in April 2006. It was directed by Shirley Serotsky with the following cast and staff:

MRS. ELSBETH	Heather Dilly
MRS. MERRIWEATHER	Sandra Shipley
BOY	James B. Seiler, Jr.
BOY'S FATHER	Matt Seidman
Scenic Designer	Paul Owen
Costume Designers	John P. White
	Stacy Squires
Lighting Designer	Paul Werner
Sound Designer	Benjamin Marcum
Properties Designer	Mark Walston
Stage Manager	Debra Anne Gasper
Assistant Stage Manager	Heather Fields
Assistant Stage Manager	Paul Mills Holmes
Dramaturg	Julie Felise Dubiner
Assistant Dramaturg	Joanna K. Donehower

CAST OF CHARACTERS
MRS. ELSBETH
MRS. MERRIWEATHER
BOY
MR. RUNIHURA

TIME
Now.

PLACE
The next town over.

For David Grimm

Heather Dilly
in *Sovereignty*

30th Annual Humana Festival of New American Plays
Actors Theatre of Louisville, 2006
Photo by Harlan Taylor

SOVEREIGNTY

Lights up on three doors upstage and three mailboxes downstage. The stage left mailbox has some balloons tied around it. Sounds of suburban bliss. MRS. ELSBETH gardening behind the stage right mailbox which is over stuffed with mail.

MRS. ELSBETH. The new neighbors are having a party. Nice people. Handsome young man. An architect I think. Has a young pretty wife. She's pregnant, you know. Looks like a ripe melon, not a care in the world. They already have one, a little boy and normally I'd say one is enough, isn't the green earth weighted down enough. But they have their ways over in that house and she does look happy. Nice people.

(MRS. MERRIWEATHER *opens the center stage door. Walks to her mailbox.*)

MRS. MERRIWEATHER. Good morning, Louise.

MRS. ELSBETH. Good morning, Rose.

MRS. MERRIWEATHER. The new neighbors are having a party.

MRS. ELSBETH. It looks that way doesn't it?

MRS. MERRIWEATHER. Birthday party for the boy?

MRS. ELSBETH. I think it might be a shower for the mother.

MRS. MERRIWEATHER. Why do you say that?

MRS. ELSBETH. I don't think the boy has many friends.

MRS. MERRIWEATHER. Maybe that's why she's having another baby.

MRS. ELSBETH. So the boy will have someone to play with?

MRS. MERRIWEATHER. Why else?

MRS. ELSBETH. Well they have their ways, those people.

MRS. MERRIWEATHER. Still they are nice people.

MRS. ELSBETH. Very nice. Get anything good today?

MRS. MERRIWEATHER. Bills for Bill is all.

MRS. ELSBETH. How is Bill?

MRS. MERRIWEATHER. Working hard.

MRS. ELSBETH. And Bill, Jr.

MRS. MERRIWEATHER. Rushing a fraternity so he says.

MRS. ELSBETH. Is that right?

MRS. MERRIWEATHER. As long as he's not raping young boys. (*Laughs.*) How's Tom?

MRS. ELSBETH. He's traveling.

MRS. MERRIWEATHER. Lonely?

MRS. ELSBETH. Calls every night.

MRS. MERRIWEATHER. He's a good man your Tom.

MRS. ELSBETH. As long as he's not raping young boys.

MRS. MERRIWEATHER. Exactly. Your mailbox…sure is piling up.

MRS. ELSBETH. What? Oh. Slipped my mind. You know, the garden.

MRS. MERRIWEATHER. The flowers look great, Louise.

MRS. ELSBETH. Thanks, Rose.

MRS. MERRIWEATHER. See you tomorrow.

MRS. ELSBETH. Call if you need anything.

(MRS. MERRIWEATHER *takes her mail inside, closes her door.*)

MRS. ELSBETH. Rose is mad she wasn't invited to the party. She won't say it but I can tell. I wasn't invited to the party either, but I have my garden. Unlike myself, Rose doesn't have anything to occupy her time so she tends to internalize. Like once, Tom and I had Rose and Bill over for drinks. We were having a great time, throwing back g and t's. Well, fast forward forty-five minutes and we're all naked fucking the hell out of each other when Bill gets on his knees and starts sucking off Tom. Well my Tom's not one to embarrass anyone, but you can tell Rose is not happy. Bill can't really hold his liquor all that well. But Rose is a doll. Practically my best friend, if you don't count Oprah.

(*A few loud thuds comes from behind the stage left door, startling* MRS. ELSBETH. *We hear a body sliding behind the door, whimpering.* MRS. ELSBETH *returns to her gardening.*)

MRS. ELSBETH. Spring. Blossoms everywhere.

Stage turns to night. Stars, crickets, then back to day very quickly. MRS. ELSBETH *is gardening.* MRS. MERRIWEATHER *is out by her mailbox, she holds some letters and a tin of chocolates.*

MRS. ELSBETH. Who sent the tin?

MRS. MERRIWEATHER. Bill, Jr.

MRS. ELSBETH. How considerate.

MRS. MERRIWEATHER. Mother's Day gift. You want some chocolate?

MRS. ELSBETH. Oh no, those are for you.

MRS. MERRIWEATHER. Please. I insist.

MRS. ELSBETH. Really, it's way too early for snacks.

MRS. MERRIWEATHER. Who's gonna know?

MRS. ELSBETH. Oh, all right.

(*She crosses to* MRS. MERRIWEATHER. *They begin to pick at the choco-*

lates.)

MRS. MERRIWEATHER. The lawn looks great.

MRS. ELSBETH. Well, it's not worth it. The stuff grows twice as fast now. Tom sprinkled too much feeder last time.

MRS. MERRIWEATHER. Well, it's the envy of the entire block.

MRS. ELSBETH. Oh Rose.

MRS. MERRIWEATHER. Chocolate makes my nipples hard.

MRS. ELSBETH. (*Changing the subject.*) Yes…um…So nice of Bill, Jr. Boys his age don't usually remember their mothers.

MRS. MERRIWEATHER. He's a sweet boy.

(*The stage left door opens. A young boy in torn, dirty clothes steps out. He looks malnourished, delirious. He walks to his mailbox. MRS. ELSBETH and MRS. MERRIWEATHER watch him, still eating from the tin.*)

(*Angry male voice from beyond stage left door: "And don't take all day, you little fucking shit!"*)

MRS. ELSBETH. The Clarks are putting in a new sprinkler system.

MRS. MERRIWEATHER. Is that right? Where did you hear that?

MRS. ELSBETH. From the Weavers. Patty and Ron drove up in their van. You could tell they were fighting, still she hits the brakes, rolls down the window and says the Clarks are tearing up their lawn and putting in new sprinklers.

MRS. MERRIWEATHER. Patty certainly runs that household.

MRS. ELSBETH. (*To the boy.*) Hello there.

(*The BOY turns around.*)

MRS. ELSBETH. Hi there.

BOY. Hello.

MRS. ELSBETH. I'm Louise. This is Rose. What's your name?

BOY. Nkundiushuti Runihura. (*Pronounced N-Koon-Deen-Shoo-Tee Roo-Nee-Hoo-Rah.*)

MRS. MERRIWEATHER. Getting the mail today?

(*The boy nods. then looks to his front door.*)

MRS. ELSBETH. How's your mom doing these days? We haven't seen her out and about lately.

BOY. Is that chocolate?

MRS. ELSBETH. Why yes, it is. Would you like a piece?

MRS. MERRIWEATHER. Louise…

(*The BOY looks towards his front door, nervous.*)

MRS. ELSBETH. It's okay. Come on.

MRS. MERRIWEATHER. If the boy doesn't want any…

MRS. ELSBETH. Well of course, he wants some…

(*The* BOY *rushes over and snatches one piece out of* MRS. ELSBETH's *hand.* MRS. MERRIWEATHER *is frightened. The* BOY *drops his mail and runs back inside his door.*)

MRS. ELSBETH. You dropped your…My God.

MRS. MERRIWEATHER. My God is right.

MRS. ELSBETH. Did you see those clothes? Did you see that face?

MRS. MERRIWEATHER. Those were my chocolates, Rose. Not yours.

MRS. ELSBETH. Rose…

MRS. MERRIWEATHER. Don't Rose me.

MRS. ELSBETH. The boy was hungry. You could practically see through his skin.

MRS. MERRIWEATHER. Oh please.

MRS. ELSBETH. Something's not right.

(*She gathers up the mail.*)

MRS. MERRIWEATHER. (*To the audience.*) Louise has had five miscarriages. Five. Every kid in the neighborhood has the face of her child. Every one of them. The fact is, no one lets their kids anywhere near her. She's a vampire and a tit tease and her womb sags. (*Back to* LOUISE.) If you want to save to the world, Louise, do it with your own chocolates. And take your mail in. It's becoming an eye-sore.

(MRS. MERRIWEATHER *takes her tin and goes inside her house.*)

MRS. ELSBETH. Rose…Rose.

(MRS. ELSBETH *takes the* BOY's *mail and walks over the stage right door. She goes to knock, then thinks again. We hear the sound of sprinklers. She places the mail in front of the door, then walks back to her yard, looks at her mailbox, then returns to her gardening.*)

The stage turns to night again, crickets and stars and then day again. The mail has been removed from the stage left door. MRS. ELSBETH *in her garden. Mail piling up by her mailbox.*

MRS. ELSBETH. They moved in six months ago. Looked a little different, sounded different. All of us peering through our windows. The Turners used to live there. They had a sign over their door that said. The Turners. First thing they did when they moved in here was take down that sign. Couldn't fit their name on a sign that size. I remember, she was wearing a big sundress and her ankles were swollen. He helped her out of the car. He's very handsome. He's an architect. They left the boy in the back of their car for hours. It was so cold outside. I don't know if they left the car heater on. I don't know if they forgot him out there or if he was being punished. Young boys do make a lot of trouble. And they do have their own ways I'm sure. You want to do things, you want to feel like you have the power. I mean the neighborhood pays for a patrol car. I mean I have a phone. I could call someone...................Tulips. They need so much attention.

> (*She hear dishes being thrown from behind the stage left door. A terrible fight, some screaming, then a large thump against the door.*)

MRS. ELSBETH. (*Ignoring the sounds.*) I wasn't always a tulip kind of girl. I used to adore the daisies if you can believe that. Then Tom and I got into swinging and I found out how much I like to be used and videotaped and I don't know, I just wanted more color in my life.

> (*From the stage right door, comes* MR. RUNIHURA. *A nice looking gentleman in a button down shirt and khaki's. He has a scratch on his face that is bleeding. One of his fists also bleeds. He walks to his mailbox.*)

MR. RUNIHURA. (*Slight accent.*) Hello.

MRS. ELSBETH. Oh, hello.

MR. RUNIHURA. Were you talking to someone?

MRS. ELSBETH. No. I don't think so.

MR. RUNIHURA. You're Mrs. Elsbeth.

MRS. ELSBETH. Why yes, I am. And your Mr. Runi...ni...

MR. RUNIHURA. Runihura. The wife and I have been meaning to have you over.

MRS. ELSBETH. Really. Me?

MR. RUNIHURA. And your husband, of course.

MRS. ELSBETH. Oh yes.

> (*She gets up from her gardening and walks parallel to* MR. RUNIHURA.)

MR. RUNIHURA. We've been so busy with the baby.

MRS. ELSBETH. Tom's been traveling a lot lately.

MR. RUNIHURA. But we're neighbors and Enjoolie and I want so very much to meet everyone. Mrs. Merriweather.

MRS. ELSBETH. Rose.

MR. RUNIHURA. You. Your husband. The Clarks across the street.

MRS. ELSBETH. You had a party the other day.

MR. RUNIHURA. Party?

MRS. ELSBETH. A party. The, uh, balloons.

MR. RUNIHURA. Balloons?

MRS. ELSBETH. On your mailbox.

> (MR. RUNIHURA *looks at his mailbox. a dark look comes over him for a moment, then he looks up and smiles again.*)

MR. RUNIHURA. Oh yes. It was my son's birthday.

> (*He pops all of the balloons.*)

MRS. ELSBETH. I was going to ask you about your son. The other day, he looked hungry, he…

MR. RUNIHURA. Do you have any children, Mrs. Elsbeth?

MRS. ELSBETH. Me? No. Tom and I haven't had any yet.

MR. RUNIHURA. That's such a shame. The only reason to live, children. Beautiful lawn you have there, Mrs. Elsbeth. The greenest I've ever seen.

> (*He turns and heads into his house.*)

MRS. ELSBETH. Oh well it's the feeder. It's…oh yes…nice meeting you, Mr. Runihura…

> (*He slams his door shut.*)

VOICE OF MR. RUNIHURA. WHERE ARE YOU, YOU LITTLE SHIT!

> (*We hear some screaming and yelling from behind the stage left door. Furniture overturned. Then silence. MRS. ELSBETH looks away from the door and over to her mailbox.*)

MRS. ELSBETH. (*To the audience.*) I got a postcard in the mail two weeks ago. The postcard was addressed to me, Louise Elsbeth and on it someone had typed the words, "help us."

> (MRS. MERRIWEATHER *comes out of the center stage door.*)

MRS. MERRIWEATHER. Good morning, Louise.

MRS. ELSBETH. Good morning Rose.

MRS. MERRIWEATHER. Beautiful day.

MRS. ELSBETH. Isn't it?

> (*MRS. MERRIWEATHER looks at* MRS. ELSBETH's *mail box. Then look at her own mail, which includes a package wrapped in black plastic.*)

MRS. ELSBETH. Anything good today?

MRS. MERRIWEATHER. (*Indicating the package.*) Maybe. How's Tom?

MRS. ELSBETH. Coming back soon. We should have drinks.

MRS. MERRIWEATHER. We should.

MRS. ELSBETH. Bring over your little package if you want.

MRS. MERRIWEATHER. Got to see if it works first.

> (*Screaming and yelling begins again behind the stage left door. The voice of a boy, repeating the word "stop." MRS. MERRIWEATHER and MRS. ELSBETH try to ignore it.*)

MRS. ELSBETH. Sorry about the chocolates.

MRS. MERRIWEATHER. Oh please. Hot flashes. It was me.

MRS. ELSBETH. No, it was me.

MRS. MERRIWEATHER. You're a love.

> (MRS. MERRIWEATHER *goes inside her house.* MRS. ELSBETH *back to her garden.*)

MRS. ELSBETH. I got another postcard the next day from the same address. Help us. You'd think she'd have the courtesy to come on by and knock. You'd think she'd at least want to save the postage.

> (*Screaming then, extremely loud thumps against the stage left door. Then some moaning.*)

MRS. ELSBETH. I don't normally get that kind of mail. Most of the time it's just bills, and catalogues, and magazines… They keep coming…the postcards. More of them everyday. Different addresses.

> (MRS. ELSBETH *picks up a few postcards, reads the addresses.*)

MRS. ELSBETH. Rwanda…North Korea…the Sudan…Kashmir. The same typeface. The same two words.

> (*Blood pours out from the top of the stage left door, running down the face and onto the floor.*)

MRS. ELSBETH. These things beyond the garden. They happen so far away. You want to do something about it…Tom and I are trying to have a baby. It's a lot of work.

> (*We hear the sound of sprinklers.*)

MRS. ELSBETH. The feeder makes the grass grow so fast. You practically have to mow it each day…

> (*Lights OUT.*)

End of Play

LISTENERS
by Jane Martin

BIOGRAPHY

A Kentuckian, Jane Martin first came to national attention for *Talking With*, a collection of monologues premiering in Actors Theatre of Louisville's 1982 Humana Festival of New American Plays. Since its New York premiere at Manhattan Theatre Club in 1982, *Talking With* has been performed around the world, winning the Best Foreign Play of the Year Award in Germany from *Theatre Heute* magazine. Her other work includes: *Vital Signs, Cementville, Keely And Du* (Pulitzer Prize nominee; 1994 American Theatre Critics Association Best New Play Award), *Jack And Jill* (1997 American Theatre Critics Association Best New Play Award); *Anton In Show Business* (2001 American Theatre Critics/Steinberg Principal Citation), *Mr. Bundy*, and *Flaming Guns Of The Purple Sage*. *Good Boys* premiered at Guthrie Theater in 2002. *Flags* was co-produced by Guthrie Theater and Mixed Blood in 2004, and her most recent work, *Sez She*, premiered at Illusion Theatre in April 2006.

ACKNOWLEDGMENTS

Listeners premiered at the Humana Festival of New American Plays in April 2006. It was directed by Jon Jory with the following cast and staff:

ELEANOR	Melinda Wade
RALPH	Mark Mineart
WALTER	Jay Russell
LISTENERS	Tom Coiner
	Lee Dolson
	Ben Friesen
	Aaron Alika Patinio

Scenic Designer	Paul Owen
Costume Designers	John P. White
	Stacy Squires
Lighting Designer	Paul Werner
Sound Designer	Benjamin Marcum
Properties Designer	Mark Walston
Stage Manager	Debra Anne Gasper
Assistant Stage Manager	Heather Fields
Assistant Stage Manager	Paul Mills Holmes
Dramaturg	Julie Felise Dubiner
Assistant Dramaturg	Joanna K. Donehower

Listeners was commissioned by Actors Theatre of Louisville.

CAST OF CHARACTERS
ELEANOR
RALPH
WALTER
VOICES FROM PHONE COLLAGE

SETTING
Somewhere.

Jay Russell, Mark Mineart; and Melinda Wade
in *Listeners*

30th Annual Humana Festival of New American Plays
Actors Theatre of Louisville, 2006
Photo by Harlan Taylor

LISTENERS

A home, represented by a single contemporary sofa and doorframe. Elsewhere, outside the "home" are three metal tables and chairs where men in dark blue suits and red presidential ties sit with large earphones, listening intently. In the blackout, we hear overlapping snatches of inane phone conversations.

WOMAN. Grandma, it's Lilian, I just wanted to wish you…

MAN. …was the corporate secretary in charge organizing the board meetings and…

CHILD. I miss you, Daddy, will you bring me a…

2ND WOMAN. You think I care? I don't care. All that talk is just…

2ND MAN. …have no idea what the article means by "insurgent," so tell Jack…

WOMAN. …something called "left weave" jeans and I'm guessing the Gap, but I…

3RD MAN. Yeah, well if you could meet us in Aruba, I know Ellen would be pleased as…

CHILD. …but you'll miss my birthday, and I want…

2ND WOMAN. …a small bag of sand from the Bay of Pigs, but who's going to…

MAN. No, not Hamas, Hamas is…

3RD WOMAN. …completely volcanic…

WOMAN. So love and kisses, Grandma…

MAN. …as far as I know, but you know me and what I know, well, hell, what anybody knows…are you still there?

(End of phone collage.)

(Lights up on ELEANOR LEFTWICH, a neatly dressed woman in her late 30s. She is on the phone.)

ELEANOR. And afterwards you fold in the beaten egg, one quarter cup of chopped chives, a touch of Tabasco, bake at low heat and…

(Two men also in dark blue suits and red ties appear at ELEANOR's door. The smaller, WALTER, incongruously wears a porkpie hat. They knock.)

ELEANOR. Oh…uhmm, sorry, Mom. You just stay right there for two shakes of a lamb's tail. (*Opens door.*) Hello.

RALPH. (*Naturally pronounced "RAFE."*) Hello.

ELEANOR. I—

191

RALPH. We—

ELEANOR. Are—?

RALPH. Actually—

ELEANOR. Could—?

RALPH. Absolutely—

WALTER. (*Bugs Bunny.*) What's up, Doc?

RALPH. Oh, let me guess. You are Eleanor Leftwich?

ELEANOR. I am.

RALPH. (*Delighted.*) Fantastic. I'm Rafe…

WALTER. Ralph.

RALPH. Rafe Aural, and allow me to say, Eleanor, I'm an admirer.

ELEANOR. An admirer?

RALPH. Your cries, murmurs and, might I say, exhortations during anal and oral sex are a treasured part of my day.

ELEANOR. I beg your pardon.

WALTER. (*Bogart.*) That's out of our hands, sweetheart.

RALPH. (*Gives* WALTER *a little hit.*) Silly. (*Brushes past* ELEANOR *into the room.*) Oh, this is lovely! Isn't this lovely, Walter? I could tell from your extensive vocabulary that you would have exquisite taste.

ELEANOR. But how…

WALTER. "But how…"

RALPH. Yes, we have our little ways. (*Holding up phone.*) Forgotten something?

ELEANOR. Oh, I'm on the phone.

RALPH. (*Holding it away from her.*) Well, if we know anything, we know that, don't we, Walter? Walter opines, by the way, that Tabasco really overpowers the recipe in an unhelpful way. (*Speaks into phone.*) Something's come up, dear, but she'll be back to you…

RALPH / WALTER. …In two shakes of a little lamb's tail.

　　　　(WALTER *snaps cell phone shut.*)

ELEANOR. You cut off my call.

RALPH. I did, didn't I? That was naughty, wasn't it, Walter?

WALTER. Very naughty, Ralph.

RALPH. Rafe.

WALTER. Ralph.

ELEANOR. Excuse me, I haven't a clue who you are?

RALPH. (*To* WALTER.) She hasn't a clue. Leftwich, you're a stitch. Honeybabydarlin'pet, you simply have to keep up here! All the little clicks, the little whirrs and

RALPH / WALTER. faint beeps?

RALPH. The nice man the city sent to check your walls for killer mold?

WALTER. (*It was he.*) Ta-da!

RALPH. Land sakes alive, we're your Listeners, girl.

ELEANOR. Listeners?

RALPH. (*Shaking a warning finger.*) Oh, there are some saucy citizens simply slathering for a good listening to!

ELEANOR. I—

RALPH. Just teasing.

WALTER. (*John Wayne.*) Just teasing, citizen.

ELEANOR. I'm afraid you'll have to leave.

RALPH. Ah, I see…but really we mustn't, we can't, we've been assigned.

WALTER. Assigned!

RALPH. Assigned. Think of it this way, Eleanor Leftwich, consider us an instrument of increased intimacy.

RALPH / WALTER. It's a lonely life, (*Cont. for* RALPH *only.*) Eleanor.

RALPH. Who really, really listens to us? Who truly wants to hear us, know us, take us seriously,

RALPH / WALTER. hang on our words—

RALPH. —regard our emotionally chaotic and badly researched opinions as having heft, value, even profundity? Family, lovers, co-workers—they don't really hear us, do they? They are locked in the hell of self, Eleanor. Sadly, only your government cares.

ELEANOR. You heard me having sex?

RALPH. (*Reassuring.*) Really, it was almost as good as being there.

ELEANOR. But isn't that illegal?

    (RALPH *and* WALTER *laugh merrily.*)

RALPH. Time for the survey.

    (WALTER *flips open a folder and clears his throat.*)

RALPH. Go it, Walter.

WALTER. Father, Shem Leftwich?

    (*The survey section is done quick tempo.*)

ELEANOR. Slaughtered in Viet Nam on behalf of the domino theory.

WALTER. Uncle, Lowell Leftwich?

ELEANOR. Butchered in Panama, lest they should invade us.

WALTER. Auntie Crystal Leftwich, battlefield nurse?

ELEANOR. Cut down in Grenada insuring hegemony.

WALTER. Brother, Lefty Leftwich?

ELEANOR. Blown to smithereens, Desert Storm, guaranteeing full misogyny for all Kuwaitis.

WALTER. Brother Al?

RALPH. Lovely vocal register, brother Al.

WALTER. Lovely.

RALPH. Lovely.

ELEANOR. Friendly fire, Afghanistan.

WALTER. Brother Joe?

ELEANOR. Beheaded, castrated, dismembered in Iraq, insuring democracy and lollipops for all Islamic peoples.

RALPH. (*Thrilled.*) Good show, Eleanor, well done. Kudos for clarity. Haven't you just come through in the clutch?!

WALTER. Dabba dabba do.

RALPH. Sooooooo…

WALTER. Sooooooo…

RALPH. Our technologies have sensibly identified you, Eleanor, as a valued citizen who just might be a little cranky. And technologically speaking…

WALTER. You're a big fuckin' winner.

ELEANOR. I am?

RALPH. You are. Your mother, your friends, that sweet State Farm agent, whose untrammeled id has given Walter and me so much erotic pleasure, have elicited only idle interest, a little credit card browsing, the odd security check. But you, my intriguing Eleanor, if I may call you so, have hit the big time, a veritable coup, your own personal Listeners…us! Take our luggage to the guest room, Walter, down the hall, second left I believe.

ELEANOR. You hear everything I say here?

RALPH. We hear everything anyone says, Ms. Leftwich, anyone of the slightest interest.

ELEANOR. And someone hears you?

RALPH. Oh, Walter hears me, don't you, Walter?

WALTER. You wascally wabbit.

ELEANOR. And someone hears Walter?

RALPH. Agent Arthur in Bangor, Maine.

ELEANOR. And Arthur?

WALTER. Ziggy in New Rochelle.

ELEANOR. And Ziggy?

RALPH. Darlene in Cuttlefish, Kansas.

ELEANOR. And Darlene?

RALPH. Ryan in Tucumcari.

ELEANOR. And Ryan?

RALPH. Heard in Burbank.

WALTER. Who's heard in Baltimore.

RALPH. Who's heard in Bethesda.

WALTER. Who's heard at the C. I. of A.

RALPH. Who's heard in the war room.

RALPH / WALTER. Who's heard by…

RALPH. (*Stops. Speaks coyly.*) Oh, I don't know…

WALTER. He doesn't know.

RALPH. —heard perhaps by he who—

RALPH / WALTER. let us say—

RALPH. —hears all.

ELEANOR. (*Amazed.*) He listens?

RALPH. In the limitless soaring freedoms of democratic process, it is the bounden duty of he who serves only at our pleasure to attend to the fall of a sparrow or the infinitesimal vibration of the Monarch's wing, dear Eleanor.

ELEANOR. (*Enthralled.*) So it's not inconceivable I could speak to him?

RALPH. Not inconceivable.

WALTER. The off-chance.

ELEANOR. So I'm not powerless? I could speak my heart, even here in the sanctuary of my home, and he who hears all might hear me?

RALPH. He might.

WALTER. He will.

RALPH. He cares.

(ELEANOR *looks up.*)

RALPH. Oh. Oh my. Do I espy upon your ivory cheek the silver tracery of a tear? Have you an unspoken sentiment, Eleanor?

ELEANOR. I can truly be heard? I never dreamed I could be heard?

RALPH. (*Shocked.*) Good heavens, Eleanor, you're not a tattooed tribeswoman of some dusky people's Banana Republic. You are the admired citizen of the most advanced society in the history of the world! Let freedom ring! Go it, Walter.

WALTER. (*Putting on earphones that have been around his neck.*) 5, 4, 3, 2, 1… (*Gives her the go signal.*)

ELEANOR. Now?

(WALTER *again signals "go."*)

ELEANOR. How should I address him?

WALTER. You swingin' dick.

RALPH. Walter! No honorifics necessary.

ELEANOR. (*Looking up.*) Sir? It's me, Citizen Leftwich.

(*A red light goes on at the desk of a Listener.*)

I mean, I'm nobody in particular, just a dental technician, sidelining in a little discreet hair removal, but I guess if…well, if you're really listening…

(*Another red light goes on.*)

I guess I'd really like to say…

(RALPH *gestures encouragingly.*)

Well, I'm kind of getting the feeling…

(*He gestures again.*)

…that you've fucked us all.

(*An alarm goes off in the distance. A curtain opens, and we see a man on a pedestal, suited as the others, in silhouette.*)

You've butchered our youth for dreams of empire, squandered our children's patrimony, enriched at untold social cost the inconceivably rich, battered our economy, ballooned our deficit, fractured our safety nets, demeaned the values that gave us pride in a national identity, fattened our cynicism…

(*A big red light.*)

…endangered our public education, made quislings of our librarians, dismantled our privacy, manipulated our fears, detained and tortured and bombed and killed men and women and children, appalled the world…

(*The silhouette figure drops his arm as a signal, and a red ring lights up on* RALPH's *hand.*)

…and all, all, all out of some blind, groping, self-serving, economic, geopolitical, theocratic impulse, untouched by real thought or empathy, at the behest of the entitled and corporate…

(RALPH *signals* WALTER, *who moves behind her.* ELEANOR *isn't focused on them.* RALPH *takes out and prepares a hypodermic.*)

…that can only end in the poisoning, beyond imagination, of our humanity and our poor earth, you stupid, boorish, vulgar, avaricious, heartless, shallow, incomprehensible, smug, smarmy, illiterate prick!!

(WALTER *grabs her from behind, covering her mouth.* RALPH *speaks admiringly while he administers the injection. She struggles but, by the end of* RALPH's *speech, goes limp.*)

RALPH. Well, by heaven, I'd have to say that's damned good listening! Shapely, passionate, indelible rhetoric, nicely phrased in its indictments. I stamp that "superior" in anyone's blue-book, Eleanor. Downright thrilling and absorbing and a by-God testament to why I got into the business.

(WALTER *releases the body, and it crumples to the floor.*)

RALPH. Good heavens, what a nasty fall.

WALTER. Kaput.

RALPH. No! You don't imagine a woman so vital and incisive with lovely breasts and a social conscience has taken her own life?

WALTER. Could be.

(*Scatters pills beside her and drops the bottle.*)

RALPH. Despair is a dangerous thing. But she wasn't boring. I enjoyed our repartee.

WALTER. Yeah, she had a mouth on her.

RALPH. Sometimes an assignment is just far too brief, Walter.

WALTER. Too brief. (*Goes for the luggage.*)

RALPH. The problem is, of course, it all ends in paperwork. (*A eulogy.*) You are, or rather were, Eleanor Leftwich, living proof that a nation's purpose can only truly be defined by an articulate and loyal opposition.

(WALTER *returns.*)

RALPH. Her sun has set while it yet was day. Sleep, oh sleep, our daughter of the republic. A scrap of scripture, Walter.

(*They stand over her, heads bowed.*)

WALTER. (*Stentorian.*) "And I say, tell it not in Gath, nor publish it in the streets of Askelon."

RALPH. You said a mouthful there, Lord. Tempus fugit, Walter. Stitch in time saves nine. (*They pick up the bags.*) Set the moral compass, bosun.

WALTER. (*Woody Woodpecker laugh, followed by Porky Pig.*) That's all, folks.

RALPH. Never all, Walter, never all. Democracy without freedoms. Still only a work in progress.

WALTER. Getting closer though.

RALPH. Not beyond our reach.

(*They are out of the house and exiting.*)

RALPH. Coming soon to an address near you.

(*Lights are dimming, shards and whispers of phone conversations rise, [see beginning phone collage].*)

WALTER. Well said, Ralph.

RALPH. Rafe.

WALTER. Ralph.

RALPH. Rafe. Up Donner, up Blitzen. Now flyaway,

RALPH / WALTER. —flyaway, flyaway all!

(*They are gone. Only the body and the voices remain. Lights out.*)

WALTER. (*Woody Woodpecker laugh.*)

End of Play

HOTEL CASSIOPEIA
by Charles L. Mee

BIOGRAPHY

Charles L. Mee has written *Big Love* and *True Love* and *First Love*, *bobrauschenbergamerica* and *Limonade tous les Jours*, *Orestes 2.0* and *Trojan Women A Love Story*, and *Summertime* and *Wintertime* among other plays—all of them available on the internet at www.charlesmee.org. Among other awards, he is the recipient of the lifetime achievement award from the American Academy of Arts and Letters. His work is made possible by the support of Richard B. Fisher and Jeanne Donovan Fisher.

ACKNOWLEDGMENTS

Hotel Cassiopeia premiered at the Humana Festival of New American Plays in March 2006. It was directed by Anne Bogart with the following cast and staff:

JOSEPH	Barney O'Hanlon
WAITRESS	Michi Barall
ASTRONOMER	Stephen Webber
HERBALIST	Leon Ingulsrud
PHARMACIST	J. Ed Araiza
ALLEGRA	Ellen Lauren
MOTHER	Akiko Aizawa
Scenic Designer	Neil Patel
Costume Designer	James Schuette
Lighting Designer	Brian H. Scott
Sound Designer	Darron L. West
Projection Designer	Gregory King
Properties Designer	Mark Walston
Company Stage Manager	Elizabeth Moreau
Production Assistants	Gabel Eiben
	Danielle Monica Long
Dramaturg	Adrien-Alice Hansel
Assistant Dramaturgs	Joanna K. Donehower
	Jamie Bragg
Directing Assistant	Irene Scaturro
Managing Director	Megan Wanlass Szalla

CAST OF CHARACTERS
JOSEPH
WAITRESS
ASTRONOMER
HERBALIST
PHARMACIST
ALLEGRA
MOTHER

A NOTE ON THE TEXT
This piece was inspired by the work of Joseph Cornell, and incorporates texts taken from his diaries and letters edited by Mary Ann Caws, some of his favorite movies, Deborah Solomon's biography *Utopia Parkway,* the writings of members of a Cornell workshop, especially Heidi Schreck, Jenny Sandman, Kristen Palmer, and Karen Hartman, the writings of Colette, and the treasures of the internet.

EDITORS' NOTE
In the interest of preserving both the flow of the play and indicating where changes of scene occurred in the original production, stage directions that open a scene are not in parentheses. Stage directions internal to the action of each scene are in parentheses.

Cast
in *Hotel Cassiopeia*

30th Annual Humana Festival of New American Plays
Actors Theatre of Louisville, 2006
Photo by Harlan Taylor

HOTEL CASSIOPEIA

A wall of stars:
the constellations
or the moon
or a vast star map of the cosmos covers the back wall
(or should it look like a Pollack painting?
splashes and droplets of white paint.).

We hear Satie's Gymnopedies *on the piano.*

A young woman on a bicycle
or a life-size paper cutout of a young woman on a bicycle
or a paper cutout of a giant owl
arcs across the sky
while he speaks.

JOSEPH. (*Sitting at a cafe table.*) There are days that I will have
a few donuts
a caramel pudding
two cups of Dutch process cocoa all milk,
white bread,
peanut butter and peach jam
a Milky Way candy bar
some chocolate eclairs
a half-dozen icing cakes from Bay West
a peach pie (6 cents.)
and a prune twist
and, on other days:
cottage cheese, toast,
bologna, jello,
fresh baked shortcake with creamy chocolate icing
Kool Aid
brownies and cherry Coke
a cinnamon donut
homemade coffee cake
the pink centers of Huntley and Palmer shortcake cookies
pancakes

> (*As he speaks a wall rises up slowly behind him*
> *of windowed cubby holes*
> *of the sort that once covered the walls of New York City's*
> *Bickford's Cafeterias,*

CHARLES L. MEE

each cubby hole containing,
behind its closed, windowed door, one item,
such as a sandwich, a piece of pie, a glass of milk.

A WAITRESS *enters, drying her hands on a towel,*
and takes out pad and pencil.)

WAITRESS. What will you have?

JOSEPH. What will I have?
I don't know.

WAITRESS. You're not hungry?

> *(Gesturing with her pencil towards the little windows.)*

Well, then,
I've got your crested cockatiel
I've got your honey colored seashells
I've got your deep sea blue sand
your dancing confetti
a toy metal horse
very nicely corroded
lead with greenish and reddish coloring
after it's been lying about washed in the sand and sea

JOSEPH. What will I do with these?

WAITRESS. You'll make a life.
Have you got a life?

JOSEPH. I'll have a caramel pudding
and a cherry Coke.

> *(The* ASTRONOMER *enters, stands to the side.)*

WAITRESS. Right.
Will you be having the whipped cream?

JOSEPH. Sure. Sure.
I'll have the whipped cream.

> *(She leaves;*
>
> *he looks after her as she leaves;*
>
> *the* ASTRONOMER *takes a seat at a nearby table*
> *several others enter and join him.)*

THE ASTRONOMER. You see, you'll be wanting to go slow with girls
because

THE HERBALIST. Because you can scare a girl

THE ASTRONOMER. You can scare anyone really.

THE HERBALIST. You can scare anyone.

THE ASTRONOMER. And you don't want always
to be looking at women out the window

THE HERBALIST. The passersby on the sidewalk.

THE ASTRONOMER. Because this can give a bad impression.

THE HERBALIST. You can scare a person.

THE PHARMACIST. Do you ever take a girl home with you?

JOSEPH. Yes.

THE HERBALIST. What do you do with her?

JOSEPH. Well.
We sit in the kitchen usually.

THE ASTRONOMER. Yes?

JOSEPH. Usually, we have tea.

THE HERBALIST. Tea?

THE PHARMACIST. That's all?

JOSEPH. And I will open the window,
so the birds can fly in
and eat crumbs from the kitchen table.

THE ASTRONOMER. Eat crumbs.

JOSEPH. Yes.

THE PHARMACIST. During the summer.

JOSEPH. Yes, well,
yes.

THE ASTRONOMER. During the winter?

JOSEPH. Well. Yes.

THE ASTRONOMER. I see.

JOSEPH. Usually, people like this.

THE HERBALIST. And then they leave?

JOSEPH. Yes. Well, by then it will be late afternoon.
So it's time to leave.

THE ASTRONOMER. Tea and crumbs.

THE PHARMACIST. Still, I like an herbal tea.

THE ASTRONOMER. A peppermint tea.

THE PHARMACIST. Or a tissane.

THE ASTRONOMER. Something made with roots and berries.

(JOSEPH, *ever a voyeur,*
watches them as they continue the conversation.)

THE HERBALIST. I would say
probably
I would have to say
licorice root
that would be my favorite root
because it contains a
thick astringent mucilage
with a little aroma
which is a very good pectoral.

THE PHARMACIST. A pectoral?

THE HERBALIST. Very good for illnesses of the chest and lungs.

THE PHARMACIST. Ah.

THE HERBALIST. And that happens to be
my own personal
preoccupation.

THE PHARMACIST. I see.

THE HERBALIST. Whereas I don't know
for you…

THE PHARMACIST. For me it would be
the hawthorn
which used to be used always
to decorate the front door on May Day

THE HERBALIST. Oh, well
but of course
also it was said to invite death indoors.

THE PHARMACIST. No.

THE HERBALIST. Yes.

THE PHARMACIST. No.

THE HERBALIST. I am afraid so.
I mean, excuse me, but
I am an herbalist.

THE PHARMACIST. Still.

THE HERBALIST. No. There is no getting around it.

THE ASTRONOMER. I would have to say
my favorite herb

would be the common quince.

THE HERBALIST. Indeed?

THE ASTRONOMER. Oh, yes,
because for two reasons
you know
it was once thought to be
the forbidden fruit of the Garden of Eden.

THE HERBALIST. I knew that, yes.

THE ASTRONOMER. And so it was served
at wedding feasts in ancient Rome.

THE HERBALIST. Of course.

THE PHARMACIST. Of course.

THE ASTRONOMER. So, to me,
it is the sexiest herb.

THE HERBALIST. Fruit.

THE ASTRONOMER. I beg your pardon?

THE HERBALIST. Fruit. It is a fruit.
Not an herb.

THE ASTRONOMER. Oh yes, fruit.
I thought we could mention either herbs or fruits.

THE HERBALIST. Well, the conversation was about herbs.

THE ASTRONOMER. And I brought the conversation around
to include fruits.

THE HERBALIST. If you are not going to stick to the point
I'm afraid
this is not my kind of conversation.

> (*He leaves;*
> *the others look around*
> *and, one by one, feeling uncomfortable,*
> *they decide to leave, too.*)

> *a crescent moon through the top of bare branches*
> *a star above it*
> *clear, fresh beauty*
> *night blue*
> *gently faded*

> JOSEPH *remains at his table.*

> *As the Bickford's windows slowly disappear*
> *a girl in tights and a tutu sings.*

These are original lyrics,
for which there is no music.

BALLERINA. The good lord makes both kinds of flowers
The good ones and the evil
The good flowers are our lifelong friends
The evil our undoing

The tawny gray, the regal royal
The creeping and the bloody red
The kidney-shaped
The wrinkle-leaved
The sugar-bearing, evergreen

White-haired scarlet leaf
Yellow-green serpentine
The bristle-like horney-headed
Helmet shaped ripening fruit

Smooth spiral
Openmouthed
The star burst
Winter flowering

> *A paper cutout cockatiel descends from the flies*
> *and an old newspaper ad for the Hotel Eden—*
> *partly obliterated by big splotches of white paint—*
> *is projected.*
>
> BALLERINA *comes for tea.*
> *She is carrying a book on erotic art*
> *and a mocha cake.*

BALLERINA. Joseph?

JOSEPH. Yes?

> *(He stands.)*

BALLERINA. Were you expecting me?

> *(He takes several steps backward*
> *unable to help himself*
> *in his embarrassment and shyness.)*

JOSEPH. Oh. Yes. Expecting you.

BALLERINA. Had you forgotten I was coming today?

JOSEPH. No. Oh, no.
I've been looking forward to it.

> *(He stands motionless.)*

BALLERINA. I've brought some cake.

JOSEPH. Ah. Cake.
I love cake.

BALLERINA. Chocolate mocha cake.

JOSEPH. Chocolate mocha cake.

BALLERINA. Shall I get some plates?

JOSEPH. Oh. Yes. I'll get them.

> (*He returns with plates.*)

Shall I cut the cake?

BALLERINA. Thank you.

How are you?

> (*He cuts the cake very carefully
> as he speaks.*)

JOSEPH. How I am.
Yes.
Well.
Some days
I will wake up in the morning
feeling serene it may be
having a vision of the house
trees, grass,
well, bushes in flower
in the early morning air
forever inviolate
this is so much better than the mornings of anxiety
the nervousness
feelings of reversal
sadness
so much so
sometimes
I will have to sit on the edge of my bed
for a few hours
waiting for the time of lifting
waiting for the time of evenness
the time of naturalness
arriving in the mental clearing
which also
on some mornings
I can induce
by spending some time standing at the sink

shaving
taking some time dressing
and then
if I make a trip down to the water
the colony of beautiful laughing gulls
I will be free of confusion
migrating birds—scattered drifts of them heading South
way up like specks against pink glow
salvaging these moments
I think of
celestial blue heavens, golden constellations,
the Milky Way star dust
the girl seen through the window of Bickford's cafeteria
a young girl
sharp features
pleasant expression after a very hot working day
black dress
such gracious qualities of serenity
that I felt ashamed of any inner complaining
and then
the sustained mood of calmness on returning home
this is OK
and the evening
the smell of night on a scarf or a handkerchief

What I saw today
I saw
thru the cellar window
the squirrel and the catbird
a robin at the bird table under the quince tree
with its petals falling
the rose pink of azalea bush in full bloom

BALLERINA. I'm going to wear a newspaper hat
because the sun is so bright.

JOSEPH. Yes.

I have some pictures.

　　　　(*He shows her.*)

BALLERINA. What will you do with them?

JOSEPH. I will keep them because…

because then I will have them.

　　　　(*We do not see his* MOTHER
　　　　but only hear her voice say.)

HIS MOTHER'S VOICE. Joseph?

JOSEPH. Yes.

HIS MOTHER'S VOICE. Did you have a guest?

JOSEPH. Yes, mother.

(BALLERINA *leaves*.)

HIS MOTHER'S VOICE. Did she wash her hands at the sink?

JOSEPH. I think she did.

HIS MOTHER'S VOICE. And dry her hands on the dish towel?

JOSEPH. Yes.

HIS MOTHER'S VOICE. Then you must boil the dish towel.

JOSEPH. Yes, mother.

> *A black and white film flickers on the back wall—*
> *the 1945 movie* To Have and Have Not,
> *starring Humphrey Bogart and Lauren Bacall,*
> *and* JOSEPH *speaks in sync with Bogart.*

INTERVIEWER. Browning, Marie. American. Age twenty-two. How long have you been in Port au France?

MARIE. I arrived by plane this afternoon.

INTERVIEWER. Residence?

MARIE. Hotel Marquis.

INTERVIEWER. Where did you come from?

MARIE. Trinidad, Port of Spain.

INTERVIEWER. And before that, from where Mademoiselle? From home, perhaps?

MARIE. No. From Brazil, Rio.

INTERVIEWER. Alone?

MARIE. Yes.

INTERVIEWER. Why did you get off here?

MARIE. To buy a new hat.

INTERVIEWER. What?

MARIE. To buy a new hat. Read the label, maybe you'll believe me then.

INTERVIEWER. I never doubted you, Mademoiselle. It was only your tone that was objectionable. I'll ask you again. Why did you get off here?

MARIE. Because I didn't have money enough to go any further.

INTERVIEWER. That's better. Where were you when the shooting occurred?

MARIE. I was—

HARRY. You don't have to answer that stuff.

INTERVIEWER. Shut up, you.

HARRY. Don't answer it.

INTERVIEWER. I told you to shut up.

HARRY. Go ahead, slap me.

INTERVIEWER. Come come, Capitan. This is not a brawl. We merely wish to get to the bottom of this affair.

HARRY. You'll never do it by slapping people around. That's bad luck.

INTERVIEWER. Well, we shall see. If we need to question you further, you will be available at the hotel?

HARRY. Well, I don't know how I'm gonna go any place when you have my passport and all my money.

INTERVIEWER. Well your passport will be returned to you. And as for the money, if it is yours, that will arrange itself in good time.

HARRY. Would you suggest I see the American consulate and have him help you arrange it?

INTERVIEWER. That is your privilege. By the way, what are your sympathies?

HARRY. Minding my own business.

INTERVIEWER. May I—

HARRY. And I don't need any advice about continuing to do it either.

INTERVIEWER. Good night, Capitan.

HARRY. Come on, let's get out of this.

MARIE. Say, I don't understand all of this. After all, I just got here.

HARRY. You landed right in the middle of a small war.

MARIE. What's it all about?

HARRY. The boys we just left, joined with Vichy. You know what that is?

MARIE. Vaguely.

HARRY. Well, they got the Navy behind them, I think you saw that carrier in the harbor?

MARIE. Yeah.

HARRY. And the other fellows, the ones they were shooting at, they're the free French. You know what they are.

MARIE. It's not getting any clearer.

HARRY. Well anyway, most of the people on the island, the natives, the patriots, are for De Gaulle, but so far they haven't been able to do anything about it.

EDDIE. Harry! Harry! Are we in trouble?

HARRY. No, Eddie.

EDDIE. Well, I seen them guys pick you up and I was scared.

HARRY. Well, everything is all right. You go on back and get some sleep.

EDDIE. Well, I'd have got you out, Harry. You know me.

HARRY. Yeah, I know you Eddie. You go on back to the boat.

EDDIE. Say, Harry could ya—

HARRY. No.

EDDIE. But—

HARRY. No more tonight, Eddie. Beat it.

> *A black and white photograph—*
> *with a musky light blue overlay—*
> *of a painting of a Renaissance princess*
> *is projected on the back wall.*
>
> *A huge yellow cork ball.*
>
> *A train whistle quietly*
> *the sound of a locomotive.*
> *JOSEPH goes to his brother ROBERT*
> *who lies in bed*
> *huddled against the wall.*

JOSEPH. Robert?
Robert?
May I bring you anything?
I will care for you, Robert
I will care for you
I will care for you and care for you forever
and not just because I'm your brother
but because I love you.
you will never be left alone
because I will always be here for you
I will be here for you forever
you don't need to worry
you never need to worry

you will be warm enough
there will be things for you to eat
and I will talk to you
so you won't be uninterested in your life
I will talk to you about the things I see
what I have done
where I have gone during the day
the pharmacy

>   (*He talks and talks*
>   *until* ROBERT *falls to sleep.*)

(I took the 7 train today from Queens to Manhattan
and I went to Bickford's cafeteria on 42nd Street.)
I had a ringside seat by the window
at Bickford's cafeteria today
the June Dairy truck
unloading into the basement in front of the plate glass window
a girl fixing her white kerchief and hair
a girl with a red scarf, well groomed
a Chinese girl in a striped sweater, with an exquisite profile
a girl in a white blouse on the escalator
a girl in a pink linen skirt reading a thick tome on Freudian theory

and out the window:
a blonde child looking from out of the window of a taxi
up 8th avenue—

on the sidewalk
a woman with chestnut hair worn down her back—
a light blue sweater—
high cheek bones
boney frame
wan
emaciated

I felt a graciousness and wonder all over again
at the impact of these "meetings"
their sudden significance

the face in the driveway across the street
the sudden surprise and
happy confusion
trying to place it

a surprise blue skirt
white blouse
graceful simplicity with that impact of surprise

Beth—do you remember the girl I call "Beth?"
walking up Lexington avenue about 56th
with a friend
almost sunny

A sunny Tuesday
high noon
the face in the crowd beaming across an intersection
one's own steps turned back

three different appearances of Joyce
in baby blue dress
from endearing to mocking

a group of older girls
and some baby lambs

Courtesy Drugs checkout girl
also seen in Food Shop
piled up hair again
warm light brown corduroy slacks
no socks but the same dreamy docileness
the immense innocence
and beauty of expression
warmth in her contacts in Food shop

Are you asleep, Robert?
Are you asleep?
I will be here all night if there is anything you need.
I will bring you tea in the morning.

Shall I open the window?

> (*And he pulls the covers up to keep* ROBERT *warm
> very carefully, meticulously, tucking the covers in
> just under* ROBERT's *chin.*)
>
> *The faint bluish suggestion of storm clouds
> emerging from tunnel.*

THE HERBALIST. A window is a lovely thing.

> (*Surprised,* JOSEPH *turns his attention at once
> to these people talking—the voyeur again.*)

THE PHARMACIST. A lovely thing.
I myself have a shop with a window
and what I like to put in the window of my shop
I like to put a glass beaker
or a vial of some sort
with an emerald green liquid in it

or a deep blue
because people will look at that

THE HERBALIST. Or sometimes I will put a white clay pipe in my window

THE ASTRONOMER. Or balloons.

THE PHARMACIST. Balloons.
Balloons are always good.

THE HERBALIST. Or…
a forest of twigs
green-leaved twigs
a crescent moon

THE PHARMACIST. crumbled pieces of paper with text on them

THE HERBALIST. fussy old wallpaper with birds on it

THE PHARMACIST. a music box wrapped in paper with old printed text on it

JOSEPH. birds

THE PHARMACIST. a paper cockatiel

THE ASTRONOMER. a whiffle ball

JOSEPH. small wrapped packages
with ribbons on them
packages of words, bits of text

THE ASTRONOMER. the stars
a map of the starry sky
the milky way

JOSEPH. sand

THE PHARMACIST. seashells

JOSEPH. broken glass

THE PHARMACIST. a wine glass

THE PHARMACIST. an engraving of a girl caught in the act of drawing

THE HERBALIST. Renaissance women

THE ASTRONOMER. children
girls
young women
flowering trees

JOSEPH. wooden benches under a quince tree
children's blocks
with pen and ink sketches of owls and ferns and songbirds on them

an 18th century man in a snowcovered forest
a star in a box as though found under a bridge

THE PHARMACIST. This will catch the eye of your typical passerby.
He will be looking in the window
and thinking
if I had one of those
then I'd have a complete life.

> (*A* YOUNG GIRL *enters,*
> *takes hold of the ballet barre*
> *and does her ballet exercises,*
> *while a pianist plays for her.*

> *Or it could be that* CAROLEE SCHNEEMAN *enters naked*
> *with her cello,*
> *sits and plays Bach.*
> *A* GIRL *enters,*
> *takes off her tutu and leotard,*
> *and gets into street clothes*
> *while we listen to the cello.*)

THE ASTRONOMER. There was a time
when you came indoors from the fields
you would expect to see
traces of human occupation everywhere;
a fire still burning in the fireplace
because someone meant to come right back;
a book lying face down on the window seat;
a paintbox
and beside it
a glass
full of cloudy water;
flowers in a cut glass vase;
an unfinished game of solitaire;
a piece of cross-stitching
with a needle and thread stuck in it;
building blocks
or lead soldiers
in the middle of the library floor;
lights left burning in empty rooms.
This was the inner life.

We miss it.

> (*The* GIRL *leaves.*

> *And, if* CAROLEE SCHNEEMAN *was playing the cello,*

then she leaves.)

JOSEPH *sits at the kitchen table,*
his head in his hands,
in despair

while we hear one of Joseph Cornell's favorite singers,
Kathleen Ferrier, sing—
on an old, scratchy, badly preserved record album—

> *Where'er you walk,*
> *cool gales shall fan the glade;*
> *trees where you sit*
> *shall crown into a shade.*
> *Trees where you sit*
> *shall crown into a shade.*

(This song is G.F. Handel, Semele,
and is taken from a CD album called Songs My Father Taught Me,
put out by Gala records.)

A star map is projected,
along with black and white engravings
of the bull of Taurus
and the fish of Pisces
and a huge silver ring is suspended in midair.

*Two artists—*MATTA *and* DUCHAMP—
sit in the garden talking.

MATTA. What sort of future do you see?
what sort of future of humanity and of the world

DUCHAMP. what new forms

MATTA. what new visions

DUCHAMP. this will be the job of the artist

MATTA. this will be the artist's only job

DUCHAMP. because the great changes in the world
the changes of consciousness
the changes of our sense of life itself
will not come from the reasoned arguments
of political scientists or philosophers
but from the visions of artists

MATTA. or is this a promise that has failed, or is failing?
new visions are easy to come up with
but the world goes on ignoring the best of them
the world is littered with so many utopias

DUCHAMP. so many visions of wondrousness
so many great ideas

MATTA. and even ideas that were possible at one time or another
beautiful things

DUCHAMP. or never mind the great ideas
just life itself
the moments of life itself
transporting things
things that will last a moment
and then vanish forever
vanish forever
how does one cherish even what has happened
let alone what might have happened
how does one relish it
how does one relish life itself
it slips through the fingers so quickly

MATTA. this is where the work comes from
if one is an artist
from the shooting stars
water in a stream
a love
a young girl
a woman
a ballerina on the stage
snow flakes
a girl I saw in a window
Hedy Lamarr on a bicycle

JOSEPH. do you know Anne Hoysio
she works in a factory where I work
and I gave her a box that I had made
a box containing
a picture of a dog
a young girl
skyscrapers
a dark blue night sky
lauren bacall behind a glass frame
a ball
and I think she may have liked it
although
the truth is
she has hardly noticed me
before or since

she gave me a Christmas card
which I have saved in a special place
and I take it out from time to time to look at it
because
she was important to me
and her card is signed, you see,
it is signed
"Anne (tester.) (Allied.)"
tester in parentheses
and Allied in parentheses
because
you see
she thought she needed to identify herself to me
she thought our friendship was so insignificant
that I wouldn't know who she was
unless she reminded me
that she was a tester in the factory at Allied
where we worked
her Christmas card was
a sort of business Christmas card
that's how I guess she thought of it
but to me
I've saved it all these years
and I take it out from time to time
not just on Christmas
to look at it
to remember her

> *We see*
> *skyscrapers*
> *a dark blue night sky*
> *lauren bacall behind a glass frame*
> *an orange ball.*

> *Is LAUREN BACALL present?*
> *Or do we only hear her voice?*

JOSEPH. Ms. Bacall, as the character in the movie,
you recall how great it was to be beautiful.
As someone who was a sex symbol yourself,
what are your views on that?

LAUREN. To begin with,
I never thought I was beautiful.
Sorry, guys.
I wish I thought I was divine.

Listen,
I would've been a much happier person
had I been able to look in the mirror and say,
"Gee, you are great!
Love your looks!"

JOSEPH. But,
you were called The Look.
You were the one who said,
"Put your lips together and blow."

LAUREN. Well, I'll go along with that.
But beautiful, no.
In movies, when somebody new comes along,
plays a part and it happens to click,
there is a tremendous exaggeration
about what you are,
what you have,
what this sudden new person is.
In my case, I was announced as the Second Coming.
I was this combination of Garbo and Dietrich
and Bette Davis and Mae West
all rolled into one—
and that was just in one movie.
Now, you know damn well
there was no way I was any of that.
Then came the second movie,
Confidential Agent.
It was a disaster, and I was a disaster,
and they said, "Oh, we made a terrible mistake."

JOSEPH. Ms. Bacall—may I call you Lauren?

LAUREN. I beg your pardon?

JOSEPH. Are there parts of you in Hannah?

LAUREN. Well, I certainly recognize the woman's insecurity
and her fear of what's to become of her
on a personal level.
I recognize certain
confrontational moments that I've had
with my own children.
I know what it feels like
to want your child to do something
and have them not do it.

JOSEPH. You've written about how happy you were

with Humphrey Bogart
and how difficult it was for you after his death

LAUREN. Well, it's been hyped so much.
But, of course,
it was a great love story.
Listen, I lucked out at a very young age;
it's been downhill ever since.
What can I say?
Then again,
I had what some people never have,
so I can't complain.

JOSEPH. Mother, why do you kick girls out of the house?
Why are you rude to them?
Do you not want me to have any friends?
And then, if you let them come
and sit with me in the garden
do you remember the time
you were washing dishes at the sink
and you emptied the dishpan out the kitchen window
and it splashed down like a waterfall
and soaked the girl who was talking to me in the garden
why did you do this?

> *He is in a corkmaker's shop*
>
> *an immense white-painted cork ball descends from the flies*
> *and whirls of wire—as though watch springs—*
> *and from beneath the stage rises*
> *a huge cordial glass with a turquoise egg suspended in it—*
> *or blue sand fills it half-way.*

JOSEPH. I am looking for a....
a present

CORKMAKER. For a girl?

JOSEPH. For someone.

CORKMAKER. But is it a girl?
That is to say, do you want something for a girl
or for a man?

JOSEPH. for my brother

CORKMAKER. I see. And what is it you would like?

JOSEPH. what do you have?

CORKMAKER. I have a little train you can wind up
that goes around a track

and a...

JOSEPH. do you have a clock?

CORKMAKER. a clock

JOSEPH. yes

CORKMAKER. we don't have clocks
what would your brother do with a clock?

JOSEPH. I would like a clock for myself
because
sometimes it seems to me
my life is going by so quickly
and I don't know what is happening
I think
if I could slow it down
I would notice it
I would feel OK about it
before it's gone

BALLERINA. Have you been looking for me?

JOSEPH. well. have I been looking for you?
Yes, well, I don't know.

BALLERINA. You can't be sure.

JOSEPH. No.

BALLERINA. You can't be sure.

JOSEPH. You see, I have obligations.

BALLERINA. I see.
I thought I'd like to come to tea.

JOSEPH. Oh, tea. Well.

BALLERINA. That would be alright?

JOSEPH. Oh.

BALLERINA. Shall I come for tea, then?

JOSEPH. Oh, yes, well, of course.

She does, instantly.

BALLERINA. Where shall I sit?

JOSEPH. At the table here.

BALLERINA. OK.

JOSEPH. Shall I open the window?

BALLERINA. If you like.

JOSEPH. I have only one tea bag.

BALLERINA. We can share it.

JOSEPH. Will you have something to eat?

BALLERINA. I've brought a cake.

JOSEPH. Oh.

BALLERINA. Chocolate cake.

JOSEPH. Oh. Good.

BALLERINA. When I was a girl,
I suddenly realized that I loved to run fast at night
so I wrote my mother that I wanted to be
a ballerina.
I had never seen a ballet
but I had three favorite dancing records at boarding school:
The Grand Canyon Suite
The Fighting Song of Notre Dame
and something by Beethoven.

Later, when I was eleven,
we came to New York
and we obtained a scholarship for me
at the School of American Ballet.
I say we because it's good to have a mother behind you
if she's not too
        (*She laughs.*)
too much of a ballet mother.

The fact that I didn't know entirely the technique—
I sort of made some of it up—
I think Mr. Balanchine was interested in that
that little offbeat part of me
because the slight
peculiarities
of a dancer were interesting to him.
Otherwise you could have a plasticine doll you know
go through the positions.
But.
So.
I think he liked that.

My first piece was called The Unanswered Question
which
actually Charles Ives the composer had a very
mystical

he was very
attached
to this composition of his
some of it I believe was even supposed to be
improvised
and it was mysterious
and he chose that piece for me.
I was held aloft by four men
I never touched the floor
and there was someone on the floor
sort of trying to reach me
always
and I regarded the four men as my spaceship
The best part was when I was standing
on the two men's shoulders
and Balanchine said to me: just fall back!
So in the first rehearsal I looked around
to make sure the men were there to catch me
and then I just slowly—
oh, that was fun.

Then Balanchine revived The Somnambulist for me
and in that ballet
The poet that I—the sleepwalker—
am so deeply in love with
is stabbed by my jealous husband
and he's lifted—
the somnambulist carries the poet backwards
offstage
in her arms.
And Balanchine always had me exit backwards
because you know
well
because I didn't need to see a doorway
to go through it.

I've had a big problem with depression but—
That's why I like to dance.
Even now, I take ballet class every day.
To normalize my psychotic instincts.
I'm just mad for pliés, tendus.
we are—
we're animals.
We have to run fast.
We have to swim,

we have to walk,
we have to dance,
we have to dance.

And now
the world has come around to thinking that muscles
are very important.
However old you are.

(OR *ELSE THE BALLERINA SAYS.*)

I miss postcards.
You know.
Postcards are unique, and no one sends them any more.
It just isn't done.
And I often wonder: why not?
Has someone taken a moral position?

With a novel or a book you always come to the end,
but you can just keep reading or writing one postcard after another and
never come to the end.
Each one of them unique—and never an end
This is a kind of pleasure we simply don't know any more,
though it seems harmless enough when you think about it.

There's no point to it, and yet it's such a pleasure.
It's not what you would call goal-oriented,
that's the pleasure of it, I suppose,
you just take it for its own sake.

And I like that you can never tell
which is the front and which is the back of a postcard.

JOSEPH. No.
Is this how you are?

BALLERINA. How do you mean?

JOSEPH. Is this how you are all the time
or just with me?

BALLERINA. How am I?

JOSEPH. Oh. Fine. Good. Excellent.
Odd.
A little odd.

BALLERINA. Good.

> *Debussy.*
> *A rain of soap bubbles,*
> *a grandiose cloud of cumulus over treetop.*

JOSEPH. Robert? Robert?
Are you warm enough?

I've brought you some things.
Some watch parts
a coiled spring
you see?
a beautiful thing
some stamps,
marbles,
a gold-colored bracelet
a painted wooden bird
a cut out metal harlequin
marbles
candies
bubble pipes
a thimble
some bits of broken glass
scrimshaw
whales' teeth
left over buttons
spools of thread
feathers
sequins
a metal ring
a cork ball
a music box
these are for you

I love you, Robert.

> (*He sits at the kitchen table,
> lost.*)
>
> *A wall of musical notes
> a box lined with musical notes, also its door
> the door opens and someone is inside
> a piano player playing ballet class music*
>
> *a couple dances
> or several people dance
> a romantic dance.*

THE ASTRONOMER. Most people feel that,
gee,
somebody must know all about that,
some university or something.
The fact is, no, they don't.

THE HERBALIST. Even about common species?

THE ASTRONOMER. Even the common birds.

THE HERBALIST. For a person just getting started watching birds,
what advice do you offer?

THE ASTRONOMER. First thing I'd tell them is
"Get some binoculars."
If you play tennis,
you get a tennis racquet.
If you go skiing,
you get skis.
If you go birdwatching,
you get binoculars.

THE PHARMACIST. "Enjoy watching the birds,
and don't be intimidated."

THE HERBALIST. Sometimes I hear a kind of
contempt
for people who enjoy birds only in the backyard,
as if they weren't real birdwatchers.

THE ASTRONOMER. Lillian and I have found
that some people tend to make a hierarchy
out of different ways of watching birds.
But there is no hierarchy.
There are various areas and ways
that people enjoy birds,
and we're all under the same tent.
It isn't something at the top
and something at the bottom.

THE PHARMACIST. It's a sphere. It's not a ladder.

THE ASTRONOMER. We always talk about cooperation,
not competition.
We're getting the language of heirachy
out of our language
In referring to birdwatching.

THE PHARMACIST. And we use the words
birdwatching and birding
interchangeably.
We feel that people are participating
in both activities
in the enjoyment of watching birds,
and both those terms describe that,
even though some people want to split them

and make a lot of different definitions.
We're all under one big tent!

THE HERBALIST. Yes, right. With the birds!

THE PHARMACIST. That's right.

THE ASTRONOMER. And we have one thing in common.
We all love birds.

> *A movie is projected—*
> *the 1938 movie* Algiers,
> *starring Charles Boyer and Hedy Lamarr.*
> JOSEPH *speaks simultaneously with Boyer.*

BOYER. So, you wanted to take another look at the strange wild animal.

LAMARR. Strange. But not so very wild.

BOYER. How do you like my cage?

LAMARR. I don't know—yet.

BOYER. How do you like Algiers?

LAMARR. I don't like traveling—makes me homesick.

BOYER. Does it?

LAMARR. If I can't see Paris when I open my eyes in the morning
I want to go right back to sleep. Do you know Paris?

BOYER. Do I know Paris?
La Rue Samaritan.

LAMARR. Champs Élysée.

BOYER. Gare du Nord.

LAMARR. L'Opéra.
Boulevard Capucines.

BOYER. L'Abays.
La Chapelle.

LAMARR. Le Montmartre.

BOYER. Boulevard Rochcouchoir.

LAMARR. Rue Fontaine.

BOTH TOGETHER. La Place Blanche.

BOYER. What a small world.

LAMARR. Cigarette?

BOYER. Thanks.
Got a light?

LAMARR. We are a long way from home.

BOYER. Mm-hmm.
Excuse me.

Well?

GUY. He still thinks he's playing his last card.
Merde.

BOYER. I'll tell her you said so.

GUY. No, no, I mean the rock she's wearing.
Now, if it was me, I'd get that first
and then do the fancy stuff afterwards.

BOYER. Shut up.

GUY. You can't talk to me like that.

BOYER. You heard me. Shut up.

GUY. OK.

LAMARR. He was talking about me?

BOYER. He was worried about you.

LAMARR. About me?

BOYER. All that stuff you have on.

LAMARR. Oh, that's nice of him.

BOYER. You're not worried yourself?

LAMARR. No. Not while I'm with you.

BOYER. Right.
This is something.

LAMARR. Isn't it? And it hardly weighs anything. Look.

BOYER. At least 20,000 francs, hmm?

LAMARR. Add a zero.

BOYER. Oh, I mean—what I would get for it.

LAMARR. Oh!

BOYER. Here. Put it on again.

LAMARR. You put it on.

(*Dance music comes up.*)

BOYER. Want to dance?

LAMARR. Yes.
They dance.

(JOSEPH *watches them a long while as they fade*
or
JOSEPH *dances with someone, or he dances alone.*)

Debussy or Chopin
the big dipper
a birdcage
painted white
which descends over the front of the stage
filling the proscenium arch
the bird has gone from the cage.

THE HERBALIST. Do you come back often?

JOSEPH. No.
I've only come back for the funeral.

THE HERBALIST. I see.

JOSEPH. Otherwise
I haven't been back since my father died
when I was seven.

THE HERBALIST. So young!

JOSEPH. And that was when we moved
and we left a good many things behind
in the attic.
But otherwise I haven't missed things so much.
The front yard
which sloped down from the front of the house
toward the corner.
And the big tree in the front yard.
I've never had a fireplace since that time.
I would like to have a fireplace.
Otherwise I haven't missed anything
except my father.

THE HERBALIST. You miss him.

JOSEPH. Oh, yes.
After he died
our lives were never the same again.

MOTHER. Joseph?

JOSEPH. Yes?

MOTHER. What is this you've left on the kitchen table?

JOSEPH. Oh. Have I left something?

MOTHER. You're not a child.

JOSEPH. No.

MOTHER. And yet it seems
you leave things on the table
you leave things on the chairs
you leave things on the cabinet
you leave things on the floor

JOSEPH. I'm sorry, mother.

MOTHER. And what?
Is the faucet fixed?
Have you fixed it?
Or have you called the plumber?
I will be right if I blame you for everything.

JOSEPH. I'm sorry, mother.

MOTHER. And do I not always do everything for you?
Here.
I've read the newspaper for you
and I have clipped out the articles
you will want to see.

(*She reads the headlines from the clippings.*)

JUDY HOLLIDAY'S GONE AND BROADWAY WEEPS
SEA SHELL MINIATURES STILL HOLD OLD CHARMS
PAN AM HELIPORT TO OPEN

JOSEPH. Judy Holliday is gone?
Has she died?

MOTHER. Yes.

JOSEPH. Oh.
Sometimes a person will wonder:
what does art matter
compared with the sad prospect of a life
unlived?

> *Ice cubes*
> *a diamond necklace*
> *velvet.*

MARIANNE. I've enjoyed our letters.

JOSEPH. Oh, I'm sorry.

MARIANNE. Sorry?

JOSEPH. I didn't mean to impose.

MARIANNE. Impose. No. Certainly not.

I only wonder if I did something inconsiderate
to have made you
disappear
the way you did
I had thought we had quite a
heartfelt exchange
so that
after I sent my last note to you
I waited
two years
for a reply.
So I wondered:
what had I done wrong?

JOSEPH. Oh.
No.
You did nothing wrong.

MARIANNE. I wrote a poem for you.

JOSEPH. Oh, you did?

MARIANNE. Yes.

JOSEPH. Would you read it to me?

MARIANNE. I'm not sure.
Because, sometimes, you know
I have trouble with the meaning of things

You'll notice how—
when you make a sentence,
all the words depend on each other.
It's like when you move your arms.
        (*Watching the gesture as she makes it.*)
You can't get from here to there without going in between.

And then you might take away one word,
and then everything you say is nonsense.
you define something in a certain way;
and poof there you are:
you've created a whole society, really, haven't you?
And what did Aristotle say?
Men are social animals:
We become what we make of ourselves in our relationships.

You know 200 years ago,
in the time of Marie Antoinette,
all the women covered their faces with white lead
so their hair fell out and they went completely mad.

It's simply what they did.

Because they thought they should.
And those who didn't were beneath contempt.
This is how it was for men and women.
These are simply things one does.

Take shoes, for example.
I often worry whether I have enough pairs,
or too many,
or the wrong sort,
whether they go with things,
or no one wears them any more –
you know, the heels are too high,
or they don't wear red, or alligator –
whether things are, you know,
too short or too long
or you know they shouldn't be embroidered,
you know or too baggy
or it shouldn't have a fur collar—
It's more than I can worry about all the time,
So now I just get what I want and sometimes I don't wear it.

JOSEPH. But, still,
Would you read the poem to me?

MARIANNE. You want me to?

JOSEPH. Yes.

(*She takes a moment, and then.*)

MARIANNE. You look at the branches of the camphor tree,
and you see how tangled they are.
they make a person feel estranged from the tree
and yet
it's because the tree is divided
into so many branches
that
sometimes
the image of the tree is used to describe
people in love.

JOSEPH *and* GORKY *are sitting at the kitchen table*

having two cups of tea
made with one tea bag.
We watch as JOSEPH *pours two cups of hot water from a pot.*
Then he dips a teabag into his teacup
then dips it in GORKY's.

GORKY. I was born Vosdanik Adoian
at the turn of the last century
in Khorkom,
a now destroyed village
in the western Armenian province of Van,
part of the Ottoman Empire.
I didn't speak until I was 6.
My father left my mother, Shushan, and her children
to find work in America,
promising to send money so they could join him,
which he never did.

After the siege of Van City by the Turks,
with my family
I fled the Turkish slaughter of Armenians by trekking east.
My mother had already endured unspeakable horrors.
Years earlier, her father, a priest,
had been killed and his body nailed to the door of his church,
and she had been forced by the Turks
to watch her previous husband murdered.
Now she starved herself to give her children
what little food there was on the long march.
Broken and impoverished, she died,
while I was by her side.

Where am I now?
My studio has burned down
with most of my work still in it.
An operation for rectal cancer
has forced me to use a colostomy bag.
I am a fastidious man.
I find this unbearable.
I pushed my wife down the stairs in a rage
when I was drunk.
Now she is gone.
I have broken my neck and my painting arm
in an automobile crash.
I don't sleep well
and I have headaches.
My wife has run off with Matta.

And I have nothing left but to hang myself.

JOSEPH. I work in the basement.
That's where I keep all my materials
for my work.

And I think:
What am I doing?
I've lost my way
why don't I give it up?
there are times I get so lost
I don't know what to do
I've gone so deep, so far
I don't know if I'll ever find my way out again
and then: what's the point?
is this useful?
does anyone care?
I get up in the morning
some days I just weep and weep
is everything I do just written on water?
but what else can I do?
just because another artist is incredibly famous
doesn't mean his work is destined to fall
into oblivion in another generation
and my work will endure
is this any way to spend a life?
I'm living my life in a basement.

> *Music.*
> *snow on glass with a hole at the center*
> *for an* ACTRESS *to look through*
>
> *as she sings a pop song*
> *maybe Cole Porter.*

ACTRESS. What is this thing called love
This funny thing called love
Just who can solve its mystery?
Why should it make a fool of me?

I saw you there one wonderful day
You took my heart and threw it away
That's why I ask the lord in heaven above
What is this thing called love?

I saw you there one wonderful day
You took my heart and threw it away
That's why I ask the lord in heaven above
What is this thing called love?

JOSEPH. Sometimes, mother,
we have a peaceful exchange

MOTHER. and we like that

do we not like that?

JOSEPH. Yes. Yes, we do,
but more often
you criticize my behavior
your criticisms fill the air like
like musical darts

MOTHER. Not like darts.
Oh, Joseph, not like darts.

JOSEPH. you say nothing without an edge
glowering at me from across the room
resentful when you are not included
belligerent
like
like
like Queen Victoria

MOTHER. Queen Victoria.

JOSEPH. what you require
it seems to me
is absolute sexless loyalty

MOTHER. No.

JOSEPH. and then there will be times
we sit together in the back yard

MOTHER. in the warm weather

JOSEPH. Yes

MOTHER. idyllic

JOSEPH. Yes
and then you will somehow say
"I haven't had one word from Mrs. Duchamp
for the letter I took such pains with
and also I wonder if she ever got the little gift
in my last gold and silver Lord and Taylor gift box
People could take a minute or two
to acknowledge little kindly things their friends do"
and then the complaining and criticism
has begun again

MOTHER. Joseph.

JOSEPH. so that no one would ever know
who you really are
the intensity of your inner life

MOTHER. Oh.

JOSEPH. the letters that you write me sometimes
for no reason at all
do you know that I mark on them
"read again"

MOTHER. No.

JOSEPH. to remind myself
to read them again and again and again
because then I see you love what I love

MOTHER. we are kept alive by the same things

>   *An entire back wall of the theatre*
>   *with bottles with things in them*
>   *or the entire fabulous window of a pharmacy*
>   *or the fantastical window of a Paris shop*
>   *or a thousand sorts of watch springs.*

JOSEPH. Of course, I wouldn't want to be presumptuous.
Giving advice to you.
A person of a different generation.
What I think
may no longer be useful.

THE GIRL. Still…

JOSEPH. Still,
if I were to say anything to you
it would be:
do what you love
not what you think you should do
or what you think is all you can do
what you think is possible for you
no
do what you love
and let the rest follow along behind it
or not
or not
because
even if it doesn't follow along behind
you will have done what you've loved
and you know what that is
you know better than anyone what you love
and a life centered around your love
cannot be wrong
cannot finally be disappointing

THE GIRL. Easy for you to say.

JOSEPH. No. No, it isn't.

> *The back of giant silver watch with a glass back*
> *is projected on the back wall.*
> *Its round frame is filled*
> *with deep blue sky and stars*
> *and the constellation Taurus in white etching.*

JOSEPH. Robert, are you asleep?
Are you asleep?
I've brought you some things.
You see:
a metal ring
a piece of string
a cork ball
a wooden dowel
a clock face
a little box
Robert.
Now then
don't leave me, Robert.
Who will I care for?
Who will I give things to?
Who will talk to me?
Because
we've had a lifetime together
without you
our lifetime
is gone.

> *(The train comes crashing through the wall*
> *its whistle screaming*
> *steam engine pounding*
> *hissing steam*
> *roaring and slamming*
>
> JOSEPH *pulls the sheet up to cover* ROBERT *completely*
> *and then sinks to the floor weeping.)*

THE ASTRONOMER. One time
long ago
not far from here
the poet Simonides
was gathered with his friends
for dinner at a palace in the hills
across this valley.

Simonides stepped outside onto the terrace
for a moment
for a breath of air,
and in that moment
an earthquake
shook the villa
and brought it to the ground.
All Simonides' friends were crushed to death,
their bodies mangled and torn apart,
not even their own families could recognize them.

But Simonides could picture in his mind's eye
just where each one of his friends had been sitting,
and as he recalled them one by one
their bodies could be
pulled out from the rubble and identified.
And from this moment
came the beginning
of mankind's desire to remember
exactly
how the world has been
at one moment or another.

And so Simonides
instructed his neighbors
how to build their own palaces of memory,
how to build each room
how to furnish these rooms
with the faces and figures of their friends,
events of their lives,
their treasures,
books, poems,
each room given things of singular beauty
or distinctive ugliness,
to make them vivid
unforgettable
memories disfigured,
faces splashed with paint
or stained with blood
each moment suspended
in this geometry of memory, thought
and feeling.

> *A movie is projected—*
> Algiers *again, with Boyer and Lamarr.*
> JOSEPH *speaks simultaneously with Boyer.*

BOYER. You're beautiful.
That's easy to say.
I know a lot of people have told you.
But what I'm telling you is different, see?
For me you're more than that.
For two years I've been lost.
Like walking in my sleep.
Suddenly I wake up: that's you.
I don't know what I've been doing all that time
waiting for you without knowing it.
Do you know what you are to me?
Paris.
That's you.
Paris.
With you, I escape. Follow me?
The whole town—a Spring morning in Paris.
You're lovely.
You're marvelous.

(Cut to: he kisses her.)

LAMARR. It's late. I must go.

BOYER. Suppose you don't come tomorrow.

LAMARR. Suppose I don't.
Can't you ever get away from the Casbah?

BOYER. Why do you ask?

LAMARR. Can't you?

BOYER. No. I'm caught here.
Like a bear in a hole.
Dogs barking.
Hunters all around.
No way out of it.
Do you like that?
Maybe it's lucky for you.

LAMARR. I don't like it.
It's not lucky.

BOYER. You are right.
If you don't come back I might do anything.
I might go down to the hotel to get you.

LAMARR. Tomorrow, Pepe.

BOYER. Tomorrow?

LAMARR. I never break a promise.

A black and white engraving of Andromeda
amidst the stars
is projected on the back wall.

JOSEPH. The fact is, of course,
I am not a good prospect for you.
I am too old for you.

LEILA. I don't think so.

JOSEPH. I am twice your age.

LEILA. Well,
not quite twice my age.

JOSEPH. You see.

LEILA. No, I don't.

JOSEPH. I will be decrepit and whatnot
while you are still just beginning your life.

LEILA. I'd like to begin it with you.
The only thing I regret
is that you won't live forever
because
I will miss you.

JOSEPH. A girl like you
anything is possible for your life

LEILA. I don't think so.

JOSEPH. Yes.
For you
it is.
A life of possibility.

LEILA. Then I'd like to be with you.

JOSEPH. You can always be with me
the way you are with Bleecker Street
or Bank Street
Broadway south of Houston
those shop windows
Debussy
Mallarmé
Fanelli's on the corner of Prince and Mercer
the little store nearby where you can find
star fish
butterflies in little boxes
driftwood

and in the antiques store
the things from Asia
inlaid wood
a thousand little drawers
you have a good sense of mortality
in these streets
stopping in the cafes
looking at the light on the buildings
in the late afternoon
when it is already nighttime down below
lights coming on in the shops
and still afternoon in the sky above
this is how I spend my time
and I never grow tired of it
I can see it again and again
it only fades
in a hundred years
when new windows
take its place.

The fact is,
I've spent my life looking for true love
and never found it.

LEILA. I thought you had.

JOSEPH. Have I?

   (*A very long silence.*)

Yes.

   (*A wall of stars*
   the constellation Andromeda
   or the moon
   or a vast star map of the cosmos covers the back wall
   We hear Satie's Gymnopedies *on the piano.*)

End of Play

THE SCENE
by Theresa Rebeck

BIOGRAPHY

Theresa Rebeck's past New York productions include *The Water's Edge, Spike Heels, Loose Knit* and *The Family of Mann* at Second Stage; *Bad Dates* and *The Butterfly Collection* at Playwrights Horizons; and *View of the Dome* at New York Theatre Workshop. *Omnium Gatherum* (co-written with Alexandra Gersten-Vassilaros, and finalist for the Pulitzer Prize) was featured at the Humana Festival 2003, and had a commercial run at the Variety Arts. *The Scene* is being produced at Second Stage as part of the 2006-2007 season. In television, Ms. Rebeck has written for *Dream On, Brooklyn Bridge, L.A. Law, Maximum Bob, First Wave, Third Watch,* and *NYPD Blue,* where she also worked as a producer. Produced features include *Harriet the Spy, Gossip,* and the independent feature *Sunday on the Rocks.* Awards include the Mystery Writer's of America's Edgar Award, the Writer's Guild of America award for Episodic Drama, the Hispanic Images Imagen Award, and the Peabody, all for her work on *NYPD Blue.* She won the National Theatre Conference Award (for *The Family of Mann*), and was awarded the William Inge New Voices Playwriting Award in 2003 (for *The Bells*). Ms. Rebeck holds a PhD. from Brandeis University in Victorian Melodrama. She and her husband Jess Lynn have two children, Cooper and Cleo.

ACKNOWLEDGMENTS

The Scene premiered at the Humana Festival of New American Plays in March 2006. It was directed by Rebecca Bayla Taichman, with the following cast and staff:

CHARLIE	Stephen Barker Turner
LEWIS	David Wilson Barnes
CLEA	Anna Camp
STELLA	Carla Harting
Scenic Designer	Paul Owen
Costume Designer	Catherine F. Norgren
Lighting Designer	Tony Penna
Sound Designer	Matt Callahan
Properties Designer	Jennifer Dums
Fight Director	Cliff William III
Stage Manager	Brady Ellen Poole
Production Assistant	Danielle Teague-Daniels
Dramaturg	Mervin P. Antonio
Assistant Dramaturg	Jamie Bragg
Casting	Vince Liebhart
Directing Assistant	Shirley Serotsky

CAST OF CHARACTERS
CHARLIE
LEWIS
CLEA
STELLA

SETTING
New York City. The present.

David Wilson Barnes, Stephen Barker Turner, and Anna Camp
in *The Scene*

30th Annual Humana Festival of New American Plays
Actors Theatre of Louisville, 2006
Photo by Harlan Taylor

THE SCENE

ACT I

Scene 1

CHARLIE, LEWIS *and* CLEA. *A corner of a party, loud music, talk, laughter.* CHARLIE *and* LEWIS *hold drinks in their hands.* LEWIS *is clearly interested in* CLEA; CHARLIE *is not.*

CLEA. I love the view here.

LEWIS. (*Surreptitiously checking out her butt.*) Yeah, awesome.

CLEA. I mean, mind blowing, right, it's just so surreal, the lights and the water, it's like unbelievable. I love this loft! Do you know the guy who lives here? He must be incredible. Because I have just no idea, I came with a friend, who knows, like, everybody and I know she told me it was somebody in the fashion industry who I just so had never heard of, my bad. 'Cause he's like, what, like clearly so talented, this place is so beautiful. The water, the air. It's just so surreal.

CHARLIE. How is that surreal?

CLEA. What?

CHARLIE. The air and the water, you said that before, that you found it surreal. How is air and water surreal?

CLEA. Oh you know, it's—just—wow! You know.

CHARLIE. (*To* LEWIS, *annoyed now.*) You want a refill? What is that, a mojita?

LEWIS. Yeah, great.

CHARLIE. How about you, I'm sorry, what's your name again?

CLEA. Clea.

CHARLIE. Would you like a mojita, Clea?

CLEA. No no, I don't drink. My mother was an alcoholic. I mean, she was a wonderful woman and she really loved me but it's like alcohol is so deadly, I mean at these parties sometimes when I'm at a party like this? To stand around and watch everyone turn into zombies around me? It just really triggers me, you know? You go ahead. I mean, that's just for me, I don't impose that on people or anything.

LEWIS. I mean, it's not like, I'm not like a huge drinker, or—

(CHARLIE *laughs into his drink at this.*)

CLEA. Oh good, because you know, I was at this party last week it was such a scene, there were so many people there. You know it was this young director, he's got like seven things going at once, off broadway, can you imagine, the energy level of someone like that? Anyway, it was his birthday party, and they rented out the top two floors of this loft in Chelsea, it was this wild party, like surreal, and then at one point in the evening? I just realized, that everyone was just totally shitfaced. I mean I don't want to be reactive in situations like that, I don't like to judge people on a really superficial level or anything but it was kind of horrifying. I mean, not that I—you know, drink, you should drink! Enjoy yourselves!

(CHARLIE *shrugs*.)

CHARLIE. Yeah, well, I think I'm gonna head out. Nice to meet you. "Clea."

CLEA. Oh. Whoa. I mean—what does that mean?

CHARLIE. (*Annoyed now.*) What does what mean?

CLEA. "Clea." I mean, "Clea." I mean, whoa—

CHARLIE. Is there a problem?

CLEA. You tell me. You're the one who's all like, "Clea." "Nice to meet you."

CHARLIE. What are you even talking about?

CLEA. Nothing. It just struck me as a little edgy, that's all.

LEWIS. You want me to get those drinks? Why don't I do that? I mean you got to at least talk to Nick, he's gonna show up.

CHARLIE. I'm not talking to Nick. I'm leaving. (*To* CLEA.) "Nice to meet you—" is "edgy—"

CLEA. Well, you're totally giving off a vibe here, I'm not making that up. And that is so fine, I mean I do not judge.

LEWIS. Look, Nick's here. Hey Nick—

CHARLIE. I'm not talking to— "A vibe?"

CLEA. Oh is "vibe" like a totally uncool word, in your little tribe—

LEWIS. Hey, Nick!

CHARLIE. No no, it's got a real seventies charm that I find particularly captivating in someone who wasn't born until nineteen eighty-two—

CLEA. Oh, I'm young, well, I guess you're not, huh, that's really the problem isn't it?

(*A beat.*)

LEWIS. Whoa.

CHARLIE. There's no problem, Clea. I don't know you. I came by my friend's loft—his name is Edward, by the way, and he's an actor, he's not in "the fashion industry," he's a very fine stage actor even though he's not doing seven off-Broadway shows at once—

LEWIS. Look, look, look—

CLEA. Yeah, whatever—

CHARLIE. I'm here because my friend asked me to come by, and I did that and now I'm going. Nice to meet you.

CLEA. If there isn't a problem, what are you so bent out of shape about?

CHARLIE. You're really a piece of work.

LEWIS. Charlie.

CHARLIE. What? She's a fucking idiot!

LEWIS. Hey, whoa, are you—

CLEA. No. It's okay. There were, obviously, there were some things said here, that maybe rubbed you the wrong way and I am totally willing to talk about that. I mean I apologize for that. But you were like jumping all over me because I said surreal, and I just started to feel stupid. So I apologize. If I was edgy or something.

LEWIS. Look, it's okay.

CLEA. Maybe I should get some vodka or something.

CHARLIE. I thought you didn't drink.

CLEA. I don't! I mean, I really don't. Hardly ever.

LEWIS. You want me to get you a vodka?

CLEA. Would you?

LEWIS. Sure.

(*He goes. After a minute,* CHARLIE *sighs, makes another move to desert her.*)

CHARLIE. Listen, I really do have to…

CLEA. I totally understand. This is your friend's party, you should go, go, you know a ton of people here probably. You need to talk to Nick, that's clearly a big thing, or something.

CHARLIE. Nick's an asshole.

CLEA. Whatever.

CHARLIE. Look—Are you here alone?

CLEA. No! God, no, I came with a friend, I don't know where she is. She's like the total scene-machine.

CHARLIE. Can I ask—I mean—Why do you talk like that?

CLEA. (*Defensive but firm.*) I talk the way I talk. I'm not apologizing for that. I mean, I apologize for before, acting like a little edgy, but language is a totally idiosyncratic and very personal, very organic function of you know, someone's humanity, so I'm not apologizing for my language.

CHARLIE. Okay.

CLEA. Okay what?

CHARLIE. Okay nothing. That's actually a fairly coherent and legitimate point.

(LEWIS *returns with three drinks. He hands them around.*)

CLEA. Thanks.

(*She downs the drink.* LEWIS *and* CHARLIE *watch her.*)

CLEA. (*Continuing.*) Wow! That is… good. Ah. Wow. Mmmm.

LEWIS. (*Cautious.*) Should I get you another?

CLEA. No, I just want to feel this one first. I never drink. My mother was an alcoholic so I have to be like totally careful.

LEWIS. So where are you from, Clea?

CLEA. Ohio. Isn't that hilarious? Plus I just got here, like, what, six months ago? It's a lot, I mean, to get used to. But it's so alive, just walking down the street, the energy. I'm like from, you know, the middle of nowhere, and I land here and it's so much more intense than even you think. Not like I'm some sort of cornball. But more like I'm alert, you know, really on fire with how amazing it is to be here. Because my experience, already, and don't take this personally, but people here are like not awake. To what—I don't want to sound judgmental because that is so not what I'm about but like what I mean is, I had this job interview yesterday, or the day be—no yesterday, I'm pretty sure, I had this amazing opportunity to work on this talk show, not that I think television is really a good place for anyone but I'm like trying to be open, really open, and anyway the agency sends me in to talk to this person who is like, she does something, I can't even tell what it is, for this talk show, like these people go on the television and interview movie stars or you know important people. She's the person who books, you know, she books people.

LEWIS. Really? 'Cause—

CHARLIE. Yeah, so you went in—

CLEA. Yeah, so I'm walking around this television studio, and there's like lights and you know "people" and everyone is so phony and intense, you just want to puke, like, what is supposed to be going on in a place like that? It's just like a void, with a lot of color in it. Totally bizarre. And this woman is so into it. Her name is like "Stella," and everything is just do this, be perfect—

LEWIS. Stella?

CLEA. Right? Right? And she could not be more like a Nazi priestess or something, she is so worked up over these phone lists and highlighting in blue and mint green who needs to get returned, who hasn't returned, just utter crap—oh and on top of it all, she's in the middle of one of those adoptions, she's one of those infertile women who is like adopting an abandoned baby from China and those calls go on the special list, like lists are the holy grail to this total Nazi, like the lists and the movie stars and this invisible baby in the middle of China is like, you know, life to her. And I'm like—look around you! This city is so alive and you're just like—I don't know. Wow I think that vodka just hit, I so don't drink. Do you know what I mean? About being alive, I mean?

LEWIS. Uh—you're alive, but Stella—

CLEA. Was totally not.

LEWIS. You know, I—I—I think I should tell you. I think I know that person.

CLEA. Stella? You know like, Stella the Nazi priestess from T.V. Land? Really?

LEWIS. Yeah, I, I think I do.

CLEA. Come on. Like, that is so wild. How do you know her?

CHARLIE. I'm married to her.

(*There is a pause while* CLEA *takes this in. Blackout.*)

Scene 2

STELLA, CHARLIE *and* LEWIS, *doing shots of tequila in* STELLA *and* CHARLIE's *apartment. They trade off the bottle, and speak on top of each other.*

STELLA. (*Pouring a shot.*) What did she call me? A "Nazi priestess?"

CHARLIE. A frigid Nazi priestess—

LEWIS. Infertile. An infertile—

CHARLIE. It was "frigid."

STELLA. Stop it, god, you guys— Why didn't you tell me about this last night?

CHARLIE. You were asleep. Did you want me to wake you up and tell you I met some girl at a party who said you were a frigid Nazi priestess?

LEWIS. It wasn't frigid!

STELLA. Why are you defending her?

LEWIS. I'm not! I'm just striving for a shred of accuracy or something—

CHARLIE. Frigid.

LEWIS. Infertile.

CHARLIE. Frigid—

LEWIS. Infertile!

CHARLIE. Frigid—

STELLA. (*Overlap.*) Yeah, okay, I got it, okay, stop it! What a bitch. I mean, I was incredibly nice to this stupid person, I mean she was patently stupid and I was so nice, and now I find out she's what, offended, she's morally offended by my phone lists and my highlighters? Everyone in New York has phone lists, how are you supposed to remember who you have to call back? And excuse me but having blue and green highlighters makes me a Nazi, and the fact that I don't kill Jews is irrelevant? She sounds like a genius. She can hardly speak, as I recall. She looks great in black and she can't speak the English language, she'll do just fine in New York.

CHARLIE. I shouldn't have told you.

STELLA. Why shouldn't you tell me? Why didn't you tell me when you got home, you met someone who called me a frigid—

LEWIS. Infertile! Infertile!

STELLA. Why were you even talking to this stupid person—

CHARLIE. She was interesting, in a vapid way.

STELLA. She was a moron who looks good in black.

LEWIS. She wasn't a moron. She's pretty.

STELLA. Oh, for heaven's sake. I've had such a shitty day. With my high-lighters, me and my highlighters trying to take over the world and buy Chinese babies for some sinister fertility ritual. Like it's better to leave them in orphanages. Children all over the world who need homes and if you decide to take one in, it must be because you're some frigid crazy workaholic bitch who wasn't woman enough to, you know, have her own.

CHARLIE. Stop! Stella. Just stop, okay?

STELLA. Sorry. Sorry, Lewis.

LEWIS. It's okay.

STELLA. Are there chips? Maybe some chips would cheer me up. Did you go to the grocery store?

CHARLIE. No.

STELLA. Oh, Charlie, come on—I have to work all day, trying to take over the world with my highlighters, couldn't you at least go to the grocery store?

LEWIS. I'll go to the corner and get some chips.

STELLA. Would you?

LEWIS. Absolutely.

STELLA. Thank you, Lewis. You are so nice to me.

LEWIS. I'll get the chips.

(*He stands, grabs his coat and goes. There is a moment of silence.*)

STELLA. I had a horrible day.

CHARLIE. I know.

STELLA. That idiot not showing. Not your idiot. I'm moving on to my idiot. Didn't show. All the shit I had to go through to get her to do us, six dozen white lilies in her dressing room, do you know what that many lilies smells like? It's enough to truly knock you out, like a disease, that many flowers. And I'm not even talking about all the stupid candy we had to buy. M&M's. Reese's cups. Twix. Why do these people think it's so cool to eat bad chocolate? Could someone, and I mean, I literally had to turn her fuck-ing dressing room into a kind of physical representation of a complete psychotic break, lilies and bad chocolate and an EXERCISE MACHINE—she was only supposed to be in there for an hour and a half, and she needed her own STAIRMASTER, with the chocolate, what's the plan, to eat the mounds of chocolate, while you're ON the stairmaster? Turns out there was no plan, because—she didn't show.

CHARLIE. You told me. A couple times.

STELLA. I told you eight times. I'm turning into one of those people who say things over and over and then you have to tell them so kindly, yes you told me, like they've gone senile—this happened to my mother, after she turned fifty, she told the same story over and over and over again, it was so dreary—it was like oh, and now mom's gone insane, she's not just a pathetic nut, now she's a boring pathetic nut, telling the same story, over and over and over again—

CHARLIE. Stella. Have a drink.

STELLA. I'm half smashed already. That idiot didn't show. She did not show!

CHARLIE. You told me this morning she wasn't going to show. I mean, there's no real surprise here, is there? This is the fourth time—

STELLA. Yes, it is the fourth time, it is the fourth time she's fucked us and they insist that I book her anyway! And then it's my fucking fault we have a hole in the schedule. And there's not even a hole, I back us up every time with that idiot who makes the low-carb pasta dishes, why do people believe that? Low-carb pasta? Why do they—

CHARLIE. Stella—

STELLA. But it's so demeaning, to put that on television, it's just demeaning. These people are all such liars. Low-carb pasta? And it's pathetic, these women sitting out there, so hungry for this specific lie, you can eat pasta and still lose weight, that's like pathetic, it's not pathetic, it's sad, if you think about it too long, it is so sad all those women sitting out there in the house, yearning for life to be just that little bit easier. It's probably one of the few things they have to look forward to, a nice plate of pasta with a little red sauce—only most of them, they don't go for the sensible red sauce, they go for the alfredo, or the carbonara, I actually had to do a low-fat carbonara show once.

CHARLIE. I know.

STELLA. Oh god. I want to have compassion for these people, I feel bad—

CHARLIE. Stella—

STELLA. That they think this is a cool thing to do with their time, go and be the studio audience for a stupid talk show!

CHARLIE. Honey—

STELLA. Because they think it means something, to be on television—only you weren't, really, you just sat there while someone else got to be on television. It's so sad. It's so so sad.

CHARLIE. No more tequila for you.

STELLA. I'm fine.

CHARLIE. Well, I'm suicidal.

STELLA. But I don't really feel sorry for them.

CHARLIE. You shouldn't!

STELLA. Oh my god of course I should. These are people who deserve compassion, these fat people who feel terrible about themselves because we're the ones, we're constantly putting on television show things like low-fat carbonara, low-fat foie gras, like this is some kind of good idea, to rip the pleasure and essence out of everything, that's how horrible it is to be fat. I mean these people didn't ask to be fat! And they're just surrounded by a culture—everything, everything—tells them they're worthless because they're fat! If that's not worthy of compassion, what is?

CHARLIE. Stupid people are destroying this planet. I don't have to have compassion for that.

STELLA. Low-fat foie gras. You know that's coming. That's just, out there somewhere, someone's going to try to stuff some poor duck full of low-fat corn, and tofu. You just know it.

(CHARLIE *laughs.* STELLA *laughs. He kisses her.*)

CHARLIE. You need to take a day off.

STELLA. Oh, god, you think?

(*They continue kissing. It starts to heat up.* CHARLIE *tries to take off* STELLA's *shirt. Laughing, she pushes him away.*)

STELLA. (*Continuing.*) Stop it, Charlie! Lewis is going to come back any minute. Good heavens.

CHARLIE. What did you say? "Good heavens?"

STELLA. I said let go of my shirt!

CHARLIE. I'm sure Lewis would love to see you without your shirt on—

STELLA. Oh my god. No more tequila for you.

(*She wiggles away from him.*)

CHARLIE. You should have come to that party with us last night. I mean, it was horrible, and boring and a complete waste of time, there was no one to talk to other than a bunch of feckless drunks and this idiot girl, plus everyone was about fifteen years younger than me, so I felt like a freak—

STELLA. Yes, I should have come, it sounds terrific.

CHARLIE. I know! It's ridiculous. But rich people's apartments are so strangely comforting. This guy Edward's hooked up with is some sort of gazillionaire, this place is freakishly opulent. Heated tiles in the bathroom, a fucking Picasso on the wall. Not a good one, but it was a real Picasso. Why is it that real art makes real people feel phony? Real clothes, too. This guy knows how to dress. Edward's taken to wearing silk.

STELLA. Edward?

CHARLIE. Right? It looked good on him. He looked good. He looked rich. The whole place was so, we were so high up. I mean, really, in the stars. I love that about New York, when you get to go to one of those parties way above the rest of the city, there's something so surreal about it. Not surreal. Oh god. I did not mean surreal.

STELLA. It actually does sound kind of surreal.

CHARLIE. No no. No. Let's be precise. What's surreal, if anything, is one's internal state in a situation like that. Everyone acts like surreal is some sort of definition, an image is surreal, water or or or air, how can that be surreal? Water and air, that's the definition of real. Surreal is more the connection. Or not.

STELLA. What are you talking about?

CHARLIE. (*Laughing at himself.*) I have nooo idea.

STELLA. So, did you talk to Nick?

CHARLIE. I haven't been to a party like that since I did that sit com. Remember, when we were stuck out in L.A., and we had to keep going to all those parties in the hills—

STELLA. Those parties were hideous. You hated those parties.

CHARLIE. The food was great at those parties. And the flowers, also great, and the pools—

STELLA. All those people constantly sucking up—

CHARLIE. But they were sucking up to me.

STELLA. Oh my god. You hated every second of that—

CHARLIE. I did not hate everything.

STELLA. So tell me what Nick said.

CHARLIE. You know what we should do, Stell? We should take a trip. We should blow out the bank account and go somewhere great, Paris, or Saint Petersburg, or Florence, stay at the Four Seasons, eat incredible food, wallow in bed, buy you expensive earrings, drink wine on some gorgeous town square somewhere—

STELLA. What's the matter, Charlie?

CHARLIE. Nothing's the matter! People take vacations, Stell. Come on. It would be so great to get out of this place for just a week. It would just be fun. Couldn't you use a little fun? Not thinking about all those lunatics for a whole week. A week in Florence. The Uffizi. Wine on the Piazza.

STELLA. Stop it.

CHARLIE. I'm not going to stop it. The Medici Chapel.

STELLA. Charlie, we can't just—

CHARLIE. Sure we can. We could go for two weeks. Leather gloves. Gorgeous earrings. Botticelli.

STELLA. (*Laughing.*) This is not—it's just not—

CHARLIE. Yes it is. It is. Say yes. Say yes. Say "sí." Say "sí, Charlie."

(*He starts to kiss her. She laughs and kisses him back. It starts to heat up.* LEWIS *calls from the hallway.*)

LEWIS. (*Calling.*) Can I come back now?

CHARLIE. Go away!

STELLA. Charlie…

CHARLIE. Go away! Go away!

STELLA. It's fine, I'm done melting down. I need some food, I have to eat something.

(*She stands, goes to the door and opens it.* LEWIS *brings in chips.*)

LEWIS. I didn't know what kind. They had all these different flavor nachos. Like, fake guacamole and fake ranch, and fake chili something, fake onion something, fake lime…

(*He hands them all out.*)

STELLA. Oh god this is so nice, and horrifying at the same time. You are so nice to just buy all these chips for me.

(*She smiles at him.*)

CHARLIE. I'm starving. We should order something real.

STELLA. (*Eating chips.*) So did Nick even show up at Ed's stupid party?

LEWIS. Yeah, he was there.

STELLA. So what did he say, how did it go?

CHARLIE. (*Slight beat.*) I didn't talk to him.

STELLA. What?

CHARLIE. I didn't get a chance.

STELLA. You didn't talk to him?

CHARLIE. I didn't stay that long.

STELLA. But that's why you went.

CHARLIE. I wasn't in the right mood.

STELLA. What kind of "mood" do you have to be in to—

CHARLIE. Oh for god's sake—

STELLA. Oh for god's sake, what? (*Beat.*) Charlie?

CHARLIE. I didn't talk to him. I didn't want to talk to him, so I didn't talk to him.

STELLA. Well, that's just brilliant.

LEWIS. Are you hungry? Maybe I should get some like real food.

STELLA. Yeah maybe you should.

CHARLIE. No, don't go, you don't have to—

STELLA. Yes, go, Lewis—

CHARLIE. We're not getting into this.

STELLA. We're not?

LEWIS. It wasn't the right moment, Stella, it really wasn't. Nick was like surrounded by all these people and to even get to him was just—

CHARLIE. (*To* LEWIS.) Do not excuse me to my own wife!

STELLA. Well that's really nice.

CHARLIE. We are not talking about this, Stella!

STELLA. You can tell me about the person who called me a frigid Nazi priestess but you can't—

CHARLIE. There's nothing to tell. He showed up. I was in a bad mood, so I didn't talk to him.

STELLA. Well then you have to call him—

CHARLIE. I'm not calling Nick—

STELLA. He's got a pilot, Charlie—

CHARLIE. I know all about that, Stella. You've told me about—

STELLA. Oh don't do that—

LEWIS. Listen, you guys, maybe—

STELLA. He loves you. You have to remind him—

CHARLIE. Nick does not—

STELLA. You went to high school with him! You were best friends for—

CHARLIE. Oh my god. We were never, ever—

STELLA. Yes you were and you're a terrific actor, he knows how good you are, he knew you when you were—

CHARLIE. (*Bitter.*) When I was working?

STELLA. (*Unflinching.*) Yes. When you were working. A lot. You're a wonderful actor, Charlie, come on, you have to fight for yourself—

CHARLIE. Talking to Nick at a party is not going to get him to give me a part on his pilot!

STELLA. Well, if you don't talk to him he's certainly not going to give you a part, I can guarantee you—

CHARLIE. Oh yeah he really is desperate to have people he knew in a previous life suck up to him at parties—

STELLA. (*Firm.*) People like that, Charlie. These people, these T.V. people like it when you suck up—they like it—

CHARLIE. Oh. That's why I should do it—

STELLA. You should do it because you need a fucking job—

CHARLIE. (*Overlap.*) Because sucking up to assholes so that you can work in television is clearly something that's worked out so well for you—

STELLA. It's certainly worked out well for you, since I pay all the bills around here.

    (*Beat.*)

LEWIS. You want some chips, Stell? Charlie? These guacamole chips are really…

CHARLIE. Shut up, Lewis!

STELLA. Could you please stop taking this out on Lewis? He is not the problem here.

CHARLIE. I'm well aware.

STELLA. (*Beat, then.*) Nick—

CHARLIE. (*Strained.*) Nick doesn't have a pilot. They just say that, people run around this fucking city saying things like "he has a pilot," "he has a go picture" "it's got a greenlight," when it's all just crap, it's just not even, it's lying taken to it's natural conclusion, these people are lying to make themselves feel better and they don't even know that they're lying and then everybody else around starts to tell the same lie and it's never true. That's the fucking punchline. Everybody's running around like psychotic sheep, bleating, "He has a pilot! He has a pilot—"

STELLA. He does have a pilot.

CHARLIE. Oh, god—

STELLA. You need a job!

CHARLIE. I know I need a job!

STELLA. Why would it kill you—

CHARLIE. I don't know, Stella!

STELLA. You just have to talk to him at a party—

CHARLIE. (*Furious.*) I am not talking to Nick! I'm not talking to that asshole! Do you understand me? I am not talking to Nick.

    (*He goes. Blackout.*)

Scene 3

CLEA *and* LEWIS, *in* LEWIS's *apartment. There is a cheese plate on a table. Lewis tries to light a candle with an automatic candle lighter, but it will not light. He finally gives up on it.*

LEWIS. Can I get you a drink? Vodka, you're a vodka girl, right?

CLEA. Water would be fantastic. Just a glass of water. I really don't drink.

LEWIS. Oh I know, I just, at Edward's party the other night you were like, you know—

CLEA. I was not drunk. At all. I hope you don't think that. Because I totally—

LEWIS. No no. I just meant you had one or two, so I thought that "no drinking" thing was not like a hard and fast rule or anything.

CLEA. (*Indignant.*) Is this a problem for you? Is it like important to you that I drink? Because that is so not something I feel comfortable with.

LEWIS. (*Alarmed.*) No! Oh my god of course not!

CLEA. I mean I asked for a glass of water and you're turning this into some major moral crisis here.

LEWIS. No—

CLEA. And I completely object to being called a "Vodka Girl." I mean, I told you before, my mother is an alcoholic so it's just not something I can be casual about, and for you to like insinuate, whatever, that I was drunk or something at that party—

LEWIS. No no, that's not what I meant at all. It's just, when you said "water," I just—it doesn't seem...

CLEA. Doesn't seem what, like you could get me drunk on water? Do you find like, drunk women attractive?

LEWIS. (*Sad.*) I was just, no!— I was just going to say that water doesn't seem festive. It seems so plain. I know everybody drinks it now, out of bottles and everything, but it just always to me it just seems so—plain.

CLEA. Plain is good. Plain is strong. Water is the strength of the earth. I don't find that "plain." I find that inspiring.

LEWIS. I know. I know! (*Beat.*) Let me get you a glass of water.

(*He goes, to get her water.*)

CLEA. Wait a minute. I'm sorry. I'm sorry, I'm a little, reactive. You're right, I said I'd come over for a drink and water, it's just not nice or something, I know you're trying to be real nice and I'd love a vodka. I had a real ridiculous day, vodka is actually an excellent idea. Maybe put some ice in it.

LEWIS. Okay.

(*He goes off. She looks around the apartment, calls after him.*)

CLEA. So. How's your friend the Nazi priestess?

LEWIS. (*Calling back.*) Oh, she's, you know, she's really not that bad.

(LEWIS *reenters with a glass of vodka, and ice. He hands it to her, pours her a drink.*)

CLEA. I know! I feel so terrible, I was totally exaggerating that interview I had and the whole thing was like, you know, just the sort of thing you say when you're not thinking!

LEWIS. Well, you didn't know—

CLEA. No, but your friend did! And he just let me keep going! It was just like a little hostile, you know. To let me go on like that. I was like, ouch! Got a little problem in the sack with the old wife, maybe?

LEWIS. No, no—not at all—they're really tight, they've been together—

CLEA. Oh totally, I didn't mean—

LEWIS. Forever! Ten years or something. And they're adopting this baby. They're great.

CLEA. Hey, what do I know. (*She downs her drink.*) Oh. Wow. Mmm. That is so—wow.

LEWIS. (*Disturbed now.*) He was just tense, that night. About other stuff.

CLEA. Look—don't treat me like I'm stupid. I mean, I think I know the difference between tension and hostility. So it's not like I'm stupid.

LEWIS. I don't think you're stupid!

CLEA. Well, you're acting kind of—

LEWIS. No, no—

CLEA. Because I really object to that. A lot of people treat me like I'm some sort of flake because I look a certain way, and that is just, I don't want to sound like some hideous feminist, but I will not be treated like a stupid person. I want to be clear on that.

LEWIS. God, no! I wouldn't have asked you to come over, if I thought—

CLEA. Well, good. Because I respect what you are saying, but I'm just, you know, your friend has like a lot of angry energy. Which I like! I mean, it's not like I'm saying that's a bad thing, if he's married to a screaming woman who is like obsessed with phone lists and highlighters—

LEWIS. She's really nice—

CLEA. Oh totally. I so totally get that. I'm just saying. I don't judge him if he's hostile about it.

(*There is an awkward pause.*)

LEWIS. I'm gonna get myself a drink. Can I refresh that for you? You know what, I'm just going to bring the bottle.

(*He goes.* CLEA *considers the cheese plate for a moment.* LEWIS *reenters, pouring himself a stiff drink, and watches her.*)

LEWIS. (*Continuing.*) Would you like a piece of cheese, or—

CLEA. Oh god no. I am totally on a diet. Food is like disgusting to me.

LEWIS. It is?

CLEA. Oh my god, are you kidding? Most of the things people put in their mouths is like totally just like eating death. That's how bad our food is for us. Do you not know this? They proved, somebody proved that eating is killing people. And that if you eat like hardly anything? Just like lettuce and maybe a few vegetables or something, everyday, that could make you live to be like a hundred and fifty years old. This is true, I read about it in the *New York Times*.

LEWIS. Eating—

CLEA. Is terrible for you. Don't do it.

LEWIS. Wow.

CLEA. Isn't it?

LEWIS. Yeah, that's—'cause everything I've heard before this, you know, food is considered to be life-sustaining.

CLEA. Well, except didn't you suspect that it was probably bad for you? All those people getting fat, all over America, just like buying food from grocery stores or going into restaurants where they give you these portions, and everything has chemicals in it, or who knows what, who knows what they put in our food anymore.

LEWIS. Wow. Not eating makes you live forever. Who, uh, knew.

CLEA. Well, I know it sounds weird but… (*Suddenly spooked.*) You know what? Forget it. I'm sorry. This is, I should go—

LEWIS. No! Why?

CLEA. I don't feel right, this just doesn't feel right.

LEWIS. Come on, you just got here! Have another drink—

CLEA. I don't really drink. I'm feeling embarrassed now, that I have to keep telling you that.

LEWIS. Please. I really like you. I, I want you to stay. Please.

CLEA. You just want to sleep with me.

LEWIS. What—that is—no!

CLEA. You don't want to sleep with me?

LEWIS. I didn't say that—

CLEA. See? This just happens to me all the time. Just, everyone just wants to sleep with me. Every guy I meet, it's just, I don't know what to do about it—because I am like, a very sensitive person—

LEWIS. I didn't just—invite you over here for sex, if that's what you think—

CLEA. It is what I think! It is!

LEWIS. No, no. No, no no—no—

CLEA. Oh, please—

LEWIS. No! I really like you. I think you're really interesting. I do.

CLEA. It's just, everybody just falls in love with me all the time. So many guys are just obsessed, and I—I mean, I'm just overwhelmed. I'm from Ohio, it's different there. I feel very out of control here.

(There is a long pause while LEWIS *tries to figure out what to do next.)*

LEWIS. Would you like a glass of water, or something?

CLEA. Maybe some vodka, I don't know. I'm kind of tense.

(He nods, and pours her a drink. He hands it to her. She holds it.)

LEWIS. Here, sit down. Come on, sit down.

CLEA. It's just been a very confusing day.

LEWIS. What happened?

CLEA. I don't want to talk about it.

LEWIS. *(Nice.)* Come on. I'm interested.

CLEA. *(Sudden.)* Would you like to kiss me?

LEWIS. *(A beat.)* Is this a trick question?

CLEA. You just, you seem like a really nice person, and I would really like it. If you would kiss me. If you're interested.

LEWIS. Yes, I'm interested! But I don't want to—you know—

CLEA. Do you think I'm a freak, or something? Because I've been freaking out here?

LEWIS. No, you just said that you were overwhelmed by men showing too much sexual interest in you, so I—

CLEA. I know, I know, I did just say that. But I would really like it if you would kiss me. I just think it might make me feel better, or—forget it—

LEWIS. No! No. No! It's okay. Really.

(He sets his drink down, takes her from her, sets it down, leans in carefully and kisses her.)

LEWIS. *(Continuing.)* How's that?

CLEA. It's nice.

(She kisses him again. They start making out. There is a knock at the door.)

LEWIS. Go away!

CHARLIE. Hey Lewis! You in there?

CLEA. Oh my god, is that your friend?

CHARLIE. Come on, you got to let me in, man—

LEWIS. Go away, Charlie—

(She pushes away from him.)

CLEA. No, it's fine, it's fine—you have to let him in, please, he's your friend! I'm fine! Let him in.

*(*LEWIS *goes to the door, and opens it.* CHARLIE *enters, carrying a script.)*

CHARLIE. I saw that shithead Nick. I went and had fucking lunch with that fucking shithead.

(He sees CLEA.*)*

CLEA. Hi.

CHARLIE. Oh. Hi! (*He is not happy to see her.*)

LEWIS. Clea just came over for a—

> (LEWIS *tips his head toward the open door, indicating that he would like* CHARLIE *to leave.* CHARLIE *railroads over him, not noticing.*)

CHARLIE. That fuckhead. I said, did I not say, he is a fuckhead? I told her that this would be a waste of my fucking time. I told everyone. Did I not? Did I not? What is this, vodka?

> (*He picks it up and uncorks it, then proceeds to drink from the bottle as he rants.*)

CHARLIE. (*Continuing.*) Because he is a fuck. You know this to be true. I mean, in high school he was a fuck, and in college, he was a fuck, and time is not a friend to people like that. I mean, it's not like they mellow. It's not like they ripen, like a good bottle of wine! No no no, Nick is still Nick, only more so. And now someone has actually told him that they are going to make his fucking pilot, which was just what Nick needed to really put the final touches on his complete lack of character! Give him a shred of power over hopeless and desperate people, that'll really make him shine! Not that I even believe it. I don't give a shit how many people say it. I do not believe that they are going to make his fucking pilot! Which by the way, he gave to me, to read, so on the sidewalk, outside the restaurant, after our cappuccinos, he took off and I opened it up and I read it, and I'm sure you'll be stunned to hear that it is utter mindless, soulless, uninspired, unoriginal, bereft, soul-sucking crap. Which is the only thing that makes me think he might actually be telling the truth. The fact that his fucking pilot is so irredeemably awful, such a complete expression of the bankruptcy of the American character, that alone argues for the shred of a possibility that he is flirting with the truth for once in his life, with his assertion that they are going to make his astonishingly shitty pilot. It is so bad, there actually is a possibility that they're going to make it. Against all my better judgment, I truly have to concede that.

CLEA. Wow.

CHARLIE. Oh you have no idea. This is the tip of the iceberg. This day was, I actually had lunch with that asshole at a place called "Grind." "Grind." Next thing you know they're going to be calling restaurants things like "Hot" "Wet" "Fuck me," someday we are all going to be forced to have lunch with assholes at some restaurant called "Fuck Me!" Nick of course is on his cell phone for a full five minutes before he can even say hello. Five minutes of the finger in the air, twitching— (*He sticks his finger in the air, twitches it.*) While I sit there grinning, like a SCHMUCK, it's okay, man, I know you got to hang on this endless phone call 'cause you're so fucking important, you're a completely essential piece of the whole mind-numbing motor that keeps capitalism itself running, you're the guy, you're the guy, and I'm just some stupid SHITHEAD who needs to lick your ass—

LEWIS. Hey, Charlie—

CHARLIE. C'mon I'm not making this up! I'm not even exaggerating! It was like a scene out of some bad Nineteenth Century novel, or a good one, even, *War and Peace*, he's Prince Somebody and I'm the bastard son of Somebody Else, who remembers, except for the licking of the ass part. Except if we were in Russia, in the Nineteenth Century, there would be a form for it all, a ritual, a way to keep your dignity while you said, please your highness, save my fucking worthless piece of shit self. Give me some money. I'm fucking broke, I'm not a man, GIVE ME SOME MONEY. And if you do, I will go to Siberia for you, I will face Bonaparte with my bare hands, I will fling myself into the abyss, just give me some fucking money so that I don't have to—Plus he's thin! Did I tell you this? You remember Nick, he was just like a normal guy, right? Aside from being a fuck? He's lost like forty pounds. And I mean, he was normal, before, it's not like he was fat, he was just normal so now he's like—it's like his face is just sitting right on his skull. You're like talking to a really skinny skull version of who Nick used to be. And he's dressed all in black, this bizarre black suit with a black silk t shirt under it, so he actually does look like one of those freaks from a vampire movie, do they honestly think that looks good, in Hollywood? They must! I don't know. I don't know. So then he orders like a huge slab of red meat, because that's all he can eat, apparently. That's how he got so thin, by eating only raw meat. I swear to you, I am not making ONE WORD of this up. And I'm completely, I am just trying to stay focused on the sucking up end of the conversation, trying not say anything truthful, just stay in the conversation, let him know that I'm a total failure of a human being, but I also know and appreciate that fact that he is not.

LEWIS. Charlie—

CHARLIE. Oh, stop it, don't even, that is completely what those conversations are about! That is what they are about! And I'm doing it, I am absolutely humiliating myself so that I can get Nick to give me an audition for a teeny tiny part in a pilot I don't even believe exists, when he looks at my plate and says, "I could never eat that. That is just too rich." I mean, he's got a slab of red meat the size of Nebraska sitting on his plate, and I've got a plate of mushroom puree, sitting in front of me. Mushroom puree, with about five or six itty bitty scallops on top of it, I got so fucking self conscious about how fucking thin he was, that I ordered a completely girly meal, scallops in mushroom puree, just so I wouldn't have to think about that crap while I castrated myself for this— this—skull-person—and then he—he—

(*He stops himself. Sits. Takes a big hit off the vodka bottle.*)

CHARLIE. (*Continuing.*) Sorry. Forget about it. I don't even know what I'm saying.

CLEA. No. Are you kidding? That was incredible. What you just said. That was—wow. I'm like tingling.

CHARLIE. Oh, good. (*Then.*) Am I interrupting?

CLEA. No!

LEWIS. Well, kind of—

CHARLIE. Oh, shit—

CLEA. No, it's fine—

CHARLIE. You're, like, having a drink here—

LEWIS. Yes.

CHARLIE. I'm sorry. I'll take off.

CLEA. God no, that was horrible what you just went through! You have to stay with your friends and just like, at least stay, and and and stay, until you feel like a human being again!

CHARLIE. Thanks, but—

CLEA. (*To* LEWIS.) He should stay, right? You can't send him back to the Nazi priestess at least until he just relaxes or—

LEWIS. She's really not that bad—

CHARLIE. No, she's great. She's great.

CLEA. Oh I know. I totally know. But come on. Should I get you a glass? So that you don't have to keep—

(*She gestures, drinking from the bottle.*)

CHARLIE. Maybe that's a good idea.

CLEA. Totally. They're like in here, right? I'll get another glass.

(*She goes. There is a long moment of silence.* LEWIS *looks at him, not amused.*)

CHARLIE. You said you asked her for drinks, I didn't know that meant today.

LEWIS. Yes! Today! Today!

CHARLIE. Come on, you're not actually getting anywhere are you?

LEWIS. Yes, I am, I was, at least, I don't seem to be anymore—

CHARLIE. She's a fucking moron, Lewis—

LEWIS. I don't care!

CHARLIE. You want me to take off?

LEWIS. Yes! No. I don't—she's very—sensitive. If you left, I don't think—I don't know—

CHARLIE. I'm sorry, man—

CLEA. (*Reentering.*) What are you sorry about?

(*She takes the vodka bottle from* CHARLIE *and pours him a drink.*)

CHARLIE. Just about coming over here and losing it.

CLEA. Don't apologize! Are you kidding! You are so in touch with your feelings.

CHARLIE. That's not actually something you want to say to a guy, to make him feel better. That's not actually considered a compliment, on our planet.

CLEA. Well, you are so just wrong about that. Because if you lose, like, knowing who you are? If you lose that? You're lost. And then the bastards like Nick, they just rule the world.

CHARLIE. They already rule the world, Clea.

CLEA. They don't rule you.

(*She hands him his drink.*)

CHARLIE. Yeah, uh, thanks.

CLEA. Besides, it's so great you came by because I totally need to apologize. That stuff I said the other night? I mean, whoa. My bad, my total bad.

CHARLIE. It's okay.

CLEA. That's very very decent of you to say. Because I felt terrible afterwards, I was being so rude about everybody. Especially your wife! The things I said! Here—

(*She pours him more vodka.*)

CHARLIE. Look, forget it, would you? We all say shitty things about people we don't know. It's the only true pleasure left in the world, trashing other people. Especially when they have something you want: Money. Or power. Or just, coherence—

LEWIS. Hey, Charlie maybe we should—

CHARLIE. (*Complete overlap, revving again.*) Not that I think Nick is coherent in any way, any larger cosmic truth has evaded Nick altogether—

LEWIS. Yeah, but I just don't know that—

CHARLIE. (*Complete overlap.*) But he's still the object of desire, isn't he? Him and that fucking pilot. He could be shooting kiddie porn as far as anyone's concerned and I still have to suck up, don't I, that's how degraded this whole fucking planet has gotten, SUCK UP to assholes like Nick because they have something you must want even though you don't, you don't want it, everyone just thinks, god, it's like we don't even know how to have a real DESIRE anymore! It's all the opposite of enlightenment, remember when that was a goal? Nowadays if someone said to you, what you want out of life? And you said, I don't know, enlightenment, what do you think would happen? WHAT DO YOU THINK WOULD HAPPEN? These are the fucking end times. The entire fucking culture has devolved to such a point that what we WANT, what we DESIRE isn't love or passion or sex or money, it's MEANINGLESSNESS. And that's what I'm supposed to sell myself for. Time to sell it, my heart, my soul, my common sense, my hope, my dreams, my pride, anything that means anything at all to my little pre-conscious, subconscious self, all of it goes on the auction block for what? That's what I want to know. What am I supposed to get? To give up everything? What do I get? (*Beat.*) I have a feeling we're gonna need more vodka. You got another bottle back there?

LEWIS. Sorry.

CLEA. Can you, can you go get some?

LEWIS. Oh—

CHARLIE. No, no—god, I'm sorry—I got to get out of here, I'm just—

CLEA. No no please. Don't be ridiculous. I'll go—

LEWIS/CHARLIE. No—no—no—

    (*Beat.*)

CLEA. Just I mean, for vodka.

CHARLIE. I'll go, it's fine. Really. There's a liquor store just a couple blocks, besides, I'm the one sucking it down.

CLEA. You're in crisis! You just got here, and you're wrecked! Lewis, can you go?

    (*Beat.*)

LEWIS. Maybe we should go to dinner.

CLEA. All three of us? Do you want to?

CHARLIE. (*Slight beat.*) You know what? I'm going to take off—I really—

CLEA. Stop it! That is insane. Besides, I totally want to hear about all of this. I mean, you have no idea how inspiring it is to hear you just talk! To someone like me? Because I am so new here, I mean, I just came like minutes ago from Ohio and the whole world seems so—just insane, you know— I am so confused like all the time—and then I listen to you, and I know I'm not crazy. (*To* LEWIS, *gushing.*) Doesn't he make you feel like that? Just less crazy?

CHARLIE. Actually, Clea, I am being alarmingly self-indulgent, and I need to go home.

CLEA. If you wanted to go home, wouldn't you have been there by now? And you are not being self-indulgent. I think it's sad that you think that. Because you're like on fire. They don't deserve you.

LEWIS. They, who?

CLEA. None of them.

LEWIS. Maybe we could all go. For the booze, I mean.

CLEA. Do you need money?

LEWIS. No!

CHARLIE. That's a good idea, we'll all go.

CLEA. But that doesn't make any sense. Besides, you must be starving! All you had for lunch was a couple of scallops and some mushrooms. Aren't you hungry?

CHARLIE. Yeah, but—

CLEA. (*To* LEWIS.) Could you pick up some pizza, too? There's like a stand down on there someplace, right?

LEWIS. I thought you only ate vegetables.

CLEA. Not for me! I can't eat a thing, I am so totally bloated right now. But I would have another drink. I mean, I don't drink, I really don't? But sometimes it clearly is just what has to happen. It'll only take you like a minute, right?

LEWIS. Yeah. (*Beat.*) Yes! Sure!

CLEA. Great!

LEWIS. Yeah, okay. I'll be right back.

(*He grabs his jacket and goes to the door, where he turns and looks at them.*)

LEWIS. (*Continuing.*) I'll—be right back!

(*He goes, shutting the door behind him.* CLEA *turns to* CHARLIE, *smiling.*)

CLEA. That is incredible, the way you define things with so much fire. I really can't even, I mean, it's totally overwhelming.

CHARLIE. Yeah.

(*He smiles at her, brief, looks away, at the cheese plate, then stands, moves away from her.*)

CLEA. You knew I was going to be here, didn't you?

CHARLIE. What? No.

CLEA. I could tell. When you walked in.

CHARLIE. No, that's—

CLEA. You're lying.

CHARLIE. You know what? I'm taking off.

CLEA. That's not what you want to do.

CHARLIE. Actually, it is. Just tell Lewis—you don't have to tell him anything, he will be so relieved I'm gone, he won't care.

(*He heads for the door.*)

CLEA. You spent the whole day doing things that made you feel shitty about yourself. Why don't you just do something you want to do?

(*She gets close to him. He takes a step back.*)

CHARLIE. You're on a date with my best friend.

CLEA. So?

CHARLIE. So I think I'd like to pretend that I still have a shred of integrity—

CLEA. Why?

CHARLIE. Because—you know—because I don't have much else left.

CLEA. You don't know what you have. Because nobody has been telling you. They've just been telling you what you're not. Why don't you try being what you are?

(*She starts to kiss him. He pushes her away for a moment. Then, he leans in and kisses her, pushing her back to the couch. They land on the couch and start to make out in earnest. Blackout.*)

End of Act I

ACT II
Scene 1

CHARLIE's *apartment. CLEA and CHARLIE are having sex on the couch, and elsewhere. They are both in a half state of undress, as if they hit the ground running. It is quite athletic. After an extended and quite vocal climax, they collapse.*

CLEA. Oh, god. Don't stop. No, don't stop. Don't stop!

CHARLIE. You got to give me a minute here, Clea.

CLEA. No, don't stop—

CHARLIE. How old did you say you were?

(*He means it half as a joke, but it does stop her.*)

CLEA. No no don't do that. Don't categorize me.

CHARLIE. (*Still breathless.*) Asking you how old you are is categorizing?

CLEA. You're trying to define age as a life characteristic. As like, something that says something about a person.

CHARLIE. It does say, how old you are.

CLEA. No, it doesn't. It really doesn't. You say, "how old are you" like I'm young and you're old, like that's some joke, because you think you're old? But you're timeless. You're like this incredible lion who's been stalking the earth since the dawn of nature, or something.

CHARLIE. Tell me, do you actually believe all this crap that you keep spouting?

CLEA. Of course I believe it. Maybe you should try believing it, too. Why wouldn't you want to believe that you're a timeless lion? Isn't that better than thinking you're some old loser who can't get a job?

(*She climbs on him and starts to kiss him. He pushes her away, sudden, stands and puts his pants on.*)

CLEA. (*Continuing.*) No no. Don't do that. That's what I'm saying, that's not who you are!

CHARLIE. We have to get you out of here.

(*He starts to dress, and straighten out the room again.*)

CLEA. We just got here.

CHARLIE. And now we have to go.

CLEA. You said she was going to be at work, all afternoon, she's off screaming somewhere, come on, you said, we have all afternoon. Be a lion.

CHARLIE. I think we've had enough of the lion, Clea.

CLEA. I haven't. I mean it. I can go all day, and all night, I could go a whole weekend. Have you ever done that? Just, spent a whole weekend inside, doing things…

CHARLIE. Don't you get sore?

CLEA. You want to find out?

CHARLIE. Jesus! You're like, it's like talking to a porno movie—

CLEA. You are so hung up about the way I talk all the time!

CHARLIE. Well, it's very unusual, Clea, to find someone so remarkably uninhibited in so many ways—

CLEA. Yeah but you always turn it around, like you don't like it. You make it sound like it's maybe not so great, the way I am. That I'm sort of stupid, or just stupid or something—

CHARLIE. "Voracious" is actually the word I was thinking of.

CLEA. Yeah, like that's a bad thing. But you know what? You like it. It's actually driving you crazy how much you like it. Why can't you just say it? If I'm voracious then you're something that wants voracious more than anything it ever saw before.

CHARLIE. How can you know so much and so little at the same time?

CLEA. You have no idea, how much I know. Come on. We have all afternoon.

(*She kisses him. He is increasingly a lost man. He tries to push her away.*)

CHARLIE. We do have all afternoon. Just, not here.

CLEA. Ohhh please…

CHARLIE. Listen to me. This is my apartment.

CLEA. I know. I love it that you brought me here. It's so hostile.

CHARLIE. You are really something.

CLEA. Yes, I am. And you're the one who brought me here, to have sex in your apartment.

CHARLIE. Stella could just walk in on us—

CLEA. (*Laughing.*) That would be hilarious.

CHARLIE. Yeah, no, it wouldn't.

(*He pushes her away, firm. Looks at her, suddenly simple and clear and a little desperate.*)

CHARLIE. (*Continuing.*) I mean, you understand what this is. We're clear on what this is, right?

CLEA. Relax. I know what this is. You're at a place, so am I. This is that place.

CHARLIE. Yes.

CLEA. It's what you need and I want, and that's why it's so hot. Trust me. I understand what this is.

CHARLIE. Good.

> (*Unsure, hoping that was clear, he leaves the room. She watches him go, goes to her purse, and takes out an apple, starts to eat, and call to him in the next room.*)

CLEA. (*Yelling.*) You know what we should do tonight? My friend can get me into this party. It's up on the upper west side so it is totally not like a really hip scene or anything, but there's going to be some movie stars there, she wouldn't tell me who, but they also have this hot tub there? On the roof. She went to a party at this place a couple weeks ago, and everyone takes their clothes off and gets in the hot tub. And then they have these cater waiters come around, I'm not kidding, with sushi. So you sit in the hot tub and like talk and eat sushi naked. It sounds so nineties, doesn't it? Movie stars and sushi in a hot tub? Maybe they'll play R.E.M. on the "record player." Or do lines of cocaine. It's so unbelievably retro, a hot tub on the roof. I soo want to go.

CHARLIE. (*Entering.*) I've been to this party.

CLEA. Get out.

CHARLIE. I swear to god, I went to that party twenty years ago. Riverside Drive, ninety-six or seven and Riverside.

CLEA. I don't know.

CHARLIE. Sushi and cocaine in the hot tub on the roof? I went to that party. No kidding. I was doing this play off Broadway, and one of the other actors knew somebody who was going to this party, on the upper west side. This rich guy, nobody knew his name, and the place is like a mansion, right, he owns the whole building and it's got art deco everything, completely tasteless. The place was huge, like five floors, people screwing in corners of the den and the living room, there was a three way going on in one room, I'm not kidding, real hedonistic shit. And then there's that the hot tub up there on the roof with the greenhouse. (*Laughing now.*) He's got a fucking greenhouse up there, growing cactuses and hibiscus, something, I can't believe I remember this, everybody was completely coked out of their minds, like all night, till five, six in the morning. That's how stupid we all were. It's amazing most of us are still alive. I was such hot shit. That play was unintelligible but I got amazing reviews, and I was… the world was on fire for me, boy. Sushi and cocaine and whatever I wanted. God that was fun. That was really fun.

CLEA. Well, guess what, it's your lucky night. Because you can go to that party again. With me.

CHARLIE. (*Reality check.*) I can't go to a party with you.

CLEA. Why not?

CHARLIE. Because I can't.

CLEA. It'll be reallly fun. That's what you said, it was reallly fun.

CHARLIE. I'm not going to a party with you, Clea!

CLEA. No one will see us! That's the whole point, that scene is completely over, so it won't matter!

CHARLIE. Great.

CLEA. You said yourself, the guy who owns this place is so nobody on earth that is important, just some rich guy with a lot of money and a house with a hot tub, we can totally just go together. I mean, with my friend, we can dump her when we get there, which will be fine with her, she dumps me all the time.

CHARLIE. Look, I have—a life, Clea.

CLEA. Don't you mean, a "wife?"

CHARLIE. Yeah. That's what I mean. And like you said that scene is over. I'm not going to a party with you.

(*He continues straightening the apartment.*)

CLEA. No, come on, forget about her! You should see how much happier you are when you forget about her. We don't have to go to any party. Let's just pretend we're at a party. We're in the hot tub right now. No. No. Let's skip the hot tub. I like the sound of those rooms, where people are just doing things, in the middle of somebody's house, who they don't even know whose house it is. Let's just think about doing it in front of everybody, in somebody else's room…

(*She reaches up and kisses him. He kisses her back. As things are heating up again, the door opens. STELLA enters, and sees them. She stops. After a moment, she speaks.*)

STELLA. Charlie. I'm here.

(*This is the first CHARLIE and CLEA are aware of her entrance.*)

CHARLIE. Shit.

CLEA. Oh. Shit. Wow. This is so—embarrassing.

CHARLIE. Stella.

STELLA. What are you doing, Charlie?

CHARLIE. Nothing. No—this isn't—

STELLA. What, what it looks like? It isn't what it looks like?

CHARLIE. Stella—

STELLA. In my home? You brought— to my home?

(CLEA *starts to laugh, embarrassed. She tries to stop herself, but simply can't.*)

CLEA. I'm sorry. Oh, I am so sorry. But this is just hideous. Oh my god. Wow. It's just so, horrible, and embarrassing.

STELLA. What is she doing here? Don't tell me what she's doing here, I can see what she's doing here. Get out of my house. GET HER OUT OF HERE.

CHARLIE. You have to go.

CLEA. Oh, look. I mean, this is horrible, right, but there's no reason to get all, like, rude. Things have happened here, obviously, but it's not like that's somebody's fault. I mean, I am so not interested in some kind of a ridiculous scene.

(She stands and looks for her clothes.)

STELLA. Oh she's a brain surgeon isn't she? Yeah, this makes complete sense now. I can see why this happened.

CLEA. See this is what I'm talking about! People getting all insulting in a situation like this, why? Is that supposed to help? Because I don't think that is in the least bit helpful.

STELLA. Charlie, get her out of here!

CHARLIE. Clea. Just go.

CLEA. Why should I go? I mean, I was invited here. You and I are doing something here. You made a choice, Charlie, that involved me and not her, and that choice made you happy for the first time in whatever, I mean, you were like fucking miserable until I showed up.

STELLA. Why are you talking?

CLEA. I'm talking because I have something to say!

STELLA. You don't have anything to say! You don't know anything! And you're in my house! This is my house, I pay the rent here, that is my husband, you don't have any rights here!

CLEA. I've been fucking him all afternoon and you haven't. That doesn't exactly give me no rights.

(She sits on the couch, defiant. STELLA looks at CHARLIE, stunned.)

CHARLIE. I'm sorry. Clea. You have to go. We have things, Stella and I have things we need to—this shouldn't have happened, this way, at all, and, and—

CLEA. But it did happen. And you were the one who made it happen. So "should," I think "should" is a very useless word in a situation like this.

STELLA. Charlie?

CHARLIE. I'm sorry. I'm completely in the wrong.

CLEA. Stop. Just stop, already. "In the wrong?"

CHARLIE. (*Furious.*) Clea, do not interfere in this!

CLEA. She's the one who's interfering! Come on, things were fine until she showed up!

CHARLIE. Stop acting like an idiot!

CLEA. You're the one who's being an idiot! "In the wrong?" You're just going to give away your power like that? To her? That's what she wants, that's what she's been about this whole time, I pay the rent, I want a baby, go suck up to stupid crazy Nick because me and my highlighters rule the world, what about what you want?

STELLA. Is that what you told her? This person, this, you told her—what did you tell her? Why do I care what you told her, that's clearly the least of, we're married, we've been married for—

CHARLIE. (*Overlap.*) No. No, I did not tell her—this is not, this was not meant to be anything, Stella, this was a mistake—

STELLA. A mistake is forgetting my birthday, Charlie. I don't know what this is. (*She sits, desolate.*)

CLEA. Charlie, are you coming?

CHARLIE. What?

CLEA. Look, we're doing something. Right? We were doing something, before she barged in.

STELLA. I live here! Are you insane? Because you sound insane. You're having an affair with an insane person. Maybe I'm the insane person, I can't, I don't even know, I have, there are—I don't, was your life that bad that you had to let this into it?

CHARLIE. No.

STELLA. Ten years, ten years! You can just, for this? This thing, this isn't a person, even, I don't know what she is—

CLEA. Okay—

STELLA. You shut up! You've ruined my life, I don't have to take care of your feelings! Charlie, say something, please! What happened? Why did you do this? Were there other ways I should have taken care of you?

CLEA. He's a man, he doesn't need a mommy.

STELLA. You know, I will hurt you. I will find some sort of weapon, there's got to be something somewhere, a knife or a vase, anything really is starting to look good, and I will hurt you and we will all end up in the Daily News. I promise you, I am not kidding. You need to get out of my house, right now. RIGHT NOW.

CLEA. Look at you, you don't even get it yet! You're just acting like a man, threatening violence and oh you're in charge of everything, why don't you just start waving your highlighters and screaming Heil Hitler? If you knew how to keep him, you would've. Look at him! He's just like totally silent around you. He's nobody with you. Let me tell you something, he isn't like that with me. With me, he's a lion, roaming the earth. With me, he's a god!

STELLA. You have got to be fucking kidding me!

CLEA. You don't make him feel the way I do. You don't even begin to know how. So you can go ahead and hit me, or hurt me, or whatever, be violent, just like a man? But that's what your problem is. I'm going, Charlie. You know where to find me.

(*She goes. There is a long moment of silence.*)

STELLA. Why?

CHARLIE. Don't ask why.

STELLA. (*Suddenly furious.*) Don't ask—why? "Why" is off the table? You just completely—that was the most humiliating—I'm humiliated, Charlie! I'm, I'm everything is, my whole life is suddenly not even—and for that? And I'm not allowed to ask WHY?

CHARLIE. This is just, I can't—I can't...

STELLA. Stop being such a fucking coward and say something!

CHARLIE. You're too competent.

(*There is a silence at this.*)

STELLA. What?

CHARLIE. Everything. Gets done. Even when you hate what you're doing, you get it done. You're like a machine. Everything gets done.

STELLA. (*Almost in tears, suddenly.*) I'm not a machine. That's a lie.

CHARLIE. You're coherent. Everything coheres, and I, I can't— anymore—because I'm—and you're perfect. Your feelings are perfect. Your work is perfect. You hold down a job you think is stupid and it frustrates you in the perfect way. Even in how you're not perfect, even in how things get to you, you're just, even your neurosis is perfect. You're so fucking competent, you don't ever expect too much out of life. You handle all of it. Even this. Even this! I'm watching you—you're handling it. You're already going to forgive this. THAT WAS A FOREGONE CONCLUSION. And then I'll have that, too. Your competence, and your forgiveness. Oh and your money, let's not forget that.

STELLA. So this is my fault?

CHARLIE. (*Snarling.*) No! It's my fault! It's my crime! And I own it! It's the only thing you left me, the ability to fuck up, and I want it! It's mine! This fucking disaster is mine, and you can just keep your fucking hands off of it!

STELLA. I don't understand why this is happening. Why are you talking to me like this?

CHARLIE. I'm talking to you like this because this is who I am! And I'm sick of pretending to be perfect, like you, because that is not the person I want to be!

STELLA. This is some sort of fucking mid-life crisis. You want to fuck idiotic twenty somethings because that's what everybody else does, there isn't even a shred of originality in this—

CHARLIE. I wasn't looking for originality, Stella. I was looking to feel like someone who still had a shred of life in him!

STELLA. And fucking great looking idiots is the only way you can do that? Are you kidding me? I mean it. You don't like your life so you honestly think that screwing that girl—that girl who can hardly speak— who has no character or substance or anything—that that is going to do something for you, make you whole, make you understand who you are in the world—

CHARLIE. I don't want that. Don't you understand?

STELLA. This is just, it's just self-loathing, Charlie! You're projecting your self loathing all over the rest of us and destroying everything so you can destroy yourself—

CHARLIE. Thanks, Stell, that's really, this is a thrilling moment to be psychoanalyzed—

STELLA. What else am I supposed to do?

CHARLIE. Nothing! Don't do anything! And don't explain this because I don't want to understand it! I just want to feel something. Remember when you felt things?

STELLA. I feel things!

CHARLIE. Honey, you feel unhappy. You feel competent. You feel like a wall.

STELLA. Don't you tell me what I feel. I feel disgust!

CHARLIE. You know what? She's right about one thing. If you want me to stay, you really don't know the first thing about how to make that happen.

(*He heads for the door.*)

STELLA. Where are you going?

CHARLIE. I'm going to a party.

(*He slams the door. Blackout.*)

Scene 2

STELLA *and* LEWIS, *in* LEWIS's *apartment. She is nervous, bereft.*

STELLA. Thanks for letting me come over, I...

LEWIS. No, sure, thanks for calling. You look great.

STELLA. I look like shit.

LEWIS. Well, no. You feel like shit. But you look great. Come on in, come on in.

STELLA. Have you heard from him?

LEWIS. No.

STELLA. Do you know where he is?

LEWIS. Stella…

STELLA. Is he living with her?

LEWIS. I don't know. That seems…

STELLA. I know, but where else would he be?

LEWIS. I don't know.

STELLA. How did this happen? So fast? Didn't it happen so fast?

LEWIS. Yes. It did.

STELLA. Did you know it was going on?

LEWIS. I…

STELLA. You did.

LEWIS. I thought, there was one night, here, a couple weeks ago. I thought something might…

STELLA. How long ago?

LEWIS. A couple weeks. Three weeks?

STELLA. Was it going on, then, is that what you mean? He was already, three weeks ago?

LEWIS. I don't know. Maybe it started that night, I don't—do you really want to—

STELLA. Yes. Yes! I want to, I can't—there's so much, you go, we had a good marriage. I thought. There was so much bile, when he, I'm too competent. That's what he told me. With so much hatred, I didn't… I thought he loved me.

LEWIS. He does love you.

STELLA. He's gone, Lewis! I called his cell phone, a bunch of times. I left utterly humiliating messages, please call, please come home, we have to talk, and and and nothing. I don't even know where he is. Do you think he's with her? Why would he be with that person?

LEWIS. I don't know.

STELLA. I mean I guess she's pretty. She's just so—but she is pretty. Is that enough?

LEWIS. No.

STELLA. Do you think she's pretty?

LEWIS. No.

STELLA. But she's attractive. She's sexy.

LEWIS. No.

STELLA. I walked in on them. Did he tell you?

LEWIS. I haven't spoken to him.

STELLA. Then how do you know where he is?

LEWIS. I don't, Stella. Sweetie. I don't know.

STELLA. I know, I'm sorry, I'm sorry, I shouldn't be dumping this on you.

LEWIS. That's not—

STELLA. I should go. I should go home. I'm afraid to go home. I don't know where my husband is.

(*She starts to cry. Lewis goes to her, puts his arm around her. She sobs into his shirt.*)

LEWIS. I would like to kill him.

STELLA. No. It's okay. It's not okay, it's so confusing. I'm sorry, I don't want to get snot on your sweater.

LEWIS. It's okay. I'm going to get you a glass of wine.

(*He goes. STELLA sits alone for a moment. She starts to cry again, then dries her eyes, shakes herself. She reaches into her purse and pulls out a manila envelope. She sets it on the coffee table, then takes it back and holds it to her chest. LEWIS returns, carrying two glasses. He sees her, takes a moment, then proceeds.*)

LEWIS. (*Continuing.*) Hey.

STELLA. Oh. Thank you. I'm sorry about all this, Lewis. I just didn't, I needed to see you and think about how normal my life used to be, when something like this happens, all of a sudden everything you thought you knew, it's all, I'm too competent. Did you know? I didn't know. I'm too—

LEWIS. Sweetie, there's nothing wrong with you. He's going through something, it doesn't have anything to do with you. You're perfect.

(STELLA *reacts, upset.*)

STELLA. That's what he said! That's why he hates me now!

LEWIS. He doesn't hate you.

STELLA. Oh god I'm sorry I'm being such a, oh, I don't want to drown in self-pity, that's so repulsive, I hate it when people do that. I'm just very confused.

LEWIS. Have some wine.

STELLA. (*With a shred of irony.*) Yes, that will help, won't it. Alcohol is so useful when you just want to clear your head.

(*She takes a drink.*)

LEWIS. (*Cautious.*) What's that?

(*He points to the envelope.*)

STELLA. It's the baby.

LEWIS. What?

STELLA. My baby. They sent me, when you do these international adoptions, they send you pictures, when they've picked out your baby. So. They sent me pictures of my baby.

(*Upset, but trying to stay on top of it now, she tries to open the envelope. She can't manage it.*)

LEWIS. Here. Let me.

STELLA. I'm sorry.

(LEWIS *opens the envelope and takes out several photographs, and a document of several pages.*)

LEWIS. She's beautiful.

STELLA. Isn't she beautiful?

LEWIS. Beautiful.

STELLA. She's, they send you that packet, when they pick your baby—I just told you this already, I'm sorry, I started doing that—repeating myself all the time—like my mother, my crazy mother does that—

LEWIS. Does Charlie know…

STELLA. I told him. I mean, I called him, and I told him. That we have to let them know. If we want her or not. I left a message on his cell phone.

LEWIS. And he didn't…

STELLA. No. Nothing. (*Beat.*) I don't know what's happened. To my life.

LEWIS. You can do it anyway. Can't you? You went through the whole process. They approved you.

STELLA. They approved both of us, and I don't know where he is! I don't know where that girl lives, I even tried to track her down through the stupid temp agency and they wouldn't give me the information and I told them off and canceled our contract with them. I did. Without consulting anyone, I just—I'm acting like a crazy person and I don't care. I would go over there and beg him, just—how can I, I would anyway, my pride is, I don't care. Do think this is why? That he didn't want the baby?

LEWIS. I don't know why, Stella. You want my opinion, he's completely lost his mind, leaving you for anybody for any length of time is just about the most insane thing I've ever heard of. Ever.

STELLA. I'm not going to be able to get her. Am I. They won't give her to me, now. And all I'll have, ever, is that stupid job that I hate, I hate that job—

LEWIS. You'll get her.

STELLA. Nothing. All I'll ever have, is nothing.

(*She is utterly bewildered with grief.* LEWIS *sits there, bereft for a moment.*)

LEWIS. (*Blurting.*) It's my fault.

STELLA. Oh, Lewis, don't be ridiculous.

LEWIS. It's true. All of this, with Charlie, he didn't even—when he met her, he couldn't stand her. I was the one who brought her into our lives—

STELLA. No—she was just there—

LEWIS. I did, I asked her over. Because I didn't care, I knew that she was—some kind of succubus—and I wanted her anyway, that's why he even saw her again, he wouldn't have, if it wasn't for me. He wouldn't have.

STELLA. (*Beat.*) You asked her…what did you ask her?

LEWIS. (*Beat.*) Nothing.

STELLA. Your apartment? You said that before. She was in your apartment. Because you were on a date with her?

LEWIS. No. I mean, it doesn't matter. It doesn't…

STELLA. Well, what was she doing here then? If you weren't on a date with her?

LEWIS. I was just, you know, I invited her over for a drink.

STELLA. And Charlie, you invited him over—

LEWIS. No, he just came by. And… she was there.

STELLA. Because you invited her.

LEWIS. Yes.

STELLA. Why did you invite her?

LEWIS. I know, it was stupid, I just—

STELLA. You wanted to, to fuck her.

LEWIS. No! Well, of course I—Stella, this isn't—useful—

STELLA. Useful! And being useful has worked so fucking well for me up to this point! She was here because you, you wanted her too, that monster, I mean, she is just a fucking nightmare—of a human being—and that didn't matter, did it—

LEWIS. Stella, this isn't, there's no point to this—

STELLA. THERE'S NO POINT TO ANYTHING, LEWIS, HAVEN'T YOU NOTICED? I'm sorry. I know, I'm being, I don't have to apologize, to you, you ruined my life—

LEWIS. I didn't, you know I—

STELLA. Fucking men, you fucks, you always stick together—

LEWIS. That is not—

STELLA. Not what, not useful? Christ. My head is going to explode. You and Charlie. Want her. Want her. That's what men want.

LEWIS. It isn't! You are what I wanted, but I couldn't have you because you're married to my best friend!

STELLA. (*Reeling.*) Stop it, you liar, you're a fucking liar!

LEWIS. (*Furious.*) It's true, you know it is, that's why I invited her—

STELLA. You invited her because—fuck you, who cares why you did it. You just did it—

LEWIS. Stella—

STELLA. Fuck you, you invited her in, why, why was she here for him to see again, why was she here, it was because you—you were the one—

LEWIS. No—

STELLA. You just said it yourself! I have to get out of here. I have to go. I can't… I can't…

LEWIS. Stella—

STELLA. Shut up. Shut up. Don't talk to me. Don't ever talk to me again.

(*She takes her pictures and papers, clutches them to herself, and goes. Blackout.*)

Scene 3

CLEA's *apartment. It is a mess.* CHARLIE *lies on the bed. There is a big bottle of vodka on the floor next to him. He pours himself a very stiff drink—a huge drink—which finishes off the bottle.*

CHARLIE. (*Calling.*) We need more vodka!

CLEA. What?

CHARLIE. (*To himself.*) We need more vodka.

(*He drinks, then—.*)

CHARLIE. (*Continuing; calling.*) So what'd you think of Nick?

CLEA. (*Off.*) What?

CHARLIE. (*Yelling.*) Nick. I saw you talking to him. At that party last night.

(CLEA *enters, dressed in black, to go out. She is jazzed, happy.*)

CLEA. I thought he was fine.

CHARLIE. He's an asshole.

CLEA. Well, that's a little reductive.

CHARLIE. Reductive?

CLEA. (*Friendly.*) Yeah, you know, like, reductive. Reductive. Like, judgmentally reductive.

CHARLIE. It's judgmentally reductive to call an asshole an asshole?

CLEA. (*Cheerful.*) Look I don't even know the guy. I just think defining any human being by one word, one demeaning sort of reducing word is something I don't want to be involved with.

(*She hunts under the couch for shoes.*)

CHARLIE. Yes, you have very high moral standards.

CLEA. I'm not trying to be judgmental! That's what I'm saying!

CHARLIE. Do you even know what reductive means?

CLEA. Somebody's in a bad mood…

(*She leans over and kisses him. He starts to drag her back onto the bed, but she pulls away.*)

CLEA. (*Continuing.*) Ooooooooh, I can't, Charlie. I have this thing I have to do.

(She slips on her heels, then goes to the wall, picks up makeup and jewelry off a bookcase there and finishes getting ready to go out.)

CHARLIE. What thing?

CLEA. It's like a dinner thing, with one of my girlfriends. I told you about it.

CHARLIE. Yeah, but all you say is it's a "thing." It's not exactly specific. It's like the opposite of specific. The only way you could say less is to say nothing at all.

CLEA. Which I know you would think was just fabulous since you think the way I talk is so stupid.

(He grabs her.)

CHARLIE. You look like a spider tonight. Getting ready to go out and sting some poor unsuspecting but delicious victim—

(He starts to kiss her. She pulls away.)

CLEA. Charlie, wow, you know, this is, you are acting, I think you have had a little too much vodka or something.

CHARLIE. We're out of vodka.

CLEA. That's not exactly a surprise. I mean, the way you've been sucking it down lately is a little—

(Beat.)

CHARLIE. No, go on.

CLEA. I am not criticizing. I mean, obviously you were in a very wrong place with the Nazi priestess and that was totally sucking you dry for how many years, I think it is obvious that I have had a lot of sympathy for you coming out of that situation, and I have been very supportive even through all this self-undermining behavior because of what you've been through.

CHARLIE. You didn't like Stella, did you. Met her for fifteen minutes and you just couldn't stand her.

CLEA. Need I point out, neither can you.

CHARLIE. You don't know anything about anything.

CLEA. Oh brother. This is exactly what I mean about the vodka. No one made you do anything. You were very clear about what you wanted from this situation! Do you not recall saying to me, you just wanted to be clear?

CHARLIE. Yes I recall that.

CLEA. Well.

(She finds her purse and starts to go.)

CHARLIE. Can I borrow twenty bucks?

(She turns at this, startled.)

CHARLIE. *(Continuing.)* We need more vodka.

CLEA. You want to borrow money? From me? For vodka? Like, I don't have a job.

CHARLIE. Neither do I.

CLEA. So use a credit card.

(*She starts to go again.*)

CHARLIE. She cut them off. None of them work anymore.

(CLEA *turns on this, startled.*)

CLEA. I just—wait a minute. All of your credit cards? You have like six.

CHARLIE. All of them. None of them. Work.

CLEA. The Nazi priestess—

CHARLIE. Stopped them.

CLEA. So you don't have any money.

CHARLIE. Nope.

CLEA. Well, what does she expect you to live on?

CHARLIE. Not her, apparently.

CLEA. What a bitch.

CHARLIE. What did you say?

CLEA. Well, it's just so passive-aggressive.

CHARLIE. I think cutting off all my credit cards would be considered aggressive-aggressive, Clea.

CLEA. Which is why you're not with her. So, look— (*Digs in her purse.*) I don't have a lot of money because as you know I just came here a few months ago, from Ohio, and I have not yet found a job that I think is something I could really get excited about but I do have some money. My mom sends me a check once in a while. Here. I mean, that is terrible, what she did.

(*She holds out a bill. CHARLIE stares at it, takes a breath, then takes it, looks at it.*)

CHARLIE. This is a ten.

CLEA. Well, I don't have a ton of money, Charlie, I think that's obvious. And due respect, given what I've gone through with my mother, I don't really want to just give you all my money, to just get drunk with.

CHARLIE. Not that you're judging.

CLEA. Well—you don't—like—expect me to support you now? You don't expect that, do you?

CHARLIE. No. I don't.

(*He pockets the bill, and downs the rest of the vodka. She watches him, uncomfortable.*)

CLEA. So, like—where are you going to live, now?

CHARLIE. (*A beat.*) Are you kicking me out?

CLEA. Well, I think it's obvious that you can't stay here forever.

CHARLIE. Not to argue semantics, because that is in fact a dicey proposition with the likes of you, Clea—but there is a rather large difference between "forever" and "now."

CLEA. You're so drunk, I can't even talk to you.

CHARLIE. I'm not drunk. I wish I was drunk but unfortunately (*Yelling, suddenly.*) WE ARE OUT OF VODKA.

(*She stares at him, shocked.*)

CLEA. Did you just raise your voice to me?

CHARLIE. Yes I did.

CLEA. (*Hushed and pious.*) Because that is—unacceptable. I do not yell. No one in my family ever yells. That is not something I can accept in any way.

CHARLIE. Soooo…stealing other people's husbands for the sheer fun of being a bitch is okay, but RAISING YOUR VOICE is pretty much crossing the line.

CLEA. (*High and mighty.*) I am asking you to leave.

CHARLIE. Yeah, we'll get to that in good time, I'm sure, but I have a question first. Who are you going out with? Are you going out with Nick?

CLEA. (*Caught, tossed.*) That is just—I'm going out with friends! I told you!

CHARLIE. (*Yelling now.*) So cheating on me with that shithead NICK is all right, but YELLING IS OFF THE TABLE.

CLEA. Cheating on you? CHEATING? This exclusive and, and proprietary language is really so retro—

CHARLIE. Call it whatever you want—

CLEA. You were the one who wanted to be clear!

CHARLIE. (*Furious, yelling.*) All right then, as long as we're arguing semantics, why don't we just call it lying? Is that okay? Lying to my face while you go off to fuck my total nemesis?

CLEA. Like you even care—

CHARLIE. MEN ACTUALLY DO CARE ABOUT THAT SHIT, CLEA.

CLEA. You have to leave! This yelling is terrible! I am not a violent person and I do not accept it in the people I care about!

CHARLIE. That's easy enough to pull off, because you don't care about anybody! Do you? It's fantastic! You look like that, you screw like a bunny, and you have no soul! Seriously. It is awe-inspiring. That no soul thing? You make it quite, it's very seductive. Letting go. Forgetting that you ever wanted anything else. Because what else is there? Except looking like that. Being hot shit. At a really great party. Inside the void.

(*He stands on the bed, lost inside himself.*)

CLEA. I do not know what you are fucking talking about.

CHARLIE. What are the odds.

CLEA. Well, I cannot have crazy people living in my apartment and just yelling at me, whenever they feel like it. Here's another ten.

(*She reaches into her purse and holds out another bill.* CHARLIE *stares at it.*)

CLEA. (*Continuing.*) Take it.

(CHARLIE *does not take it. She finally throws it on the ground.*)

CLEA. (*Continuing.*) I don't care if you take it or not, you crazy loser. But you better not be here when I get back. Or I'm calling the cops.

(*She goes. After a moment,* CHARLIE *reaches down and takes the money, pockets it. Blackout.*)

Scene 4

A remote corner of a party. STELLA *is there, with* CHARLIE. *He is a mess. They stare at each other for a long moment of silence.*

CHARLIE. Hi.

STELLA. Charlie. Edward didn't tell me he had invited you. I didn't think, we asked so many people if they knew where you, where you—

CHARLIE. No. I just heard from someone, you know, I bumped into a friend of his on the street, and he mentioned that Edward was, you know... you know, you look great. How have you been?

STELLA. How have I been? Terrific. Being abandoned by my husband was a trial at first but over time it forced me to do some real soul searching and I think I've grown as a result.

CHARLIE. You're still working for that talk show.

STELLA. Oh for heaven's sake. It's been months, Charlie. You disappear for months, and now you just show up like like like—did you get my messages at all? I left like, a hundred messages, maybe, on your cell phone. Didn't you—did—

CHARLIE. Yeah. I got them. For a while. I mean, my cell doesn't work anymore. They cut it off, when I stopped paying. When you stopped paying.

STELLA. Well, what was I supposed to do? I didn't know if you were dead or alive, or if, or if—

CHARLIE. (*Overlap.*) No, you did the right thing. You should have cut me off, long before you did. You did the right thing.

STELLA. You look like shit.

CHARLIE. Yeah, right. Right? (*Beat.*) Look, can I borrow a few bucks?

STELLA. What?

CHARLIE. I'm really broke. I mean, it's temporary, but a few bucks would really help right now. There's kind of a housing situation...

STELLA. A housing—where are you living?

CHARLIE. I'm with friends…

STELLA. Charlie. Are you homeless?

CHARLIE. No, I'm with friends! I said, I'm with friends! It's okay. If you don't have any on you, that's all right. I'll pay you back.

STELLA. Why didn't you come home?

CHARLIE. (*A beat, then.*) I wrecked it. It wasn't there anymore. It wasn't what I wanted. I thought nothing would be better.

STELLA. Is it?

> (LEWIS *appears, with* STELLA's *wrap. He doesn't see* CHARLIE *at first.*)

LEWIS. Sorry that took so long. To get to the wraps I had to get by three girls who were throwing up, and one who was shooting up.

CHARLIE. Edward's parties are great, aren't they?

LEWIS. (*Stunned.*) A total blast.

CHARLIE. Hey, Lewis.

> (*He reaches over; they shake.*)

LEWIS. Charlie. (*To* STELLA.) You okay?

CHARLIE. (*Distracted.*) Yeah, great! I mean, I was hoping to find Clea here, but she's, who knows where she is…. I'm telling you, she's really a piece of work. You were so better off out of that. I did you a favor, man, I really did.

LEWIS. (*To* STELLA, *quiet.*) Do you want to go? We can go, right now.

STELLA. I don't know.

CHARLIE. No, god, come on, I can find Clea later, it's so great to see you guys! You look great. Stell, you look terrific.

LEWIS. (*To* STELLA.) We should go.

CHARLIE. (*Snapping.*) She's my wife! Would you stop telling her what to do! I mean what the fuck are you… what… what the fuck is this?

> (*For he now sees that they are holding hands.*)

STELLA. We're going to China, Charlie. Next week. Lewis and I are going to China to get my baby.

CHARLIE. Together?

STELLA. Yes. Lewis and I are going to China together.

CHARLIE. Well, that's just classic. How long did you wait, huh, Lewis? A week, two weeks, how long did it take you to start moving in on my wife?

STELLA. You have no right to even ask—

CHARLIE. How long did it take you, Lewis?

LEWIS. Three weeks.

CHARLIE. Three weeks! Wow, that's, you know, admirable self-restraint.

You know, you really gave it time then. Good for you. Three weeks. That was loyal.

LEWIS. You're not allowed to expect loyalty after what you did!

CHARLIE. Not from you, clearly!

LEWIS. This is such a distortion.

CHARLIE. Make your excuses! You stole my wife.

STELLA. He didn't steal me.

CHARLIE. Oh yeah, he loves you. He really really loves you, that's really what's going on here. Love will find a way. I'm so happy for you both.

STELLA. (*Furious at this.*) Well, what was I supposed to do, wait for you? Wait for you to to—come to your senses and and—what was I supposed to do? You just threw me away like it was all nothing, Charlie! How could you? How could you. Neither of us were perfect, but what we had was real.

CHARLIE. I DON'T WANT ANYTHING REAL. Where do you, where where do you think you are, anyway? Have you been out of the house lately? Have you been to Times Square? It's fantastic! You look up, and they're everywhere. Movie stars. TV stars. Underwear models. Those crazy rap people nobody understands, they're everywhere. Three and four stories tall, hovering over everything, like gods. Laughing. All of them, laughing at us. Because they know. All these fake people are having a more real life than we are! Real? Why should I want to be real? Fuck reality.

(STELLA *reaches over, touches his heart for a moment, then turns and goes back into the party.* CHARLIE *starts toward her;* LEWIS *steps between them.*)

LEWIS. Leave her alone, Charlie. Leave us alone.

(*He follows* STELLA *off.*)

CHARLIE. Wait. Wait wait wait.

(*Silence. Completely alone now, he paces, impatient and agitated. Several times he tries to get himself to go back into the party; he cannot. Finally he looks out at the night, stares at the river beneath him. After a long moment,* CLEA *enters, in a beautiful black dress.*)

CLEA. I heard you were looking for me. I saw the Nazi priestess and your friend; they looked pretty cozy. Anyway, they told me in front of Nick that you were out here looking for me. And I have to say it's really a problem, okay? I mean, Nick is completely allergic to you now because that lunch you had, you weren't exactly subtle. So make it fast.

CHARLIE. (*Abrupt.*) I need that money.

CLEA. What?

CHARLIE. We racked up a lot on my credit cards. I need that money back. Fifteen hundred, at least. To start.

CLEA. Fifteen hundred dollars? I don't even know you!

CHARLIE. You know me. You spent all my money. You took me from my wife. You're here with my ex-friend Nick—

CLEA. "Ex-friend," who you always called "the asshole—"

CHARLIE. (*Anger rising.*) He is an asshole!

CLEA. (*Sharp.*) Well, that asshole is my boss. I am his personal assistant.

CHARLIE. And what kind of sexual favors did you have to perform to get that plum job?

CLEA. I did pretty much the same thing I did for you, only this time, it got me somewhere. I can't be seen with you.

(*She starts to go. He grabs her, a little too violent, and pushes her back onto the deck.*)

CHARLIE. Wait wait wait—

CLEA. Get out of my way, Charlie.

CHARLIE. No wait! Forget about the money. Please. I just to talk to someone for a second, I'm out there by myself all day and I I, Lewis and Stella were here and they left, and I just can't go back down there by myself. I can't go back down.

(*He doesn't move. She sighs, frustrated.*)

CLEA. Oh, boy. Look. I'm sorry you're like not having a good time right now, I really really am. Now get out of my way.

CHARLIE. Because, to be that alone. People everywhere, and no one who sees you. With recognition. It's you!

CLEA. Okay. Earth to Charlie.

(*Still abrupt, almost violent, he takes her by the arm and leads her back to the railing.*)

CHARLIE. And I'm just starting to see, just now even, what's wrong with all of this, this fall into narcissism—

CLEA. CHARLIE.

CHARLIE. Is how lonely it is. Aren't you lonely?

CLEA. (*Startled.*) Am I what?

CHARLIE. Lonely. That's the problem. That's what's wrong with it. All of it. We're not meant to be this lonely, and you and I, we, we went to this lonely place together, and I just think that, I know, there's nothing between us, but maybe—we could, we could help each other out of it. If we just had a cup of coffee. Or even, not even a cup of coffee. Maybe just a glass of water. If we started that simply, and had a glass of water. Together.

CLEA. You want me to have a glass of water with you?

CHARLIE. Holy beggars did this. They just ate and drank the simplest, people would give them what they could, from the earth, and it was like a connection—

CLEA. This isn't funny.

CHARLIE. To the self, and others, connection for people who have no place in the world. Which none of us, really, none of us do.

CLEA. Let go of my hand.

CHARLIE. No, listen—to my heart. Listen.

CLEA. I said LET GO!

(CLEA *shoves him away.*)

CLEA. (*Continuing.*) Get it together, would you? God, you're a mess, you're really just a wreck and there's a party going on in there, Charlie! Get a clue! There are four casting agents in there! Plus Nick—okay I'm going to tell you this I don't know why because you so don't deserve it but he fact is, he still needs somebody to play the homeless guy in the third act and it's only two lines so I could get him to just give it to you if you would just—just tell Nick how much you love the pilot, he will really like that. You know part of the reason he gets so edgy with you is because he thinks you're really talented, like fucked up but talented and honestly, if you just said some nice things it would solve everything! Just don't talk about having a glass of water with him, okay? That is too nuts. Holy beggars, also off the table. Okay? Okay, Charlie? Honestly, you are so much work, I'm going to have to have a massage for a week to get over this. It's a party. Okay, Charlie? It's a party.

(*She pushes by him, back into the party.* CHARLIE *watches her go, then looks out over the water.*)

CHARLIE. It is surreal. That's exactly what it is.

(*He leans back, looking into the doorway, considering whether or not he will re-enter the fray. Blackout.*)

End of Play

SIX YEARS
by Sharr White

BIOGRAPHY

Sharr White's plays include *Six Years* (30th Anniversary Humana Festival of New American Plays at Actors Theatre of Louisville); *The Dream Canvas* (downtown New York at Todo Con Nada); *The Last Orange Dying* (off-Broadway at the Ohio); *Safe from the Future* (off-Broadway at Raw Space); *Heaven and All Things Lovely* (far above Broadway in the Mariott Marquis, room 3806); *Iris Fields* (Lincoln Center Theatre Directors Lab, Key West Theatre Festival); *Satellites of the Sun* (finalist, Princess Grace Award); *The Escape Velocity of Savages* (Dr. Henry and Lillian Nesburn Award as part of the Julie Harris Award in Playwriting); and *Achilles in Sparta* (a play for young performers at Denver Center Academy). Mr. White is a member of the Ensemble Studio Theatre's Playwrighting Unit in New York, and a company member of Apartment A Productions in Los Angeles. He is a recipient of a 2006 New York Foundation for the Arts fellowship.

ACKNOWLEDGMENTS

Six Years premiered at the Humana Festival of New American Plays in March 2006. It was directed by Hal Brooks with the following cast and staff:

PHIL GRANGER	Michael J. Reilly
MEREDITH GRANGER	Kelly Mares
TOM WHEATON	Harry Bouvy
JACK MUNCIE	Frank Deal
PEG MUNCIE	Marni Penning
DOROTHY	Stephanie Thompson
MICHAEL GRANGER	Isaac Gardner

Scenic Designer	Paul Owen
Costume Designer	Catherine F. Norgren
Lighting Designer	Tony Penna
Sound Designer	Matt Callahan
Video Content Designer	Joanna K. Donehower
Properties Designer	Mark Walston
Fight Director	Cliff Williams III
Samba Coach	Christina Ingraham
Stage Manager	Nancy Pittelman
Production Assistant	Megan Schwarz
Dramaturg	Julie Felise Dubiner
Assistant Dramaturg	Joanna K. Donehower
Casting	The Orpheus Group
Directing Assistant	Emily Wright

CAST OF CHARACTERS
PHIL GRANGER
MEREDITH GRANGER
TOM WHEATON
JACK MUNCIE
PEG MUNCIE
DOROTHY
MICHAEL GRANGER

Each scene of this play occurs six years beyond the scene proceeding, beginning in 1949, and ending in 1973. The ages and dispositions of the actors should be such that they can be aged convincingly throughout the course of the play; Phil and Meredith span from 27 to 51 years old.

For reasons of efficiency, the same actress may play the roles of Peg Muncie and Dorothy. The sets are intended to be minimal.

SCENES
Act I

A motel room in a small town outside St Louis, Missouri, 1949

Phil and Meredith's small home in St. Louis, Missouri, 1955

Split stage: a Chicago cocktail lounge / Phil and Meredith's St. Louis bedroom, 1961

Act II

Phil and Meredith's modern St. Louis home, 1967

A motel room in Vacaville, California, 1973

Michael J. Reilly, Marni Penning, Harry Bouvy, and Frank Deal
in *Six Years*

30th Annual Humana Festival of New American Plays
Actors Theatre of Louisville, 2006
Photo by Harlan Taylor

SIX YEARS

ACT I

Scene 1

Night. Heavy rain. A motel room on the outskirts of St. Ann, Missouri. It is 1949, and everything in the room exudes the hopeful newness of postwar construction; taut, optimistic bedspread; smart drapes; dim, stylish lamps; thin, new carpeting. As if in direct contrast with the surroundings, a suitcase so ragged that it is close to useless lies open on the bed. Its owner is in the bathroom. Water runs in the sink.

There is a nervous knock on the door. After a few moments, another. We hear a key in the lock and MEREDITH GRANGER, *twenty-seven, enters. She is completely soaked through; pinned-up hair, careful dress, a stylish but now-ruined coat, a soaked handbag. She shuts the door and stands in silence, shivering and dripping as she listens to the water run in the bathroom.*

The water shuts off and we're left only with the sound of the rain. The bathroom door opens and PHIL GRANGER *enters in trousers and undershirt. A towel is slung over his shoulder and bits of shaving cream adhere to his face. He is a worn and weary twenty-seven with the bearing and looks of one much older. They stare at one another.*

MEREDITH. I'm...I'm...

> (MEREDITH *suddenly changes her mind about having appeared. She quickly turns and makes for the door.* PHIL's *voice stops her.*)

PHIL. (*Hollow.*) —Something—uh...happened? To the car? There was a *car*, wasn't there?

> (MEREDITH *turns back, utterly unsure of what to do.*)

MEREDITH. (*Nervous torrent.*) I uh...I just never...there was rationing and all and I just...there was this...bedroom set that was so pretty and I thought we'd never really begun furnishing our...and so I sold it and now we have this bedroom set and no car which is fine because I'm in town now I'm not at your mother's—at *your*—out at the farm...I've taken a room and it just made sense because we didn't have any. —Furniture.

(*Miniscule beat.*) June—June Whitley—ran in and announced you were back, just like that, and the whole shop turned and looked at me and I...I didn't want to be in a car with any of them, not with news like that, so I...uh...ran. (*Miniscule beat.*) The whole *world's* buzzing.

PHIL. Hank and Snow saw me. At the bus station.

MEREDITH. June Whitley sure made a big deal over...wondering why it looked like you were…headed to the *Starlight*.

PHIL. I…I just wasn't really ready to—

MEREDITH. —The…manager…gave me a key. I told him…uh…that I was…that I'm your…

> (*Slight pause.*)

PHIL. You're…you're wet.

MEREDITH. (*Quickly.*) —I knocked! And when you didn't answer, I—

PHIL. —Do you…want…to take off your—

MEREDITH. —I don't know. I don't know if I'm staying. I mean…long enough…I mean for very… (*Taking him in.*) I just…can't believe…

PHIL. (*Trying desperately to sound normal.*) —I saw the funeral notice. In a newspaper somebody'd dropped. The *Dispatch*, of all things. In the…the Kansas City bus station.

MEREDITH. (*Disbelief.*) Kansas City? This whole time?

PHIL. —Just for the last few weeks. I was uh…I had a…. (*Staring at the water dripping from her.*) —Do you want a…I…I have clean towels…

MEREDITH. —No…No, I…

PHIL. (*Straightforward.*) —They come free with the room here.

> (*Pause.* MEREDITH *takes a small step towards him.*)

MEREDITH. I'm *sorry*.

PHIL. What for.

MEREDITH. About your *mother*.

> (PHIL *moves to the bed. He sits and digs into his bag for a flask.*)

PHIL. (*Struggling.*) I'm a bit of a wreck, Meredith.

MEREDITH. (*Approaching him.*) What are you doing here? Why haven't you just—

PHIL. —I didn't know she was—

MEREDITH. —Your mother was so…worried.

PHIL. Meredith, I…

MEREDITH. —Where've you *been*, Phil?

> (PHIL *considers this for a small beat, then shakes his head.*)

MEREDITH. The room I'm letting, it's at the Fulton's, you remember George Fulton, he was two grades behind us, well he—

PHIL. —Meredith—

MEREDITH. —joined up a year after you did—

PHIL. (*Short.*) —I remember George Fulton.

> (*Slight pause.* PHIL *is unable to look at her. She tries again.*)

MEREDITH. And I have a job that everyone finally approves of. You remember Mrs. Sampson's dress shop, well…well it's a nice little boutique now and…and I'm measuring the ladies and bringing them tea…. I…I just couldn't stay out there with your mother after everyone started….

PHIL. (*A blank admission.*) —Of course.

MEREDITH. (*Struggling against defeat.*) Do you…do you want me to go?

(*Pause.* PHIL *struggles to give some response.*)

MEREDITH. (*With finality.*) I only thought that…if I could just *see* you, then you could tell me *yourself*, that's all. I'm sorry.

(MEREDITH *turns and makes for the door again.*)

PHIL. (*Quickly.*) —Tell you what.

MEREDITH. (*Stopping.*) —Whatever you haven't been able to. Uh…for the last…six years.

(PHIL *stares at the trail of water that leads to* MEREDITH's *coat.*)

PHIL. —It's dripping…your…your coat is dripping.

(MEREDITH *stares at him. She decides to take off her coat. It is a quietly daring act which will leave her looking somehow unprotected.* PHIL *stands and goes to her, as if small social mores are all he has left. An awkward exchange occurs,* PHIL *trying to take her coat,* MEREDITH *trying to do it herself while holding her handbag, etc.*)

MEREDITH. No, you don't have to—

PHIL. —I'll—

MEREDITH. —If you just—

PHIL. —Here, *I'll* take it—

MEREDITH. No, I *have* it, I just…

PHIL. —No, the *other* arm—

MEREDITH. —It's soaking *wet!*

(*Slight pause. They stand awkwardly. He holds her coat.*)

PHIL. Well let me hang it up at least. That's what people do, right? They hang up coats?

(*She gives a small nod. He goes to a closet and hangs it.*)

MEREDITH. (*Bravely.*) I wanted to bring a couple of your suits.

PHIL. (*As if he's never heard the word before.*) Suits?

MEREDITH. (*Struggling not to lose control of her emotions.*) I don't know why I figured you might…need that…black one…

(PHIL *at last understands what she means. As if by rote, he turns to comfort her.*)

MEREDITH. —No, don't. —DON'T!

(*He reacts almost childishly to her tone, dropping his arms and turning from her.*)

MEREDITH. (*Surprised at herself.*) —I'm sorry, I uh…

PHIL. No. No, it's OK.

MEREDITH. I just don't really know what this means. You *do* understand…

PHIL. …Yes.

MEREDITH. Are you…

PHIL. I don't know.

MEREDITH. Were you planning on…

PHIL. I don't know.

MEREDITH. Well…can you at least…tell me…how long…

PHIL. No.

MEREDITH. Can you…can you tell me…anything at all?

PHIL. Meredith, I…

MEREDITH. You what.

PHIL. I don't know.

MEREDITH. (*Briefly letting a deep anger slip out.*) Well how do you expect to just show up here and not at least have some idea HOW LONG YOU'RE STAYING…for people, Phil. Because we're going to want to know that. — And don't say you don't know again! (*Long pause. then, almost softly.*) Mrs. Fulton, she's kept all the things in George's room; the trophy from that freshman game…all sorts of things. She…she asked me to ask you if…

PHIL. (*Tersely.*) I never saw him.

MEREDITH. Everyone came home, Phil.

PHIL. —I know.

MEREDITH. And those *cards* the…hospital sent said you weren't…so we didn't know…*why*…you would be…there. You…you don't have any…?

PHIL. (*Almost resentfully.*) —No, Meredith.

MEREDITH. You stopped writing to us in '44. We thought you were *dead*. The same thing happened to Mrs. Fulton except there was a *reason* for it because George Fulton actually *is* missing, but you…Can't you just tell me where you've *been*?

(*Slight pause. PHIL searches for some explanation.*)

PHIL. (*Almost childish.*) A lot of places.

MEREDITH. That's *it*?

(*Slight pause. PHIL thinks, then nods. MEREDITH gathers herself, attempting as best she can to become businesslike. She brings her handbag to a small desk.*)

MEREDITH. So. I had some papers drawn up. But there was no way to finalize everything… I ran to Mrs. Fulton's and… Look. I thought that if this was going to be the only time I would ever…I uh…they're divorce papers.

PHIL. (*Again, as if not immediately recognizing the meaning of the words.*) Divorce papers.

MEREDITH. Your mother...thought that...

PHIL. (*Not quite alarmed.*) *My* mother?

MEREDITH. Yes, that...well, it's just...I mean—*I* thought too. That if...if something...if someone else were to—for me—and something were to happen, you know...if I were ever to have... Well I would never be able to...remarry.

PHIL. (*Fear and a long-forgotten taste of jealousy rising through him.*) Do you...have...is there...anyone...

MEREDITH. (*Quickly.*) No! Gosh no, Phil, I...*no*, I've been...

PHIL. —You've been what.

MEREDITH. (*Almost to herself.*) —Nothing, never mind, I...I don't think I should tell you certain things. It's too much.

PHIL. (*Intently.*) Certain things like *what?*

MEREDITH. Things that might make me seem...*desperate.*

(MEREDITH *opens her handbag and takes some folded papers out. She turns to* PHIL *as she opens them. Water gushes out of the sodden mass.*)

MEREDITH. (*Meekly.*) Oh.

(*Slight pause.*)

PHIL. I don't suppose you'd like a drink.

MEREDITH. I'd like a drink very much.

(PHIL *turns and disappears into the bathroom.* MEREDITH *calls after him.*)

MEREDITH. Because I'm...I'm *not.*

PHIL. (*Offstage.*) Not what.

MEREDITH. —Not desperate!

PHIL. Over *what.*

(PHIL *re-emerges with two motel glasses.*)

MEREDITH. (*Carefully.*) Over *you.* I don't want you to think that I've rushed right over to claw at you or something. I've only come so quickly because... well who knew if you were just going to turn around and...

PHIL. (*Knowing.*) Yes.

MEREDITH. (*Softly.*) I...I feel like I just...want to look at you. Can I look at you?

PHIL. (*Miniscule pause, then quietly.*) Yes.

(MEREDITH *takes him in. She almost raises her left hand as if to touch his face, but then thinks better of it. She still wears her wedding ring.*)

MEREDITH. (*Plainly, quickly.*) There was that movie starring that fellow who had his hands shot off, you know the one that won the award, and there was this article in Life about him, how they made him new hands out of hooks and they showed him playing with his wife and his daughter and they all had these terrible smiles on their faces and I kept thinking what if you had something shot off like that, I supposed maybe that's what made you stay away but that didn't make sense because everything they sent…said just…exhaustion…

(*Pause. MEREDITH gulps her drink without flinching.*)

PHIL. Do you want another?

MEREDITH. No thank you.

(*Slight pause.*)

PHIL. (*At last truly focusing on her.*) What things?

MEREDITH. What?

PHIL. What things do you not want to tell me?

MEREDITH. (*Almost shyly.*) Oh well I'm sure I'm supposed to bluff or be a tease with you or something make you think all the guys are chasing me home every night that's probably what the girls would tell me to do but I…the truth is…I'm not making plans. In any way to be with…anyone else. That's what I don't want to tell you. (*The dark truth.*) That I never want to be with anyone else.

(PHIL *goes to pour himself another drink, but his flask is empty.*)

MEREDITH. Here…

(MEREDITH *efficiently reaches into her purse and comes out with her own, much larger flask. She pops the top, pours one for both* PHIL *and herself, then sticks it back in her purse. She whirls back to* PHIL. PHIL *stares. She catches herself.*)

MEREDITH. We all just do what we can, right?

PHIL. Sure.

(*They actually each smile a little.*)

MEREDITH. (*A little more confidently.*) You don't think it makes me seem…desperate? What I told you, I mean.

PHIL. No, Meredith.

MEREDITH. You don't…think that I'm clawing at you?

PHIL. No, Meredith.

MEREDITH. Poor Mrs. Fulton….*She* drinks. She drinks *plenty*. Some nights I help her out of her chair and upstairs and in the mornings we both pretend not to remember.

(*The following exchange is almost, though not quite, a shy seduction; we see the demure push and pull of a couple who once shared many things.*)

PHIL. And what do *you* do?

MEREDITH. About…

PHIL. You said we all do what we can.

MEREDITH. Oh. Well I…I just work in the dress shop.

PHIL. And then what?

MEREDITH. I…I stay late. I…Most nights I'll close up. And even then sometimes I'll stay. It's nice when things…empty out, I guess.

PHIL. And then what?

MEREDITH. And then I go home.

PHIL. Every day?

MEREDITH. I listen to the radio with Mrs. Fulton, but it's not much fun since Fred Allen went off. In fact it's not terribly fun at *all*, Mrs. Fulton, she…she's so…(*Slight pause.*) George…George was in the 29th.

PHIL. (*Not unkindly.*) Someone sent me a letter.

MEREDITH. (*Desperately relieved.*) So you…you did at least *read*? Your *letters*?

PHIL. (*Intently.*) Every one.

MEREDITH. When I told Mrs. Fulton it appeared you'd come back, she… she wanted to go to the bus station right away. She thought *George* might've…that some…*miraculous*…

> (PHIL *reaches out and moves a lock of* MEREDITH's *wet hair away from her face. It is the first time she has felt him touch her in six years.*)

MEREDITH. You look…older.

PHIL. (*Quietly.*) You don't. Not a day.

MEREDITH. (*Admitting a terrible, long-held fear.*) Phil? You're not already…? You haven't…? Has there been…anyone?

PHIL. No, Meredith.

> (*She nods in relief. She begins crying.* PHIL *looks surprised, like he's forgotten that people actually do that. He puts his arms around her with a tentative, wooden awkwardness.*)

MEREDITH. Why were you in the hospital?

PHIL. You sure do look beautiful, Meredith.

MEREDITH. (*Fighting to regain control of herself.*) What's…*exhaustion*. We thought after you'd had a good rest… And we couldn't travel of course because… And then we got the *release* notice and we just…

PHIL. You look more beautiful than I can remember.

MEREDITH. Why didn't you come *home*?

> (*Pause.* PHIL *struggles to answer.*)

PHIL. It's…*hard*…for some fellows to… (*Slight pause.*) …and…and so they…

(*Pause.* PHIL *shakes his head, unable to articulate. He takes his towel and sets it into* MEREDITH's *hands. She wraps it around herself. Sensing an opening, she gently, insistently, presses him.*)

MEREDITH. Hard for some fellows *what.* So they *what.*

(*Pause.* PHIL *shakes his head.*)

MEREDITH. (*Hopefully.*) There are people who care about you, Phil. There are people, friends, people you know who don't want anything other than to know you're safe. It's…it's like a miracle. That you're even here. Don't you know that? We'll…give you whatever you need. We'll give you plenty of room to…to figure things out. You can go out there to the farm and…and…

PHIL. (*Almost fierce.*) —It's not that, Meredith!

MEREDITH. (*Long-suppressed anger, building to a devastated crescendo.*) Well what is it, then? You have to tell me what it is! I've been alone in this…*Goddamned town* too long to let you go again without knowing what it is! The war comes and we lose everybody, and we suddenly have to be…! And we are! All of us! Even June Whitley and Mrs. Fulton, and me, little Meredith! And the girls in town used to be so…but now that their husbands have come back they've all turned into cats again and I'm the one they talk about because *my* husband isn't dead or wounded or missing, he just hasn't come *home* yet, and I just…haven't known what to do with this *goddamned*…!

(MEREDITH *sobs, desperately tugging at her ring as if attempting to commit to some grand, dramatic gesture, but the ring foils her and refuses to come off. Finally, she stops trying. Her sobs subside.*)

PHIL. (*Haltingly.*) This…this fellow on a bus not long ago. He was talking at me. He was saying had I noticed how hard it was to know where the good places to eat were along the road. And I…said that I had. And he said he was going to open a whole bunch of restaurants and put them along the highway. And all these restaurants would be exactly the same, so no matter where you were, you would get the same great food.

MEREDITH. (*Quietly.*) Is that so?

PHIL. He…he told me the word of the future is 'big'.

MEREDITH. (*Almost resentfully.*) There are a *lot* of words for the future.

PHIL. He said now is the time to move on big ideas or see the world move on without you.

MEREDITH. —It's just talk, like anything else!

PHIL. (*A deep admission of failure.*) I…I don't have any big ideas, Meredith.

MEREDITH. (*Softening, insistent.*) I don't *care* if you do.

PHIL. I feel…like…some sort of a…. I just feel so behind that no amount of…running will catch me up to it.

MEREDITH. Maybe you need to just stay in one place for a little while.

PHIL. I was... Meredith...I was... uh...I...I...

(PHIL *attempts desperately to articulate his greatest shame. Sensing the importance of what he is about to say,* MEREDITH *moves closer to him.*)

MEREDITH. (*Quiet.*) What are you trying to...

PHIL. *That's* why I was in the hospital. Because I...

(*Pause.* PHIL *is unable to say it.* MEREDITH *reaches over and takes a corner of* PHIL's *towel. She gingerly wipes a bit of remaining shaving cream from his neck, then from his cheek. It is a gesture of the most profound acceptance. She lowers her hands.*)

PHIL. Everything seems so *wrong.*

MEREDITH. I don't *care* what you've done.

PHIL. I can't explain it.

MEREDITH. You don't *have* to.

PHIL. The world just...keeps...moving on, doesn't it?

MEREDITH. Yes it does. Whether you're ready or not.

PHIL. (*Building to a quiet emotional crescendo.*) I thought between being over there and coming back I could...have a minute. To take a breath somehow. I thought maybe everybody could have a minute to...to let...what we've been through...sink in. I don't even know what that means. I guess that's what I've been trying to do. Let it all sink in. But everything just moves so fast. The clothes keep changing. The cars keep rolling off the production lines. The houses keep going up. And...you let yourself be taken away from it all for long enough, you find when you come back that you...just...don't fit there anymore. You find that there's another puzzle piece that's been made in your shape and it's been stuck in the picture without you.

MEREDITH. (*Quietly.*) It's OK Phil.

(*Pause.* PHIL *sits on the bed.*)

PHIL. You...you don't think maybe you wouldn't...want me to leave so you could maybe find someone who wasn't...

MEREDITH. Who wasn't what, Phil?

PHIL. Who wasn't...uh...so...uh...so goddamned broken?

(*Long pause.*)

MEREDITH. Can I...Can I put my...my arms...around you?

(PHIL *adjusts himself just enough to signal yes.* MEREDITH *sits on the bed next to him. She puts her arms around him, tentatively at first, and then tightly.*)

PHIL. It's just that you're so young.

MEREDITH. I don't feel it.

PHIL. You're so full and pretty. You're not used up yet, like that Mrs. Fulton.

MEREDITH. I haven't had quite enough heartbreak yet.

PHIL. (*Pulling away from her for a moment.*) That's what I'm saying. Don't you see?

MEREDITH. I just think that…that I might have enough if you go away again.

PHIL. I…I can't promise you that.

MEREDITH. I'll take a maybe. I'll take just a night and a day so long as it's a night and day of maybe.

    (*Pause. MEREDITH reaches up and lets her hair down. Pause. PHIL reaches up and feels it.*)

MEREDITH. So…a night and a day?

PHIL. Maybe.

MEREDITH. And maybe then…another?

PHIL. Meredith.

MEREDITH. And one day…maybe even yes. (*Quickly, hopefully.*) Yes, Phil. Just say yes. It's easy.

    (*She puts her arms around him again. She rocks him.*)

PHIL. Meredith…

MEREDITH. —Yes! Shhh. Yes. Shhh. It's me, remember? Remember me? It's me, Phil. Say yes to me. Say yes to me.

    (*She rocks him for a long time. The lights fade.*)

Scene 2

In the dark, we hear the frantic sounds of a rare 1940s big-band Samba. the lights rise to reveal the living room of PHIL and MEREDITH's cozy St. Louis house containing a not terribly ill-matching couch, chairs and coffee table. A well-stocked bar unit occupies a special place, like a small shrine. Even more revered in its placement onstage is a credenza unit with its top open revealing a state-of-the-art hi-fidelity record player. Sleeves of records are neatly catalogued in matching storage units to either side of the credenza. Dessert plates and half-full cocktail glasses fill most of the available surfaces.

MEREDITH's older brother, JACK, dances his wife, PEG, onstage with a drunken sense of abandon. At thirty six, JACK is a habitual and breathtakingly unsuccessful salesman; jovial and loud-talking even as he moves from scheme to scheme. PEG, thirty-two, is prim and groomed, and her loyalty to JACK is inexplicable, and often total. They work their way across the stage and exit, only to dance back on a few moments later. Their dancing is light-hearted and joyful, and they are very good—reveling in show-off, almost comical maneuvers.

Following them onstage with a valise and rolled map is TOM WHEATON, thirty-two, good-looking, slightly uneasy in his association with JACK; *admiring* JACK's *bluster, but uncomfortable with the lack of modesty associated with* JACK's *personality and profession.*

All are dressed well, almost too well for an informal supper. It is a warm summer night in 1955.

JACK. (*Derisively to* TOM, *voice raised over the music.*) In the *water?*

TOM. (*Rhetorically.*) From a seventeen *thousand* acre plant?

JACK. They shut it down in '44!

TOM. Things leak! I don't know, munitions chemicals, *TNT*, whatever they—

JACK. —now that's just the most—

TOM. —My wife's skin is *yellow*, Jack. OK? Almost orange.

JACK. Well heck it's probably *jaundice!*

TOM. (*Almost furious.*) —Jaundice! It's…it's not…! My wife doesn't have—

PEG. (*To* TOM, *mollifying.*) —He's only saying it would be nice if she were *here*, Tom, that's all! (*Quickly, insisting.*) —Aren't you sweetie, aren't you saying that—

TOM. (*Almost to himself.*) —Well she doesn't have jaundice—

JACK. It ruins the symmetry of the *pitch*, that's all!

TOM. (*Present again, derisive.*) Symmetry!

JACK. —Three couples! Three gals and three fellas! *You* show up alone like a sore *thumb* and now everyone's *tense!*

TOM. (*Incredulous.*) Because my *wife* is sick?

(MEREDITH *enters. A very well-dressed thirty-three, she exudes a hopeful confidence, at times genuine, at times strained, as if willing the world around her to become a place her husband can more easily move through.*)

MEREDITH. Jack, let up on him for crying out loud!

JACK. Well here we've got the idea of a lifetime and he's thrown off the symmetry!

MEREDITH. Just *relax*, Jack, you'll have your *say*, I *swear* you drive into people like some mad bulldog— (*Calling offstage.*) —Hon, what are you doing?

PHIL. (*Calling back, almost a reprimand.*) Nothing! What do you think! Listening!

MEREDITH. (*Cheerfully overcompensating.*) We're out here again, Phil, so why don't you come and join us?

PHIL. (*Enthusiastic, vulnerable, as if explaining a deep, newfound love.*) …but just *listen*…! Just stop and…and *listen* to it will you!

(PHIL *enters with a small stack of records in his hands. Also now thirty-three, his plain trousers, open-collar white shirt and workman's boots act in stark contrast to the clothing of everyone around him. He moves to a chair by the cre-*

denza and begins flipping through the other albums. JACK, TOM *and* PEG
give each other looks, trying to decide how to move forward.)

MEREDITH. (*Chatty attempt at defusing tension.*) So Phil bursts in with this
new crate of records and announces...*I just want you to appreciate*...how'd you
say it, Phil?(*Imitating* PHIL.) ...*this is the moment. Right now. That Brazilian Jazz
came to America.*

PEG. (*Following* MEREDITH's *lead.*) Well! Well...So many...things...to appreciate tonight!

MEREDITH. —Turns out there's this guy! Charles Cloud, Phil? Who in-
troduces him to some...*Brazilian* at Ford...

PHIL. (*Listening.*) ...Ricard.

MEREDITH. *Whoever*, turns out he's a fanatic like Phil and shipped these
records all the way up just to trade for American jazz and he heard Phil had
some—

PHIL. (*Proud.*) —reel-to-reel of Monk and Bird at Monroe's! Offered the
entire crate!—

MEREDITH. —and I'm saying oh gosh, because Phil's promised —you've
promised to stop—and he says *Look Em! Jazz is over for me! American Jazz at
least. From now on it's all Brazilian!*

PHIL. (*As if everyone knows what he's talking about.*) Because Charlie Parker's
dead, that's what I'm saying, and his sidemen are taking heroin or whatever
and the whole scene is circling the drain now! Just *listen* to this...one and two
ba da da da da! —

(PHIL *obsessively observes the rhythm through the next exchange.* PEG,
thinking she's found the way in, urges the men into action.)

PEG. (*Pandering.*) —Gosh, but it...it sure *is* great, Phil. Why...let's everyone
get a little more dancing in while we have the chance! Tom, get up and—

TOM. —No, I—

MEREDITH. (*Joining in.*) —oh, come on, Tom—

(MEREDITH *pulls* TOM *up as* PEG *and* JACK *dance again.* TOM
half-heartedly goes through the motions with MEREDITH. *As the others
swirl around him,* PHIL *makes a vain attempt at waving them to a halt.*)

MEREDITH. —besides I'm going to hear this a hundred times by tomorrow morning, I may as well dance while I still like it—

JACK. (*Barely hiding his contempt.*) —*See* Tom? You *see?* What's *next?* Toy
trains? Bird watching? Farm team *baseball's* out, we already went through that
at *dinner*—

(PHIL *rips the needle off the record player and slams the lid of the hi-fi down.
He turns to them, aching with fury.*)

PHIL. —YOU KNOW WHAT? FORGET IT. FORGET THE WHOLE
FUCKING THING. IF NOBODY'S GOING TO LISTEN TO THE

FUCKING THING, THEN I'M NOT GOING TO PLAY IT!

> (*Silence. Everyone freezes at* PHIL'*s outburst.* PHIL *angrily takes the record off the turntable and replaces it in its sleeve. He begins flipping through the pile of records, concentrating on them as he talks.*)

PHIL. (*Quietly, quickly.*) This is what's the matter with people, Meredith, they can't just stop for a fucking minute, one fucking minute, to fucking appreciate something. Somebody pours their fucking heart into something and people just jabber away until it's over and then it's all gone and that's it! They've missed it! It's like people aren't comfortable unless there're sound waves coming out of their fucking necks! All I was saying was to listen to the goddamned thing, but can anybody do that? Can they just do that one simple thing?

PEG. (*Quiet offense.*) Oh *my.*

> (*Pause. Everyone stares at* PHIL, *who continues flipping through the records. From another room, a small boy begins crying.*)

MEREDITH.   (*Disappointment.*)   Oh,   Phil.   (*Rushing   offstage.*) …Mikey…MICHAEL…I'm *coming…*

> (*Uncomfortable pause.* JACK *and* TOM *see this as their opening. They circle* PHIL.)

PEG. (*To the room.*) Maybe…those drinks just need freshening up, fellas, and we'll all just…

JACK. (*Quieting her.*) Peg.

TOM. (*Sharing a glance with* JACK.) Phil, we didn't mean to—

PHIL. (*Tersely, quietly.*) —Forget it.

TOM. We just liked it that's all and so—

PHIL. —I said forget it so let's forget it.

TOM. Look. Just tell us what we can do, Phil. You know? To get you to…I mean you bring out your…baseball cards at dinner, OK, and then there was the fuel-efficient carburetor issue and…well I guess we didn't appreciate that correctly either, but we…we…*tried* to listen to you. And now with the *music,* we—

JACK. —We just think we have a good *idea,* Phil, and—

PEG. —Oh Phil, they've been talking about it for days!—

PHIL. (*Quietly.*) Has he told you? Tom? About the guy? Convincing him the government was researching avocado oil as a substitute for gasoline?

JACK. (*Angrily.*) Oh for cryin' out loud!

PHIL. *That* was a good idea too—

JACK. (*Pleading.*) —that's just a—

PHIL. —He wanted…I don't know how much. To buy a whole orchard of trees that didn't produce anything in California. Cash, of course. Personally

I've…I've—

JACK. (*Going for the throat.*) —and what, I suppose you're providing for my sister? Are you? On the assembly line at Ford when you have a thousand acres—

PHIL. (*Squaring off with him.*) —I guess that's between me and your *sister*, isn't it!

TOM. OK guys, I think we're all just getting a little hot under the collars here…

JACK. (*Turning on* TOM, *meanly.*) Yeah? You think that Tom? Really?

TOM. (*Privately.*) Fuck you, Jack.

JACK. (*In* TOM's *face.*) Fuck you too!

PEG. (*Halting them.*) —Boys, please, everybody's handsome.

JACK. (*Breaking from* TOM, *dropping all pretense.*) You know what, Tom? Forget him. Forget the whole— (*Suddenly.*) —I told you he's got no sense! This is all just the biggest…

PEG. —Well! Well look at the time! Jack, let's go, you can talk about this in the morning.

JACK. No I think I want to stay a little while! Have another drink of Phil's liquor! Here in my sister's house!

> (MEREDITH *appears in the doorway.*)

MEREDITH. (*Coolly.*) It's his house, Jack, I just own all the furniture. (*To* PHIL.) I can't find his space book.

> (PHIL *stands. He glances at everyone in the room. He exits quietly.* MEREDITH *stands in the doorway.*)

JACK. (*Homing in on her.*) Come on, Meredith, what are you doing? You who see potential in everything. You're just gonna let him pass on this? What else is he gonna do with his life, huh? Get himself drunk at night—

MEREDITH. —oh *that's* the pot calling the kettle black—

JACK. (*Picks up a record, tosses it aside.*) —get all wrapped up in…whatever weirdo obsessed—

MEREDITH. —The thing that kills *me*? Is that as soon as you get one of your *schemes* together—

JACK.	**PEG.**
—this isn't about any scheme—	—Meredith, no, it's up-and-up, honestly it is!

MEREDITH. —I'm sorry, Peg, I wish I could say otherwise, but it's always been something or other with him, and what am I supposed to think?

TOM. (*Jumping in.*) —it's just that it's a uh…it's a solid plan, Meredith. It really is.

MEREDITH. That's beside the point, Tom. Look. Phil's…found something. That works. OK? You take the ten thousand directions he's running in and you put it together and somehow, it...it works. He's...he's...holding himself together! So how dare you...come here and...and...

> (PHIL *reappears in the doorway. Almost as if he wishes he were invisible, he goes to the record player, picks up a new record from the stack and examines the sleeve. He takes the record out of the sleeve and swaps it with the one on the turn-table. Soft music plays. Everyone stares. Embarrassed silence.*)

MEREDITH. (*Re: their son; returning to a delicate social pretense.*) How is he?

PHIL. (*Quietly, still examining the sleeve.*) The book was under the bed.

MEREDITH. (*To the others.*) There's this space book...

PHIL. (*Quietly.*) ...*Young Adventurer's Pocket Book of Space Travel.* Not up to par with the other space books out there, you know, it's...it's...pulpy, but he...he uh...

> (*Long pause.* PHIL *is drawn into an intensely emotional reverie.*)

TOM. (*Carefully.*) Phil? Meredith? I just want to...I want to pick up where we left off at dinner. Can I...can I...change gears here? (*To everyone.*) Does anyone object if I...? I brought a map along, Phil. Uh. If that's OK.

> (*Pause.*)

MEREDITH. Phil?

PHIL. (*Quietly, snapping out of it.*) Look, I...I'm sorry. About everything. I don't know what... I uh...OK? But I am. Uh. Sorry about it.

MEREDITH. (*To* TOM.) Sure, Tom. Sure. You...you show him what you...you go ahead.

> (*Relieved,* TOM, JACK *and* PEG *eagerly leap into action.* PEG *clears glasses and plates from the coffee table,* TOM *unfurls his map on it,* JACK *takes off his sport coat and they all rendezvous at the couch as* MEREDITH *leads* PHIL *to a solitary chair facing the three of them. She stands nearby, as if on guard.* JACK *takes a breath and jumps directly into salesman mode.*)

JACK. It's like this, Phil. People're wanting things right now—

TOM. (*Quickly, quietly, with a nice smile.*) —Jack, would you shut up? Just for a minute?

> (JACK *opens his mouth like he's going to protest, then claps it shut. He sits.*)
> (TOM *leans over the map.*)

TOM. OK, here it is. St. Louis. The river. Your land. Now, the route of the highway is—

> (TOM *takes out a pen and draws a line down the map.*)

JACK. (*Can't help himself.*) —The first interstate highway to be installed in the U.S. of A, Phil. You think about that.

TOM. —Right past with a quarter mile buffer, OK? At forty five miles per with no stop lights, you'll be able to hit downtown in twenty minutes.

(*Everyone stares at* PHIL.)

PHIL. Go ahead.

TOM. (*Gaining steam.*) Now like we said during dinner, we don't have capital. So what we want is you to come in with us on this thing as a... Well look. We take a loan out against your land. With that financing, we use Levittown as a model like everyone else is doing—

JACK. —How many men on that line over at Ford got a house they can call their own?

TOM. Almost none, Phil. Say we price these just within reach at eleven thousand dollars—

JACK. —Eleven thousand! But where we really make our money? We set up a private loan company, see, which bundles loans and delivers them to the bank, who charges us an administrative fee, but essentially we're the *lenders.* So not only do we get the cash up-front from the house, we're loaning the buyer the money they're giving us! That same house'll pay off for—

TOM. —With that first two million in the bank we can build about five hundred houses. We gross five point five million dollars—

JACK. —A hundred and twenty percent profit per house and all we need is the land, that's what we've been telling you. We'll do everything. Everything, Phil. All you have to do is show up at the bank with us. Put your Hancock on some papers.

TOM. St. Louis is changing, Phil. People do want things. A yard. Convenience. Safety. That's what we're talking. It's happening everywhere else and people want it here, too.

(*Pause. Everyone stares at* PHIL.)

PHIL. (*A careful edge to his voice.*) That's it?

TOM. I mean that's just the beginning, but there's...there's paperwork. But uh...

PHIL. (*Almost friendly.*) So...It's going to be what. House house house house house? Spread out? Over the entire thing?

PEG. Oh well there's a cute little area for shops and stores they've been talking about, Phil, and—

(JACK *grabs* PEG's *leg tensely.* PEG *self-consciously claps her mouth shut.* TOM *smoothly attempts to keep everything on track.*)

TOM. That's right, Phil. And a clubhouse. Maybe a few of them. With swimming pools. Like little...country clubs. If you will. Right around the corner from people.

PHIL. OK. So...house house house swimming pool house?

(*Miniscule pause.* JACK *and* TOM *glance at each other. An air of panic begins to dominate the sales pitch.*)

JACK. (*Condescending, to* PHIL.) It's far more complicated than that—

PHIL. (*Rising, approaching the coffee table.*) Well right Jack, OK? I would…uh…assume. That a two square mile development would be—

TOM. (*Trying in vain to keep everything afloat.*) —The figures are great, Phil. If we can get anywhere close to the figures, we'll—

PHIL. (*Picking up the map, examining it.*) —I'm not talking figures, I'm talking about you building an entire city from—

JACK. —Exactly! A brand new city! Everything clean, everything safe!—

PHIL. (*Intently.*) —Could you stop with the sales routine for a minute? Could you?

TOM. What can…what can we do? To…to convince you of our good intentions here.

PHIL. I believe in your good intentions fellas, but you know what they say about that.

JACK. All we're really asking is that you come on board for the…the concept, Phil—

PHIL. —Really! Wanting to build some houses! Gee, you want to—! (*Tossing the map back down, angrily.*) —because that's…that's not a concept! That's barely even an idea! Do you have *anything*? Beyond your good intentions? Studies? Sketches?

MEREDITH. Go easy, Phil…

PHIL. (*Resentfully.*) No! These guys walk in here like a couple of hack brush salesmen and try every line in the—*How many guys at Ford have houses, Phil, People're wanting things, Phil,* but they don't have the slightest…I suppose you're just "idea men"? Is that it?

JACK. That's…that's right! We're…!

PHIL. —So I'd like to see some *ideas*! Sketches! Houses! Clusters! Streets! Stages! Parks! The way you talk, you'd think I have…drool coming out of my mouth! I worked construction all over for four years fellas, so I think I know which way is up, and I think I know when some guys are feeding me a line of bull, so I'd like to see some studies! And I'd like to see—what do you call it, Meredith?

MEREDITH. (*Sweetly.*) A business plan.

PHIL. —I'd like to see one of those! And I'd like to see if you really mean what you say about selling houses to my friends on the line at Ford because I bet you don't realize half of 'em are negro. And I happen to want to look my friends in the eyes when I talk to them about this!

JACK. (*To* PEG.) What kind of Communist bullshit is this?

> (PHIL *turns on* JACK, *trembling, as the house explodes into a cacophony of overlapping voices. through the next sequence,* PHIL *and* JACK *will press violently towards each other.* TOM *will hold* JACK *back,* MEREDITH *with cling desperately to* PHIL.)

PHIL. —How…*dare* you! Not in *my* house! Not in *my*—

JACK. (*To* MEREDITH.) —I mean don't you get tired of this routine!? This incessant crackpot—

PHIL. —JUST BECAUSE I—

MEREDITH. —Phil!—

PHIL. —I AM NOT SOME—

MEREDITH. —Phil, calm down!—

PHIL. —THIS IS A…! I'M NOT NUTS! I'M NOT NUTS! JUST BE-CAUSE I HAVE QUESTIONS!—

(MICHAEL *calls from offstage.*)

MICHAEL. —Daddy…!

(*Long pause. The men stop, quietly panting. Pause.*)

MICHAEL. Daddy…!

MEREDITH. (*Fiercely, to* JACK.) This is why you've made a shambles of your life, Jack, you've got to push everybody past the edge. (*To* PHIL.) Phil, you go put your son to bed again.

(PHIL *seems to sink back into himself once more. He exits.*)

JACK. (*Turning on* MEREDITH.) But this is what I'm talking about!

MEREDITH. —I don't want to hear it anymore!—

JACK. —But I mean really! *I* was over there, Meredith! You know? Look at *me*! I'm *fine*! I was on *Utah Beach*!

TOM. (*Quiet disgust.*) Bullshit, Jack.

JACK. I *was*! Even got a little jar of sand I've been saving!

TOM. You landed two days after D-Day!

JACK. Day after, day of, I don't really see the difference!

PEG. —She's right, Jack, that's about enough—

JACK. (*Turning meanly on* PEG.) —Won't you shut the hell up when I'm talking for the last time!

PEG. (*Shocked.*) What did you say?

(*Slight pause. JACK realizes he's overdone it and quickly switches tactics to one of honeyed kindness.*)

JACK. Look Meredith, I know I've been involved in a few things, but…but I'm just the kind of guy who—

(PEG *gets up and gathers her hat and purse.*)

JACK. —Wait a minute, where're *you* going?

PEG. (*Quietly, firmly, to* JACK.) I suppose you think you think you can speak to me like that anytime it's convenient.

JACK. Peg, it was just a—

PEG. —Save it, will you. I can't pretend anymore tonight. You're drunk and obnoxious and I'm taking the car.

JACK. *I'm* drunk?

PEG. (*Fishing in* JACK's *sport coat for keys.*) Oh, I *wish* I were drunk! And you'd better pray I can get the sitter to stay or we'll be dealing with an eight year old at six AM. (*To* JACK.) I'm talking about Jackie *Jr.*, if you're wondering. (*To everyone.*) I'll be thrilled if I never have to hear about construction or houses or loans again, I've heard nothing but for two months. This is almost as bad as the canned hamburger idea.

JACK. (*To everyone.*) It was a hamburger. Already cooked and in the can, even had the grill marks on it. You just pull the lid back and pop it in the oven. It was going to work. It was going to be big—

PEG. Good night, Meredith, thank you for…oh gosh.

(*Slight pause.* PEG *looks pained. She exits.*)

JACK. Wait a minute! Peg—I'll be right back, don't anybody—Peg…!

(JACK *follows her out.* PHIL *appears in the doorway. Long pause. He goes to the hi-fi and calmly flips the record. Quiet guitar music begins again.* PHIL *sits in his spot near the hi-fi and concentrates on a plain brown record sleeve.* TOM *clears his throat and stands awkwardly.*)

TOM. Well that went up like a lead balloon.

MEREDITH. (*Bustling after him.*) Oh sit, Tom, it wasn't so bad.

TOM. (*Small laugh.*) That was…terrible. Really. Just. Terrible.

MEREDITH. (*Cheerfully.*) But it *wasn't*. Was it, Phil. Truly.

PHIL. (*Regarding the album.*) …I can't figure out who this is.

(*Distracted,* PHIL *rises and exits again.*)

MEREDITH. (*Following him for a few steps.*) Can't you find some way to figure it out in the morning? Tom's still here.

PHIL. (*Offstage.*) I'm calling Ricard.

MEREDITH. Who?

PHIL. The guy!

MEREDITH. You'll see him *tomorrow.*

PHIL. (*Offstage.*) For *fuck's sake*! Can I call him? Can I do that?

MEREDITH. (*Reprimanding him through the doorway.*) Don't you for fuck's sake me, I just don't want to be up until three in the morning listening to you…catalogue…every single record!

TOM. …But really, thanks for a swell dinner, I'm just…sorry we botched it so badly—

MEREDITH. —Absolutely not Tom, just…will you sit? It's just a little downturn, you can't go throwing in the towel at the first sign of trouble or this thing will never get off the ground, will it.

TOM. Well maybe it doesn't…deserve to. I don't know, I'm… (*Honest, al-*

most good-hearted admission.) …I'm just not cut out for this sort of thing.

MEREDITH. (*Soothing him.*) You're doing *fine*, Tom. I just…think you should ask…my opinion, I've been here the whole time, haven't I?

> (MEREDITH *pours an indiscriminate glassful of something into a seemingly random glass, presses it into* TOM's *hands and leads him to the couch.* TOM *doesn't sit.*)

TOM. You mean…you're saying you…what…want to be…?

MEREDITH. Yes, Tom. Involved. I do. I mean I don't think there's any other way to move forward…do *you?*

> (TOM *almost laughs again and then shakes his head.*)

MEREDITH. What.

TOM. Just…forget it. Jack's right, we should drop the whole thing. I mean…it's…it's a construction project.

MEREDITH. So? I own a successful business, don't I?

TOM. Sure, but no bank would…I mean no offense. I mean hell, you're…a…well you own a *dress* shop, Meredith.

MEREDITH. Oh *relax*, I'm not going to make you fellows walk in front of a bank president with *me*, I'm not an *idiot*, but…but…I think I can…guarantee Phil's consent. I mean…so long as there's some sort of agreement. Beforehand. Between you and…and Jack and me.

TOM. What…what sort of…

MEREDITH. (*Competently, swiftly, as if she's planned it all out.*) Well Phil would obviously require a majority share, he's assuming absolutely all of the risk, I think that's not even negotiable. That is if you were to forgo forming a limited partnership I guess you'd call it and go right on to…setting up a…a proper company. I mean. With…with voting stock. And… (*Suddenly modest.*) …and everything.

> (TOM *looks strangely at* MEREDITH.)

TOM. Uh. (*Sounding her out.*) OK, but say we do. And…there is. All of that. Don't you think that if we went to the bank right now as individuals, me, your brother and Phil…well…

MEREDITH. —Well what?

TOM. I mean we've got to face facts here. Jack and Phil…they'd…get laughed out of the place.

MEREDITH. (*Telling herself as much as him.*) There's nothing wrong with Phil, Tom.

TOM. Come on, Meredith, you… (*Realizing she's serious.*) …Sure. …I mean *I* know Phil's fine…

MEREDITH. …It's just that he's…better than he's ever…he's not… He's being very…*careful*. With us.

TOM. I'm only saying that with a project this large, you...I mean there are *approvals*, there are...you know, city *agency* stuff, it really helps if the principles are...upstanding.

MEREDITH. (*Keeping herself from becoming offended.*) Phil's upstanding, Tom.

TOM. (*Approaching* MEREDITH *earnestly, sitting.*) Look. I like Phil. We used to be friends. I was...over there. I...think I...know. The sorts of things. He must have been through.

> (*Long pause.* MEREDITH *stares hard at* TOM. *Her coded answer is couched in a measured, false cheerfulness that almost fails to cover a deep, irrepressible sadness.*)

MEREDITH. I sure...I sure do hope Mary starts feeling better, Tom. We...we sure were sorry she couldn't come.

> (*Long pause.* TOM *stares back at* MEREDITH, *realizing that he's breached a forbidden topic.*)

TOM. (*Quietly.*) Sure. (*Politely backing off.*) —Sure, Meredith. She's...on the mend. We hope. (*Understanding that he should get back to business.*) Uh. So I'm sorry. Perhaps then I'll just—

MEREDITH. (*Bravely keeping her cheerful facade in place.*) —Yes, Tom. Why don't you—

> (TOM *opens his valise and takes out a typed sheet of paper and a pen. In the middle of this,* PHIL *will step quietly onstage, limply holding the brown record sleeve. It is obvious he has heard the majority of this conversation, and yet will choose to keep his roiling emotions to himself.*)

TOM. —scratch out a few things and I'll just write your name in here under Phil's, how's that? It's a simple statement of intent, really, about future partnership, so we can...well...put that business plan in shape. In...in good faith.

> (TOM *holds the sheet out to* MEREDITH.)

MEREDITH. (*Lost in thought.*) I'll have Fred Maples look it over in the morning.

TOM. Actually a...a signature might be—from both of you—Just to signal...

PHIL. (*Surprising them both a little.*) Baden Powell. (*Off their looks.*) His name is uh...Baden Powell. He's uh...he's a songwriter. Plays guitar. A guitar player. Uh. With...uh...

MEREDITH. (*Kindly, sadly.*) Phil?

PHIL. (*Quiet.*) Yeah.

MEREDITH. (*As if to a child.*) Do you...do you want to put the record down for a minute? Do you? Please?

> (PHIL *unquestionably obeys her.* TOM *stands, awkwardly. Slight pause.*)

TOM. On second thought. Well. Well look. Phil. I know you both...have some…

MEREDITH. (*Ushering* TOM *to the door.*) We do, Tom. Don't you worry. And I'll get the paperwork to…

TOM. (*Twisting to make any last contact with* PHIL *over the deal.*) —Sure. Yes. I mean as soon as you…but…but uh…. Well.

>(TOM *exits. Silence.* PHIL *marches restlessly about the stage, from chair to hi-fi to bar, as if he can't quite figure out how to put things in order.*)

MEREDITH. You're…Phil? You're…how are you…doing?

PHIL. (*Stopping.*) I know.

MEREDITH. You know what.

PHIL. (*Angrily.*) I know people think I'm…*sick*, Meredith.

MEREDITH. Are you? Would you even…be able? To tell me?

PHIL. I'd be sick if I…*didn't* have questions, wouldn't I? I'd be sick if I…*didn't* feel the way I feel. I'd be *sick*. But look. Here I am, Meredith. I…I…get up. In the morning. Don't I. I put my own shirt on. Comb my own hair. I know the way to go when I leave the house. I bring my own money home and it's just the same color as anyone else's. I…don't see terrible things when my eyes are open anymore. I'm…here. And you're here. And Michael's here. And I'm good to you. What more am I supposed to do but that?

>(MEREDITH *sits* PHIL *down in his chair.*)

MEREDITH. (*A deal.*) You just…just hold it in, then, sweetheart. You feel these things come up and you just…for me. For Michael. If you can just concentrate. A little more. I'll take care of everything so long as you do that.

PHIL. (*Hollow, almost bewildered.*) I'm not sick, Meredith.

>(MEREDITH *takes him in her arms. She rocks him.*)

MEREDITH. Shhh shhhh, I know, sweetheart. Shhhh shh shh. I know. (*Breaking from him, taking his head in her hands.*) Look at me. Look at me.

>(*Slight beat.* PHIL *does look at her.*)

MEREDITH. I love you, Phil Granger.

PHIL. I know.

MEREDITH. I always have.

>(PHIL *reaches out with both hands and brings* MEREDITH's *face to his. He stares at her.*)

PHIL. Meredith?

MEREDITH. (*Hopeful.*) Yes, sweetheart.

>(MEREDITH *watches as* PHIL *fights for something to say. At last, he realizes he cannot find the words. She catches her breath and sadly, kindly, rises.*)

MEREDITH. I'm going to go check on him.

>(PHIL *nods. She moves offstage. Stops. Turns to him.*)

MEREDITH. Turn…turn out the light? If you're up late?

(PHIL *nods again.* MEREDITH *turns and flips out the lights.* PHIL *remains in the spot of a single lamp. She exits. The light fades.*)

Scene 3

In the dark, we hear a track from John Coltrane's Blue Train. *As the lights rise, we see a split stage.*

Stage right is a bedroom, well-designed with recognizable modernist pieces; bed, side-tables, vanity, a small selection of liquor bottles and glasses. A man's suit jacket, shirt and undershirt are draped, neatly folded, over the back of a chair. MEREDITH *reclines nervously on the still-made bed in modest lingerie.*

Stage left is the suggestion of a modern bar/lounge circa early sixties with Sputnik-style lighting. PHIL, *extremely well-dressed, sits next to* DOROTHY, *early thirties, who exudes a cool and cynical sexuality. In his every aspect,* PHIL *exudes a profound, infectious excitement, one that is at once charismatic, exhilarating, child-like and needful. It is a joy driven by a deep sense of emotional release. It is late January, 1961.*

PHIL. *Ask not what your country can do for you?* You know? I mean…I mean. About time. Right? About time. But not in this fall-in-line-with-every-damned-fool-headed-witch-hunt-your-country-forces-you-to-embark-on kind of…of…*zealotry* that we've had for the last…what. Eight? Ten? *Years?* You know? With that Dick Nixon attack dog barking down everybody's door? *Ask what you can do for your country* and what was it? *Together what we can do for the freedom of man?* I mean look, if that's not a call to *service!* You know, finally these…mean little men have been *beaten* and this country's ready to be *worthy* of service again. And I can *say* that, see? I'm *allowed* to say that. Because I've—Look. A nation…a nation has to *earn* service, that's all I'm saying, you can't…stand up with a bullhorn and a club and demand that the believers rip the non-believers limb from limb like we've been doing. Neighbor turning neighbors in! And if you so much as have a wayward thought? You know? But we've said enough is enough, haven't we, and here we are! And all of a sudden? Today? Tonight? I want…I want to buy it! I want to bite into it and chew it and swallow it, like everybody else! By God it's like he said, the torch has been passed! It has! Born in this century. Tempered by war. Disciplined by a…a hard and bitter peace? Boy wouldn't it be great to…to…to be…someone. Who can believe in that again.

DOROTHY. (*Coolly charmed.*) Yeah? Believe in what, fella?

PHIL. Something! Anything! Tonight! This minute!

DOROTHY. (*An admission.*) Well I *suppose* it's exciting.

PHIL. —Is that what you think?

DOROTHY. (*As if no one's ever asked her before.*) Well I…

PHIL. (*Earnest.*) I really want to know.

DOROTHY. I mean like it or not there *is* a glamorous feeling to it all—

PHIL. —Right! That's what I'm saying! Look. First thing I did when I got in was buy a copy of *Life*—

DOROTHY. (*Almost catching his enthusiasm.*) —I mean of course they're in *Life* Magazine, they're just so…*Life*—

PHIL. —plus a whole stack of things. The *Times*, the *Tribune*, the *New Yorker*, you name it, I brought it to my room and I…. You know how long it's been since I've read anything but the sports pages? Here, close your eyes.

DOROTHY. (*Truly amused.*) Close my…

(PHIL *pulls a square of newspaper from his pocket.*)

PHIL. Listen, I just want you to listen.

(DOROTHY *actually closes her eyes.* PHIL *speaks as if he's committed the passage to memory.*)

PHIL. *Together let us explore the stars, conquer the deserts, eradicate disease, tap the ocean depths, encourage the arts and commerce. Let both sides unite to heed in all corners of the earth the command of Isaiah—to "undo the heavy burdens and let the oppressed go free."*

(DOROTHY *opens her eyes, inexplicably moved.*)

PHIL. Right. You see?

DOROTHY. (*Laughs, in spite of herself.*) What are you, some sort of a preacher?

PHIL. You know who I am? I'm a guy who's been sitting in his office all day. Biggest office you've ever seen. A little…lounge area, bar setup, little patch of green carpet for putting—all mine, and what've I been doing? Where've I *been*? Where've any of us *been*? Do you ever feel that way?

DOROTHY. What way?

PHIL. Like you've been…sleepwalking! (*Beginning a proclamation.*) —Deirdre!

DOROTHY. —Dorothy—

PHIL. —DOROTHY! It's a brave new world, I'm telling you! —Ulp!

(PHIL *suddenly slips halfway off his chair.*)

DOROTHY. Hey, you OK? That martini going to your head already?

PHIL. (*Almost bewildered, getting himself straightened out.*) I just…can't explain what's happening to me, it must have been the flight.

DOROTHY. (*This explains it.*) Oh, so you're a *New York* fella.

PHIL. —St. Louis.

DOROTHY. Little *fancy* flying from St. Louis, ain't it?

PHIL. —That's my wife all over for you, I schedule a train ride, after she talks to the secretary, it's first class with a car and driver at the other end.

DOROTHY. Must be rough.

PHIL. It's like living in the future. (*Fighting to regain his exuberance.*) Hey! Here's a question for ya'. You like *architecture?*

DOROTHY. (*Laughing at him.*) Gee I…I don't rightly know.

PHIL. Tell you what! We'll run a cab along Lakeshore, I just read about some buildings going up, real space-age stuff! And then we'll have a night on the town! Tell me where you want to eat! Wherever you want, I'll take you!

DOROTHY. Gee, that sounds awfully swell fella, but I'm—well I'm meeting some friends here soon, that's all, a few girls I know—

PHIL. —Bring 'em! Bring everyone! I…I feel…I feel like being around *people* tonight.

DOROTHY. You mean *girls*. You feel like being around girls.

PHIL. It's not *like* that. *Honestly* it's not I…I'm *married.*

DOROTHY. (*Knowing.*) Sure fella, you keep telling me that, I've heard it before. (*Business.*) Tell you what, if you're serious about dinner I'll phone Nancy just to give her a warning that there's a night on the town in store, how's that?

PHIL. That's…well that's fine.

DOROTHY. (*Getting up.*) But if she's against the idea, then you find your own way tonight, alright?

PHIL. Alright, but look. I…I don't want you to think I've got some…*idea.* I don't have *any* idea.

DOROTHY. (*Dry.*) Yuk yuk.

> (DOROTHY *picks up her bag and takes a few steps upstage. She stops, turns around, comes back, and kisses* PHIL *on the cheek.*)

PHIL. What's that for?

DOROTHY. It's because the fella I had a steak with *last* night made me go Dutch. Don't go anywhere, OK?

> (*The lights rise slightly on the other side of the stage.* MEREDITH *rises nervously and quickly checks her hair and complexion in the vanity mirror.* TOM WHEATON *enters in just a robe.* MEREDITH *whirls nervously to face him. Pause.*)

TOM. (*Nervous anticipation.*) Are you OK?

MEREDITH. I could…I could use a drink.

> (*Pause.*)

TOM. Sure.

MEREDITH. The uh. The scotch? No ice.

> (*Pause.*)

TOM. Sure.

> (TOM *pours two stiff drinks. He turns to* MEREDITH. *Pause.*)

TOM. Look. We could *still* just—

MEREDITH. —No.

(TOM *approaches* MEREDITH *and sets one of the glasses in her hand. He touches her cheek. He kisses her lightly. She kisses him back, lightly, then suddenly with a surprising ferocity. He takes the drink out of her hand and turns to set it on the side-table.*)

MEREDITH. No! —Sorry. I uh…

TOM. —Of course. Sorry. Sure.

(TOM *hands her the drink back.* MEREDITH *gulps it and hands the glass back, jiggling it to signify more. He turns to refill it. She goes to the bed and nervously pulls the covers back.* TOM *turns to her with the fresh drink. She whirls to meet him. They stare at one another.*)

MEREDITH. Can I have a cigarette first?

TOM. Uh…of course.

(TOM *shakes his head before gamely moving to a side-table, opening a cigarette box and holding it out to her.*)

MEREDITH. (*Taking one.*) What.

TOM. …Nothing.

MEREDITH. Tell me.

(TOM *lights a bed-stand lighter and holds the flame out at arm's length for her.*)

TOM. …It's not an execution, Meredith.

MEREDITH. (*Quickly, lighting cigarette.*) I *want* to. I *told* you I wanted to and I *meant* it. OK?

TOM. Sure.

(MEREDITH *smokes. Beat.*)

MEREDITH. So I…guess…you wouldn't be able to…stay.

TOM. (*Proud of thinking ahead.*) I sent the kids to their grandmother's.

MEREDITH. (*Officially cheerful.*) …I see. Good. Uh. (*Business.*) And I should let you know that I have to get myself together on the early side because I'm…well I'm having Michael picked up at the bus station, he's returning from his first big class trip, a…well a whole inaugural week in Washington.

TOM. —That's…that's fine.

MEREDITH. (*Conflicted pride.*) He's Accelerated Learning, Tom.

TOM. …You've mentioned.

MEREDITH. Very…highly principled. Christ, I don't know how he got so principled. Or hell, I suppose it's entirely obvious. An upstanding…Accelerated Learning…chip off the old block. (*Realizing she's off-track.*) Sorry! I'm sorry, here… (*Putting out her cigarette.*) OK?

TOM. (*All is forgiven—it's the moment he's been waiting for.*) Yeah. OK.

(*With an almost adolescent eagerness,* MEREDITH *climbs into bed and*

TOM *takes off his robe and slings it over the back of a chair. He whirls to her, stares, and then halts himself.*)

TOM. So...you *haven't* ever...?

MEREDITH. (*Definitive.*) Let's just do this, Tom. I want to do this.

(*Pause.* TOM *approaches her, eager again.*)

MEREDITH. (*Quickly.*) Well I mean...do you *really* want to know? If I've...

TOM. (*Stopping.*) I don't know. Uh. I guess.

MEREDITH. Well. ...I have, then. I have. Once. Um. Just so you know. But it was only once. OK?

(*Slight pause.*)

TOM. (*Quietly, disappointed.*) OK.

MEREDITH. Why? Did you?

(*Slight pause.*)

TOM. Yeah. Once. When Mary was...was sick. I did. She was sick for so long, I uh...

MEREDITH. (*Confessional, introspectively needful.*) —I had this... It was...It was...random. Almost. I never thought I could *be* someone who... I don't know. Phil was at the office. And I uh...took myself to lunch. A *nice* lunch. And there was this *fellow.* At the table next to mine. And he talked. *I* talked. We *talked* to each other. It was so...*he* was so...*attentive*, Tom.

TOM. Does Phil know?

MEREDITH. (*Quickly.*) Look, it was *more* than once, OK? With this fellow. OK? It went on for while. But it *was*...just one fellow.

(*Pause.* TOM *gulps his drink.*)

MEREDITH. And one evening...late afternoon, rather. He was driving me back to my car. And by God if we didn't...Phil was—I don't know what I was thinking, I knew he'd be picking Michael up from—well they—Christ, there they were, coming the other way. And uh. And I know Phil saw me. Michael I'm not so sure about, but uh...but...lately he's certainly been... (*Pause.*) Are you...does that make you...

TOM. I don't know. No. I guess.

MEREDITH. Gosh, did you ever...? Did you ever just feel like...you'd gone so far you...might as well...just go all the way?

TOM. (*Quietly.*) Sure.

MEREDITH. Phil was home when I got in. Puttering around, trying to...have something. *Interesting.* To say to Michael, which doesn't matter because the boy *idolizes* him, and I went upstairs and showered and our help, Sally, had dinner on and...not a *word!* Not a word. But that's Phil all over, isn't it. Anyway, it's over. Partly because it was the best thing to do, partly because I…I don't know. How do you let something like that go unpunished?

TOM. When.

MEREDITH. (*Consoling.*) It doesn't matter.

TOM. Tell me when.

MEREDITH. Uh. Almost three… (*Pause.*) Well three weeks ago.

TOM. (*Struggling for something to say.*) Fuck.

MEREDITH. *TOM.*

TOM. I mean really. Fuck. Just…. Fuck.

MEREDITH. So what? What does it matter?

TOM. (*Standing, putting on the robe.*) I don't know.

MEREDITH. What, you have some image of me as being…pure as the driven *snow*? I'm here with *you*, aren't I? And what do you think I'm *doing* here?

TOM. I just thought that…That you were…

MEREDITH. —That I was *what.*

TOM. …at the end of things.

MEREDITH. —It's complicated. You should know how complicated it is.

TOM. What's that supposed to mean, are you or aren't you?

MEREDITH. It means *maybe* I am. What do you want me to tell you? Yes Tom, I've been growing fond of you? For years? That I…think you're a good person? That I admire the way you raise your children? That Michael likes you and…Is that what you want to hear? That after tonight I'll visit Fred Maples and have papers drawn up so Phil can have something waiting for him when he gets back, and…and suddenly you'll have three children instead of two! Are you ready for that? Are you telling me you've been waiting for me? To be finished with him, is that what you're saying?

TOM. I don't…I don't…need. To be *ridiculed*, Meredith.

MEREDITH. I'm not ridiculing you!

TOM. Well I can tell at least that you think that idea…is ridiculous.

MEREDITH. —Wait, so it's *true*?

(*Pause. TOM turns and exits.*)

MEREDITH. Tom!

(MEREDITH *sinks slowly down in front of the vanity. The focus shifts to stage left as* DOROTHY *reenters.*)

PHIL. (*Excited anticipation.*) So?

DOROTHY. Oh, she'll be here.

PHIL. (*Like it's the best news he's ever heard.*) Good! Good! We'll go out and have a great time!

(DOROTHY *smiles and shakes her head.*)

PHIL. What.

DOROTHY. Are you for real? Are you?

PHIL. (*Innocently.*) What do you mean?

DOROTHY. I dunno, look, I'm sorry, but I guess I've seen one lounge too many because I see a married guy like you and all I can think of is getting pawed at all night. So…sorry if I've been a little rough with you, that's all.

PHIL. (*Happily.*) Rough? You weren't being rough!

DOROTHY. —Wasn't being rough, my kind of fella, you sure you're married?

PHIL. (*Enthusiastically.*) Of *course* I'm sure, I've got a *kid* even! A *boy*! Twelve years old…Look, I admit I'm in a funny mood, but I'm…I feel…I don't know—I feel *excited* tonight!

(DOROTHY *laughs.*)

PHIL. What.

DOROTHY. You know what fella? There's something about you? I'll tell you what you come across as. To a girl like me. —Of course, I know you're from out of town and you have to take into account the lounge atmosphere and everything…

PHIL. What.

DOROTHY. To me? Right now? You're coming across like you're maybe the loneliest guy in the world?

PHIL. (*Laughing, though unable to fully cover the truth of it.*) What? What makes you say that? Because well I've got…I've got plenty to do.

DOROTHY. (*Immediately sorry she's said anything.*) —I didn't mean it like you *don't.*

PHIL. —I've got… well my *son* for instance! Which can be a *lot*, you know—

DOROTHY. —I didn't mean to get you all excited, fella, I was just *talking* that's all—

PHIL. —I mean, well. …I mean he's *Accelerated Learning*! In school, so I…I try to keep up! So I'm…well I'm taking *classes*! There's this new community college and…well I sneak off during the day and…I mean I have to find *something* to talk to the kid about, don't I, so I'm taking…well, trigonometry and engineering and…and…Medieval history. Uh. This…*this* semester.

DOROTHY. (*Amused.*) Yeah? How're your grades?

PHIL. Uh. Straight A's.

DOROTHY. I rest my case.

PHIL. (*Momentarily deflated.*) Yeah, shit, it sounds pretty bad, doesn't it?

DOROTHY. Sorry.

PHIL. (*Devastated admission.*) I mean *I* know I bore the kid! I bore him to *tears*! But he's…he's really *good* about it! I mean he *wants* to like me. You know? He wants to *know* things about me…he's just so full of these…*questions*! (*Suddenly.*) —You know what he did? He's gone and written to all these damned *military* academies.

DOROTHY. —Well that's all about girls, take it from me, they really go for that, God knows I did a lot.

PHIL. —Yeah, but *military* academies! If his mother ever finds out…! —She should never have kept that *picture*, there's this picture he found, I took it after basic training— (*Suddenly desperately hopeful.*) —but you know what I'm gonna *do*? I'm gonna talk to him about this *Peace* Corps idea, you heard about this? *Ask what you can do for your country*, right? Right?

DOROTHY. (*Gently.*) Hey. It's OK, fella. It's OK. You OK?

(*Pause. PHIL isn't, and he struggles to hide it.*)

PHIL. Sure. Well…well sure. Fine! I'm fine. Let's have another round, huh?

DOROTHY. Hey. I lost my…my brother. Bill. In Italy. If that's what this is all about.

PHIL. Oh I'm…I'm…

DOROTHY. And I just want to say that…well that…well you're not alone. Even if you might be…lonely.

(*Pause.*)

PHIL. I was in the lounge. At the airport today. And I see a guy. A guy I used to know. Robert Kilner. By God if that's not Bobbie Kilner. And…and I go over to him. And I call out…Bobby. And he doesn't look at me. And I get closer, and I get this big dumb grin on my face and I spread my arms out and I shout Bobbie. Bobbie Kilner! And this fellow…he looks at me. Like I'm some crazy man. Right? And he says to me that he thinks I have the wrong guy, but I won't let it go. I say no. You're Bobby Kilner, First Division, 16th Infantry regiment, etc. etc. you old so-and-so, you can't pretend you don't know me and… and…the guy…the guy who I thought was Bobby. He gets this look in his eyes. His eyes sort of soften up on me. And he says real softly. Well. Sure. OK, Mac. I'm Bobby. And he gets up and he…shakes my hand and we…catch up. He tells me where he's been and what he's been doing, and I sort of tell him the same. And there's this announcement made and he…he shakes my hand again and says…says…real genuine…says it's…it's really good to see you again, Phil. Real good. I'm real glad you said hello. And I turn around and I'm walking back to the lounge and…and damned if I don't stop dead in my tracks. Because this guy…he can't be Robert Kilner. Because Bobby Kilner…His face. His face…came off. Of his head. At Aachen. He looked around a corner and there was a boom and he…looked back at me. Before he dropped. And there wasn't anything under his helmet. The damndest thing. And so this guy…he couldn't have been Bobby Kilner, could he, because they can't do things like that. And I...Dorothy, I...I went into the men's room and I...well I...I wept. For a bit. I locked myself in and I...wept. I'm not afraid to say it. I did. And when I get out of the bathroom. There's this...shine. To the lights. And everything seems to be in this...focus. Like I've put on eyeglasses. And I...well I decide against having another drink. And I...I walk out on the tarmac and get on the plane. And we take off and climb up past the cloud layer. And I...and we outrun the clouds so that I can see the fields down below and the roads, and...and this voice. Comes to me. And it sounds like my voice. And I realize that I'm talking to myself. I can hear myself saying. I am Phil Granger. It's 1961. I live in a large house outside of St. Louis. I have a beautiful wife and a son who both love me. And uh...and I'm alive. I'm alive. I'm alive and I'm here and I...I lived.

(*Long Pause.*)

DOROTHY. (*Falsely apologetic.*) Oh. There she is. My friend. Over there. (*Waves.*) Well she's not waving back, but... (*Waves again.*) Nancy! Nancy! No, she's...well look let me just—

PHIL. —That's...that's not your friend, is it.

DOROTHY. Well...well of *course* it is. That's her right over *there*, she's...with the...

PHIL. —You didn't even go call her, did you.

DOROTHY. Well I called her. Of course I called her.

PHIL. But that's not her.

DOROTHY. (*Not unkindly.*) Look. Sometimes a girl just...likes to go out and have a nice time, that's all. A little laughing. A little eating. Like you said it would be. Things are hard for people. Yours truly included. I'm sorry. I just thought this was gonna be...

PHIL. Sure.

(DOROTHY *rises, picking up both her coat and purse.*)

DOROTHY. You...you OK fella?

PHIL. Sure. Yeah, yeah. Yeah, I'm OK.

DOROTHY. I'll just... Um... ...Well. Pretend like I'm coming right back, OK? People don't stare too much if you do that.

(DOROTHY *exits. The focus shifts to stage right.* TOM *comes out of the bathroom and starts dressing.*)

MEREDITH. You understand this makes you exactly like everyone else around here, Tom. You're shocked, *shocked*, to discover I've had an affair as you stand there drinking my husband's scotch, I mean really. And after admitting you yourself had an affair on your dying wife.

TOM. That's a low blow.

MEREDITH. The truth is never low, it's just the truth.

TOM. Look. It does sound…completely absurd. But I just thought. Meredith, of all people. If I were to…. Well she's the type who only has room for…one…person. In her life. And I thought…if you were willing to…with *me*. Then that person would be—

MEREDITH. Oh Tom…

TOM. —I don't need that. I don't need a tone of pity from you, Meredith.

    (TOM *continues dressing. He stops.*)

TOM. Why don't you divorce him?

MEREDITH. You'd think that would be better than the way I've been treating him, wouldn't you.

TOM. This…this *fellow*. Did you…did you *want* to stop seeing him?

MEREDITH. It's just that…it seemed like a good arrangement.

TOM. Well I'm not really too good at arrangements.

    (MEREDITH *stands up. She drains her drink.*)

MEREDITH. (*Sharply.*) Well that's that then, isn't it.

TOM. Well now. Now wait a minute—

MEREDITH. —Button your shirt, Tom.

TOM. Well *look*. Look, I'm…I'm…

MEREDITH. Go on, it's just like un-buttoning except in reverse. And then we'll shake hands and see each other around the office, how's that?

TOM. (*Quietly.*) Jesus Christ, Meredith, I'm not some *general contractor*, you don't have to talk to me like that.

MEREDITH. …Sorry. Sorry about that. I just…I…I…gosh I just…life is uh…a real balancing act around here, that's all. You'll forgive me I hope.

TOM. Look. Maybe if I had a little more time to get used to the idea, I could…

MEREDITH. You're very kind, Tom. But it's OK. (*To herself.*) We're all going to be…OK.

    (TOM *exits as the lights iris down to a pool of light around* MEREDITH. *The phone on* MEREDITH's *vanity begins to ring. She turns to it.*)

MEREDITH. Yes hello? …I'm sorry I can barely… Yes. Yes, of course I'll accept.

    (*A phone booth appears in a pool of light on the apron of the bar side of the stage.* PHIL *stands at the phone, shivering, his sport coat collar turned up.*)

PHIL. It's…it's *me*.

MEREDITH. (*Sadly amused.*) Hi, Me.

PHIL. I'm calling you. From *Chicago*.

MEREDITH. I *know* sweetheart, I *sent* you there, remember?

PHIL. —Are you *lonely*, Meredith? Is *that* what it is?

MEREDITH. (*Beat, then almost lightly.*) That's a can of worms, don't you think?

PHIL. Is it because it's lonely being with *me?*

MEREDITH. (*Not wanting to be drawn in.*) It's more than a call from Chicago will take care of, Phil.

PHIL. —I want to come home.

MEREDITH. (*Miniscule beat.*) When.

PHIL. —Now. I'm going to catch the overnight.

MEREDITH. (*Reluctant.*) I'm having Michael picked up tomorrow and I want to be here waiting—

PHIL. —Why don't you go yourself for once? You can pick me up beforehand, the train comes in early. I don't want to be at any furniture convention, I don't want to shake hands or take business cards—

MEREDITH. —I don't know, Phil.

PHIL. (*Dropping the bomb.*) Have you stopped seeing him?

MEREDITH. (*Miniscule, dreadful, pause.*) Look. OK? I—

PHIL. —I'm not so dead inside that the idea doesn't…*kill* me, Meredith.

MEREDITH. I've…I've—

PHIL. —Are you going to leave me?

MEREDITH. (*Miniscule pause, still avoiding the conversation.*) Yes why don't you come home. On the overnight.

PHIL. If you left me, I don't know what I would…

MEREDITH. —I know, Phil.

PHIL. I…Meredith. No matter what…I've always…I will always…I'll always…

(*Long pause.*)

MEREDITH. I'll…I'll arrange to have you picked up at the station.

PHIL. Sure. Arrange for that.

MEREDITH. Or…sure. I suppose I could. Meet you myself.

PHIL. And then we'll meet Michael. That'll be good. The three of us? All together? Don't you think? (*Pause.*) Don't you think? (*Pause.*) Meredith? (*Pause.*) Don't you think?

(MEREDITH *quietly sets the receiver into its cradle.* PHIL *slowly lowers the phone from his ear. They both look up from their pools of light on opposite ends of the stage, their eyes meeting across a thousand miles of darkness. The lights fade.*)

End of Act I

ACT II

Scene 1

Dusk. A late-July Sunday in 1967. We are in the suggestion of PHIL *and* MEREDITH's *large modernist home. A television set in a corner shows images of rioting in Detroit; towering flames, looters being sprayed with fire-hoses, burning police cars, crowds in the streets.*

As the lights rise, we see a tall, breathtakingly young soldier in dress greens standing in the middle of the room, breathing hard, as if he's been running, although now he is deeply arrested by the images. This is MICHAEL GRANGER, *17.*

Outside, we hear the searching shouts of MEREDITH *and* PEG.

PEG. Michaaaaaaal?

MEREDITH. Michaaaaaaal!

PEG. Michaaaaaaal?

MEREDITH. Michaaaaaaal!

(JACK *marches in and comes to a halt when he sees* MICHAEL. JACK *is now in his late forties and grayer and far heavier than when we last saw him. Though he tries to project the contrary, he can't help but give the impression of a man who has slowly, over the years, become broken.*)

JACK. Hey!

(MICHAEL *turns. He and* JACK *regard each other for a moment.* MICHAEL *runs quickly out.*)

JACK. HEY!

(*We hear a bedroom door slam closed.* JACK *wheels around and dashes to a doorway that leads outside.*)

JACK. (*Calling out.*) WELL HE'S COME BACK INSIDE FOR CRYIN' OUT LOUD! PEG? MER!

(*Exiting as he calls through a different doorway.*) Phil! He's back inside now! Will you at least talk to him?

(MEREDITH *enters, followed closely by* PEG, *both groomed for a summer occasion. Now forty five,* MEREDITH *has kept her figure even as her hair has taken on substantial gray streaks, which she has elected to keep, and which she works into her hairstyle with elegant effect.* PEG *is a more humbled version of her former self, having endured years of changing fortunes.*)

PEG. Stop, Meredith! Mer, *stop!* (*Catching her, an authoritarian voice of reason.*) You *listen* now, I won't have you going after that boy any *more*, it's not his *fault*—

MEREDITH. (*Controlled fury.*) —HE forged the signature, Peg! HE snuck off to basic training! HE'S the one who treats his mother like some…*STRANGER*—

PEG. —and we agreed that you would leave him *be* tonight! Didn't we!—

MEREDITH. (*Avoiding* PEG, *calling offstage towards* MICHAEL's *room.*) —and HE'S the one who will come back to the dinner table and *apologize*, and let my guests finish what they've come to *propose*!

PEG. (*Calmly, reprimanding.*) —Honestly, Meredith, you ought to be ashamed—

MEREDITH. —ME!—

PEG. —You can't bear to face Phil so you go after the *boy*, it's just so...*animal*! (*Off* MEREDITH's *protest.*) —It *is*! You've got to get PHIL to talk to him, he's the only one Michael will listen to!

MEREDITH. —I KNOW! I know. But every time I open my mouth and try to... Well you saw him! Just...sitting deaf and dumb with a FORK in his hand through the whole conversation!

(*Staring in disbelief at the TV.*)

I mean my...Gosh...it's like the whole world is...

PEG. (*Softly.*) Meredith? Meredith.

(PEG *approaches* MEREDITH.)

MEREDITH. (*Still at the TV.*) I won't let him, Peg. I won't.

(PEG *puts her arms around* MEREDITH, *but* MEREDITH, *barely able to contain her iron-clad composure, pushes* PEG *away.*)

MEREDITH. I'm...I'm...well I've got to get my face together...

(MEREDITH *dashes offstage with* PEG *on her heels.*)

PEG. —Mer? Oh!—

MEREDITH. —No! I'm fine!—

PEG. —Oh, hold on, sweetheart...Meredith?—

(PHIL *enters, futilely concentrating on his tie.* JACK *follows.*)

PHIL. Every time, without fail! The two of you come to dinner and there's a fucking ambush!

JACK. It was MEREDITH's idea, Phil!

(PHIL *wheels darkly to face* JACK.)

JACK. I mean it was *my* idea too. And PEG's. We all—

PHIL. —Can't a guy just have a nice farewell dinner? With his son? Can't he? Without there being some—

JACK. (*Almost pleading.*) —Yeah, but this time is different! I wish I could just...peel it all back and show you what's in my...my *heart*, Phil, we're not putting together some...*scheme* this time! —there isn't anything in it for us, not at all! I know I always say that, but... We just want you to *talk* to him! Just...*talk*!

PHIL. —Yeah, but you had to do this during his last dinner? Jack? You couldn't've screwed everything up for us *yesterday*?

JACK. Well we would have been glad to, but my sister invited us here *tonight*, Phil.

PHIL. (*To* MEREDITH, *offstage.*) MER! TIME CHECK! THAT PLANE'S NOT GOING TO WAIT!

MEREDITH. (*Sobbing.*) HOW WOULD I KNOW, PHIL! HOW THE HELL WOULD I KNOW ANYTHING, WHY DON'T YOU LOOK AT YOUR DAMNED WATCH!

PHIL. I…! (*Feeling his empty wrist.*) Oh. I've lost my watch. (*To himself.*) I need a drink. (*To* JACK.) Pour me something.

> (JACK *goes to a small bar setup.* PHIL *starts searching the room for his watch.*)

JACK. Don't do this. Don't pretend I'm some…half-wit! Like I've got nothing to *say*!

PHIL. —On the rocks!

JACK. (*Pouring.*) Look, Phil. Just listen. How many times have you bailed me out? How many?

PHIL. I wouldn't know anymore.

JACK. (*Setting a glass in* PHIL's *hand.*) Right! Right, you see? And I've always tried to pay you back the best I can, but you know how things go.

PHIL. (*A stare and a gulp, then.*) Yes I do.

JACK. So…so I'm…I'm trying to pay you back *now*. That's what I'm saying. We're talking about your son.

PHIL. —Are you out of your…! The kid just told you! At dinner! You drove him out of our *house* with that talk!

JACK. And *Meredith's* son. He's her son too, Phil.

PHIL. But what do you expect me to *do* about it!

JACK. We've found an honorable solution. That's all we're saying.

PHIL. —Honorable!

JACK. (*Emotional, letting years of ruined opportunity spill out.*) Look, I know what you think of me! I know what you think of my whole *family*, but Jackie Jr., he's *not* me. He's not just some…fuckwit dodger…running up to Canada to have fun! He's organizing people! Kids just like Michael!

PHIL. (*Breathing heavily.*) Look. My wife and me. We have to get our son to the airport. And there are a lot of things. That I'd like to concentrate on in the few minutes that we have left with him. If that's OK with you.

JACK. (*Intently.*) —So listen to what we're *saying*. Peg and me, we will *drive* him to Toronto. Jackie Jr., he's got a whole network of guys up there, ready to help him out.

PHIL. (*Quietly.*) —He enlisted. He *enlisted*. He went and forged my signature and he's taken basic training and he… I mean…HE'S GOING!

JACK.
Yeah, but who for? You think he's doing it to impress his *country*? Do you? He's just a…a scared kid! And he's waiting for you to talk him out of it! ARE YOU LISTENING TO ME?

PHIL.
MEREDITH?
(*Pulling at tie.*)
Jesus Christ—This damned…!

PHIL. (*To* JACK, *furiously.*) Please, Jack! Please! Just…just…shut! Up! Please! Will you do that!

(*Pause.*)

JACK. (*Quietly, with a broken dignity.*) You don't have to talk to me like that. Like a…like some…some kind of dog. For *once* in my life, I…I got something to tell you that…that *matters*. Somethin' that…

(*Slight pause.*) …aw, what's the use. I'm sorry for you, Phil.

(JACK *exits.* PHIL *looks helplessly around the room. All the life just seems to spill right out of him. He pours himself a tall scotch. He throws it back. He goes to pour himself another, but his hand starts shaking uncontrollably, then his arm, then his knees. He braces himself against the bar and then sinks to his knees, putting his hands up to his chin as if to pray.*)

PHIL. God! God! You…you… (*Defiantly.*) …fucking…*cocksucker!* (*Pleading command.*) I don't even *believe* in you, but you'd better keep him safe! You keep my son safe! Keep him safe!

(PEG *enters.*)

PEG. (*Startled and embarrassed.*) …Oh.

PHIL. (*Covering, quickly drying his eyes.*) I…I'm looking for my watch. Watch fell off somewhere and I just can't find it.

PEG. Are you all *right*, Phil, you're—

PHIL. —Damned tie, it's…it's too tight for my throat!—

PEG. —Your *collar's* all wrong, you have it all *buttoned* wrong. Here…

(PEG *goes to* PHIL, *she helps him adjust his tie.*)

PHIL. (*Helpless.*) I keep tying it and re-tying it and the damned thing looks good in the mirror and then by God a second later it's—

(*Suddenly engrossed by the TV images.*)

PEG. —It's OK, you're just nervous! (*Off* PHIL's *stare.*) …What. What is it.

(PEG *follows* PHIL's *gaze. The television images have turned to fighting in Vietnam.*)

PHIL. (*Lost in the glow.*) Damned…*Kennedy.* LBJ.

PEG. (*Quietly.*) —Please, Phil. *Please* think about it. *Please.*

PHIL. It was going to be…a new world. Don'tcha' remember? Doesn't anybody remember?

(*Suddenly enraged, pulling at his tie.*) Goddamned tie's goddamned choking me to fucking death, Peg!

(*Running offstage.*) What's the matter with this…goddamned…!

> (MEREDITH *enters quickly, but she too is immediately arrested by the images of fighting.* PEG *glances at the TV.*)

PEG. Well *this* will never do.

> (PEG *moves to the TV and changes the channel. A banal commercial plays.*)

MEREDITH. (*Mournfully.*) He…He won't open the door for me. He won't even talk to me.

PEG. (*Insistently.*) Mer.

MEREDITH. (*Quietly.*) I know.

PEG. (*Finality.*) So you go get Phil and you march him in there and you get him to speak to that boy for you.

MEREDITH. (*Quietly.*) I'm…I'm…*afraid.*

PEG. (*Comforting, moving her to a chair.*) I'll mix you another drink. A little something.

> (*They share a small, terribly sad laugh.*)

MEREDITH. I've…I've ruined *everything.*

PEG. Nonsense! —Maybe just a little something. —A little gulp.

MEREDITH. From the day he came home from the…recruiter's office, I've been…by *both* of them! Well how am I *supposed* to take news like that? How am I supposed to…to…be *cheerful* about it! And now I'm living in this house, *my own* house, like…like…not *even* as if I were the enemy—if that were the case I would be relieved—but…almost like I don't even exist at *all!*

> (PEG *brings a drink to* MEREDITH *and kneels down next to her.*)

PEG. Here. Here. You drink this up. Go on.

> (MEREDITH *takes the glass. She swallows the drink.* PEG *takes the glass back.*)

PEG. Mer. We're…we're…. Me and Jack. We're right here. We'll *be* right here. Right behind you. So you…you go ahead and be as afraid as you'd like. (*Finality.*) But you speak to him. You do that.

> (PHIL *enters, pulling at his tie—a new one. He stands helplessly in front of* PEG.)

PEG. (*Rising.*) What is it *now* Phil.

PHIL. Necktie again.

PEG. (*Helping him.*) Well what's the matter with *this* one?

PHIL. (*Obsessing.*) How should I know? Do I look like a maker of neckties? Do I know what particular stitch is out of place that would make a fucking necktie pull at my damned throat in such a way that—

PEG. —Phil, can you stop for a minute? Can you do that?

(*The commercial on the television has been replaced with Walter Cronkite at his news desk followed by images of fighting in Vietnam again.* PHIL *is suddenly engrossed, almost paralyzed by the images.*)

(PEG *glances at* PHIL *and then stares at* MEREDITH. MEREDITH *stares nervously back at* PEG. *Then both* PEG *and* MEREDITH *turn their eyes towards* PHIL. JACK *enters with car keys, defeated.*)

JACK. It's no use. We'd better get on the road…we've got a long…

(JACK *stops. Glances at* PEG *and* MEREDITH, *and suddenly understands. He too stares at* PHIL. PEG *urges* MEREDITH *to speak.*)

MEREDITH. Ph…Phil?

(PHIL *doesn't look at her.*)

MEREDITH. (*Emphatically.*) Phil…

(*Long pause.* MEREDITH *can't continue.* PEG *turns off the television.* PHIL *glances up at everyone.*)

PHIL. Why are you looking at me? Don't everyone look at me. What have I done that you should all look at me?

MEREDITH. (*Carefully.*) You…you haven't done anything, sweetheart. That's…*that's* why we're all looking at you.

PHIL. Well what do you suggest I be doing, Meredith? Huh?

MEREDITH. —*Don't*, sweetheart, *don't* do that.

PHIL. —Don't do *what*? What am I *doing*? Just what sorts of things am I *supposed* to be doing!

MEREDITH. I…Phil? I…I want you to… (*Glancing at* PEG, *who urges her on.*) …to go! Go in! There! To…to *Michael's* room. And…and I…I want you to…to *tell* him. For *me*. That you…*don't want him to go!*

PHIL. (*Almost bewildered.*) He doesn't want to go to *Canada*, Meredith.

MEREDITH. But maybe. Maybe he thinks…*you* want him to…go over there.

PHIL. Why would *I* want him to go over there?

(JACK *and* PEG *leap to* MEREDITH's *side, desperately hopeful.*)

MEREDITH. Then if you don't *want* him to! Ask him to go to *Canada*!

PHIL.	**MEREDITH.**
But he wants to go over there, Meredith.	But what if he really doesn't?
(*Miniscule pause.*)	
PHIL.	**MEREDITH.**
But he wants to go, Meredith.	But what if he…
(*Miniscule pause.*)	

PHIL.	MEREDITH.
But he wants to go, Meredith.	I JUST WANT YOU TO TALK TO HIM! TALK TO HIM! YOU GO IN THERE AND TALK TO HIM!

PHIL. I'VE TALKED TO MY SON! He doesn't want to go to Canada! He wants to go find out what it's like to kill some Gooks! What do you want me to do, march in there and tell him everything he's about to go through is for…for…for nothing? Meredith? Is that the last thing you want him to hear from us?

MEREDITH. —Yes! *Yes!* Because it *is* for nothing! It's for *nothing!* And I'll be *damned* if my son's going to become YOU for nothing!

PHIL. IT'S NOT FOR NOTHING! IT'S NOT FOR NOTHING! BE-CAUSE LOOK AT MY LIFE! Because my friends died by the fuck-ing…armful! Sc…sc…scared! K…k…k…k…k…KIDS! Just trying to keep their sh…sh…SHIT TOGETHER SO THEY CAN MAKE IT HOME OK AND GETTING MUTIL…MUTIL…MUTIL…CUT TO PIECES AND…AND…SHITTING THEIR PANTS WITH…WITH FEAR! AND IF WE DIDN'T BELIEVE ALL THAT WAS FOR SOMETHING… IF ALL OF THAT WASN'T FOR SOMETHING…! IF MY SON'S NOT GOING TO VIETNAM FOR SOMETHING…. Oh…Jesus! …*fuck!*

> (PHIL *staggers back and clutches desperately at his chest.* PEG *and* JACK *rush to him and sit him down in a chair.* MEREDITH, *however throws up her arms in furious exasperation.*)

MEREDITH. Oh hell, Phil!

> (PEG *and* JACK *loosen* PHIL's *shirt as he grabs frantically at them.*)

MEREDITH.	PHIL.
(*To* PHIL.) What. What are you doing *this* for, Phil? —He needs some water, Peg, could you run get him some water?	(*To* JACK *and* PEG.) No. No. No. I'm OK. I'm fine. I'm OK. Just got to…got to sit. Jesus Christ, what's the matter with me.

PEG. (*Running off.*) I'll get some water!

JACK. (*Following.*) He doesn't need water, he needs a damned *doctor!* I'm calling a doctor!

> (MEREDITH *is left alone with* PHIL. *Hiding an intense worry behind her anger, she storms to the chair and bends over him.*)

MEREDITH.	PHIL.
(*Stern.*) Goddamnit Phil, let's loosen the Goddamned shirt! Loosen it up! Now you take a deep Goddamned breath and you	(*Struggling.*) Jesus Christ I think I…yeah, let's…loosen it up! Loosen it up! Jesus Christ, I…I got to…tryin' to! Tryin' to

get it together, Phil.
(*Almost ritualistic.*) Get it together.
You get it together and keep it
together. OK. OK. OK.

breathe! Take a deep breath and…
(*Almost ritualistic.*) …get it together.
Gonna do that. Gonna keep it
together. OK? OK? OK?

(*A pause. Panting, MEREDITH straightens as PHIL straightens in his chair. The familiarity to each other of the final words have made us realize that this is something they've done many times before. They regard each other, recognizing in a terrible way the shared intimacy of the exchange that has just passed. PHIL opens his arms and leans forward to her, in desperate need. MEREDITH is almost drawn in, but then jumps back, regaining her full fury.*)

MEREDITH. I CAN'T!

(*MEREDITH moves as far away from him as she can. She hugs herself. PHIL stares helplessly. Their son MICHAEL, concerned, appears in the doorway with a duffle.*)

MICHAEL. Dad?

(*MEREDITH turns and stares at PHIL. This is the moment.*)

MEREDITH. (*Pleading.*) Phil?

(*Silence. PHIL is frozen*).

MEREDITH. (*Emphatically.*) Phil.

(*PHIL looks at her, as if snapped out of a trance.*)

MEREDITH. Phil…

(*PHIL understands. He half-rises out of his chair towards his son before looking at him. He stares at MICHAEL, caught halfway between rising and sitting. A short, agonizing pause as he takes in the sight of his son. He sinks back down in his chair and covers his face with his hands in complete failure. Choking back sobs, MEREDITH dashes to MICHAEL and throws herself into his arms. Blackout.*)

Scene 2

Night. Heavy rain. A motel room in which the décor of two eras seem to collide, with aged mass-production 1950s prints and furnishings standing out among cheaper, newer additions. As if in direct contrast to the surroundings, an expensive set of luggage lies strewn across the bed and various surfaces. Their owner is in the bathroom. Water runs in the sink.

There is a light knock on the door. After a few moments, we hear a key in the lock. PHIL opens the door. He hesitates in the doorway for a long moment, then finally steps in and closes the door behind him. He is a soaked, exhausted fifty-one years old, heavier again since the last time we've seen him. He stands helplessly in front of the closed door.

The water in the bathroom shuts off and we're left only with the sound of the rain. It is February 15, 1973. Pause.

PHIL. (*Hoarsely.*) Mer…. (*Emotional, clearing his throat.*) M…Meredith?

    (MEREDITH *steps into the lighted doorway of the bathroom. She wears a long bathrobe. A towel wraps her wet hair. Long pause.*)

MEREDITH. (*Unhappy surprise.*) What are you…

    (*Pause.* MEREDITH *glances quickly at the telephone. She lunges for it, but* PHIL *anticipates her.*)

MEREDITH. NO! NO PHIL! NO!

    (*They struggle.* PHIL *wrests the phone out of* MEREDITH's *hands. He yanks the cord out of the wall.*)

MEREDITH. HELP ME! SOMEBODY HELP Mmmmfff…!

    (PHIL *puts his hand, hard, over* MEREDITH's *mouth. She struggles.*)

PHIL. No! Enough! No more! No more! Stop it! Stop it! Stop!

    (*He presses his hand harder and talks almost soothingly to her the way one might to an animal.* MEREDITH *struggles intermittently through the next beat.*)

PHIL. Right? OK? I'm gonna…OK? Let go? And…and I don't want any…raised voices, I don't want any screaming, I'm not here to…I just…I need everything to stop. For a second. Just for a second. —I'll stop too. We'll both just…OK? I'm going to lift the hand?

    (MEREDITH *nods.* PHIL *gingerly lifts his hand.*)

MEREDITH.	**PHIL.**
(*Venomous.*) Get out of here! What are you even doing here, you…you…crazy…	(*Reflexive anger.*) It's you! It's you!…you've been…and you can't even…!
	(*Instantly repentant.*) —Sorry. I'm sorry.

MEREDITH. —Don't tell me that!

PHIL. —*Sorry*—

MEREDITH. —I said *don't tell me that*, you don't tell me that *any* more.

    (*Commanding.*) Let go of me.

    (PHIL *lets go. She pulls herself to her feet. So does he.* MEREDITH *takes stock of the room.*)

MEREDITH. (*Regaining control.*) Put the phone back in the wall.

PHIL. (*Innocent.*) It's broken.

MEREDITH. Way to go Phil.

PHIL. Don't start with that chickenshit…*bullshit!*

MEREDITH. How did you get the key. Give it back.

PHIL. I told the office that—

MEREDITH. —They should have called—

PHIL. —I told them not to *bother* because I—

MEREDITH. Put it on the *desk* there, Phil. I mean it.

 (*Pause.* PHIL *reaches over, hesitates, and drops a motel room key on the desk.*)

MEREDITH. Now go. You go. Now. And we'll…we'll…forget about the whole thing.

 (*Pause.* PHIL *turns. He opens the door. The sound of the rain overwhelms us. He steps into the night and shuts the door.* MEREDITH *turns and sits on the bed. She puts her face in her hands and cries. The door slowly opens and* PHIL *steps back in, even more soaked than before. He slowly shuts the door and stands in front of it again.*)

PHIL. (*Quietly defiant.*) No.

MEREDITH. What no. No what.

PHIL. No I'm not going to.

 (*In a fury,* MEREDITH *rises and pounds on* PHIL *with her fists.*)

MEREDITH. GET OUT OF HERE. YOU GET OUT OF HERE.

PHIL. No.

MEREDITH. I'LL TELL THE POLICE! AND THEY'LL TAKE YOU AWAY! I'LL SAY YOU'RE VIOLENT! I'LL PUT YOU IN PRISON!

PHIL. I don't care.

MEREDITH. I'LL KILL YOU, PHIL! I'LL STAB YOU IN THE HEART! DON'T THINK I WON'T DO IT!

PHIL. I don't care.

MEREDITH. I'LL KILL MYSELF THEN! I WILL, I SWEAR TO GOD, AND THEN WHAT'LL YOU HAVE? NOTHING! NO SON! NO ME! NOBODY! NOTHING!

PHIL. No.

 (*Long pause.* MEREDITH *breaks from him.*)

MEREDITH. I thought you put the key on the desk.

PHIL. That was the key to *my* room.

MEREDITH. What do you *mean* the key to…

 (*Realizing.*) —*you're* not…

PHIL. —I'm three doors down.

MEREDITH. (*Flabbergasted.*) You…I don't…You're not going to start this up again!

PHIL. I'm *better*, Meredith.

MEREDITH. Then what are you…! I can't believe you have the *nerve* to…!

PHIL. Listen! I'm…I'm uh. I…have a…a doctor. That I have appointments with. Every week. He's a… Back home. A psychiatrist.

MEREDITH. See? See? I knew it! You're…

PHIL. (*Righteous.*) CAN'T YOU JUST STOP? WHY DOES EVERY LIT-
TLE INCH OF GROUND HAVE TO BE SOME…SOME…THAT
DOESN'T MEAN I'M CRAZY! THAT MEANS I'M GETTING BET-
TER!

MEREDITH. AND YOU FOLLOWED ME ALL THE WAY OUT
HERE TO TELL ME THAT!

> (*Slight pause.*)

PHIL. (*Caving.*) OK, *yeah*, well that's…*that's*…

MEREDITH. Right. People don't *do* that. Don't you understand? People
don't do *half* the things you do.

PHIL. (*Innocent.*) I mean I just…! I drove! For…one day! And when I got to
the place where you'd stayed that night, I…! And then I drove another day,
and then…! I didn't mean to go all the…! But then I thought you know,
halfway through… Hell, it was actually kind of a nice vacation you were on,
Meredith, and—

MEREDITH. —How did you—

PHIL. —That Bank *Americard.*

MEREDITH. (*Actually confounded.*) Are you kidding?

PHIL. No. It was easy. You should really use cash if you want to run away.

MEREDITH. (*Skeptical.*) Really!

PHIL. Every hotel. Every gas station. Every restaurant. I'm not lying, I
stopped there.

MEREDITH. Bullshit!

PHIL. Bullshit!

MEREDITH. Tell me your favorite.

PHIL. Uh. Green River. In Utah. I don't know what you had, but I got the
hamburger.

MEREDITH. The hamburger was your favorite?

PHIL. It was dry.

MEREDITH. Then why'd you like it.

PHIL. (*Dryly.*) I like a dry hamburger.

> (*Pause.* MEREDITH *stares, resenting the impulse to be charmed by him.*)

MEREDITH. You kill me, you know that?

> (*She breaks from him and picks up the broken telephone. She wraps the cord
> around the phone.*)

PHIL. Can I have a towel?

MEREDITH. (*Slamming the phone back onto the desk.*) Go to hell, why don't
you.

> (*Pause. They gather themselves.*)

PHIL. *Tom.* Let them…give me my membership back.

MEREDITH. He *shouldn't* have.

PHIL. The…that jackass *manager* kid—

MEREDITH. (*Like he's forgotten the name a thousand times.*) —Edward?—

PHIL. —picks up the phone when I go in and calls Tom. You ever hear of probation? At a country club? But guess what, I'm allowed to have lunch there again! My own club that was built in my name with my own…! And I groveled! In order to have a dried out turkey sandwich and a cold cup of soup across the room from a *sneak* who—

MEREDITH. (*Sharply.*) —we had our settlements, Phil.

PHIL. (*Regaining a false calm.*) Anyway, I uh…declined. Very nicely. To join him. Tom. I thought it was very polite of him to ask, though. And I was very nice in return, I didn't…I didn't…

MEREDITH. That's not a miracle, you know. Being civil.

PHIL. Sometimes it is. When your whole life disappears it is. You try it sometime.

MEREDITH. (*Almost childish.*) I *have. I* can do it.

PHIL. *Really!* You call that *civil!* So you're suggesting that I use *your* behavior as a model to follow. You know. To prove to everyone I'm not the way you *say* I am.

MEREDITH. People *do* things, Phil.

PHIL. Yeah? Why is that a reply I'm not allowed to use for *myself? (Miniscule pause.)* Just give me a towel, will you?

MEREDITH. (*Finality.*) I'm…I'm sorry, Phil, I…

> (*Pause.*)

PHIL. (*Back on the trail.*) Tom. Told me. Uh. That you'd left him.

MEREDITH. That's none of your business.

PHIL. (*Childish.*) It is if *TOM* told me.

MEREDITH. Then it's just *information*, Phil, that's all, it's not your *business,* it doesn't give you the right—

PHIL. —what *denies* me the right—

MEREDITH. —you made an agreement—

PHIL. WELL YOU MADE AN AGREEMENT TO ME, MEREDITH! WHAT ABOUT THAT! WHAT ABOUT THAT AGREEMENT!

MEREDITH. (*Almost calmly.*) I'm not going to go into this.

> (*Long pause.*)

PHIL. So uh…he's uh…he's devastated. Tom. I…uh…had a…pretty hard time. Uh. Feeling sorry for him, though, I'll tell you that.

MEREDITH. So what about this makes you better, Phil.

PHIL. Well nobody *else* was looking for you! What was I *supposed* to—

MEREDITH. —I left a note!

PHIL. —A note! You don't get a note like that and…! I mean he was just sitting there! At the…at the…! Crying into his soup! And you've packed your bags and…and…! Well people…don't get to just… disappear! Without someone looking for them! They don't! Especially not…you! *You* disappear, you deserve to have someone looking for you! It's the least they can do! And he was just…! Just…! How dare he!

> (*Long pause.* MEREDITH *looks for a split second as if she could melt before bitterly fighting to regain herself.*)

MEREDITH. Well I'd be lying if I didn't admit I wasn't a little impressed.

PHIL. I didn't do it to impress you.

MEREDITH. (*As if she's caught him.*) Following me all the… Phil? You could have just called that credit card a month from now to see where I'd—

PHIL. —It wouldn't have mattered because by the time I got to Reno I figured it all out.

MEREDITH. Don't pretend to be so—

PHIL. —I'm not pretending anything! I'm *serious*, you don't think I—!

MEREDITH. —I think you have to believe that you know me! I think you have to believe you're still intimately connected with me with so you won't feel…as lonely as you really are! But I've—

PHIL. (*The trump card.*) —I've been in this motel since *yesterday*, Em. So in a way, actually, you followed me.

MEREDITH. (*Confused.*) How did you…

PHIL. I can put two and two together. I saw the headlines. The route you were on was heading right for it.

MEREDITH. (*Flatly.*) Right for what.

PHIL. (*Knowing he's caught her.*) Travis Air Force Base.

> (*Pause.*)

MEREDITH. That's…well that's *ridiculous*, I wouldn't—!

PHIL. (*Bitter.*) Of *course* not! Because you're not the *crazy* one! You wouldn't drive all the way across the country to see…

MEREDITH. You're *sick*, Phil. You're…

PHIL. —So you were just taking a random…very *long* route—

MEREDITH. (*Desperate denial.*) —Yes! I was!

PHIL. —That just happened to take you past Travis Air Force Base the morning the first POW'S were coming home? (*Pause.*) I was *there*, Em. *Today.* I saw you. You were standing over by the fence. Pretending to wave at someone so you'd blend in.

MEREDITH. (*Quickly.*) You're *obsessive*, Phil, you've been—

PHIL.
YOU'RE THE OBSESSIVE…!
YOU'RE THE OBSESSIVE!
I GET PEGGED AS THE SICK
ONE ALL THE *TIME* WHICH
IS MIGHTY *CONVENIENT*
CONSIDERING YOU'RE THE
ONE WHO CAN'T LET GO OF HIM!
YOU DROVE ALL THE WAY
OUT HERE! TO WATCH A BUNCH
OF KIDS YOU DON'T EVEN
KNOW COME HOME FROM
VIETNAM WHEN OUR SON HAS
BEEN DEAD FOR *SIX! YEARS!*

MEREDITH.
—You shut up!
Shut up! You don't know anything!
What do you know!
You don't know why!
You don't know anything!

(MEREDITH *covers her ears and runs into the bathroom, sobbing.* PHIL *follows her to the door and shouts through it.*)

PHIL. AND I'LL TELL YOU! I AM SICK TO DEATH OF BEING HELD TO BLAME! I WAKE UP EVERY DAY AND I DON'T KNOW WHO TO MOURN THE LOSS OF! YOU OR HIM!

(*Saddening.*) But I'll tell you it sure does put a little extra sting in the cuts knowing you've made every arrangement possible to see that I am somehow punished.

(PHIL *sits on the bed. Long Pause. The sobbing eventually stops.* PHIL *looks over into one of the open suitcases. He lifts out a framed picture. He stares at it. He rises and sets the picture on the dresser. Long Pause.* MEREDITH *opens the bathroom door. She reenters.*)

MEREDITH. (*Sadly unapologetic about her misplaced punishment.*) Someone's got to be held accountable, Phil.

PHIL. And I'm the logical choice?

MEREDITH. You're the only one I can find. So I'm sorry. I mean what am I gonna do, write to my senator?

PHIL. I have an idea. Why don't you divorce your husband and dismantle every sliver of his life you can possibly get your hands on. Oh, sorry, I forgot, you've already done that. Well in that case why don't you attempt to commit him as a severe obsessive because he's completely unable to accept being blamed for the death of his son. Oh my apologies, you've already tried that, too. But you know I think you're right about your ex-husband's mental state. Because a well-adjusted person would accept the accusations you've leveled against him! But not Phil! Phil's got to reject them! Because he's a nut-case! And to cement it all, he makes a couple of very public scenes, one of which involves throwing an entire banquet table full of shrimp and cheese through his club's window and into the pool during his ex-wife's engagement party! So now he's a fucking pariah! And you know what? He deserves to be! Because you know what else? His son's death and mutilation in the central highlands of Southeast Asia is his! Fucking! Fault!

(*Pause.*)

MEREDITH. (*Bare.*) I'm…I'm…

PHIL. What! Sorry? Are you sorry? And why would you be sorry? Because our lives have been torn to bits? Or is it that after everything that's been done, you still don't feel any better?

MEREDITH. Why did you come here?

PHIL. Because this time you're wrong. And if you're going to live the rest of your life without me, I want you to know in no uncertain terms that you're doing it for the wrong reasons.

MEREDITH. (*Almost pleading.*) I left him, didn't I? Didn't I do that?

PHIL. Why.

MEREDITH. Because…because.

PHIL. Well you're setting records left and right. People talked enough about the first divorce. How bad is this one going to be?

MEREDITH. I don't know.

PHIL. What are you going to blame *him* for?

MEREDITH. Something, I'm sure.

PHIL. They'll hound you out of St. Louis for good. Forget going near the club again.

MEREDITH. Yeah. Well it doesn't really matter, does it? I could go anywhere and nothing would ever be…

(*Realizing what she's about to say.*)

PHIL. (*Emphatic. He's won.*) Yeah. That's right.

(*Pause. MEREDITH sits on the bed. There is a tone change now, a hesitant, yet easy intimacy between them.*)

MEREDITH. I…I had a long time to think on the way out.

PHIL. Yeah.

MEREDITH. I… It's funny, Phil. I…I did…think. Of you. Quite a lot.

PHIL. Yeah?

MEREDITH. I started wondering. About the years after the…well after the war. About…where you might have been.

PHIL. (*Quietly.*) Yes.

MEREDITH. I…liked…feeling a little…lost. I liked…how you start to wonder about all the places you pass through. What your life might be like if you stopped there for a while. How long you could last there before you catch up to yourself. And…if that would be…OK. In the end. If you did. Wherever there is.

(*Slight pause.*) The West. Is a strange place, isn't it.

PHIL. Utah sure is beautiful.

MEREDITH. Too barren.

PHIL. I like Colorado.

MEREDITH. Except that I'm tired of being…cold. In the winter.

PHIL. The grapevines here…

MEREDITH. I've never seen grape vines.

PHIL. (*Plainly.*) They had them in Sicily.

MEREDITH. That doesn't…? That wouldn't…? It doesn't remind you of…?

PHIL. It was a long time ago.

MEREDITH. Not really too long, Phil.

PHIL. Can I please have a towel? Please?

(*Pause. MEREDITH stands and goes into the bathroom, returning with a towel. PHIL stand and meets her in the middle of the room. She holds it out to him. He takes one end of it, delicately. She doesn't let go of her end.*)

PHIL. (*Quietly.*) When you left me. You told me that I just didn't live for you the way you lived for me. But you never understood I think that you were the only…

(*Miniscule pause.*) And thinking of us. Today. The both of us standing in the rain at the base. You over by the fence in the crowd. Me watching you, near the parking lot. The both of us waiting for the transport to land so that…we could watch…three hundred other people…get their children back. I realized that…dying, Meredith. Is not the ultimate sacrifice. Uh.

(*Miniscule pause.*) We are.

MEREDITH. They all looked so…

PHIL. …Yeah.

MEREDITH. You looked like that, Phil.

PHIL. Yeah?

MEREDITH. And Michael would have…and then…and then I would've had two. And I would have taken you both of course… But somehow. When it turned out I just had the one again…it was just more than I could…

PHIL. I know.

MEREDITH. I'm only fifty-one, Phil. I might be…

PHIL. What.

MEREDITH. …Ready.

PHIL. For what.

MEREDITH. For…I don't know. One last…hoorah. Or maybe…my first hoorah ever.

PHIL. What am I supposed to do with that?

MEREDITH. I don't know.

> (PHIL *sits on the bed again.* MEREDITH *slowly sits next to him. They don't touch. They both stare straight out.*)

MEREDITH. Phil, I'm—

PHIL. —I know. Me too.

MEREDITH. There's been so much—

PHIL. —So just forget about it.

MEREDITH. I want to.

PHIL. Then why don't we?

> (*Pause.* PHIL *reaches over and takes* MEREDITH's *hand.*)

MEREDITH. Because it's not as easy as just saying 'we' again.

PHIL. Why not?

MEREDITH. Well because it's…it's not. It would be…ridiculous.

PHIL. Maybe to people in St. Louis. But uh. Nobody knows us here, Em.

MEREDITH. You're not saying you would…. I mean that really would be a little crazy, wouldn't it?

PHIL. Everybody thinks I'm crazy anyway, so it's no skin off my back. Besides, it's not like we just met each other or anything. I mean are you really that different?

MEREDITH. No.

PHIL. Neither am I.

MEREDITH. That's what I'm afraid of.

PHIL. We'd just be…a…couple. From the Midwest. Taking in the sunshine. Getting…drunk in the afternoons. Doing things we…we…we could have done. We could…have someone…send some trucks! I don't know, arrange the packing! Change our addresses! My God, it would be simple!

MEREDITH. (*Falling for it.*) I'm not going to fall for this.

PHIL. Can't we just…give ourselves a night and a day?

> (*Slight pause.* MEREDITH *looks at* PHIL.)

PHIL. You owe me a maybe.

> (*Pause.* MEREDITH *reaches over and lightly touches* PHIL's *face.*)

PHIL. And then maybe…another. Remember?

MEREDITH. Phil…

> (PHIL *embraces her.*)

PHIL. It's me, remember? Remember me, Meredith? Say yes to me. Say yes to me.

> (*The lights fade.*)

End of Play

NEON MIRAGE
by Liz Duffy Adams, Dan Dietz, Rick Hip-Flores, Julie Jensen, Lisa Kron, Tracey Scott Wilson, and Chay Yew

BIOGRAPHIES

Liz Duffy Adams is a New Dramatists Resident Playwright who has received a New York Fellowship for the Arts Award, the Frederick Loewe Award, and the Will Glickman Award. Plays include *The Listener* and Humana Festival finalists *Dog Act, One Big Lie,* and *Wet or Isabella The Pirate Queen Enters The Horse Latitudes.* Publications include *Poodle With Guitar And Dark Glasses* in Applause Books' *Best American Short Plays 2000-2001* and several plays with Playscripts, Inc. Adams has been in residence at Portland Center Stage's JAW/West, Bay Area Playwrights Festival, Portland Stage Company's Little Festival of the Unexpected, Djerassi Artists Residency Program, and the Millay Colony For the Arts, and is a graduate of NYU's Experimental Theater Wing and Yale School of Drama.

Dan Dietz's plays include *Dirigible, Blind Horses, Tilt Angel,* and *Americamisfit,* and have been seen in New York, Los Angeles, and points in between. His play *tempOdyssey* received a rolling world premiere from the National New Play Network in 2006-07, premiering at Curious Theatre (Denver, CO), Studio Theatre (Washington, DC), Phoenix Theatre (Indianapolis, IN) and New Jersey Rep (Long Branch, NJ). Mr. Dietz has been honored with a James A. Michener Fellowship, a Josephine Bay Paul Fellowship, and the Austin Critics Table Award for Best New Play. He is a two-time finalist for the Princess Grace Award and a nominee for the Oppenheimer Award, the Osborn Award, and the ATCA/Steinberg Award. His short play *Trash Anthem* received the 2003 Heideman Award from the Actors Theatre of Louisville. Mr. Dietz is a Core Member of the Playwrights' Center and a Resident Company Member of Salvage Vanguard Theater.

Rick Hip-Flores has written music and lyrics to *Neon Mirage* (Humana Festival, 2006), *My New York* (Vital Theater), *Dido and Aeneas* (Prospect Theater), and the Columbia *Varsity Show.* He has also composed scores for *Tartuffe* and *As You Like It* (Worth Street Players). He is a member of the BMI Lehman Engel Workshop in New York. As a musical director, recent credits include *Jacques Brel is Alive and Well...* (Off-Broadway revival), *Singin in the Rain* (Northshore Music Theatre), and the Neil Sedaka musical *Breaking Up is Hard to Do* (Actors Playhouse). Other New York and regional credits include *Laugh Whore, Beauty and the Beast, Altar Boyz, Last Five Years, Shakespeare on Broadway, 8 by Tenn, Fame, Henry and Mudge,* and *A Christmas Carol.* Rick is the resident musical director for Musicals Tonight, where he interprets lesser known works by Porter and Kern.

Julie Jensen has a Ph.D. in theatre from Wayne State University in Detroit, and has taught playwriting at seven different colleges and universities. She worked as a writer in Hollywood for five years and until recently directed the graduate playwriting program at the University of Nevada, Las Vegas. She is now Resident Playwright at Salt Lake Acting Company. Ms. Jensen is the recipient of the Kennedy Center Award for New American Plays (*White Money*), the Joseph Jefferson Award for Best New Work (*The Lost Vegas Series*), and the LA Weekly Award for Best New Play (*Two-Headed*). She has received the McKnight National Playwriting Fellowship (*WAIT!*), the TCG/NEA Playwriting Residency (*WAIT!*), and a major grant from the Pew Charitable Trusts (*Dust Eaters*). Her play, *Two-Headed*, was included in the volume *Best Plays by Women, 2000*, and she has twice been nominated by the American Theatre Critics Association for the best new play produced outside of New York (*Last Lists of My Mad Mother* and *Dust Eaters*).

Lisa Kron has been writing and performing theater since coming to New York from Michigan in 1984. Her play, *Well,* opened on Broadway at the Longacre Theater in March of 2006 and received two Tony nominations. It premiered at the Public Theater in Spring 2004 and was listed among the year's best plays by the *New York Times*, the *Associated Press*, the *Newark Star Ledger, Backstage* and the *Advocate*. Her play, *2.5 Minute Ride* premiered in New York at the Public Theater in 1999 and received an OBIE Award, Drama Desk and Outer Critics Circle nominations, an L.A. Drama-Logue Award, a GLAAD Media Award and was named the best autobiographical show by New York Press. Ms. Kron is also a founding member of the OBIE and Bessie Award–winning theater company The Five Lesbian Brothers. She is the recipient the Cal Arts/Alpert Award, as well as grants and fellowships from the Creative Capital Foundation, New York Foundation for the Arts, NEA/TCG, the Guggenheim Foundation and the Lucille Lortel Foundation.

Tracey Scott Wilson's current work includes *The Story*, which was first produced at The Joseph Papp Public Theater/NYSF, and transferred to the Long Wharf Theatre. *The Story* has since been produced at thirty theatres nationwide. Additional productions include *Order My Steps* for Cornerstone Theater's Black Faith/AIDS project in Los Angeles; and *Exhibit #9*, produced in New York City by New Perspectives Theatre and Theatre Outrageous; *Leader of the People* produced at New Georges Theatre; two ten-minute plays produced at the Guthrie Theatre in Minneapolis; and a ten-minute play produced at Actors Theatre of Louisville. Ms. Wilson has had readings at the New York Theatre Workshop, New Georges Theatre, The Joseph Papp Public Theater and Soho Theatre Writers Centre in London. She earned two Van Lier Fellowships from the New York Theatre Workshop, a residency at Sundance Ucross, and is the winner of the 2001 Helen Merrill Emerging Playwright Award, the 2003 AT&T Onstage Award, the 2004 Whiting Award and as well as the 2004 Kesselring Prize. Ms. Wilson holds a Master's degree in English Literature from Temple University.

Chay Yew's plays include *Porcelain, A Language of Their Own, Red, A Beautiful Country, Wonderland, Question 27 Question 28* and *A Distant Shore*. His other work includes adaptations, *A Winter People* (based on Chekhov's *The Cherry Orchard*) and Lorca's *The House of Bernarda Alba,* and a musical, *Long Season*. His work has been produced at the Joseph Papp Public Theatre, Royal Court Theatre (London), Mark Taper Forum, Manhattan Theatre Club, Wilma Theatre, Long Wharf Theatre, La Jolla Playhouse, Intiman Theatre, Portland Center Stage, East West Players, Cornerstone Theatre Company, Perseverance Theatre, Singapore Repertory Theatre and TheatreWorks Singapore. He is also the recipient of the London Fringe Award for Best Playwright and Best Play, George and Elisabeth Marton Playwriting Award, GLAAD Media Award, APGF Community Visibility Award, Made in America Award and Robert Chesley Award. He's under commission from Oregon Shakespeare Festival, Alliance Theatre and Writer's Theatre.

ACKNOWLEDGMENTS

Neon Mirage premiered at the Humana Festival of New American Plays in March 2006. It was directed by Wendy McClellan with the following cast and staff:

Drift, Liz Duffy Adams
Woman...Robin Grace Thompson

MGM Grand, lyrics/music by Rick Hip-Flores,
text by Julie Jensen
Singers.. Company

Breaking Even, Dan Dietz
Leo.. Ben Friesen
Lola...Lauren Bauer
Larry .... Michael C. Schantz

Paradise, scene by Tracey Scott Wilson,
underscoring by Rick Hip-Flores
Mother .... Melissa Dowty
Princess...Kim Carpenter
Queen...Eva Gil
Michelle..................................... Stephanie Thompson

Charity, Lisa Kron
Clay...Lee Dolson
Merlene ....Ashanti Brown

Air Conditioning, Rick Hip-Flores
Bugsy... Aaron Alika Patinio
Gangsters... Company

Don't Talk, Don't See, Julie Jensen
Wanda ....Keira Keeley

Montecore, Lisa Kron
Tiger 1 ....Toby Knops
Tiger 2 ....Tom Coiner

The Electric Former Feminist Studies
Major Bares It All For You, Dan Dietz
Gina...Sarah Augusta

Imelda and Cher, Chay Yew
Eileen Katigbak .... Elizabeth Truong
Tibo Katigbak .... Aaron Alika Patino

Some Such Luck, Liz Duffy Adams
Sherri ....Eva Gil
Roy...Bryan Manley Davis

Gestures, Chay Yew
Chloe .... Cindy N. Kawaski

Lion Tongue, Julie Jensen
Our Girl..Kim Carpenter
Campy Guy .... Cliff Williams III

Show Me That Smile, Rick Hip-Flores
Kathleen... Stephanie Thompson

The Odds Aren't Good, Rick Hip-Flores
Woman.. Melissa Dowty
Man...Lee Dolson
Chorus .... Company

Dog Shot, Dan Dietz
Schultz.. Isaac Gardner
Deangelo.. Michael C. Schantz

Ghosts of Las Vegas, scene by Liz Duffy Adams,
underscoring by Rick Hip-Flores
Kathleen.. Stephanie Thompson
Rick...Tom Coiner
Ghost of Elvis..Bryan Manley Davis
Slot Pullers.. Company

Scenic Designer ....Paul Owen
Costume Designer.. John P. White
Lighting Designer..Nick Dent
Sound Designer ....Benjamin Marcum
Properties Designer .... Jo Cunningham
Music Director..Rick Hip-Flores
Stage Manager...Megan Schwarz
Dramaturg .... Adrien-Alice Hansel
Dramaturg Assistants ....Joanna K. Donehower, Jamie Bragg
Directing Assistant...Jessica Franz

Ben Friesen and Lauren Bauer
in *Neon Mirage*

30th Annual Humana Festival of New American Plays
Actors Theatre of Louisville, 2006
Photo by Harlan Taylor

Neon Mirage

Drift
by Liz Duffy Adams

A YOUNG WOMAN—*could be a man just as easily—talking to the audience. Quiet.*

So, I'm drifting across the desert. Really drifting, eddies of air, little air currents above the dessert floor, 'cause, you know, semi-corporeal. Don't even worry about it. It's night; well, it's always night now. The worst happened—didn't you really know it would?—and now everything rests in the sweet clasp of night, all the time, forever as the sands drift, everywhere. I drift across the desert and in the distance I see... something... glittering in the starlight (oh, there's still starlight, it'll be a lot longer before those nightlights go out.), and BANG WOOSH I'm suddenly a lot closer. (I can do that, we can, it's a thing, don't even.) Ohhh, man, what am I looking at. How can this be. Big sandblasted monuments rising out of the sands. A spidery pointy metal tower, all rivets and swooping struts. A hard-jawed metal woman as high as the tower, holding up a dead torch, pocked to hell by the blowing sands. A sketch of a ruined temple, palm trees, gods in skirts. Something went on here. Something, huh, something strange. Here are traces, here are remnants. Was it trash? Was it sacred? These things existed in the world, I recognize them, but they don't belong here, all together in this western desert. There's a bridge, I know that bridge. Once it was a symbol of something that couldn't be sold, to define gullibility. But that bridge was far away, spanning liquidity near a liquid plain. Now it's nothing, is dust in a river of dust near a sea of dust, we few sad remnants drifting by. We're not ghosts, not quite. There are ghosts here, I can smell them. Papery smell, the sand has leached the highs and lows away. But they still linger. Spectral arms reaching up, pulling down. Over and over. A shiver runs up my semi-corporeal spine. I recognize my ancestors. I recognize the authors of my fate, all our fates. (*Whispers.*) *You fucking assholes. What did you build here? What did you throw away, in a timeless fever? You gambled our world. You lost.* They don't answer. They can't hear me. And who am I to scold and preach? I don't take any chance, I don't gamble on fate. Fate's come and gone on this dusty globe. I'm just a trace, a remnant. But if you don't believe me when I tell you what's coming... I've got a bridge I can sell you.

At The MGM Grand

Lyrics and music by Rick Hip-Flores
Scene by Julie Jenson

Blackout, Drumroll. KATHLEEN *center stage in an elaborate costume.*

COME ON IN
DON'T BE SHY
ALL THE PLEASURES HERE ARE YOURS TO TRY
COME AND FEEL YOUR HEART EXPAND
AT THE MGM GRAND.

TAKE A CARD
WIN THE POT
MISTER, EVEN YOU HAVE GOT A SHOT.
DON'T YOU WANT TO PLAY YOUR HAND
AT THE MGM GRAND.

COME SPIN THE WHEEL,
AND SOON YOU MAY FEEL A TINGLE
IF YOU SUCCEED
THE FUN'S GUARANTEED
IT SAYS SO ON OUR SHINGLE.

SO TAKE A ROMP,
HAVE A FLING
WATCH OUR LOVELY SHOWGIRLS DO THAT THING,
OVER WHERE THE BOOZE IS CHEAP
AND THE WOMEN ARE TANNED
EVERYBODY WANTS A PEEP
AT THE MGM GRAND!

> (*During the following monologue, other actors come out on stage, some serving drinks and hors d'oeuvres to audience members, some holding cards and chips, some dressed as Vegas showgirls, and some doing performance stunts.*)

CAMPY GUY. Yes, of course, sweetheart, we're all from somewhere. Some little place that's grimy and grey. But now you're here, right here. In the *lap* of the lion, in the *heart* of the strip, on the *back* of the dream.

You wanna be rich, you *are.* You wanna be loved, you're *on.* You wanna be free, you're *out.* You wanna get hitched, you're *in.* The sky's not the limit, it's just the beginning.

So what do you want? A fling, a fuck, a flirt? You got it, sweetheart. Everyone loves you. Everyone's free. Everyone wants to take you home. And remember, honey, what happens in Vegas, stays in Vegas. That's what the lion says. (*Growl.*)

And yes it's hot, it's supposed to be hot. Vegas is…hottt. It sizzles, it fries. It bakes, it burns. It is hot. We're all hot. So very, very HOTTT.

 (CHORUS *sing Back-up vocals on this refrain.*)

HAVE A DRINK,
TRY A SMOKE,
ANYTHING YOU WANT, UNTIL YOU'RE BROKE
IF YOU ARE, WE UNDERSTAND
AT THE MGM GRAND

CATCH A SHOW
HEAR THE PRAISE,
SEE THAT CIRCUS ACT THAT'S ALL THE CRAZE
FRONT ROW TIX ARE IN DEMAND
AT THE MGM GRAND

GET WHAT YOU WANT
IT'S NOT AT THE MONTE CARLO
COME, STOP ON BY
WHERE BETTING IS HIGH
ONLY THE PRICES ARE LOW.

SO MAKE A FRIEND,
FIND ROMANCE,
EVERYONE LOOKS HAPPY, AT A GLANCE
YOU WON'T SEE THE SUNSHINE BEAM
WITH YOUR HEAD IN THE SAND
EVERYONE IS FREE TO DREAM
AT THE MGM GRAND.

 (*Dance/music break.*)

COME SPIN THE WHEEL,
AND SOON YOU MAY FEEL A TINGLE
IF YOU SUCCEED
THE FUN'S GUARANTEED
IT SAYS SO ON OUR SHINGLE.

SO MAKE A FRIEND,
FIND ROMANCE,
EVERYONE LOOKS HAPPY, AT A GLANCE
YOU WON'T SEE THE SUNSHINE BEAM
WITH YOUR HEAD IN THE SAND
EVERYONE IS FREE TO DREAM.
AT THE MGM GRAND.

BREAKING EVEN
by Dan Dietz

A posh Las Vegas hotel room, including a bed and a dining table with a chandelier hanging above it. Door opens, LEO enters. He looks around, smiles. He sets down his suitcase, opens it, and pulls out a length of rope with a noose on the end. He climbs up on the table, attaches the noose to the chandelier, gives it a good tug. He pulls out an envelope labeled "SUICIDE NOTE," removes the letter inside, and reads it aloud.

LEO. To Whom It May Concern,

Vegas is the City of Luck, and mine has always been bad. The day I was born in this lousy town, the doctor dropped me on my head. He then handed me to my mother, who, woozy from too much anesthetic, dropped me on my head. My father scooped me up, slipped on a discarded surgical glove, and dropped me on my head. That was the best day of my life. Since then, I have had twenty-seven broken bones, twelve broken hearts, and one botched circumcision. The Universe Punishes Me Nonstop For No Good Reason And I Just Can't Take It Anymore. Tonight I decided to give Vegas one final chance. I took every penny I own into the casino downstairs and bet it on a roll of the dice. I think you can guess what happened.

Signed,

Leo, the Unluckiest Man in the World

(Satisfied, LEO places the note back in the envelope, tucks it into his front pocket, and fits the noose around his neck. He closes his eyes, braces himself to jump off. Sound of a toilet flushing. LEO freezes. The bathroom door opens and LOLA comes out. She goes straight to the bed—without noticing LEO—sits down, and pulls out an envelope labeled "SUICIDE NOTE." She removes the letter inside and reads it aloud.)

LOLA. To Whom It May Concern,

Vegas is the City of Luck, and mine has always been good. The day I was born in this crazy town, the doctor dropped me on my head. My parents promptly filed a malpractice suit that kept us comfortably well off for the rest of our lives. Since then, I've aced every exam without even studying, found eleven winning lottery tickets lying in the gutter, and won the World Ping Pong Championship playing with my eyes closed—*twice*. The Universe Rewards Me Nonstop For No Good Reason And I Just Can't Take It Anymore. Tonight I decided to give Vegas one final chance. I took every penny I own into the casino downstairs and bet it on a roll of the dice. I think you can guess what happened.

Signed,

Lola, The Luckiest Woman In The World

(*Satisfied,* LOLA *places the paper back in the envelope and sets it on the bedside table. Then she pulls out a massive handful of pills, gulps them down with a glass of water, and lies down, eyes closed. Pause.*)

LEO. Hello?

(LOLA *bolts upward and screams. Startled,* LEO *cries out and falls off the table, noose around his neck. He starts choking.*)

LOLA. Oh my god! Let me help you. (LEO *frantically motions "no."* LOLA *drags a chair over and puts* LEO*'s legs on it so he can stand.* LEO *pulls his legs off and begins choking again.*) Quit struggling! Do you want to die? (LEO *nods vigorously. He points to the letter sticking out of his pocket.*) You're an inch away from asphyxiating and you want me to open your mail? (LOLA *grabs his legs and forces them back on the chair.*) There! Now stand up. Stand up! (*Finally,* LEO *sighs and stands on the chair. He stares at her resentfully.*) Well, the least you could do is thank me. I just saved your life.

LEO. (*Throwing the letter at her.*) THANK YOU!

(*She reads the note.*)

LEO. My entire life I've gotten up every morning and endured whatever bazooka-sized misfortune Lady Luck decided to hurl my way. But when I finally decide to quit her game of karmic dodge ball once and for all, guess what? They've double booked my hotel room! Lady Luck fucks me again! (*He gestures hugely, loses his balance and falls off the chair.*) OW!

LOLA. (*Finishing the note.*) This is incredible.

LEO. (*Holding his ankle.*) Make that twenty-eight broken bones.

LOLA. All my life, I've felt completely alone. Lost in a shower of money, power, prestige…

LEO. Am I supposed to feel sorry for you?

LOLA. Do you know what it's like to live in a world where no matter how hard you don't try, you can't help but win?

LEO. Do you know what it's like to live in a world where if there's even the tiniest chance for some horrific catastrophe to befall you… (*He sits in the chair, the leg breaks and it collapses.*) OW!

LOLA. But that's just it. Ever since I figured out how empty my life was, I've been praying for someone who could make me feel full.

LEO. Twenty-nine.

LOLA. Oh, Leo, don't you see? After years of loneliness and wandering, Vegas has finally brought us together.

LEO. Why? So I can watch you succeed while I fail?

LOLA. No! So we can help each other succeed! And fail!

LEO. Failing sucks, don't go there.

LOLA. I want to go there. I want to build a house, settle down, and raise a family there. How dreamy it must be! To pluck failures from life like ripe fruit from an orchard! (*She makes a plucking gesture.*) Pluck last place. (*Pluck.*) Pluck Miss Congeniality. (*Pluck.*) Pluck you!

LEO. Pluck me?

LOLA. Pluck you hard.

LEO. Do you mean what I think you mean?

LOLA. You bet I do. Marry me, Leo!

LEO. (*Recoiling.*) WHAT?!

LOLA. Vegas has given us the gift of a lifetime. And I want a lifetime to savor it with you.

LEO. I don't know, this is all so sudden.

LOLA. The best things in life are sudden. Rainstorms that come crashing down out of a clear blue sky, // the first sweet birdsong that pierces the morning air, the moment when every friend you ever had comes leaping out from behind the couch to yell "Happy Birthday!"

LEO. (*Overlapping at //.*) Yeah, but in my world the rainstorm causes me to lose control of my car, swerve off the road and crash into a tree, killing the bird as well as the friend who was sitting next to me, giving me directions to the surprise par—

(LOLA *suddenly kisses him. It's a great kiss.* LEO *blinks in amazement.*)

LOLA. See? No pies in the face, no falling pianos. Just a kiss. How do you feel, Leo?

LEO. (*In wonder.*) Like I just got dropped on my head. (*Jubilant.*) Let's do it. Let's get married!

LOLA. Oh, shit!

LEO. Is that a yes?

LOLA. No: those pills I took.

LEO. Oh, shit! 911. I'll call 911. (LEO *rushes to the phone, picks it up.*) The line's been chewed through by rats!

LOLA. What are the odds?

LEO. Welcome to my world.

LOLA. (*Dreamy smile.*) It's wonderful.

LEO. Okay. You wait here, and I'll run downstairs and… (LEO *trips and falls facedown on the floor.*) Thirty!

LOLA. (*Swooning hard now.*) Leo, it's too late…I'm going…

LEO. Then, then…I'll go with you!

(He grabs the noose. The chandelier comes crashing down.)

LEO. Damn!

LOLA. Lie down with me, Leo. Let my last moments in Vegas be here in your unlucky arms.

(LEO *lies down on the bed, and holds her.*)

LOLA. I love you, Leo, the Unluckiest Man in the World.

LEO. I love you too, Lola, the Luckiest Woman in the World.

(LOLA *reaches up, makes one final plucking gesture, and dies.* LEO *holds her tight, in quiet misery. The door opens.* LARRY *enters, carrying a suitcase. He goes to a chair, sits, opens his suitcase, and pulls out a revolver. Then he pulls out an envelope labeled "SUICIDE NOTE," removes the letter inside, and reads it aloud.*)

LARRY. To Whom It May Concern,

Vegas is the City of Luck, and mine has always been ordinary. The day I was born in this boring town, the doctor pronounced me to be of exactly average weight, height, health and temperament. Every day since then, I've done exactly what was expected of me, exactly when it was expected of me. The Universe Punishes Me With Nonstop Banality And I Just Can't Take it Anymore. Tonight I decided to give Vegas one final chance. I took every penny I own into the casino downstairs and bet it on a roll of the dice. I broke even.

Sincerely,

Larry, the Least Interesting Guy in the World

(*Satisfied,* LARRY *places the note back in the envelope, tucks it into his front pocket, and places the revolver to his head. He braces himself.*)

LEO. Hello?

(LARRY *screams, turns, and fires the revolver.* LEO *clutches his chest and falls against* LOLA. *A huge smile spreads across his face. He dies.* LARRY *stares at* LEO *and* LOLA, *then down at the revolver in his hand.*)

LARRY. Cool.

PARADISE
by Tracey Scott Wilson

Lights up on a woman.

MOTHER. Mary, Mary, Mary, where are you? No, no, no, Mommy's not mad at you anymore. I'm not mad honey at all. Come on baby. Come on. I have some exciting… No, no, I don't want to read you a bedtime story right now. Because I have something I want to tell you baby. It's important. We're moving. Yes…yes, but listen baby Daddy is not going with us. Oh, no baby. Don't cry. Don't cry. Shhhhh. Shhhhh. I'm going to tell you a story. OK? No, not those stories. Because you know what happens already… The princess runs away and happy ever… Well, this is a special story, Mary about a very special place far, far away called Las Vegas. Snuggle in honey. And I'll tell you all about how an unhappy princess discovered this wonderful, magical land. You see, once upon a time there was a princess and the princess. Princess Annie was her name. Yes, just like Mommy's name. Try not to interrupt anymore OK honey? OK. Princess Annie was a sad little girl and she lived in a sad little land with sad pathetic people.

(*Lights up on* PRINCESS ANNIE.)

PRINCESS ANNIE. Annie is my name and it is really a shame/That people in this land are all so dumb and bland.

MOTHER. The people in the town were mean, mean, mean…

(*Lights up on* PRINCESS ANNIE.)

PRINCESS ANNIE. If you are just a bit different in dress, style or speech. They yell and scream…

(*Lights up on* CHORUS. *From here on chorus can be used as background in town and Las Vegas scenes.*)

CHORUS. …How dare you try and breach/Our rules, our manners, our language are perfect in every way/Keep acting up little girl/You'll regret it someday.

MOTHER. So Princess Annie didn't have many friends and her family, well her family was no help at all. Her mother the Queen, who looked and sounded a lot like grandma, was a wicked old hag. She never gave poor Annie a moment's rest.

(*Lights up on* QUEEN.)

QUEEN. Why must you be so weird dear and your look so severe?/If you dressed a little nicer the townspeople would not sneer/The devil's got your mind/Your body/And your soul/Get on your knees and pray the Lord will make you whole.

MOTHER. So Princess Annie was very unhappy. Her Daddy? Her Daddy was away. King Daddy was very, very busy with diplomatic business. Diplomat is when you have to go to different countries and solve problems. That's right baby. No, your Daddy is not a diplomat. (Pause.) But he does go away a lot. It's called a bender. Anyway just when Annie thought she would die of loneliness she made a friend, Michelle.

(*Lights up on* MICHELLE.)

MOTHER. Michelle was just like Mommy. I mean, Annie. Michelle liked to dance and sing and sometime even…

(MICHELLE *screams at the top of her lungs.*)

MOTHER. She'd scream just because she wanted to. Annie and Michelle got along great.

ANNIE AND MICHELLE. Hear Ye! Hear Ye! All you small-minded folks/Michelle and Annie are here and we are no joke/We drink. We party and occasionally smoke/If you don't like it why don't you choke.

MOTHER. The townspeople didn't like Princess Annie hanging around Princess Michelle. And Michelle, well, her castle was not a very happy place. Michelle's mother...

(*Lights up on* MICHELLE's MOTHER.)

MOMMY. Michelle! Michelle! Michelle!

MOTHER. ...was not very nice to her.

MOMMY. Get off your big fat fanny/Mommy needs a drink?/Hey don't stand so close, God, do you stink!/And be quiet for God's sake. Don't make so much noise!/Your Uncle Fred is passed out/You seen my sex toys?

MOTHER. So one night Michelle decided to run away.

(*Lights up on* MICHELLE *and* ANNIE.)

MICHELLE. Come with me.

PRINCESS ANNIE. Can't.

MICHELLE. I've got to flee.

PRINCESS ANNIE. But if you go.

MICHELLE. Yes?

PRINCESS ANNIE. What will I be?

MICHELLE. Then come.

PRINCESS ANNIE. I'm scared.

MICHELLE. To run away from home?

(ANNIE *nods.*)

MICHELLE. Don't be. I'll protect you. You'll be safe. Like a bee in a honey comb.

MOTHER. So off they went. They got into a big, beautiful bird and flew and flew and flew. And when Annie peered down from the bird's wing, the first thing she saw was lights. So many beautiful bright lights blinking and flashing. Mary you wouldn't believe it. And when the bird landed... Well, to Annie it was a paradise. It was not like her town at all. Her town that had one school and one store and one movie theatre. This place had a thousand stores, a thousand movie theatres and a thousand...Well, I don't know how many schools they had but I'm sure it was a bunch. Annie and Michelle had so much fun. Doing what? Well...They played games.

(ANNIE *and* MICHELLE *mime gambling.*)

MOTHER. ....and saw shows...

(ANNIE *and* MICHELLE *clap like audience members.*)

MOTHER. ...and they...

(ANNIE *and* MICHELLE *make out with male* CHORUS *members.* MOTHER *looks at them.*)

MOTHER. Uh...they danced. It was the best time Princess Annie ever had but then Princess Annie and Michelle ran out of money.

PRINCESS ANNIE. Why did you gamble our last twenty dollars?

MICHELLE. What would we have done with it anyway?

PRINCESS ANNIE. Eat! We could have gotten something to eat.

MICHELLE. We can still eat.

PRINCESS ANNIE. How?

(MICHELLE *looks at two johns beckoning them.*)

PRINCESS ANNIE. No.

MICHELLE. (*Shrugs.*) See ya.

MOTHER. So Princess Annie called up the Queen and the Queen whisked her back to the tiny, tiny kingdom and Annie settled down just like the Queen and townspeople wanted.

QUEEN. My prayers have been answered. You're my sweet little girl/Your behavior no longer makes me want to hurl.

PRINCESS ANNIE. So Annie finished school/And soon after married/ She followed all the rules/Never did she tarry.

MOTHER. So Annie lived. Not happy or sad just somewhere in between. But then one day Princess Annie got a letter in the mail.

MICHELLE. Hey! Remember me!

MOTHER. And Princess Annie started to remember all the things she hadn't known she'd forgotten. She remembered laughter and fun and freedom. And she thought maybe she could have that again.

MICHELLE. Come down to Vegas. I can get you a job in one of the hotels. It's just like you remember it. Even better. Oh, I don't drink no more. Done with that. (*Pause.*) You're the only true friend I ever had.

MOTHER. And you know what happened then Mary? Princess Annie went to Vegas with her beautiful daughter and they lived happily ever after because Princess Annie could be herself there. She could laugh as loud as she wanted and dance and sing and no one would try and stop her with gossip and stares and whispers. Doesn't that sound wonderful honey? Doesn't Las Vegas sound like a wonderful place? Las Vegas. Come on say it with me. Las Vegas. That's where we're headed baby. (*Pause.*) Paradise.

CHARITY
by Lisa Kron

The lobby of the Bellagio Hotel. MERLENE ODUMS, *her 7-year-old son,* CLAUDE, *and her 9-year-old daughter,* ANTOINETTE, *wearing tee-shirts, shorts and flip-flops and carrying plastic supermarket bags containing all that's left of their belongings, and holding glossy folders with the Bellagio logo on the front are listening, wide-eyed and a bit shell-shocked, to* CLAY ERICK-SON, *a hospitality specialist wearing jeans and a blue blazer.*

CLAY. Okay, so in your packets you will find your room key, a map of the strip, your vouchers for the world famous Bellagio buffet and, complements of Mr. Wynn, tickets to a very special show called "O."

(*Leaning down to talk to* ANTOINETTE.)

Do you know what "O" is about honey? It's a show all about water!

(CLAUDE *and* ANTOINETTE *look at their mother, their eyes fill with confusion and tears—and a touch of incredulity.*)

MERLENE. They're a little frightened of water right now Mr. Erickson. We was floating on a mattress for 5 days.

CLAY. Believe me, I know. I can't even imagine what that was like for you, Mrs. Odums. But that's why we thought this might be good. Therapeutic, right? (*To* ANTOINETTE.) See that water can be fun. We're going to have grief counselors sitting in the row behind you. Okay?

MERLENE. Okay. Thank you.

CLAY. (*Handing* MERLENE *an envelope.*) Mr. Wynn thought you probably needed a little fun. So this is $50 in cash, mad money as it were, and

(*He pours a big pile of chips into each of the children's hands.*) $200 in chips which you can use in any of the Wynn hotel/casinos. Normally kids aren't allowed in the casinos but we feel a natural disaster this big calls for an exception.

MERLENE. Can I just cash them in for the money?

CLAY. Um. Well, when Mr. Wynn gives out chips, which he very seldom does by the way, he expects that you'll use them to play in his casinos.

MERLENE. No disrespect but we're not much in the mood for gambling right now, Mr. Erickson.

(CLAY's *cell phone rings.*)

CLAY. Uno momento. (*Into cell phone.*) Yep?... You're kidding... Now? That is fantastic!... She said that?...Wow! Okay. Thanks.

(*Snaps his cell phone closed.*) O. Kay. So. Mr. Wynn is on his way down right now and I am very excited to tell you that Mr. Wynn's co-sponsor in this hospitality package, Ms. Celine Dion, is on her way over here with Mr. Wynn right now. She says she would consider it an honor to meet you.

MERLENE. Thank you but could we just go to our room?

CLAY. Um. Okay. I'm not sure if you understand but Ms. Dion is coming over from Caesars. She just doesn't do that. She doesn't leave Caesars.

MERLENE. Please tell her thank you but me and my children got to rest.

CLAY. Okay, um, Ms. Odums, can I speak frankly with you?

MERLENE. Okay.

CLAY. It would be really nice if you could thank Mr. Wynn and Ms. Dion when they get here. It's fine that you haven't thanked me because I'm just the conduit for their generosity but I really think it would be nice if you acknowledged what a terrific thing they're doing here.

MERLENE. (*Fighting a losing battle to hold her temper.*) Can we stay here permanently?

CLAY. Of course not. What do you mean?

MERLENE. This is the third city we've been to in five weeks Mr. Erickson. We don't need to gamble or see shows. We need an apartment and I need a job. My kids need to go to a school and not get pulled out after 10 days.

CLAY. We're holding out a helping hand, Mrs. Odums but you're also going to have to show some initiative. Okay? Celine Dion and Steve Wynn cannot magically change your life for you, can they?

MERLENE. I actually think that they could. I think they're richer than God and they could get me an apartment and a job here at the Bellagio in billing or shipping and receiving. And that's all I would need.

(CLAY's *cell phone rings.*)

CLAY. (*Into cell phone.*) Yep. Super. (*Snaps the phone shut. Addresses* MERLENE.) Mr. Wynn and Ms. Dion are in the building so we need to put our happy faces on, okay?

MERLENE. I'll put on a happy face when you get me an apartment.

CLAY. (*With urgency, almost pleading—he needs to get the situation under control before Steve Wynn and Celine Dion show up.*) That's not our responsibility. Okay? We're doing all we can for you.

MERLENE. You know what I'm doing right now?

CLAY. What?

MERLENE. I'm showing some initiative. There's lots of jobs here. Get me one.

CLAY. Okay, Listen. There is a process. You have vouchers, right? From the government, for an apartment.

MERLENE. I've been to seventeen apartments! Three already here in Vegas and I only been here half a day! Eight in Houston and six in Oklahoma. They tell me—we can give you this apartment if you show us a birth certificate and certify that you never committed a felony.

CLAY. Calm down, Ms. Odums.

MERLENE. You calm down! Are you a felon, Mr. Erickson?

CLAY. No.

MERLENE. No?

CLAY. No!

MERLENE. Me either! I ain't got no birth certificate. My whole life was washed away! All I wanna do is take care of my children!

(*The* CHILDREN *begin to cry.* MERLENE *glares at* CLAY. *His cell phone rings*)

CLAY. Oh shit. (*Into cell phone.*) Yeah. (*Alarmed.*) What? A riot? Where? (*To* MERLENE.) There's some kind of riot.

MERLENE. (*Frightened.*) What?

CLAY. (*Listens—then to* MERLENE.) Are Mr. Wynn and Ms. Dion okay? Thank God. Guests being threatened? This is terrible.

MERLENE. Oh, Lord.

CLAY. (*Listens—then to* MERLENE.) It's on CNN. (*Listens—then to* MER-LENE.) Refugees from New Orleans are taking over the Bellagio! I thought you people were the only ones here. There must have been another big bus load brought in by the MGM or something. (*Listens—then to* MERLENE.) People reported yelling—threatening…. (*To phone.*) What part of the hotel?… (*Freaking out.*) The west entrance?! Holy crap, that's right where I am. No! I don't see anything but oh my God I don't even know which way is safe to try to get out. What is it? What do you see? (*To* MERLENE.) They're showing a loop of footage from the security cameras. (*Listens—then to* MERLENE.) A woman… crazy…

MERLENE. Oh no.

CLAY. (*Listens—then to* MERLENE.) Yelling…. (*Listens—then to* MER-LENE.) Menacing a guy in jeans and a blue blazer. (*Listens—then to* MER-LENE.) Kids, thugs, (*Listens—then to* MERLENE.) Taking everything they can carry. (*Listens—then to* MERLENE.) They're showing them with their hands full of chips….

(*Clay and Merlene look at each other - realizing what's happening at the same time. Clay looks the kids, holding the chips he's given them.*)

CLAY. Oh… Oh… (*He looks up and sees the security camera.*) It's, um…. (*Futilely points up toward the camera trying to explain. Listens.*) I'm pretty sure it's fine. I gotta go. (*He closes the cell phone. To* MERLENE, *rattled, embarrassed, trying to make light of it, awkward.*)

Wow. Weird, right? Wow. Crazy. How does a thing like that happen?

(MERLENE *puts her arms around the shoulders of her children. She looks at directly at* CLAY, *shaking her head.*)

AIR CONDITIONING
Text and Music by Rick Hip-Flores

Lights come up on three men dressed in dark designer suits and fedora hats. Among them, one BENJAMIN "BUGSY" SIEGEL *stands in the middle. They are arguing loudly, talking all at once.*

ALL. (*Ad-lib clamor.*)

BUGSY. Whoa, whoa, whoa. Fellas, one at a time. One at a time.

GANGSTER 1. (*Agitated.*) What are you doing with our money, Benny? Huh? The million bucks? This better not be just another one of your dim-brained schemes.

BUGSY. Dim-brained schemes?

GANGSTER 2. Yeah, like that time you convinced us to open up a whore-house in the middle of Pennsylvania.

BUGSY. Yeah, those people really weren't having it.

GANGSTER 2. You mean the Amish?!

GANGSTER 3. You've taken our money, you've betrayed our trust, and what have you given us? Bupkis! So give me one good reason why I shouldn't let Miles here put a hole in you so big you could read tomorrow's headlines through it.

BUGSY. (*Thinks. No answer.*)

GANGSTER 1. Plug him, Miles!

BUGSY. Listen guys, I've got something cooking here. Something bigger and better than anything we've ever pulled before.

GANGSTER 2. Well, let's have it.

BUGSY. I say we open up a club. Lots of dancing girls, big shiny bar—a mile long! Biggest casino you've ever seen! And I say we do it in Las Vegas!

GANGSTER 1. The desert?!!!

(*He pulls out a gun about to shoot* BUGSY. GANGSTER 2 *stops him.*)

GANGSTER 2. Benjamin, Benjamin. Las Vegas is no place to open a business establishment. It's the armpit of the American West! There ain't nothing there but hot air, a couple of cactus plants, some dumpy saloons—

GANGSTER 1. That does it! Plug him, Miles!

BUGSY. Wait! I got it. You say Las Vegas is nothing but hot air, right.

GANGSTER 2. Yeah, that's right.

BUGSY. Well, then I have the answer: Air conditioning!

GANGSTER 1. What did he say?

BUGSY. Air conditioning. People will come for miles to get a taste of it! We'll make back the million dollars like that!

GANGSTER 2. Well, so far, I'm not buyin'!

BUGSY. Listen.

WHAT DO YOU NEED TO MAKE A BUCK?
TO STRIKE IT RICH?
I DON'T MEAN LUCK.
AIR CONDITIONING!

HOW YOU GET THOSE PETTY PROFITS TO GROW?
HOW DO YOU BEAT THAT DESERT SUN?
NOT WITH CARD AND DICE GAMES.
TRY SOME COLD-AS-ICE GAMES
YOU'LL BE ROLLIN' SEVENS EVERY THROW!

WHAT DO YOU DO TO MAKE A SPLASH?
TO HAVE SOME STYLE?
TO SHOW PANACHE?
AIR CONDITIONING!

GIVE 'EM THE COOL, AND I'M CERTAIN THAT YOU'LL AGREE:
THAT YOU NEED A PROPER CLIMATE
IF YOU WANT YOUR BIZ TO CLIMB!
YOU'LL BE GOOD AS GOLD,
IF YOU CRANK THAT OLD AC!

GANGSTER 2. Good as gold, huh? Can you put that in writing?

BUGSY. Don't need to. It'll be written on the faces of every person who sets foot inside our club: *El Flamingo!*

GANGSTER 1. It's got a name!

GANGSTER 2. Listen Benjamin, it don't sound too bad. Only thing is, where are we gonna get enough power to run all that air conditioning in the middle of the desert?

BUGSY. Don't worry. I have it all worked out!

HERBERT HOOVER
HE COULDN'T STAND THE HEAT
BUT SOUGHT TO GAIN SOME SWEET PUBLICITY
BOLD MANEUVER:
THE WEST WAS IN A JAM
SO HOOVER GAVE A DAM
PROVIDING ELECTRICITY
TO EVERYONE IN THIS CITY!

AND SO,
THE POSSIBILITIES ARE COLDER
THE HOOVER DAM BECAME THE BOULDER
AND THINGS WENT OFF WITHOUT A HITCH.
AND THOUGH,
THE WEATHER CAN'T BE ANY HOTTA
STILL FEELS LIKE CHRISTMAS IN NEVADA
AND THAT'S WHY WE'LL BE STINKIN' RICH!
OKAY?
SO FELLAS, WHAT DO YOU SAY?

GANGSTER 2. You've saved yourself one more time, Benny. But this air conditioning scheme of yours better work or else—

BUGSY. Or else what?

GANGSTER 2. Or else you'll be running your own club at the bottom of the East River.

BUGSY. Wow! That was my other idea!
WHAT DO YOU NEED, TO MAKE A KILL
TO GIVE YOUR GUESTS
A LITTLE CHILL.

GANGSTER 1. (*Hesitantly.*) AIR CONDITIONING?

BUGSY. HOW DO YOU SELL THAT SEARING CITY OF SIN?

WHAT ARE THE PEOPLE HOPIN' FOR?
NOT A PAIR OF ACES,
JUST A COOL OASIS
AND YOUR CUSTOMERS WILL SHOUT "ALL IN!"

HOW DO YOU BUILD THE PLEASURE DOME
THAT LOOKS LIKE GREECE
AND FEELS LIKE NOME?

GANGSTER 2. (*Excitedly.*) AIR CONDITIONING!

BUGSY. GIVE IT A BLARE AND IT COMES WITH A GUARANTEE:
SINCE YOU CAN'T BEAT GOOD OL' COMFORT
IF YOU'VE CHILLED IT, THEY WILL COME.
YOU'LL BE GOOD AS GOLD
IF YOU CRANK THAT OLD A.C.!

Come on guys, help me out!

YOU'LL BE GOOD AS GOLD,

GANGSTER 1. (WHEN LIFE'S LITTLE SNAGS PRODUCE BUMPS
SOLVE 'EM ALL WITH GOOD OL' GOOSEBUMPS.)

BUGSY. IF YOU CRANK THAT OLD

GANGSTER 2. (KEEP IT BRISK AND KEEP IT BREEZY,
KEEP IT SIXTY-FOUR DEGREE-ZY!)

ALL. A.C.!
YEAH!

DON'T TALK, DON'T SEE
by Julie Jensen

WANDA *is out in front of a 7-Eleven, sitting on a newspaper stand. There is a bank of phones behind her. She's pierced, goth, about 14 years old, smoking a cigarette. Another younger girl, unseen, is with her.* WANDA *likes scaring her, showing off.*

WANDA. I own these phones. Me and Danny own em. We charge people use them, cuz a lot of business goes on outta here. 7-Eleven, across the street from the El Cortez? Think about it. People that don't want their cell phone number known. That's who uses these phones. We charge a buck use the phone. Sometimes five, depends.

You can sit up here, you want to. But don't talk to no one. Don't see.

(*She scoots over.*)

See, way it happened, I'm waiting for Danny. Like now. This guy comes up to me. Says he give me ten bucks I stay right where I am next fifteen minutes. I do it. He pays me. So whenever I'm hanging out down here, I do same thing. Sit here. Collect. Pack a cigarettes. You know.

(*She looks around. Nothing.*)

Sometimes he talks to me. I like how he talks. Can't hardly hear him.

Job is I'm here, like a signal. He makes a call, leaves the drop, then cuts. Someone picks up drop. And I got quick ten. So now I got two jobs. I got this job for him and I got the phones. Score twenty bucks half an hour.

(*She notes the other girl and explodes.*)

So what I tell you? Don't see no body. Don't talk. That's the job. Don't see a cop. Don't see a guy.

(*She slips off the newspaper stand. She's looking for someone. Nervous. She returns to her perch.*)

Danny's been in house for week, some guy beat his face. Danny likes it dangerous. Picks up trash. I tell him, you know, I tell him. But he's 14 now, can't hear.

Stay right here. Don't watch me.

(*She moves off the newspaper stand and toward the phones. Then she twirls on the girl, and explodes.*)

What I say? WHAT I SAY? Don't watch me. Don't see.

(*She's approaches someone, passes by, returns. Stands by the girl.*)

That's him. Stay right here on this box. Right where you are. Fifteen minutes. That's the job.

Don't see. Don't talk.

(*Talking low. Something to say during the wait.*)

Danny says the end of the earth already happened. When they blew the last underground bomb. Says cracked the earth and stuff is running out now, radioactive. All over everything.

(*She's studying the surroundings.*)

Once you believe that, you got a certain way of living. Like Danny. Scared of nothing. Cuz you already dead.

(*Sound of a siren.*)

Stay right where you are. Don't see. Don't talk. Ain't about you. Ain't about nothing you know.

(*Filling time. But she's scared.*)

Breatl.e. Breathe even. No face. No look on your face.

(*Siren gets louder. In front of them now.*)

(*The other girl runs off.*)

SHIT! DON'T FUCKING RUN!

(WANDA *is talking to herself now.*)

Stay where you are. Don't talk. Don't see.

(WANDA *scans the scene. Thinks about it. Gets up on the newspaper stand.*)

Where you, Danny? Don't talk. Don't see.

(*Lights pop. She is discovered with her hands up, her legs splayed.*)

(*Siren is excruciatingly loud.*)

MONTECORE
by Lisa Kron

TIGER 1 *is laying on a rock in Siegfried and Roy's Secret Garden.* TIGER 2 *enters.*

TIGER 2. Hey, man.

TIGER 1. Hey. I didn't know you were working this rotation.

TIGER 2. Yeah, I'm afternoons this week. How's the rock?

TIGER 1. Nice. Hot.

TIGER 2. (*Stretching out.*) Oh yeah. That's nice. (*Looking out.*) Hey, where is everybody?

TIGER 1. I know. Small crowd.

TIGER 2. Well, I guess it's to be expected. They'll be back in a week or so.

TIGER 1. Oh yeah, I'm not worried. (*Conspiratorially.*) You know the last thing they heard Roy say before they took him away, right?

BOTH TOGETHER. (*In a German accent.*) "Don't kill the cat."

(*They laugh.*)

TIGER 2. Yeah, kinds breaks your heart, doesn't it?

TIGER 1. Oh yeah. Well, you know how he is.

TIGER 2. Like a child.

TIGER 1. Yeah. Like a big, dumb, (*German accent.*) Homozekchoo-al chi-eelt.

(*They laugh.*)

TIGER 2. Right?

TIGER 1. Oh, shit. We're terrible. (*Getting up.*) Ready?

TIGER 2. Yep. (*Getting up.*) I gotta say, though, I'm not used to playing to half a house.

TIGER 1. I know. Sucks. But—show must go on, right?

TIGER 2. Right.

> (*They walk to the glass, and suddenly wrestle and snarl at each other for a moment. Sound of people screaming with fear and delight. The tigers go back to their rocks.*)

TIGER 1. Ah, people are easy to please.

TIGER 2. They got their money's worth last night, huh?

TIGER 1. Yup.

TIGER 2. Now that was a fun night in the theater. I'm telling you, once every 5000 shows you do a performance that really pops.

TIGER 1. (*Slightly unsettled.*) It's true.

TIGER 2. Hey, what's up?

TIGER 1. Nothing. I don't know.

TIGER 2. Did you see Montecore after the show?

TIGER 1. Yeah. Just for a minute. Backstage.

TIGER 2. Was he stoked?

TIGER 1. Yeah—but…

TIGER 2. What is it, man? What's going on?

TIGER 1. I think I'm feeling a little—I don't know—bad for Roy? Is that possible?

TIGER 2. You're shitting me.

TIGER 1. I know. It's crazy. But…

TIGER 2. I'm going to say this once and then I'm not going to say it again. What did the man expect?

TIGER 1. I know.

TIGER 2. No, seriously. What did he expect. I mean—Hello! We're TI-GERS.

TIGER 1. Yeah, but—

TIGER 2. But what?

TIGER 1. I don't know…

TIGER 2. What?

TIGER 1. Well—You can see why they anthropomorphize us.

TIGER 2. No. I can't.

TIGER 1. I think we might bear a little responsibility.

TIGER 2. For what?

TIGER 1. I mean, come on.

TIGER 2. What?

TIGER 1. We sleep in their bed with them.

TIGER 2. So?

TIGER 1. We lay around the palazzo with them like a bunch of house cats.

TIGER 2. Again I say—so?

TIGER 1. We play along.

TIGER 2. I don't.

TIGER 1. You? You leap through a ring of fire every friggin' night.

TIGER 2. Yeah. For steak. I will do anything for steak. There's no contradiction in that.

TIGER 1. I just think we romp around all day enjoying the perks of domestication and then get all indignant when they assume we're domesticated.

TIGER 2. I have never pretended to be domesticated. Okay? I don't hide my feral nature but I don't think it's necessary to go around flaunting it either.

TIGER 1. But it is. We can't keep pretending to be something we're not.

TIGER 2. Oh for Christ's sake.

TIGER 1. I think there's going to be a backlash.

TIGER 2. (*Dismissive.*) No there's not.

TIGER 1. He almost killed the guy. You don't think the humans are going to react to that?

TIGER 2. No. They've convinced themselves Montecore was trying to save him.

TIGER 1. Siegfried and Roy have. Other humans aren't like them. Maybe you haven't noticed but those two are super freaks living in a spandex fantasy world. They told the press Montecore was distracted by a lady in the front row with a "freakish hairdo." Have we ever done a show without a lady in the front row with a freakish hairdo? Hello. People. This is Las Vegas.

TIGER 2. You have got to calm down.

TIGER 1. I'm telling you, last night was a wake up call. And we are not going to be served in the long run by trying to pretend we share a value system with humans. I Don't Have A Value System. And as of today I'm going to stop apologizing for that. I want for Seigfried and Roy to see me and acknowledge me for what and who I am: A Wild Animal. Is that too much to ask?

TIGER 2. They acknowledge we're wild animals. It's on the website, it's in the souvenir books it's in the audio tour, it's written right on that interpretive panel taped to the glass for God's sake.

TIGER 1. (*Getting more excited as his theory is coming clearer to him.*) No, no, see?

This is exactly what I'm talking about. They use the term—because it's sexy, because it's titillating, because it brings people in. But then when we actually act like wild animals, oh no, they don't like that. And we pay the price.

TIGER 2. What price are we paying?

TIGER 1. Did you spend the night at the palazzo last night? I didn't

TIGER 2. So what.

TIGER 1. I guarantee you, none of us are ever going to see the inside of that palazzo again.

TIGER 2. The Secret Garden has a better waterfall anyway. Who cares.

TIGER 1. I predict the Secret Garden will be closed in six months—a year, tops.

TIGER 2. No way.

TIGER 1. And even if it's not, things still have to change. Because I don't know about you but I cannot continue to live a lie.

TIGER 2. Okay, buddy.

TIGER 1. (*With great gravity.*) We have been living in paradise. But today, for the first time I see—paradise—is a prison.

TIGER 2. (*Looking around.*) Where's that giant teething ring?

TIGER 1. (*Stands up and yells.*) LONG LIVE THE WHITE TIGERS! FREE MONTECORE!

(*Sound effect of people screaming with fear and delight and then applauding.*)

TIGER 2. It's not going to be easy.

TIGER 1. (*Roars. Sound effect again.*) Change never is.

THE ELECTRIC FORMER FEMINIST STUDIES MAJOR BARES IT ALL FOR YOU
by Dan Dietz

GINA, *mid to late 20s, stands alone in a Vegas showgirl outfit with an outlandish headdress—and no top. She has stretched a tiny towel over her breasts and is doing her best to keep them covered.*

STAGE MANAGER. (*O.S.*) Gina, baby, you're on in five!

GINA. You know those dreams where you're about to go on stage and you realize you're completely naked? But then you wake up and you realize it was just a dream? And you're really really glad because, really, how awful would that be to have to go out on stage in front of hundreds of people completely I AM AN IDIOT!

No. Breathe. (*She breathes.*) You. (*Breath.*) Are not. (*Breath.*) An idiot. (*Breath.*) You. (*Breath.*) Are a Feminist Studies Major. This is not idiocy. It's irony. The cold, brutal hook of irony snagging on your self-esteem and tugging and tugging until it finally rips it away, exposing the darkness that seethes inside your very—

STAGE MANAGER. (*O.S.*) Gina, let's go!

GINA. I never have those dreams. My dreams are always about power outages. Caused by me. In my dreams, I'm electric. A little girl shooting sparks out her eyes. My outside is cute and sweet and picture perfect, but inside I'm whirring and whirring and generating a limitless amount of energy. Appliances reach for me to give themselves life. Everything's plugged into me. My only job is keep it all running, keep the TV screens glowing and the cuisinarts kweezing and the whole world spinning round. But the plugs keep multiplying and the switches keep flicking and I'm straining and smiling and then all of a sudden, POW! The world goes black. Cold. Quiet.

And the thing about those dreams is, I can't figure out whether I'm a scourge or a blessing, angel or devil. Whether people are furious when their episode of *The Sopranos* cuts off in mid whack, or whether they're relieved. The world has finally stopped spinning. They can breathe. A simpler time dawns. And we all step out into the desert together.

STAGE MANAGER. (*O.S.*) Chop freaking chop already!

GINA. I'm an only child. My father is a dealer (blackjack, not crack, he used to say before realizing no one laughed) in this very casino. My mother cleans the hotel rooms right over my head. I'm the one that was supposed to get out of this town, supposed to make it. I laughed at the 46% undergraduate dropout rate. Not me, baby. I'm a limitless source of energy. I turned myself into pure electricity and hopped the first power line outta Vegas.

And now, three years, fifty thousand dollars in student loans and one methamphetamines addiction later *god grant me the serenity to accept the things I cannot change* HERE I AM. Sleeping in my old bedroom, working in the casino, getting ready to bare my breasts night after night so I can make the monthly payments that stretch out into my future like the very desert that surrounds me. Gloria Steinem can kiss—

STAGE MANAGER. (*O.S.*) Your ass, out on stage, NOW Gina! Curtain in sixty seconds!

GINA. The thing is…sometimes I think you need the breakdown. Terrible as it may be. The world doesn't evolve slowly. It gets stuck in the same pattern, running in the same circles, over and over, whirring and whirring til POW! A huge leap forward gets made. Boom!—The dinosaurs get ripped off the planet and mammals sprout up in their place. Zap!—The wheel gets invented. Bang!—The steam engine. The automobile. Computers. Each step a cataclysm. Leaving nothing but sand in its wake. I'm a teenager cruising the same streets over and over, desperate for a way out, Bang!—I get accepted to Brown. I keep writing the same papers again and again, jonesing for a new idea, Zap!—I take my first breath of crystal. I start spending all my money and freetime high as shit, happier and more productive than I've ever been, Boom!—I'm caught and expelled and sent to rehab and then back home to mom and dad who've spent their whole lives plugged into me, tuned into my dreams and now they look at me with eyes so hungry I could cry and I just want to show them show you all what it means to have everything you thought you were and everything you thought you'd be ripped away from you till you look like look like LOOK LIKE THIS!

> (GINA *tears off the towel and we here a loud BANG! like the biggest fuse in the world just blew and the lights go completely black. Then, slowly, we see the sun begin to dawn on a desert landscape. Pale, pale light.* GINA *stands silhouetted, looking out at the endless dunes of sand.*)

GINA. Pow.

IMELDA AND CHER
by Chay Yew

A hotel room in Las Vegas. EILEEN, *a twentysomething Filipino woman in a cleaning maid's outfit is tucking the sheets on the bed.* TIBO, *a twentysomething Filipino man catwalks from the bathroom in a yellow Versace dress into the bedroom.*

TIBO. Do I look like Madonna... or Cher?

EILEEN. (*Not looking at him.*) More like Imelda. After she got convicted.

TIBO. Feel this. I saw this in a magazine once. Versace. Four seasons ago. The fabric. Just like skin.

> (TIBO *twirls around in the room.*)

EILEEN. Tibo Katigbak, we have three floors to clean! The guests are checking in in two hours!

TIBO. Judging from the taste of her clothes, shoes and waist size... A white woman. Rich and in her forties.

EILEEN. Every room we clean, you ransack the guests' closets and try on a different dress. What's the matter with you? You'll get us fired and then what? Back to flipping burgers at McDonald's. This job is a good thing.

TIBO. This job is shit, Eileen. Not even black people want it.

EILEEN. Luxor is a good hotel.

> (TIBO *goes to the mini bar and opens a small bottle of brandy. He drinks it.*)

TIBO. How would you know? They never allow us to walk through the front door. All we ever see of this hotel is the service entrance.

EILEEN. You expect us to waltz through the front door with the guests? We don't even have enough money for the nickel slots. Tibo, get it into your thick skull. We are just hired help. And stop drinking the brandy. The supervisor will find out.

(TIBO *sits at the dresser looking at the mirror.*)

TIBO. Back in the Philippines, we said we wanted to do great things. Look at us. Not even thirty and we're changing white people's linens.

EILEEN. Someone has to do them.

TIBO. Slaves. That's what we are.

EILEEN. The slaves built the pyramids. Prisoners built the Great Wall.

TIBO. Eileen Katigbak, I didn't come to this country to clean hotel rooms. Rooms with sheets of strangers' semen, bathrooms filthy with piss and shit, towels soiled and scattered like garbage. I crossed the ocean for more than this.

(TIBO *takes a lipstick and opens it. He applies it the back of his hand and looks at the color.* EILEEN *continues to change the bed sheets.*)

TIBO. You wanted to be a doctor.

EILEEN. Why do you always stroll down memory lane when we have work to do? You know my degree from University of Luzon translates roughly to a piece of toilet paper here. All I'm qualified for in this country is to be a cleaning maid. And I make more money as a maid here, than a doctor there.

And you? You didn't even finish secondary school. All you wanted to do was sing.

TIBO. I have a beautiful voice.

EILEEN. What good is a beautiful voice if it's brown in this country?

TIBO. I have an audition next week. Backup. The next thing you know, I'll be headlining at Caesar's. Ay naku, just like Celine Dion. She made it. And she's a foreigner.

(TIBO *walks to the window.*)

The boulevard brims with so much color and sound. Sometimes, I walk down the Strip and pretend to be a tourist. Pretend I'm a guest in this country, shopping, going to see shows…

I wish we didn't come here.

EILEEN. And what do we have back at home, naku? I can't even get a job as a doctor in town. All we had was that factory job where we're paid peanuts. Twelve hours a day, under dim light, we sew and assemble shirts for Gap and Banana Republic. Over here, we can afford these shirts.

TIBO. From factory outlets!

EILEEN. At least we now have money to buy them! Back home, we can't even feed our family. Here we don't even need to buy food—

TIBO. Because you steal leftover food from the banquet hall buffet—!

EILEEN. That's not stealing! No one eats the food anyway! The hotel throws away all that wasted food. Why not take it—?!

TIBO. From garbage dumpsters—!

EILEEN. It's clean—!

TIBO. Like filthy rats—!

EILEEN. I'D RATHER BE A SERVANT HERE THAN DIE HUNGRY AND POOR BACK IN THE PHILIPPINES!

(*Silence.*) Tibo, don't spend so much time dreaming the American Dream. The American Dream is for Americans only.

(*Silence.*)

TIBO. Come on, try it.

EILEEN. Try what?

TIBO. A dress.

EILEEN. No.

TIBO. There's a Donna Karan in the closet.

(TIBO *goes to the closet and retrieves a dress.*)

Ay naku, China silk! A whole month's pay check!

EILEEN. Put it back.

TIBO. Don't you want to at least try it on?

EILEEN. We'll get fired if they found us—

TIBO. We're finally in America and this is Las Vegas. For one minute, we can be white people. We can be Americans.

EILEEN. I don't know…

TIBO. Try it.

(EILEEN *hesitates. She stares at the Donna Karan.*)

EILEEN. Okay!

(EILEEN *takes the dress from* TIBO *and tries the dress on.*)

Well?

TIBO. Ay naku, you look like Cher.

EILEEN. You think?

TIBO. Before "Moonstruck."

EILEEN. Puta!

(EILEEN *and* TIBO *go to the window.*)

TIBO. Look at us… Imelda and Cher at the top of the world.

(EILEEN *and* TIBO *continue to look out the window.*)

EILEEN. It's a beautiful country, isn't it?

(*Beat.*)

TIBO. Come on, we have three floors to clean.

(EILEEN *and* TIBO *change the sheets on the pillows in their dresses.*)

SOME SUCH LUCK
by Liz Duffy Adams

A woman and a man in a Vegas motel room. Both young but not unscathed.

SHERRI. We burned us off some *calories* last night, you betcha. Wanna go eat?

ROY. I don't have any money.

SHERRI. Lost it, huh?

ROY. Not a damn dime.

SHERRI. Yeah?

ROY. Yeah, not a—well, I've got a dime, I've got— (*He turns out his pocket. A handful of change.*) —that, I've got…37 damn cents.

SHERRI. I can spot you breakfast. Hit the ATM later.

ROY. That isn't—you aren't—I'm not—I *don't have any money.* I lost my, what do you call it, my stake. I lost what I came here to win with. Then I went to the ATM and I took out more and I lost that. I just spent three damn days emptying my damn bank account into the gaping damn maw of this evil damn town.

SHERRI. So you go home, make more money. What's the big?

ROY. No job.

SHERRI. No?

ROY. Lost it. Few weeks ago. Laid off. Haven't found another.

SHERRI. Huh.

ROY. No home to go back to, either.

SHERRI. No?

ROY. Lost it. Couldn't make the rent.

SHERRI. Got parents can help you out?

ROY. Lost them. Couple of years ago.

SHERRI. Oh. Sorry. (*Slight pause.*) Girlfriend?

ROY. Lost her too, I lost her. So I came here and lost what I had left, which wasn't much. And somewhere in there I lost my dignity, I lost my pride, I lost my mind a little, I lost my temper once or twice, I lost my shit and I lost all hope.

SHERRI. Dang. You really are the boy with nothing left to lose, aren't ya?

ROY. I don't even know where I am.

SHERRI. You're in Vegas, guy. Would have thought that would have sunk in by now.

ROY. That doesn't mean anything to me. I got on a bus, I got off a bus, I checked in here and went up the street and started losing. And now I'm in a room with a complete stranger—I mean, I don't mean, but you are—and I look around this room and I don't recognize a thing. I'm lost. I'm lost. That's what I'm trying to… I don't know where I am.

SHERRI. Huh. I'll tell you where you are. You. Are. In. Luck.

ROY. OK, what, now you're going to sell me something.

SHERRI. Hang on, just settle down, I've got an idea coming on and I'm willing to bet you need to hear it. (*She thinks for a moment.*) This town didn't make you a loser, you walked in the biggest the loser on the strip. You came here like a homing pigeon to its coop, and gave up everything you had left to the Great American gods of luck and lucre. And for your sacrifice those gods have relented and sent you…me.

ROY. I'm sorry, I don't think I got your name.

SHERRI. It's Sherri, but that's not the point. As far as you're concerned, I am Lady Luck and you just fell right into my lap. So, here's what's gonna happen next. You're gonna take a shower, put on a clean shirt and come on with me.

ROY. Yeah?

SHERRI. Yeah. And—oh, now, anyway, what's your name?

ROY. It's Roy.

SHERRI. Roy, nice. So, OK now Roy, you're coming with me to the nearest wedding chapel, and a plump toupéed Elvis Tribute Artist is gonna say a thing or two, and I think there will probably be some cheesy music, and I think we will probably sign something. And one last strange and powerful sacrifice to the gods of luck will be made and everything will be utterly and irrevocably changed.

ROY. What?

SHERRI. We are getting married.

ROY. (*Slight pause.*) Oh, hahaha. (*It's not a joke. Well, maybe he heard her wrong.*) What? (*Uncertainly.*) I don't think so.

SHERRI. Oh, man, what good has thinking done you so far?

ROY. OK. OK, funny idea. Look, I don't know you, I don't know—anything about—

SHERRI. I got a job with the casino. I'm in the union. This is a union town, you know that? I didn't even go to college—I'm an auto-didact—that means self-taught, OK—and I got a salary and bennies and a 401K. I rent a little house with a yard of 'digenous plants, you know, cactuses and like that. Cacti. I'm saving to buy but I can carry you a while, till you get on your feet. Longer, if you want to knock me up and play house husband.

(ROY *is speechless.*)

I know, you're wondering what's in it for me, a loser like you? Well, Roy, I like your face. I like the way you screw. I've been with you almost what 15 hours and you had nothing to drink or snort or anything, so I know your loserdom isn't substance related. Anything else, I can deal. Just naturally unlucky? I can handle that. Little bit dumb? I can help you out there. All you have to do is say "OK Sherri," and your life comes up three cherries.

ROY. You're not even serious—

SHERRI. Play the odds.

ROY. This is such bullshit—

SHERRI. Raise the stakes.

ROY. You don't even know me, I don't even—

SHERRI. Throw the dice.

ROY. Sherri, for Christ's sake—

SHERRI. Roy. do you know how many gambling clichés there are in the American lingo? I can go all night.

(*Pause.*)

ROY. Look. That I'm a good screw: yeah, true, sure—and by the way, back atcha—but that's no reason. You got to ante up a better reason than that, before I get in your game.

(*They exchange a "yeah, he can sling the gambling clichés too" look. She nods a "fair enough." She thinks for a moment.*)

SHERRI. You can't live in this town without it becomes pretty obvious it's a big fat walk-in metaphor. Life's chancy. You got to be in it to win it. All that crap. Flip side, it's real easy to avoid losing. Don't play. So that's me. Nothing rocking my raft. Nice job, nice house, nice occasional fling with a friendly stranger. In a place that's all about change and violent shifts of fortune and lives transformed in a single night—I am equilibrium itself.

ROY. Good gig.

SHERRI. Yeah, it really is. But you know, the thing about perfect balance, you gotta think, sooner or later something's going to come along and knock it off center. It's just bound to.

ROY. So, you figure, fuck it up yourself before something fucks it up for you?

SHERRI. No, listen, I don't gamble, gambling is for chumps and losers— sorry, but, you know. But this is it. I'm gonna put it all on one throw. I'm gonna marry a likely stranger and take a chance on increasing my store of earthly happiness, knowing I could lose big time, lose it all. I'm betting on you, Roy. You want to bet on me?

ROY. Boy, wouldn't it be funny if I said yes? (*Slight pause.*) I could say yes, wouldn't that be…? (*Slight pause.*) I really do have nothing to lose …

SHERRI. (*Whispering.*) OK, Sherri.

(*Slight pause.*)

ROY. OK, Sherri.

(*They stare at each other, surprised and incredulous, on the verge of laughing or whooping or kissing or changing their minds….*)

GESTURES
by Chay Yew

(Note: Due to production considerations, *Gestures* was performed as a one-person piece in the 2006 Humana Festival production, rather than as the author's original two-person piece that follows.)

This play continues chronologically after "Imelda and Cher at the Top of the World."

The same hotel room. Hours later.

CHLOE, *an Asian American girl in her late teens, is wearing a simple black dress. She is plain looking. She speaks with an American accent. She looks down at the street below from the window.*

ELSIE *sits on the bed and is dressed in the same yellow dress we saw in the last scene. She wears spectacles and is smoking a cigarette; her back towards us. She sports a bouffant and is busy scribbling on her Keno card, watching the TV monitor for her numbers. The soft glow of the TV screen lights her gently.*

When CHLOE *and* ELSIE *speak to each other, their speeches are italics. When their speeches are in roman, they are speaking to the audience. When* ELSIE *is saying the numbers, it's an audible murmur. She's not addressing the audience but speaking to herself.*

CHLOE. I read somewhere that at this height…

ELSIE. 29…

CHLOE. Twenty-nine floors from the ground, say, with a mass about one hundred pounds, if a body should fall,

that after a little more than four seconds…

ELSIE. 4…

CHLOE. Its velocity would reach about 90 miles per hour. This would of course increase every instant (because of the acceleration due to gravity which is 22 miles every second).

ELSIE. 22…

CHLOE. The velocity at impact would exert a force 150 times the normal pull of gravity. And the body will increase its normal weight 150 times.

ELSIE. 15…

CHLOE. The impact at 15,000 pounds would completely puree your flesh and bones. Splat. Instant street pizza.

ELSIE. Quick Pick…

CHLOE. The consoling thing is if you jump, it's said you'd lose all consciousness. Of course, there's no one who can really verify that fact. But if you do lose consciousness, the good thing is you won't feel a thing when you kiss the pavement.

ELSIE. *Ai, Chloe, why you say things like that at dinner table? No good. Bad luck. Who going to marry a mouth like that?*

CHLOE. (*Referring to* ELSIE.) This is… my mother.

ELSIE. Please. You call me Elsie.

CHLOE. (*Indicating to* ELSIE's *dress.*) Ma, why are you always wearing that yellow tablecloth?

ELSIE. (*Ignoring* CHLOE.) She know nothing about fashion. What she know? Look what she wear. Like she at funeral. (*Whispers.*) *This is Versace!*

　　　　(ELSIE *returns to her Keno card.*)

CHLOE. She got it in Chinatown.

ELSIE. 10…

CHLOE. For "ten dolla ten dolla."

ELSIE. *What's wrong with ten dolla? Good bargain!*

CHLOE. *It smells ten dolla.*

ELSIE. *Something wrong with your nose! I smell nothing!*

CHLOE. *And it's yellow! Who wears—?*

ELSIE. *Anyone can wear black. But wearing yellow require—*

CHLOE. *Glasses—*

ELSIE. *Balls. Big ones.*

　　　　(ELSIE *snorts at* CHLOE *and returns to her Keno card.*)
2!

CHLOE. And my mother has plenty of that.

ELSIE. Quick pick!

CHLOE. She has very few interests.

ELSIE. I love Las Vegas!

CHLOE. That's one interest.

ELSIE. And Atlantic City!

CHLOE. Any place really… where there's a casino.

ELSIE. Reno! But Vegas is Paradise. Cheap food, cheap hotel, Siegfried and Roy!

　　　　(CHLOE *whispers to* ELSIE.)
Oh. How about Liberace?

　　　　(CHLOE *shakes her head.*)
Celine?

(CHLOE *shrugs her shoulders.*)

(*Beat.*)

Well, anyway, in Vegas, sometimes you can also win big money!

CHLOE. *How do you know so much about Vegas? You've never been.*

(ELSIE *points to her eyes with her two index fingers.*)

ELSIE. *See this? Eyes. There are magazines in beauty parlor.*

(ELSIE *returns to her Keno card.*)

20…

CHLOE. I'm twenty. A junior at—

ELSIE. (*Proudly.*) Stanford!

CHLOE. Majoring in—

ELSIE. (*Proudly.*) Accounting!

CHLOE. It was my mother's idea. I wanted to major in—

ELSIE. *What is environment studies? What for, environment studies? Environment fine for thousands and thousands of years and no one study it. If you want me to pay for university, pick something useful. Be doctor. Lawyer. Oh I know… Proctologist!*

CHLOE. Like her, I feel destined to live a life looking at Vegas only through tattered magazines in beauty parlors.

But, unlike her, I want to taste Vegas.

ELSIE. *Ay, Chloe! Mrs. Valdez daughter got accept into Harvard!*

CHLOE. I know she wants more of me.

ELSIE. *You know Mr. Tannenbaum son graduate Harvard last week!*

CHLOE. I'm a disappointment to her.

ELSIE. *Stanford? Ai, Chloe, you are big disappointment.*

CHLOE. I want to give her everything. Yet, at the same time, I want to kill her.

ELSIE. *Chloe, you are killing me. I am dying from disappointment every time I look at you.*

CHLOE. *Ma, why can't we go to Vegas? Take a vacation?*

ELSIE. *Ai, I don't need holiday. Don't need to go back to Hong Kong and see my sick and dying mother and my eight brothers and sisters I haven't seen in twenty-seven years. No. No. Not important. What is important is you… and university. Otherwise you end up ugly spinster cleaning hotel rooms. Is that what you want?*

CHLOE. *Why not? I thought we could—*

ELSIE. *Could what?*

CHLOE. *Spend time together—*

ELSIE. *For what?*

CHLOE. *I don't know—!*

ELSIE. *And do what—?!*

CHLOE. *Do mother daughter things—!*
ELSIE. *Like what—!*
CHLOE. *I don't know—something!*
ELSIE. *Who you think you are? We not American—!*
CHLOE. *BUT I AM! YOU MAY NOT BE! BUT I AM!*

> (ELSIE *returns to her Keno card.*)

ELSIE. 56...
CHLOE. There's no talking to her.
ELSIE. 2...
CHLOE. About two years ago, I stopped talking to her.
ELSIE. 77...
CHLOE. There was no point anyway. Her broken English And my mangled Cantonese.

> (ELSIE *scolding* CHLOE *in Cantonese.*)

Between select words the rest of the words that come out of her mouth, an alien tongue. Singsong words that bite snatch and slap. It was easier to swim in silence. So we began living a life of gestures.

> (CHLOE *smiles warmly and nods.*)

This means...
ELSIE. *No.*

> (CHLOE *holds out two fingers and circles them in front of her mouth.*)

CHLOE. This means...
ELSIE. *Dinner is ready!*

> (CHLOE *glares.*)

CHLOE. This means...
ELSIE. *What you eating? Ai, you look like Goodyear blimp! At this rate, who will marry you?!*
CHLOE. In the absence of words, we gesture.

> (CHLOE *gives* ELSIE *the third finger.* ELSIE *glares at* CHLOE.)
> (*Silence.*)
> (CHLOE *finally breaks the stare. Satisfied,* ELSIE *goes back to her Keno card.*)

CHLOE. My mother thinks I'm still at Stanford studying during spring break.
ELSIE. 52...
CHLOE. I make any excuse I can not to go home. Every cent I have goes to a bus ticket to Vegas.
ELSIE. 47...

CHLOE. I've been here five times in the last two years. And each time, I drink the shine of lights and drown in the burn of its promises. But this time, the glow of the city doesn't feel the same.

ELSIE. 34...

CHLOE. It's as if I saw the desert for the first time. I should be studying for my finals. They're coming up in a couple of weeks.

ELSIE. 3...

CHLOE. I have a GPA of 3.8.

ELSIE. 4... No... Not 4...

CHLOE. She would have preferred if I was just like...

ELSIE. (*With a sigh.*) Kenny. Good son.

CHLOE. My younger brother.

ELSIE. 4!

CHLOE. 4.0 GPA. Studying to be a—

ELSIE. Proctologist!

CHLOE. Last week, I got a B+ for my macro midterms.

      (ELSIE *staring at her Keno card.*)

ELSIE. Hmmm...

CHLOE. It's common knowledge no one hires an accountant who doesn't make perfect scores.

ELSIE. *Chloe, study hard. Must have 4.0 GPA. Remember no company hire inaccurate accountant. No client want their tax return calculate all wrong.*

CHLOE. Accountants have to be perfect. A perfect—

ELSIE. 10...

CHLOE. I should change my major.

ELSIE. 2...

CHLOE. I've always wanted to study the environment.

ELSIE. 29...

CHLOE. It's so beautiful down there.

      (CHLOE *slowly opens the hotel window.*)

ELSIE. 6...

      (*A burst of street sounds.*)

44...

      (CHLOE *stands on top of the window sill.*)

Quick Pick!

      (*She jumps out of the window.*)

36...

      (ELSIE *continues to scribble on her Keno card.*)

2…

(*The same black dress* CHLOE *was wearing flutters, like a wave, gently down from the window.*)

1…

(ELSIE *does not notice the dress.*)

ELSIE. I never come to Vegas until Chloe jump from this hotel. Five years ago. In this room.

(ELISE *shuts the window.*)

Now, every weekend I come here. Take bus from Monterey Park. (Twenty dolla. Good bargain.) I always stay here. Luxor. On 29 floor. Play Keno and spend time with Chloe here.

Ai, but I still don't know what to say her. Even when she was still breathing, we don't speak same language.

See, everything I learn from my country is old way. And everything in this country is shiny and new. Why she need burden to carry my past? All I need to do I is my duty, as mother. So I push her, push her hard, so she can be success, so she can make living after I die.

Chloe don't know but I can see in her eyes what she sees of me. Obnoxious babbling old woman with bad Chinese accent.

When I am here, I talk to her…

(ELSIE *holds out her hands.*)

With these.

(ELSIE *holds out two fingers and circles them in front of her mouth.*)

This means… *Chloe, have you eaten?*

(ELSIE *takes out a Tupperware of noodles and opens it.*)

I cook your favorite noodles. Here. Eat. Eat.

(ELSIE *glares.*)

This means… Chloe, how come you not eat? You not eat when alive. You not eat when dead. If you eat, you eat so much and then vomit in bathroom. Why? How I know? I know. I just don't say, that's all. You got that American disease. Want to be skinny like Vegas showgirl. Not good, Chloe. Not good.

(ELSIE *looks out of the window.*)

I see why Chloe always come to Vegas. This place is only place in this country she feel American. Here, everything is perfect. Is like American Dream Every job I take, every cent I save is to make sure Chloe have better life than me.

So she not dream American Dream but breathe, and live American Dream.

(ELSIE *turns to the TV screen and looks at the numbers on her Keno card.*)

I won.

(ELSIE *sits looking at her Keno card.*)

LION TONGUE
by Julie Jensen

Note: Italicized lines indicate narration or direct address.

OUR GIRL. *I'm at the entrance of the MGM Grand. Just inside the lion's mouth. Standing on the lion's tongue, as a matter of fact. The thing is, for this one, they built themselves an ugly ole lion head, and you gotta walk into its mouth to get to the casinos. I suppose you gotta walk out its ass to get to the parking lot.*

It feels like I ain't seen daylight since November. Neon's buzzing overhead. And I gotta find a phone.

Then I see this woman dressed like a circus worker. She's sweeping up cigarette butts from the lion's tongue.

A phone. I gotta get to a phone.

CAMPY GUY. A phone is the hardest thing to find in a casino, sweetheart. Who you gonna call?

OUR GIRL. Baby Jesus, asshole. None of your damn business.

CAMPY GUY. Whatever you say.

(*He shrugs and turns away.*)

OUR GIRL. (*A new tack.*) Look, I been up since Thursday. This here's Saturday morning. My feet are killing me, I smoked a six pack of cigarettes since I last slept, and I need a phone.

CAMPY GUY. All god's chillun got a problem.

OUR GIRL. It's important. Please…

CAMPY GUY. Well, we'll begin again, then. You need a phone. You need a phone for what?

OUR GIRL. I need a phone to call a hospital.

CAMPY GUY. To call a hospital. That's good. Call the hospital about what? Remember, my life is dull and I do not have meaningful work.

OUR GIRL. Call the hospital…about a test.

CAMPY GUY. Buzz! I'm sor-ry. You do not call a hospital about a test. Hospitals do not do tests. Labs do tests. Now let's begin again. Why do you want to call the hospital?

OUR GIRL. Never mind, I'll take my business across the street.

(*She turns and walks away.*)

CAMPY GUY. (*Calling to her.*) Excuse me. I have a phone. What do you think these tits are made of?

(*He reaches in and pulls a cell phone from the top of his dress.*) Now, who are you calling?

OUR GIRL. The hospital.

CAMPY GUY. That was previously established, I believe.

OUR GIRL. My old man is dying.

CAMPY GUY. Three on a scale of ten. Wanna try again?

OUR GIRL. That's the truth.

CAMPY GUY. An old story. I've heard it a million times.

OUR GIRL. My old man is dying. And I'm supposed to call the hospital every few hours.

CAMPY GUY. Two on a scale of ten. Unless he got poisoned or was shot.

OUR GIRL. He was not poisoned or shot.

CAMPY GUY. Oh, I'm so weary of the wasting deaths, the slowly dying deaths, the labored breathing deaths, the progressive weakness deaths. I know them all already. What happened to the beautiful deaths, the deaths full of song and spectacle?

OUR GIRL. My father is dying an ordinary death. In a crappy room without a view, cuz he ain't got insurance, and he dropped all his money on the wrong number.

CAMPY GUY. No beauty? No tragedy?

OUR GIRL. He's a plain old man dying a plain old death. Which doesn't matter to many people except to me and to him.

CAMPY GUY. It's your last chance to make this story beautiful.

OUR GIRL. (*Giving it a try.*) We have this habit. I call him at three when I get off shift. Check to see how his day was. Who was in to see him. What they served for lunch. I don't know. It doesn't add up to much. A habit we have.

CAMPY GUY. Meager contribution.

OUR GIRL. And I have his knife in my pocket. He used to cut willows with it.

CAMPY GUY. Sounds divine.

OUR GIRL. Fuck you, you little creep. Not everything on this earth is beautiful and brave!

CAMPY GUY. Well, it should be.

OUR GIRL. And you should be a woman!

CAMPY GUY. And who says I'm not?

OUR GIRL. (*A beat.*) Look, I know you. I know who you are.

CAMPY GUY. You don't know me. I am the sphinx, the secret of the ages.

OUR GIRL. I know you, all right. One night you went home with a sixteen-year-old boy, a virgin at the time. You sneaked into his room after his parents went to bed. The two of you had your way with each other. Afterwards when the boy got frightened and began to cry, you rocked him and hummed to him.

(*She hums "Somewhere Over the Rainbow."*)

CAMPY GUY. (*She's won.*) Which hospital?

OUR GIRL. Give me the phone.

CAMPY GUY. I'll dial the number.

OUR GIRL. Let me use the damned phone.

(*She reaches for it. He pulls it away.*)

I'm not going to steal your fucking phone.

CAMPY GUY. —she said, right before she disappeared into the crowded casino with my cellular sweetheart.

OUR GIRL. Look, here's a handful of bills, two sets of wedding rings, and a pair of come-fuck-me's.

(*She hands the stuff to him and steps out of her heels.*)

Let me use the goddamn phone.

(*He relents. She grabs the phone and punches the numbers.*)

Arnell, it's me. (*Pause.*) How's the old man?

(*Silence. She breathes deeply. She punches the phone off. Pause.*)

CAMPY GUY. What'd they say?

OUR GIRL. They're forwarding my call.

CAMPY GUY. To the head nurse.

OUR GIRL. Yeah.

CAMPY GUY. That means he's dead.

OUR GIRL. Yeah.

CAMPY GUY. Someone official has to tell you. I know all about it. I know all about how they do it.

OUR GIRL. Yeah.

(*Long pause. She's in her own world.*)

I've got my dad's knife in my pocket. It's his pocket knife, left over from when he was alive. "Cut me something, Dad, cut me a whistle." "Don't you know how to make a whistle?" he says and pops me that grin.

CAMPY GUY. (*Doing his part.*) "Don't you know how to make a whistle?"

OUR GIRL. I do, of course, know how to make a whistle. But I pretend I don't know. "No, Dad, I can't remember how to make a whistle." "Bring me my hat," he says.

CAMPY GUY. "Bring me my hat."

OUR GIRL. I bring him his hat. "We'll be back in an hour."

CAMPY GUY. (*Calling.*) "We'll be back in an hour."

(*She looks over at the guy. He looks ridiculous in his pill box hat.*)

OUR GIRL. Forget it. Sing Judy Garland for me.

CAMPY GUY. (*Singing.*) "Somewhere over the rainbow, way up high…"

(*He slows down. Now he means it.*) "Birds fly over the rainbow. Why, then, oh why can't I?"

OUR GIRL. *The two of us are staring out from the lion's mouth. A blade of lightning cuts through the sky.*

(*There is a clap of thunder and a flash of light.*)

I walk out of the lion's mouth and into the rain.

(*She tosses a look at* CAMPY GUY, *then heads out toward the rain.*)

SHOW ME THAT SMILE
by Rick Hip-Flores

KATHLEEN. DON'T LOSE HOPE.
DON'T YOU CRY, MY BABY, I'M HERE,
LET'S LEAVE OUR TROUBLES FOR A WHILE.
SHOW ME THAT SMILE.

IT'S BEEN SAID,
STORMY SKIES ARE GOING TO CLEAR
TIME TO GIVE HAPPINESS A TRIAL.
SHOW ME THAT SMILE.

SHOW ME THAT GLOW
THAT FUNNY FACE I KNOW BY HEART, AND THEN
WE'LL MAKE A START AGAIN
YOU MAY GET LUCKY AFTER ALL.

AND THEN WE'LL GO
AND LET THIS WHOLE WIDE WORLD DISAPPEAR
THROW ME A GLANCE THAT CAN BEGUILE
HONEY, YOU OWE ME,
SO SHOW ME THAT SMILE.

THE ODDS AREN'T GOOD
by Rick Hip-Flores

WOMAN. DARLING, I LOVE YOU
YOU KNOW THAT I DO,
AND WHEN YOU ASKED ME TO MARRY YOU
I WAS OVERWROUGHT
NOT A SECOND THOUGHT.
AND WHEN THE TIME CAME TO PLAN THE DAY
NEVER DID I FEEL MORE ALIVE AND GAY
IT WAS PERFECT BLISS,

TIL IT WENT AMISS.
PERHAPS YOU MISUNDERSTOOD ME
OR PERHAPS YOU'RE ALOOF AND UNKIND,
BUT WHEN I SAID I WANTED TO GET MARRIED
IN A LITTLE WHITE WEDDING CHAPEL
THIS IS NOT WHAT I HAD IN MIND...

(MAN *enters. Holding several Vegas brochures and two plane tickets.*)

MAN. Okay, "The Little White Wedding Chapel." This map says it's on the corner of Park Paseo, and Las Vegas Blvd. That's great. We should have a pretty good view of the Bellagio. Oh, and it's only a mile North of the Sahara Hotel, so we won't even have to take a cab!

WOMAN. GET MARRIED IN VEGAS?
DID I HEAR THAT
GET MARRIED IN VEGAS?
DID I HEAR YOU CORRECTLY?
THE DAY I'VE BEEN WAITING FOR ALL OF MY LIFE,
THE DAY I HAD SET FOR BECOMING YOUR WIFE
WILL HAPPEN IN VEGAS—
ARE WE FLYING DIRECTLY?
DIRECTLY TO SOME LITTLE HONEYMOON SUITE,
WITH HEART-SHAPED JACUZZIS AND ALL-YOU-CAN-EAT—
IT SOUNDS CHARMING, DARLING
AND HAPPILY FOLLOW I WOULD,
BUT TAKE IT FROM ME—
THE ODDS AREN'T GOOD.

MAN. I think we should spring for the "Lover's Package." Professional photographs, and they even provide the witness! How cool is that!

(*A* CHORUS OF BRIDESMAIDS *enter and sing backup vocals.*)

WOMAN
WHAT A WEDDING I'D PLANNED, NOTHING GRAND,
JUST THE LITTLE KIND
WITH FLOWERS AND RICE.
THAT WOULD HAVE BEEN NICE!
I SUPPOSE WE CAN STICK TO THE QUICK
NONCOMMITAL KIND
BUT SURELY OUR LOVE WILL LAST THE YEARS, DEAR
JUST THINK OF BRITNEY SPEARS, DEAR.
GET MARRIED IN VEGAS?
OH, I HOPE YOU'RE NOT JOKING!
FOR WHAT BETTER WAY FOR US TWO TO ESPOUSE?
WE'LL EVEN GET ELVIS TO READ US THE VOWS
IN GOOD OL' LAS VEGAS

WE'LL BE HAPPILY CROAKING

THERE'S NOTHING FOR WEDDINGS LIKE HOT DESERT SUN
AND SWEATING AND PEELING AND—WON'T IT BE FUN?
IT SOUNDS PLEASANT, SWEETHEART
AND SUCH AN IMAGINATIVE WHIM
BUT TAKE IT FROM ME
THE CHANCES ARE SLIM…

BUT DON'T GET ME WRONG,
I WANT US TO GO, DEAR
YOU KNOW I HAVE DOUBTS,
BUT I'M NOT SAYING NO, DEAR,
BUT I'VE DONE THE MATH
AND THE ODDS AREN'T GOOD!

DOG SHOT
by Dan Dietz

In the dark, the dull engine roar of a massive propeller-driven aircraft. Lights rise on the cockpit of a Boeing B-50 bomber. CAPT. DANNY DEAN-GELO, *late 20s, sits in the pilot seat. His co-pilot is* LT. LEONARD SCHULTZ, *early 20s.*

SCHULTZ. God, I hate these B-50s.

DEANGELO. I know. Superfortress my ass. Thing's held together with rubber bands and bacon grease.

SCHULTZ. Good de-icing system though.

DEANGELO. Who needs a de-icing system in the middle of the Nevada desert?

SCHULTZ. Ain't these supposed to be junked by now?

DEANGELO. Not until the B-47's ready. And they've already pushed that back till '52, '53…

SCHULTZ. You'd think they'd build a better stork to carry a baby this dangerous.

DEANGELO. Let's just pray it don't wake up and start crying before we drop it.

(*Pause.*)

SCHULTZ. Deangelo.

DEANGELO. Yeah?

SCHULTZ. You okay with this?

DEANGELO. With what?

SCHULTZ. This.

(*Pause.*)

DEANGELO. Ain't my job to be okay with it.

SCHULTZ. I can't get it outta my head. Those guys. Down there, waiting. In trenches. Some of them not in trenches, some of them just crouching in the sand. Like dogs. That why they're calling this one "Dog Shot" you think? Cause we're treating our own buddies like—

DEANGELO. Shut up, Schultz. Those men are seven miles out from zero. They're perfectly safe.

SCHULTZ. They start seven miles out. Then they march *in.*

DEANGELO. You a scientist?

SCHULTZ. No.

DEANGELO. Then what do you know about it?

SCHULTZ. I heard things. Guys getting sick from exposure. One guy lost his voice. It just dried up, like a…peanut.

DEANGELO. How can a voice dry up like a peanut? How can anything dry up like a peanut? What does that even mean?

SCHULTZ. You know, like a dry little peanut?

DEANGELO. Where you from again?

SCHULTZ. Iowa.

DEANGELO. Do me a favor. When you go back home, inform the Iowa Board of Education that they need to seriously reassess the curriculum out there.

SCHULTZ. Peanuts are dr—

DEANGELO. Shut up.

(*Pause.*)

SCHULTZ. I never dropped a bomb on my own countrymen before.

DEANGELO. It's a job, Schultz. You been given a job, I been given a job. You do your job, I'll do mine, life'll be a song. Got it?

SCHULTZ. Yeah. Yeah. (*Pause.*) But what if, uh…What if we didn't?

(DEANGELO *looks at* SCHULTZ.)

DEANGELO. This is a joke, right?

SCHULTZ. Yeah. Maybe.

DEANGELO. This has to be a joke. Because if it's not a joke, then you're insane.

SCHULTZ. I'm not insane.

DEANGELO. Then this is a joke. Right?

SCHULTZ. Right. Yeah. (*Beat.*) Maybe.

DEANGELO. You're actually thinking about this.

SCHULTZ. It's on my mind.

DEANGELO. Treason's on your mind?

SCHULTZ. Not dropping a bomb on my buddies is on my mind.

DEANGELO. This is great. All the co-pilots in the USAF, I get the nutjob.

SCHULTZ. I'm not a—

DEANGELO. The peanut-job.

SCHULTZ. Peanuts are dr—

DEANGELO. So what do we do then?

SCHULTZ. What do we—

DEANGELO. We don't do what we're supposed to do, what do we do?

SCHULTZ. Head for the Pacific.

DEANGELO. What, like make a hard right?

SCHULTZ. Fly it over the ocean. Drop it in.

DEANGELO. Explode the ocean?

SCHULTZ. Maybe it won't explode. Maybe it'll sink.

DEANGELO. It won't sink. It's set to detonate at fourteen hundred feet.

SCHULTZ. Great. So no one gets hurt.

DEANGELO. Right. You ever hear the word "soo-nammy," my friend?

SCHULTZ. Soo-what?

DEANGELO. Soo-nammy. It's Irish or something for "tidal wave."

SCHULTZ. What do the Irish know about tidal waves?

DEANGELO. The point, okay, the point is that if we drop it over the ocean, it's gonna make a gigantic wave that'll shoot straight for Hawaii and finish what Pearl Harbor started. Then Roosevelt will have to crawl all the way up and outta his grave to declare another day that will live in infamy and warn Americans everywhere that there is nothing to fear but Schultz and Deangelo itself.

SCHULTZ. Schultz and Deangelo themselves.

DEANGELO. Shut up.

SCHULTZ. So maybe we don't drop it at all.

DEANGELO. Then what do we do with it?

SCHULTZ. Keep it.

DEANGELO. Keep it?

SCHULTZ. Yeah.

DEANGELO. Like a borrowed screwdriver or something. Is that what you're saying?

SCHULTZ. Basically, yeah.

DEANGELO. You're saying, and I just want to, you know, paint an accurate picture for myself here so bear with me a minute, you're saying we take an atomic bomb entrusted to us by the United States of America, a weapon twice as big as the one that ended the second world war, a piece of ordinance so powerful it carries with it the distinct possibility of igniting the very atmosphere we're flying through, you're saying we take this canister of molten death and we…keep it.

SCHULTZ. That's what I'm saying.

DEANGELO. In a nutshell.

SCHULTZ. Or a garage somewhere.

(DEANGELO *looks at him.*)

DEANGELO. It's hard to believe they actually let you fly a plane.

SCHULTZ. I can fly a plane. I can fly this one right now. See?

(SCHULTZ *flips a switch and starts flying. The plane begins to turn.*)

DEANGELO. What the fuck?!

SCHULTZ. The fuel I got, I can fly it all the way to the North Pole…

DEANGELO. Schultz, take your hands off the wheel!

SCHULTZ. The South Pole…

DEANGELO. That's an order, Schultz!

SCHULTZ. I can fly around the world and never come down.

(DEANGELO *draws his service pistol.*)

DEANGELO. (*Pointing the gun at him.*) LIEUTENANT!

SCHULTZ. Which is easier, Captain? Knowing that if you pull that trigger, one guy's gonna die fast? Or knowing that if you drop that bomb, eight hundred guys will die slow?

DEANGELO. YOU AREN'T THEM, OKAY? You're up here. They're down there. You're a bird. They're a buncha dogs. And there are times in life when you just gotta close your eyes, say, "Thank you God for making me a bird," and fly on. Close your eyes. Close your eyes, goddammit! (SCHULTZ *closes his eyes.*) Now say thank you.

SCHULTZ. Thank you.

DEANGELO. Good. (DEANGELO *places the gun in his lap, reaches over, and hits the switch, taking control of the plane.*) Now get ready cause we're dropping this motherfucker. (*He gets on the horn.*) Johnny, you all set back there? Good. Open the doors, we're coming up on zero.

(*Sound of bomb bay doors opening. Then nothing but the roar of engines. After a moment,* DEANGELO *glances at* SCHULTZ.)

DEANGELO. Hey, Schultz. Buddy. Look. (SCHULTZ *opens his eyes. He's almost crying.*) Vegas.

SCHULTZ. Yeah.

DEANGELO. You know Frank Sinatra's playing there today?

SCHULTZ. No shit.

DEANGELO. The Man Himself.

SCHULTZ. What's he doing in Las Vegas?

DEANGELO. He's a has-been, so he's doing what has-beens do. He's playing Vegas.

SCHULTZ. Maybe we oughta fly over. Ask him for an autograph.

DEANGELO. I got a better idea. Let's give him ours. (*On the horn.*) Let 'er go, Johnny.

> (*The engines suddenly increase in pitch.* SCHULTZ *and* DEANGELO *lurch in their seats.* DEANGELO *makes a hard turn of the wheel.*)

DEANGELO. Look up, Frankie! You don't wanna miss this! A twenty kiloton mushroom cloud smashing into the horizon like a freight train!

SCHULTZ. Like a soo-nammy.

DEANGELO. Yeah! Your own personal soo-nammy!

SCHULTZ. Nothing to fear but Schultz and Deangelo itself.

DEANGELO. Step on stage and wait for the light, Frank. And when you see that light, start singin'!

SCHULTZ. They deserve it. The boys down there. They deserve a fucking song.

DEANGELO. That's right. For the Dog Shot boys. Start singing, Frankie! Start—

> (*All in an instant: huge explosion rocking the entire cockpit, blinding flash of light, blackout. Then in the dark, as if on cue, Frank Sinatra begins to sing….*)

GHOSTS OF LAS VEGAS
by Liz Duffy Adams

The GHOST OF ELVIS *mopes somewhere upstage. A* CHORUS OF GHOSTS, *making a non-stop series of slot-pulling gestures—reaching up, pulling down—in a languid steady rhythm, murmuring or singing.*

SLOT-PULLERS. In it
To win it
We are
In it
To win it
Minute
By minute
We are willing
To be
Rich rich rich rich rich rich rich rich rich

(*They loop this from the beginning, under the following.* KATHLEEN *enters.*)

KATHLEEN. Welcome, ladies and gentlemen, to the swingingest show on the strip, the razzest dazzest red-sweet-hottest extrava-panorama in all of this most glitter-palace of a desert city. Presenting: Ghosts of Las Vegas... Ta...da...

(*She trails off, stands off-kilter, dazedly, as the* SLOT-PULLERS *continue their low song.* KATHLEEN *snaps to and, talks over them again; at some point they trail off and stop singing.*)

Viva Las Vegas! (*The* GHOST OF ELVIS *is stimulated by this, swivels and jerks his hips briefly then subsides.*) O, Viva. Viva. You think you know what that means? You don't know. O, my beautiful Vegas, the true heart and soul of our nation. I came out of the wilderness in 1955, right off the ranch into the Lido show at the Stardust Hotel—almost, almost, maybe there was a little interregnum in less glorious surroundings, maybe I had to pay some dues in low wriggle and beer stink—but soon there I was yeah yeah yeah more exalted than all my ranchgirl dreams could ever rustle up. Adorning the bar between shows, wearing pointy lizard stilettos, cruising up and down Fremont with Darla and Jeannie in my creamy creamy Cad, neon fireworking over its fat creamy flanks... O my darling Vegas.

(*Dancing languidly to this.*) The Riviera, The Dunes, The New Capri Lounge. The Slipper, The Stardust, The Starlight Lounge. The Flame, The Sahara, The Casbah Lounge. Sans Souci, El Cortez, The Flamingo...and the Rat Pack, the Rat Pack, O, O, the Rat Pack...at The sa-sa-sa-Sands.

I kicked in '61 and Darla scattered my ashes up and down the Strip. Now I'm the spirit of Las Vegas, don't you know. You want to win you ought to whisper my name over those dice, baby. *Kathleen. Kathleen the true true spirit of The Meadows, Mama needs a new pair of pointy lizard...* But you don't know. You don't know me. I'm long long gone. (*To the* SLOT-PULLERS.) Sing your sorry song, you sorry sad fucks. (*To us.*) Ooh, sorry, that's Vegas for I love ya. (*To the* SLOT-PULLERS.) You'll never know the glory. You're a later race of pathos.

SLOT-PULLERS. In it
To win it

(*They are interrupted by a man's howl from off.*)

RICK. (*Off.*) NOOOO.

(*Slight pause.* RICK *walks dazedly in. The* SLOT-PULLERS *stop their motions, look at him.*)

SLOT-PULLERS. Here's a new one. Killed himself. (*Losing interest, returning to their gestures.*) Jerk.

KATHLEEN. Leaving Vegas on your own gun. I don't get that.

RICK. Yeeaahh...that was a big mistake. I see that now. It felt just exactly like the rightful inevitable even dramatically satisfying climax to my lifelong horror-show but just JUST as my finger tightened I thought *wait a minute no no bad idea* but somehow my finger didn't get the news in time and BLAM something kicked me in the head and the deed was done and now my name I guess is eternal regrets.

KATHLEEN. That's nothing new around here.

RICK. You're pretty. (*Slight pause.*) I shot myself.

KATHLEEN. Be cool, cat. You'll get in the ghost groove soonest. Takes a little... at first.

RICK. How long you...?

KATHLEEN. Long time, kiddo. Radioactivity caught up with me. Oh, you don't even know, do you? We used to watch the tests light up the desert, sitting outside the house in lawn chairs like the 4th of July. Big excitement for lonely ranch family. G-men came and thanked us for doing our part to protect America. But they made sure not to test when the wind was toward the money. I drifted on those safer winds to Vegas soon as I was old enough, and when I got sick they gave me fifty-thousand bucks for my trouble. I was kind of mad, then. Now... now everything seems like a dramatically satisfying story told long long ago, around some little fire in the dark. It's all apt, dig? The glow and the glitter. Radio-activity and neon bright nights. I luminesced from inside and out.

RICK. Wait, wait.... If that's all true.... If the government.... If they really.... Wait.... I forget what I was going to say...

KATHLEEN. That's the name of this town, baby. Razz and dazz and pick your immortal pocket. Don't nobody get excited. Don't nobody pay attention. Don't nobody remember what time it is.

RICK. Want to hear my life story?

KATHLEEN. I know you're a lead-sucker. What else I gotta?

(ELVIS *jerks to life, hip-swivels, drifts off again.*)

RICK. Hey. Hey, is that...?

KATHLEEN. Oh, yeah, you know. That's the local god.

RICK. God?

KATHLEEN. Not capital G, just minor local godhead, they won't let him die in peace, got him hanging around. He's a corn god, you know, one of those recycled deities, dying and coming back, you get me? Oh, you know, there's a Greek one and an Egyptian one and that one from that other desert. Everybody's got one. He's ours.

RICK.(*Singing tentatively.*) Viva Las Vegas.

(GHOST OF ELVIS *stirs to life again.*)

RICK & KATHLEEN.(*Slowly.*) Viva Las Vegas.

(GHOST OF ELVIS *winds up his pelvis.*)

RICK, KATHLEEN & ELVIS. (*Slow but building to a ghostly intensity.*) Viva, Viva, Las Vegas!

KATHLEEN. Oh yeah, those dying gods. They're always guys, you notice that? When women die they stay dead.

RICK. You look like a goddess.

KATHLEEN. Settle down, Sparky. This ain't no happy ending.

RICK. Why am I still here?

KATHLEEN. Oh, you may be dead, but you're still American, aren't ya? You didn't get your birthright, your big payoff, your happy happy happy, did ya? And you can't let go. This town's a gravity well for greedy little ghosts like you.

RICK. That sounds about right. But I'm caring about it less by the second. About anything.

KATHLEEN. Told ya. You're getting in the ghost groove.

RICK. Dance with me, while I still care a little?

> (*They dance as the* SLOT-PULLERS *sing.* ELVIS *dances too by himself. Maybe he sings* Viva Las Vegas *at the same time, a slow empty version, maybe the music fits together.*)

SLOT-PULLERS. In it
To win it
We are
In it
To win it
American god
Hear our prayer
We are willing to be lucky
Accept our humble sacrifice
And make us rich rich rich rich rich rich rich rich

> (KATHLEEN *and* RICK *dance slower, drift apart as though forgetting what they were doing. Elvis goes back to drifting around the outskirts.*)

End of Play